Sources in Modern East Asian
History and Politics

Edited by

Theodore McNelly

UNIVERSITY OF MARYLAND

Sources in Modern East Asian History and Politics

New York
APPLETON-CENTURY-CROFTS
Division of Meredith Publishing Company

ACKNOWLEDGMENTS

Pages xvi & 97: Reproduced from: *A History of the Far East in Modern Times*, 6th
Edition, By Harold M. Vinacke. Copyright © 1950, 1959, by Appleton-Century-
Crofts, Inc. Reproduced by permission of Appleton-Century-Crofts.

Page 2: Reproduced with the permission of Charles Scribner's Sons from *The Ageless
Chinese* A History by Dun J. Li. Copyright © 1965 Charles Scribner's Sons.

Page 8: From: David J. Dallin, *The Rise of Russia in Asia*. New Haven: Yale University Press, 1949, p. 21. Reproduced by permission.

Page 45: Reprinted from *A History of Japan to 1334* by George Sansom with the
permission of the publishers, Stanford University Press. © 1958 by the Board of
Trustees of the Leland Stanford Junior University.

Pages 153, 326–327: Reproduced from: *Far Eastern Politics in the Postwar Period*
By Harold M. Vinacke. Copyright, © 1956 by Appleton-Century-Crofts, Inc. Reproduced by permission of Appleton-Century-Crofts.

Page 190: From *Yoshida Kara Kishi E* by Ryosuke Nasu. Reprinted by permission of
Mainichi Shimbunsha.

Page 255: Reprinted with permission of The Macmillan Company from *The Relations
of Nations*, 2nd edition, by Frederick H. Hartmann. © The Macmillan Company
1957 and 1962.

Pages 274–275: This map is reproduced with permission from Peter S. H. Tang,
Communist China Today Vol. I: *Domestic and Foreign Policies* (Washington, D.C.:
Research Institute on the Sino-Soviet Bloc, 1961).

Page 296: From *The China Quarterly*, No. 16 (October–December, 1963), p. 61.
Reprinted by permission.

Page 303: Adapted by permission from *Dynamics of International Relations: Power,
Security and Order*, Copyright © 1964 by Fred Greene. Holt, Rinehart and Winston,
Inc., publishers.

Page 334: From: United States Department of State, *Viet-Nam: The Struggle for
Freedom* (Washington, D.C.: Government Printing Office, 1964), pp. 12–13.

Pages 342–343: From: United States Department of State, *American Foreign Policy,
1950–1955: Basic Documents* (Washington, D.C.: Government Printing Office, 1957),
Vol. I, between pp. 788, 789.

Page 351: From *Peking Review*, Vol. VIII, No. 31 (July 30, 1965), p. 12.

In memory of

ALFRED G. TAYLOR

Preface

In the study of world affairs there is no substitute for reading the documents which professional historians and political scientists use in their research. To the extent that the student is unfamiliar with primary sources, he is at the mercy of textbook writers and journalists for the interpretation of events. Only after examining the raw materials of history is he in a position to do some intelligent thinking for himself. Moreover, reading the actual statements of world leaders will give the student a vivid sense of the historical and political processes in which he himself is a participant.

This source book is designed to provide supplementary reading for courses in the history, politics, and ideologies of modern China, Japan, Korea, and Vietnam. In order to devote the maximum space to the readings themselves, the editorial notes have purposely been kept short. They summarize the recent political history of East Asia and suggest the significance and interrelations of the selections. The book is arranged in chapters corresponding roughly to the chapters in standard textbooks. A correlation chart is provided to help the student relate the selections to what he is studying in his textbook. At the end of each chapter there is a bibliography of suggested further reading. The Constitutions of Japan and Communist China are reproduced in the appendix. The maps have been selected with an eye to their accuracy, clarity, and up-to-dateness.

As is often the case with compilations such as this, there were many important materials which could not be included for lack of space. The principal criteria for inclusion were the relative importance of the political events concerned and the relevance of the documents to the causes and results of the events. An effort was made to represent a variety of points of view on controversial topics. Where several documents competed for a place, the compiler sometimes chose the less readily available document to enhance the value of the collection for the more advanced students.

The reader should, of course, be aware that most of the selections in this book were written not by impartial scholars but by politicians and diplomats who were less concerned to provide unbiased presentations of the facts than to persuade people to particular points of view. The real purposes of these writers are often hidden behind pretended objective accounts of history. To discover the underlying motives of these historical figures is but one of the challenges before the student. Other problems which he may wish to analyze are the historical situations which provided the occasion for particular documents, the extent to which the pronouncements were successful in attaining their purposes, and the consequences for the policies of the major world powers, including the United States.

In the preparation of this volume, the editor is particularly indebted to Professor Hyman Kublin, of the City University of New York, who took time from a busy schedule to make numerous suggestions for improvement. The editor also wishes to thank Professor Kenneth Folsom, Professor Chün-tu Hsüeh, Professor Marlene Mayo, and Mr. Hideo Kaneko, all of the University of Maryland, Professor Jung-Gun Kim, of East Carolina College, Dr. Hattie K. Colton, of Washington, D.C., and Mr. Walter J. Green and the staff of Appleton-Century-Crofts for their very helpful comments. The editor's wife, Myra, typed much of the manuscript, and Mr. David Atkinson helped to compile the index. The editor is grateful to the General Research Board of the University of Maryland, which supported his research on Japanese politics in the summers of 1961, 1964, and 1966.

For errors of fact or interpretation, the editor assumes responsibility.

T. M.

Contents

VII. THE DEFEAT AND OCCUPATION OF JAPAN

APPENDICES

Maps

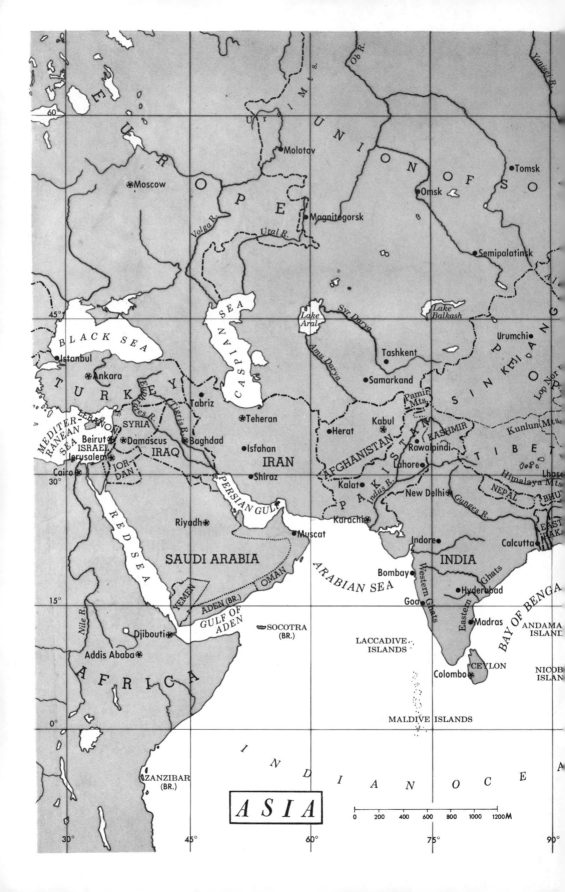

60

⊕Moscow

Molotov•

Tomsk•

EUROPE
UNION OF SO

U r a l M t s.

Ob R.

Yenisei R.

⊕Magnitogorsk

Omsk•

Semipalatinsk•

Volga R.

Ural R.

45°

CASPIAN SEA

Lake Aral

Lake Balkash

Urumchi•

BLACK SEA

•Istanbul

⊕Ankara

TURKEY

Tabriz•

Syr Darya

Tashkent•

SINKIANG

Lop Nor

Kunlun Mts.

MEDITER-
RANEAN
SEA

LEBANON

Beirut⊕
Damascus•
ISRAEL
Jerusalem⊕

SYRIA

Euphrates R.

Tigris R.

•Baghdad

IRAQ

Amu Darya

•Teheran

•Isfahan

IRAN

•Shiraz

Herat•

Kabul
⊕

Pamir Mts.

AFGHANISTAN

•Rawalpindi

Lahore•

KASHMIR

TIBET

Lhasa

Himalaya Mts.

NEPAL

BHU-

Cairo⊕

30°

JOR-
DAN

PERSIAN GULF

Kalat•

PAKISTAN

Indus R.

New Delhi•

Ganges R.

EAST
PAK.

RED SEA

Riyadh⊕

•Muscat

Karachi•

Indore•

Calcutta•

SAUDI ARABIA

OMAN

ARABIAN SEA

INDIA

Bombay•

Western Ghats

Hyderabad•

15°

YEMEN

ADEN (BR.)

GULF OF
ADEN

SOCOTRA
(BR.)

Goa•

Eastern Ghats

•Madras

ANDAMAN
ISLANDS

Nile R.

Djibouti⊕

LACCADIVE
ISLANDS

BAY OF BENGA

Addis Ababa⊕

AFRICA

CEYLON

Colombo⊕

NICOB
ISLAN

0°

MALDIVE ISLANDS

INDIAN OCEA

A

⊕ZANZIBAR
(BR.)

ASIA

0   200   400   600   800 1000 1200 M

30°

45°

60°

75°

90°

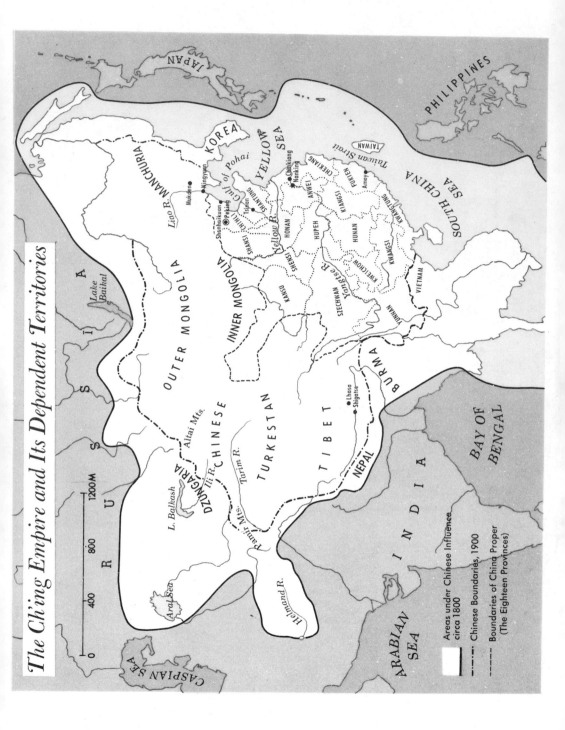

The Ch'ing Empire and Its Dependent Territories

I

Reform and
Revolution in China

The politics of modern East Asia are incomprehensible unless one has some grasp of the philosophical tradition of China. From the founding of the Han dynasty in 206 B.C. to the establishment of the Chinese Republic in 1912, Confucianism provided the ideological basis of the government and administration of the Chinese Empire. Furthermore, because of the power and prestige of China, this philosophy spread to neighboring countries and became a principal influence on the political development of Japan, Korea, and Vietnam.

Confucius (K'ung-fu-tzu) was born in 551 B.C., when the feudal order of the Chou dynasty (1122–256 B.C.) was in the throes of disintegration. He asserted that when the ruler set a good example for his subjects, who were expected to be loyal, and when the obligations of the five relationships (ruler and subject, father and son, husband and wife, elder brother and younger brother, and friend and friend) were properly fulfilled, society would be well ordered. The Confucianists held that if a king failed to rule according to virtue, he might thereby lose the Mandate of Heaven to a more virtuous man. Throughout China's history, this theory was used to justify successful revolution and the passage of political authority from one dynasty to another. The Confucian principle of government by virtue became the basis of the merit system, and from the T'ang dynasty on officials were normally chosen by means of literary examinations. (Confucian ideals are especially emphasized in Selections 5, 11, 13, 36, and 41 in this book.)

The emperor of China, known as the Son of Heaven, was lord of all "Under Heaven." The barbarian peoples looked to China, the Central Kingdom, for the rudiments of civilization, and their rulers often paid tribute to and were invested with their authority by the Son of Heaven. Nevertheless, much of the time during the past two thousand years the

3

Chinese Empire was ruled by "barbarian" dynasties, the most important being the Mongol (Yüan, 1279–1368) and the Manchu (Ch'ing, 1644–1912). The Manchus enlisted the support of the Chinese scholar-gentry class by governing according to traditional Confucian principles and subsidizing classical scholarship. The Manchu Empire included not only China proper but also Tibet, Chinese Turkestan (Sinkiang), Mongolia, and Manchuria.

However, the nineteenth century in China was characterized by internal disintegration and incursions from the West. The effort of the Manchu authorities to halt the importation of opium and the English insistence on diplomatic equality and enlarged trading opportunities resulted in the Anglo-Chinese Opium War (1839–1842). The British defeated the poorly coordinated Manchu forces and imposed the first of a long series of "unequal treaties" on China. The treaties of the Western powers with China provided for extraterritoriality (exemption of Europeans and Americans from Chinese jurisdiction), the most-favored-nation principle (which meant that future grants of privileges to a foreign country by China would automatically accrue to the other Western nations enjoying most-favored-nation treatment as well), cessions of territory, the opening of additional treaty ports, the right of Christian missionary activity, the payment of indemnities by China, and the establishment of low tariffs which could be changed only with the consent of the treaty powers (Selection 1). The unequal treaties compromised the sovereignty of China. Patriotic Chinese later came to regard them with great resentment, looking forward to the time when they might be abolished.

The Taiping Rebellion, led by Christian-influenced fanatics, ravaged much of China from 1850 to 1864. The rebels nearly succeeded in toppling the Manchu dynasty, but Chinese officials, appalled by the land reforms advocated by the Taiping and by persecution of Confucianism and Buddhism, finally organized an effective resistance. Some Western powers, fearful that the Taiping rebels might extinguish their treaty privileges, also lent support to the Manchus.

China was defeated in the Arrow War with Britain and France (1856–1860), the Sino-French War (1884–1885), and the Sino-Japanese War (1894–1895) (Chapter II, Selection 14). Russia took advantage of China's weakness following the Arrow War to acquire some 350,000 square miles of China's northeastern territories. The wars with France and Japan resulted in the loss of two of China's dependencies, Annam and Korea, and in the cession of Taiwan to Japan.

Japan's surprising victory over China in 1895 exposed the latter's weakness to the world at the very time when European imperial rivalries in Africa and Asia were keenest. The partitioning of the Manchu Empire appeared imminent, and in 1898 various European powers forced the Manchus to grant them naval bases together with railroad and mining concessions in the hinterland. To protect American commercial and missionary opportunities in China, Secretary of State John Hay in 1899 proposed that the powers agree to respect the principle of the Open Door (equality of commercial opportunity for all nations) in China (Selection 2). During the Boxer uprising in 1900, Hay further proposed that the powers cooperate with the United States to preserve China's territorial and administrative integrity (Selection 2). However, Hay's policy did not succeed in ending the occupation of Manchuria by the Russian forces, which were expelled by the Japanese in 1905; nor did the United States oppose Japan's annexation of Korea in 1910. Although the United States was less imperialistic towards China than were the major European powers, in 1898 the United States annexed Hawaii, which had been independent, and the Philippine Islands, which had been a Spanish possession. A Filipino insurrection against the newly established American rule immediately broke out and was not suppressed by the United States Army until 1902.

At the close of the nineteenth century, the once mighty and prosperous Chinese Empire was falling prey to European and Japanese imperialism. Faced with the apparently imminent partition of their country by the imperialist powers, China's leaders scrutinized their political and social institutions in order to diagnose and prescribe for their country's weakness. For example, in 1898 Chang Chih-tung,[1] the Governor-General of Hupei and Hunan, published his famous *Exhortation to Learn*, in which he urged China to avoid foreign conquest by adopting Western technology and preserving the monarchy and the Confucian ethical system (Selection 5). The Confucian scholars, K'ang Yu-wei and Liang Ch'i-ch'ao, advocated a modern constitutional monarchy. The Kuang-hsü Emperor, advised by K'ang Yu-wei, issued a series of sweeping reform decrees in 1898 (the Hundred Days' Reform), but was then placed under house arrest as the result of a reactionary coup headed by the Empress Dowager Tz'u-hsi.

The Boxer uprising, an anti-foreign and anti-Christian popular movement, endangered the foreign legations in Peking and provoked military intervention by the Western powers and Japan in 1900. The Empress Dowager and her court, which had encouraged the Boxers, were forced to flee the capital. Manchuria fell under Russian military occupation, and the Manchus had to sign the humiliating Boxer Protocol (Selection 4). Belatedly the court, advised by Chang Chih-tung and others favorably disposed to reform, abolished the traditional civil service examinations, undertook to modernize the educational system and the army, and inaugurated a program for sending Chinese youths abroad to study.

Japan's victory in the Russo-Japanese War in 1905 led many Chinese

---

[1] As a rule throughout this book, in Chinese, Japanese, Korean, and Vietnamese names, the family designation precedes the given name. The romanizations used in the editorial notes are those favored by contemporary scholarship, but the romanizations in the selections have not been altered.

to believe that by adopting a modern constitution similar to Japan's, China too might become powerful. The imperial court sent scholars overseas to study the constitutions of modern states. In 1908 the court proclaimed its Constitutional Principles (Selection 6), and announced a nine-year program that would lead step by step to a constitutional monarchy similar to Japan's. A national provisional assembly and twenty-two provincial assemblies came into being in 1910. These new representative bodies, although made up of upper-class conservatives, immediately demanded more authority than had been originally granted them and called for the prompt establishment of a national parliament and constitutional government.

In the meantime, Sun Yat-sen and other revolutionary leaders had been advocating the overthrow of the Manchu dynasty and the establishment of a parliamentary republic. Sun Yat-sen, of peasant birth, had received part of his childhood education in Honolulu, where he learned English and became a Christian. Later he received a medical degree in a Hongkong college, but rather than practice medicine, he devoted his efforts to the cause of the revolution. He traveled extensively, attempting to win the moral and financial support of the overseas Chinese for his program. In 1905 Sun and Huang Hsing, a Hunanese revolutionary, merged various revolutionary groups among the Chinese students in Japan to form the *T'ung-meng Hui* (United League) (Selection 7). At the same time, republican sentiment spread in the Chinese army.

From 1895 to 1911, a number of revolutionary outbreaks were suppressed by the government. On October 10, 1911, Chinese army units in Wuchang rebelled, and the revolution spread throughout southern China. As a last minute gesture to meet the demands for political reform, the throne promulgated the Nineteen Articles, which would establish a new constitution and parliamentary government under the Manchu dynasty. The South was soon under the control of revolutionary forces, but it appeared that they stood little chance of military victory over monarchist troops in the North. Sun Yat-sen, the Provisional President of the Republic, telegraphed Yüan Shih-k'ai, Premier of the Manchu government, and offered him the presidency of the Republic on condition that he obtain the abdication of the dynasty. The Hsüan-t'ung Emperor (Pu Yi) abdicated on February 12, 1912, appearing to transfer his authority to Yüan rather than to the Republic directly (Selection 8).

The republican assembly in Nanking elected Yüan Provisional President of the Republic. Backed by his loyal modern army, President Yüan soon displayed dictatorial tendencies. He was apparently implicated in the assassination of Sung Chiao-jen, the leader of the majority Kuomintang (Nationalist) Party. As a result, in 1913 a brief and unsuccessful insurrection broke out against Yüan. Late in 1915 Yüan attempted to reestablish the monarchy with himself as Emperor. Liang Ch'i-ch'ao, a former supporter of monarchy, led the protest against this effort to over-throw the Republic (Selection 9). Rebellions against Yüan broke out in the South, and he was forced to renounce his imperial ambitions. He died in 1916. Vice-President Li Yüan-hung succeeded to the presidency.

In 1917, during the controversy over a proposed declaration of war against Germany, the dismissal of Premier Tuan Ch'i-jui led to an uprising of northern military governors. The warlord Chang Hsün was asked to put down the uprising. On July 1, he startled the country by restoring Pu Yi as Emperor. However, faced with overwhelming opposition at home and abroad, the Manchu dynasty was overthrown only twelve days later by Tuan. Sun Yat-sen organized a separate government in Canton in opposition to the military regime in Peking. China disintegrated as each province fell under the control of one clique of warlords or another. By the end of the First World War the monarchy had indeed been over-thrown, but a viable republican regime had yet to be established.

1

The Treaty of Wanghia

July 3, 1844

The principles of most-favored-nation treatment and extraterritori-ality are provided for in the first treaty made between the United States and China. The United States did not relinquish her extra-territorial rights in China until 1943, when the two countries were allies in the war against Japan.

ARTICLE II

Citizens of the United States resorting to China for the purposes of commerce will pay the duties of import and export prescribed in the Tariff, which is fixed by and made a part of this Treaty. They shall, in no case, be subject to other or higher duties than are or shall be required of the people of any other nation whatever. Fees and charges of every sort are wholly abolished, and officers of the revenue, who may be guilty of exaction, shall be punished according to the laws of China. If the

From Hunter Miller, ed., *Treaties and Other International Acts of the United States of America* (Washington, D.C.: Government Printing Office, 1934), IV, 559–625.

The Russian Acquisitions, 1858–1860

Chinese Government desire to modify, in any respect, the said Tariff, such modifications shall be made only in consultation with consuls or other functionaries thereto duly authorized in behalf of the United States, and with consent thereof. And if additional advantages or privileges, of whatever description, be conceded hereafter by China to any other nation, the United States, and the citizens thereof, shall be entitled thereupon, to a complete, equal and impartial participation in the same.

ARTICLE XXI

Subjects of China who may be guilty of any criminal act towards citizens of the United States, shall be arrested and punished by the Chinese authorities according to the laws of China: and citizens of the United

States, who may commit any crime in China, shall be subject to be tried and punished only by the Consul, or other public functionary of the United States, thereto authorized according to the laws of the United States. And in order to the prevention of all controversy and disaffection, justice shall be equitably and impartially administered on both sides.

2

The Open Door Notes

Hay hoped that the powers would promise to respect the principle of equality of commercial opportunity for the nationals of all countries in China (the Open Door), notwithstanding the recent establishment of spheres of influence there.

SECRETARY HAY TO THE AMBASSADOR IN GREAT BRITAIN (CHOATE)

WASHINGTON, *September 6, 1899*

SIR: The Government of Her Britannic Majesty has declared that its policy and its very traditions precluded it from using any privileges which might be granted it in China as a weapon for excluding commercial rivals, and that freedom of trade for Great Britain in that Empire meant freedom of trade for all the world alike. While conceding by formal agreements, first with Germany and then with Russia, the possession of "spheres of influence or interest" in China in which they are to enjoy special rights and privileges, more especially in respect of railroads and mining enterprises, Her Britannic Majesty's Government has therefore sought to maintain at the same time what is called the "open-door" policy, to insure to the commerce of the world in China equality of treatment within said "spheres" for commerce and navigation. This latter policy is alike urgently demanded by the British mercantile communities and by those of the United States, as it is justly held by them to be the only one which will improve existing conditions, enable them to main-

From United States Department of State, *United States Relations with China: With Special Reference to the Period 1944–1949* (Washington, D.C.: Government Printing Office, 1949), pp. 414–417.

tain their positions in the markets of China, and extend their operations in the future. While the Government of the United States will in no way commit itself to a recognition of exclusive rights of any power within or control over any portion of the Chinese Empire under such agreements as have within the last year been made, it can not conceal its apprehension that under existing conditions there is a possibility, even a probability, of complications arising between the treaty powers which may imperil the rights insured to the United States under our treaties with China.

This Government is animated by a sincere desire that the interests of our citizens may not be prejudiced through exclusive treatment by any of the controlling powers within their so-called "spheres of interest" in China, and hopes also to retain there an open market for the commerce of the world, remove dangerous sources of international irritation, and hasten thereby united or concerted action of the powers at Pekin in favor of the administrative reforms so urgently needed for strengthening the Imperial Government and maintaining the integrity of China in which the whole western world is alike concerned. It believes that such a result may be greatly assisted by a declaration by the various powers claiming "spheres of interest" in China of their intentions as regards treatment of foreign trade therein. The present moment seems a particularly opportune one for informing Her Britannic Majesty's Government of the desire of the United States to see it make a formal declaration and to lend its support in obtaining similar declarations from the various powers claiming "spheres of influence" in China, to the effect that each in its respective spheres of interest or influence

First. Will in no wise interfere with any treaty port or any vested interest within any so-called "sphere of interest" or leased territory it may have in China.

Second. That the Chinese treaty tariff of the time being shall apply to all merchandise landed or shipped to all such ports as are within said "sphere of interest" (unless they be "free ports"), no matter to what nationality it may belong, and that duties so leviable shall be collected by the Chinese Government.

Third. That it will levy no higher harbor duties on vessels of another nationality frequenting any port in such "sphere" than shall be levied on vessels of its own nationality, and no higher railroad charges over lines built, controlled, or operated within its "sphere" on merchandise belonging to citizens or subjects of other nationalities transported through such "sphere" than shall be levied on similar merchandise belonging to its own nationals transported over equal distances.

The recent ukase of His Majesty the Emperor of Russia, declaring the port of Ta-lien-wan open to the merchant ships of all nations during the whole of the lease under which it is to be held by Russia, removing as it does all uncertainty as to the liberal and conciliatory policy of that power, together with the assurances given this Government by Russia, justifies the expectation that His Majesty will cooperate in such an understanding as is here proposed, and our ambassador at the court of St. Petersburg has been instructed accordingly to submit the propositions above detailed to His Imperial Majesty, and ask their early consideration. Copy of my instruction to Mr. Tower is herewith inclosed for your confidential information.

The action of Germany in declaring the port of Kiaochao a "free port," and the aid the Imperial Government has given China in the establishment there of a Chinese custom-house, coupled with the oral assurance conveyed the United States by Germany that our interests within its "sphere" would in no wise be affected by its occupation of this portion of the province of Shang-tung, tend to show that little opposition may be anticipated from that power to the desired declaration.

The interests of Japan, the next most interested power in the trade of China, will be so clearly served by the proposed arrangement, and the declaration of its statesmen within the last year are so entirely in line with the views here expressed, that its hearty cooperation is confidently counted on.

You will, at as early date as practicable, submit the considerations to Her Britannic Majesty's principal secretary of state for foreign affairs and request their immediate consideration.

I inclose herewith a copy of the instruction sent to our ambassador at Berlin bearing on the above subject.

I have the honor to be [etc.]   *John Hay*

SECRETARY HAY TO AMERICAN DIPLOMATIC REPRESENTATIVES AT LONDON, PARIS, BERLIN, ST. PETERSBURG, ROME, AND TOKYO

WASHINGTON, *March 20, 1900*

SIR: The ——— Government having accepted the declaration suggested by the United States concerning foreign trade in China, the terms of which I transmitted to you in my instruction No. ——— of ———, and like action having been taken by all the various powers having leased territory or so-called "spheres of interest" in the Chinese Empire, as shown by the notes which I herewith transmit to you, you will please inform the Government to which you are accredited that the condition originally attached to its acceptance—that all other powers concerned should likewise accept the proposals of the United States—having been complied with, this Government will therefore consider the assent given to it by ——— as final and definitive.

You will also transmit to the minister for foreign affairs copies of the

present inclosures, and by the same occasion convey to him the expression
of the sincere gratification which the President feels at the successful
termination of these negotiations, in which he sees proof of the friendly
spirit which animates the various powers interested in the untrammeled
development of commerce and industry in the Chinese Empire, and a
source of vast benefit to the whole commercial world.

    I am [etc.]   *John Hay*

3

The Open Door Notes: Second Round

The presence of foreign troops in China to repress the Boxer uprising seemed to endanger China's independence and with it the
Open Door.

SECRETARY HAY TO AMERICAN DIPLOMATIC
REPRESENTATIVES AT BERLIN, PARIS, LONDON,
ROME, ST. PETERSBURG, VIENNA, BRUSSELS,
MADRID, TOKYO, THE HAGUE, AND LISBON

WASHINGTON, *July 3, 1900*

    In this critical posture of affairs in China it is deemed appropriate to
define the attitude of the United States as far as present circumstances
permit this to be done. We adhere to the policy initiated by us in 1857
of peace with the Chinese nation, of furtherance of lawful commerce, and
of protection of lives and property of our citizens by all means guaranteed under extraterritorial treaty rights and by the law of nations. If
wrong be done to our citizens we propose to hold the responsible authors
to the uttermost accountability. We regard the condition at Pekin as one
of virtual anarchy, whereby power and responsibility are practically
devolved upon the local provincial authorities. So long as they are not in
overt collusion with rebellion and use their power to protect foreign life
and property, we regard them as representing the Chinese people, with
whom we seek to remain in peace and friendship. The purpose of the

From United States Department of State, *United States Relations with China:
With Special Reference to the Period 1944–1949* (Washington, D.C.: Government
Printing Office, 1949), p. 417.

President is, as it has been heretofore, to act concurrently with the other powers; first, in opening up communication with Pekin and rescuing the American officials, missionaries, and other Americans who are in danger; secondly, in affording all possible protection everywhere in China to American life and property; thirdly, in guarding and protecting all legitimate American interests; and fourthly, in aiding to prevent a spread of the disorders to the other provinces of the Empire and a recurrence of such disasters. It is of course too early to forecast the means of attaining this last result; but the policy of the Government of the United States is to seek a solution which may bring about permanent safety and peace to China, preserve Chinese territorial and administrative entity, protect all rights guaranteed to friendly powers by treaty and international law, and safeguard for the world the principle of equal and impartial trade with all parts of the Chinese Empire.

You will communicate the purport of this instruction to the minister for foreign affairs.

John Hay

4

The Boxer Protocol

Note the humiliations inflicted on China by the Western powers and Japan in this treaty.

FINAL PROTOCOL ENTERED INTO BETWEEN THE PLENIPOTENTIARIES OF VARIOUS POWERS AT THE CONCLUSION OF THE SO-CALLED "BOXER" TROUBLES IN 1900

(*Concluded at Peking, September 7, 1901.*)

ARTICLES

I. (*a*) Assassination of German Minister.
(*b*) Erection of monument.
II. (*a*) Punishment.
(*b*) Suspension of official examinations.

III. Assassination of Japanese chancellor.
IV. Erection of monuments.
V. Importation of arms, etc.
VI. Indemnity; payment.
VII. Legation quarter.

VIII. Razing of forts.
 IX. Points occupied.
  X. Publication of imperial edicts.
 XI. Amendments to commercial

treaties; improvement of rivers.

XII. Office of Foreign Affairs; evacuation of Peking, etc.

[Translation]

FINAL PROTOCOL

The plenipotentiaries of Germany, His Excellency M. A. Mumm von Schwarzenstein; of Austria-Hungary, His Excellency M. M. Czikann von Wahlborn; of Belgium, His Excellency M. Joostens; of Spain, M. B. J. de Cologan; of the United States, His Excellency M. W. W. Rockhill; of France, His Excellency M. Paul Beau; of Great Britain, His Excellency Sir Ernest Satow; of Italy, Marquis Salvago Raggi; of Japan, His Excellency M. Jutaro Komura; of the Netherlands, His Excellency M. F. M. Knobel; of Russia, His Excellency M. M. de Giers; and of China, His Highness Yi-K'uang Prince Ching of the first rank, President of the Ministry of Foreign Affairs, and His Excellency Li Hung-chang, Earl of Su-i of the first rank, Tutor of the Heir Apparent, Grand Secretary of the Wen-hua Throne Hall, Minister of commerce, Superintendent of the northern trade, Governor-General of Chihli, have met for the purpose of declaring that China has complied to the satisfaction of the Powers with the conditions laid down in the note of the 22d of December, 1900, and which were accepted in their entirety by His Majesty the Emperor of China in a decree dated the 27th of December.

ARTICLE I a

By an imperial edict of the 9th of June last (Annex No. 2), Tsai Feng, Prince of Ch'ün, was appointed Ambassador of His Majesty the Emperor of China, and directed in that capacity to convey to His Majesty the German Emperor the expression of the regrets of His Majesty the Emperor of China and of the Chinese Government for the assassination of His Excellency the late Baron von Ketteler, German minister.

Prince Ch'ün left Peking the 12th of last July to carry out the orders which had been given him.

ARTICLE I b

The Chinese Government has stated that it will erect on the spot of the assassination of His Excellency the late Baron von Ketteler a com-

From W. M. Malloy, ed., *Treaties, Conventions, International Acts, Protocols and Agreements between the United States of America and Other Powers, 1776–1909,* 2 vols. (Washington, D.C.: Government Printing Office, 1910), II, 2006–2012.

memorative monument, worthy of the rank of the deceased, and bearing an inscription in the Latin, German, and Chinese languages, which shall express the regrets of His Majesty the Emperor of China for the murder committed.

Their Excellencies the Chinese Plenipotentiaries have informed His Excellency the German Plenipotentiary, in a letter dated the 22nd of July last (Annex No. 3) that an arch of the whole width of the street would be erected on the said spot, and that work on it was begun the 25th of June last.

ARTICLE II [a]

Imperial edicts of the 13th and 21st of February, 1901 (Annexes Nos. 4, 5, and 6), inflicted the following punishments on the principal authors of the outrages and crimes committed against the foreign Governments and their nationals:

Tsai-I Prince Tuan and Tsai Lan Duke Fu-kuo were sentenced to be brought before the autumnal court of assize for execution, and it was agreed that if the Emperor saw fit to grant them their lives they should be exiled to Turkestan and there imprisoned for life, without the possibility of commutation of these punishments.

Tsai Hsün Prince Chuang, Ying Nien, President of the Court of censors, and Chao Shu-Chiao, President of the Board of Punishments, were condemned to commit suicide.

Yü Hsien, Governor of Shanhshi, Chi Hsiu, President of the Board of rites, and Hsü Cheng-yu, formerly senior vice-President of the Board of punishments, were condemned to death.

Posthumous degradation was inflicted on Kang Yi, assistant Grand Secretary, President of the Board of works, Hsü Tung, Grand Secretary, and Li Ping-heng, formerly Governor-General of Szu-ch'uan.

An Imperial Edict of February 13th, 1901 (Annex No. 7), rehabilitated the memories of Hsü Yung-yi, President of the Board of war, Li Shaon, President of the Board of works, Hsü Ching-cheng, senior vice-President of the Board of works, Lien Yuan, vice-Chancellor of the Grand Council, and Yuan Chang, vice-President of the Court of sacrifices, who had been put to death for having protested against the outrageous breaches of international law of last year.

Prince Chuang committed suicide the 21st of February, 1901, Ying Nien and Chao Shu-chiao the 24th, Yü Hsien was executed the 22nd, Chi Hsiu and Hsü Cheng-yu on the 26th. Tung Fu-hsiang, General in Kan-su, has been deprived of his office by Imperial Edict of the 13th of February, 1901, pending the determination of the final punishment to be inflicted on him.

Imperial Edicts dated the 29th of April and 19th of August, 1901, have inflicted various punishments on the provincial officials convicted of the crimes and outrages of last summer.

ARTICLE II [b]

An Imperial Edict promulgated the 19th of August, 1901 (Annex No. 8), ordered the suspension of official examinations for five years in all cities where foreigners were massacred or submitted to cruel treatment.

ARTICLE III

So as to make honorable reparation for the assassination of Mr. Sugiyama, chancellor of the Japanese legation, His Majesty the Emperor of China by an Imperial Edict of the 18th of June, 1901 (Annex No. 9), appointed Na-Tung, vice-President of the Board of revenue, to be his Envoy Extraordinary, and specially directed him to convey to His Majesty the Emperor of Japan the expression of the regrets of His Majesty the Emperor of China and of his Government at the assassination of the late Mr. Sugiyama.

ARTICLE IV

The Chinese Government has agreed to erect an expiatory monument in each of the foreign or international cemeteries which were desecrated and in which the tombs were destroyed.

It has been agreed with the Representatives of the Powers that the legations interested shall settle the details for the erection of these monuments, China bearing all the expenses thereof, estimated at ten thousand taels for the cemeteries at Peking and within its neighborhood, and at five thousand taels for the cemeteries in the provinces. The amounts have been paid and the list of these cemeteries is enclosed herewith. (Annex No. 10.)

ARTICLE V

China has agreed to prohibit the importation into its territory of arms and ammunition, as well as of materials exclusively used for the manufacture of arms and ammunition.

An Imperial Edict has been issued on the 25th of August, 1901 (Annex No. 11), forbidding said importation for a term of two years. New Edicts may be issued subsequently extending this by other successive terms of two years in case of necessity recognized by the Powers.

ARTICLE VI

By an Imperial Edict dated the 29th of May, 1901 (Annex No. 12), His Majesty the Emperor of China agreed to pay the Powers an indemnity of four hundred and fifty millions of Haikwan Taels. This sum represents the total amount of the indemnities for States, companies or societies, private individuals, and Chinese referred to in Article VI of the note of December 22nd, 1900.

a. These four hundred and fifty millions constitute a gold debt calculated at the rate of the Haikwan tael to the gold currency of each country, as indicated below.

Haikwan tael = marks	3. 055
= Austro-Hungary crown	3. 595
= gold dollar	0. 742
= francs	3. 750
= pound sterling	3s. 0d.
= yen	1. 407
= Netherlands florin	1. 796
= gold rouble (17.424 dolias fine)	1. 412

This sum in gold shall bear interest at 4 per cent per annum, and the capital shall be reimbursed by China in thirty-nine years in the manner indicated in the annexed plan of amortization. (Annex No. 13).

Capital and interest shall be payable in gold or at the rates of exchange corresponding to the dates at which the different payments fall due.

The amortization shall commence the 1st of January, 1902, and shall finish at the end of the year 1940. The amortizations are payable annually, the first payment being fixed on the 1st of January, 1903.

Interest shall run from the 1st of July, 1901, but the Chinese Government shall have the right to pay off within a term of three years, beginning January, 1902, the arrears of the first six months, ending the 31st of December, 1901, on condition, however, that it pays compound interest at the rate of 4 per cent per annum on the sums the payments of which shall have thus been deferred. Interest shall be payable semiannually, the first payment being fixed on the 1st of July, 1902.

b. The service of the debt shall take place in Shanghai, in the following manner:

Each Power shall be represented by a delegate on a commission of bankers authorized to receive the amount of interest and amortization which shall be paid to it by the Chinese authorities designated for that purpose, to divide it among the interested parties, and to give a receipt for the same.

c. The Chinese Government shall deliver to the Doyen of the Diplomatic Corps at Peking a bond for the lump sum, which shall subsequently be converted into fractional bonds bearing the signatures of the delegates of the Chinese Government designated for that purpose. This operation and all those relating to issuing of the bonds shall be performed by the above-mentioned Commission, in accordance with the instructions which the Powers shall send their delegates.

d. The proceeds of the revenues assigned to the payment of the bonds shall be paid monthly to the Commission.

e. The revenues assigned as security for the bonds are the following:

1. The balance of the revenues of the Imperial maritime Customs after payment of the interest and amortization of preceding loans secured on these revenues, plus the proceeds of the raising to five per cent effective of the present tariff on maritime imports, including articles until now on the free list, but exempting foreign rice, cereals, and flour, gold and silver bullion and coin.

2. The revenues of the native customs, administered in the open ports by the Imperial maritime Customs.

3. The total revenues of the salt gabelle, exclusive of the fraction previously set aside for other foreign loans.

The raising of the present tariff on imports to five per cent effective is agreed to on the conditions mentioned below.

It shall be put in force two months after the signing of the present protocol, and no exceptions shall be made except for merchandise shipped not more than ten days after the said signing.

1°. All duties levied on imports "ad valorem" shall be converted as far as possible and as soon as may be into specific duties. This conversion shall be made in the following manner: The average value of merchandise at the time of their landing during the three years 1897, 1898, and 1899, that is to say, the market price less the amount of import duties and incidental expenses, shall be taken as the basis for the valuation of merchandise. Pending the result of the work of conversion, duties shall be levied "ad valorem."

2°. The beds of the rivers Peiho and Whangpu shall be improved with the financial participation of China.

ARTICLE VII

The Chinese Government has agreed that the quarter occupied by the legations shall be considered as one specially reserved for their use and placed under their exclusive control, in which Chinese shall not have the right to reside and which may be made defensible.

The limits of this quarter have been fixed as follows on the annexed plan (Annex No. 14):

On the west, the line 1, 2, 3, 4, 5.

On the north, the line 5, 6, 7, 8, 9, 10.

On the east, Ketteler street (10, 11, 12).

Drawn along the exterior base of the Tartar wall and following the line of the bastions, on the south the line 12.1.

In the protocol annexed to the letter of the 16th of January, 1901, China recognized the right of each Power to maintain a permanent guard in the said quarter for the defense of its legation.

ARTICLE VIII

The Chinese Government has consented to raze the forts of Taku and those which might impede free communication between Peking and the sea; steps have been taken for carrying this out.

ARTICLE IX

The Chinese Government has conceded the right to the Powers in the protocol annexed to the letter of the 16th of January, 1901, to occupy certain points, to be determined by an agreement between them, for the maintenance of open communication between the capital and the sea. The points occupied by the powers are:

Huang-tsun, Lang-fang, Yang-tsun, Tientsin, Chun-liang Ch'eng, Tang-ku, Lu-tai, Tang-shan, Lan-chou, Chang-li, Ch'in-wang tao, Shan-hai kuan.

ARTICLE X

The Chinese Government has agreed to post and to have published during two years in all district cities the following Imperial edicts:

a. Edict of the 1st of February (Annex No. 15), prohibiting forever, under pain of death, membership in any antiforeign society.

b. Edicts of the 13th and 21st February, 29th April, and 19th August, enumerating the punishments inflicted on the guilty.

c. Edict of the 19th August, 1901, prohibiting examinations in all cities where foreigners were massacred or subjected to cruel treatment.

d. Edict of the 1st of February, 1901 (Annex No. 16), declaring all governors-general, governors, and provincial or local officials responsible for order in their respective districts, and that in case of new antiforeign troubles or other infractions of the treaties which shall not be immediately repressed and the authors of which shall not have been punished, these officials shall be immediately dismissed, without possibility of being given new functions or new honors.

The posting of these edicts is being carried on throughout the Empire.

ARTICLE XI

The Chinese Government has agreed to negotiate the amendments deemed necessary by the foreign Governments to the treaties of commerce and navigation and other subjects concerning commercial relations, with the object of facilitating them.

At present, and as a result of the stipulation contained in Article VI concerning the indemnity, the Chinese Government agrees to assist in the improvement of the courses of the rivers Peiho and Whangpu, as stated below.

a. The works for the improvement of the navigability of the Peiho, begun in 1898 with the cooperation of the Chinese Government, have been resumed under the direction of an international Commission. As soon as the administration of Tientsin shall have been handed back to the Chinese Government, it will be in a position to be represented on this commission, and will pay each year a sum of sixty thousand Haikwan taels for maintaining the works.

b. A conservancy Board, charged with the management and control of the works for straightening the Whangpu and the improvement of the course of that river, is hereby created.

This Board shall consist of members representing the interests of the Chinese Government and those of foreigners in the shipping trade of Shanghai. The expenses incurred for the works and the general management of the undertaking are estimated at the annual sum of four hundred and sixty thousand Haikwan taels for the first twenty years. This sum shall be supplied in equal portions by the Chinese Government and the foreign interests concerned. Detailed stipulations concerning the composition, duties, and revenues of the conservancy board are embodied in Annex No. 17.

ARTICLE XII

An Imperial Edict of the 24th of July, 1901 (Annex No. 18), reformed the Office of foreign affairs (Tsungli Yamen), on the lines indicated by the Powers, that is to say, transformed it into a Ministry of foreign affairs (Wai-wu Pu), which takes precedence over the six other Ministries of State. The same edict appointed the principal members of this Ministry.

An agreement has also been reached concerning the modification of Court ceremonial as regards the reception of foreign Representatives and has been the subject of several notes from the Chinese Plenipotentiaries, the substance of which is embodied in a memorandum herewith annexed (Annex No. 19).

Finally, it is expressly understood that as regards the declarations specified above and the annexed documents originating with the foreign Plenipotentiaries, the French text only is authoritative.

The Chinese Government having thus complied to the satisfaction of the Powers with the conditions laid down in the above-mentioned note of December 22nd, 1900, the Powers have agreed to accede to the wish of China to terminate the situation created by the disorders of the summer of 1900. In consequence thereof the foreign Plenipotentiaries are authorized to declare in the names of their Governments that, with the exception of the legation guards mentioned in Article VII, the international troops will completely evacuate the city of Peking on the 17th September, 1901, and, with the exception of the localities mentioned in Article IX, will withdraw from the province of Chihli on the 22nd of September.

The present final Protocol has been drawn up in twelve identic copies and signed by all the Plenipotentiaries of the Contracting Countries. One copy shall be given to each of the foreign Plenipotentiaries, and one copy shall be given to the Chinese Plenipotentiaries.

Peking, 7th September, 1901

Signatures and seals of Chinese plenipotentiaries

A. v. Mumm
M. Czikann
Joostens
B. J. de Cologan
W. W. Rockhill
Beau
Ernest Satow
Salvago Raggi
Jutaro Komura
F. M. Knobel
M. de Giers

[Translation]

Annexes to the final protocol (Appendix For. Rel. of U.S. 1901, pp. 319 et seq.)

No. 1. Imperial Edict of 27 December, 1900.
2. Imperial Edict of 9 June, 1901.
3. Letter of the Chinese plenipotentiaries of 22 July, 1901.
4. Imperial Edict of 13 February, 1901.
5. Imperial Edict of 13 February, 1901.
6. Imperial Edict of 21 February, 1901.
7. Imperial Edict of 13 February, 1901.
8. Imperial Edict of 19 August, 1901.
9. Imperial Edict of 18 June, 1901.

10. List of desecrated cemeteries.
11. Imperial Edict of 25 August, 1901.
12. Imperial Edict of 29 May, 1901.
13. Table of amortization.
14. Plan of the diplomatic quarter and notice.
15. Imperial Edict of 1st February, 1901.
16. Imperial Edict of 1st February, 1901.
17. Regulations for the improvement of the Whangpu.
18. Imperial Edict of 24 July, 1901.
19. Memorandum concerning court ceremonial.

5

Exhortation to Learn

1898

Chang Chih-tung

Chang Chih-tung, Governor-General of Kwangtung and Kwangsi from 1884 to 1889 and of Hunan and Hupei from 1889 to 1907, was famous for his influential memorials to the throne, the best known of which was his *Exhortation to Learn*. A practical statesman and administrator, he was distinguished by his educational reforms and for the construction of factories and railroads, including the Peking-Hankow railway. Chang was a conservative reformer. He was devoted to the Manchu dynasty, whose record, he held, was distinguished by magnanimity towards the people, and he was emphatically opposed to democracy, parliamentary government, and Western theories of freedom and individualism. He was the leading advocate of the principle of "Chinese learning for the fundamental principles, Western learning for practical application," that is, Confucian principles of politics and morality combined with Western technology and administrative methods. He was sharply critical of the rapid reforms advocated by K'ang Yu-wei in 1898, advocating instead a gradual reform based upon education. The throne was pleased with his *Exhortation to Learn*, and copies were distributed to provincial officials for reproduction. The Preface of

Excerpts from Chang Chih-tung, *China's Only Hope* [*Exhortation to Learn*], translated by Samuel I. Woodbridge (Westwood, N.J.: Revell, 1900), pp. 19–27, 31–36.

the memorial summarizes the chapters which make up the work and lists the five objects of knowledge. Chapter I, also quoted here, emphasizes the need to conserve the Manchu dynasty, the teachings of Confucius, and the Chinese race.

PREFACE

In olden times, Ch'u Chwang Wang made it his chief aim to exhort his people to diligence, and to caution his troops lest some catastrophe should suddenly befall his countrymen. In consequence of this, the kingdom of Ch'u became powerful, and the neighboring countries—Ts'i, Tsin, Ch'in, and Sung—were intimidated and held in check. An old saying runs: "If a man will not understand in what misfortune consists, disgrace is sure to follow; but if he will only face the difficulty, happiness will ensue."

In no period of China's history has there arisen an emergency like the present. It is a time of change, and His Imperial Highness, the Emperor of China, has accepted the situation by altering somewhat the system of civil and military examinations and by establishing schools. New plans are being formed for the welfare of the country by Chinese philanthropists, but these plans differ both in degree and kind. There are some who hold that the new learning will save us; others maintain that its acceptation will abrogate our old doctrines, and that we ought to hold fast the patrimony of our sages. Who can tell which is right? The Conservatives are evidently off their food from inability to swallow, whilst the Liberals are like a flock of sheep who have arrived at a road of many forks and do not know which to follow. The former do not understand what international intercourse means, the latter are ignorant of what is radical in Chinese affairs. The Conservatives fail to see the utility of modern military methods and the benefits of successful change, while the Progressionists, zealous without knowledge, look with contempt upon our widespread doctrines of Confucius. Thus those who cling to the old order of things heartily despise those who even propose any innovation, and they in turn cordially detest the Conservatives with all the ardor of their liberal convictions. It thus falls out that those who really wish to learn are in doubt as to which course to pursue, and in the meantime error creeps in, the enemy invades our coast, and, consequently, there is no defence and no peace.

The present condition of things is not due to outside nations, but to China herself. It has ever been true that the number of our able men has been proportioned to the good qualities of the government, and that morals are gauged by the conduct of the schools. In view of many facts, and with the hope of relieving our country from her present embarrassments, We, the Viceroy of the Liang Hu, have prepared this work especially for the Chinese under our jurisdiction, and generally for our countrymen in the other provinces. It consists of two parts, divided and discussed as follows:

PART I. MORAL

Subject: *Radical Principles a means of rectifying the Heart.*

Chapter I. United Hearts. It is plain that three things claim our attention just now—the protection of the Empire, the Religion, and the Race. If the hands and feet are nimble, the eyes and head will be at rest, and if the constitution is robust, the purpose will be strong. The Imperial power will increase in proportion to the number of intellectual men who come forward.

Chapter II. The Inculcation of Loyalty. The moral excellence of this Dynasty is so universally known that both ministers and people should cherish an ardent patriotism in order to conserve the country.

Chapter III. The Three Moral Obligations. The sages have always taught that the true relations existing between the sovereign and subject, father and son, and husband and wife, are of prime importance, the *radix* of propriety and the distinguishing feature between man and the brutes.

Chapter IV. The Recognition of Class. We are grieved lest the Chinese—the descendants of the gods—should be sunk in obscurity, and We write this chapter for the protection of our race.

Chapter V. Honor due the Classics. Some of our extra-canonical books are good, others are pernicious. Let not the bad obscure what is good. Doctrines that tend to disrupt ought not to be followed. Before any work is approved it should be brought to the touchstone of the Holy Canons.

Chapter VI. Centralization of Power. Differentiate between officials and people, but give direction to popular thought. We denounce republicanism as rebellious.

Chapter VII. The Proper Sequence of Things. That which enters first, dominates. A thorough knowledge of Chinese is necessary in order to a Western education. Possessing this knowledge our ancestors will not be forgotten.

Chapter VIII. Attending to what is Vital. To rejoice in the new is sweet; to love the old is bitter. If we are to preserve Chinese learning, we must find out what is important and hold to it.

Chapter IX. Cast out the Poison! The foreign drug (opium) is debasing the homes and sweeping away the lives of our people. Cut it off, root and branch!

PART II. PRACTICAL

Subject: *The Intercourse of Nations a means of Enlightenment.*

Chapter I. Beneficial Knowledge. When unknown foes assail us, we are deluded and meet with disaster.

Chapter II. Travel. Discern the signs of the times, enlarge the mind, broaden the understanding, and increase the skill and knowledge of the Chinese! Without travel in foreign countries these *desiderata* cannot be obtained.

Chapter III. The Establishment of Schools. Establish schools everywhere adapted to the present time, for putting into practice the knowledge of the graduates. Rouse the stupid!

Chapter IV. The Study of Regulations. The strength of Western countries is derived from their government institutions in which the students are required to observe stipulated rules. These have the power of conferring official rank. We should establish such institutions on the best approved methods.

Chapter V. The Extensive Translation of Books. The benefits derived from the instruction of Western teachers have their limits. Those which follow the translation of foreign books are boundless.

Chapter VI. Newspaper Reading. It is difficult to see one's own eyebrows and eyelashes, and hard to take bitter medicine. Be sensible of moral corruption and cast it out at once! Have a knowledge of outside evil and prepare a defence!

Chapter VII. Reform of Methods. Self-preservation demands something more than our old inherited principles.

Chapter VIII. Railways. Commerce is the blood and breath of a nation.

Chapter IX. Comparative Study. Know how to combine the gist of Western learning with Chinese learning, in order to enlighten dense ignorance.

Chapter X. Maintaining the Army. The despicable teaching of ease and lust is suicidal.

Chapter XI. Religious Toleration. The outbreaks of petty malignity against different sects defeat great schemes and are to be deplored.

The corollaries of these Twenty Chapters may be briefly comprehended in

FIVE OBJECTS OF KNOWLEDGE

1. Know the shame of not being like Japan, Turkey, Siam, and Cuba.
2. Know the fear that we will become as India, Annam, Burmah, Korea, Egypt, and Poland.
3. Know that if we do not change our customs we cannot reform our methods, and if we do not reform our methods we cannot utilize the modern implements of war, etc.
4. Know what is important. The study of the old is not urgent; the

call for men of attainments is useful; knowledge is pressing. Foreign education is of different kinds. Western handicraft is not in demand, but a knowledge of the methods of foreign governments is a consummation devoutly to be wished.

5. Know what is radical. When abroad, do not forget your own native country; when you see strange customs, do not forget your parents; and let not much wisdom and ingenuity make you forget the holy sages.

It will be seen then that the purport of what we have written accords well with the Doctrine of the Mean. Long ago, when the kingdom of Lu was in a weak condition, Duke Ai [B.C. 550] inquired of Confucius about government. He replied: "To be fond of learning is the next thing to knowledge. To be up and doing comes near to perfection. Know what shame is, and you will not be far from heroism." Finally the sage said: "If these principles can be carried out, although one may be stupid, yet he will become clever; although weak, he will attain to strength." These maxims were spoken in the time of Lu. How much more urgent are they now when China has become great, with her almost limitless territory and her teeming population of four hundred millions!

At the outset of this Preface We referred to a state of things that existed in the time of Ch'u. This is because We are apprehensive, lest the officials and gentry accustomed to a life of *otium cum dignitate* should be indifferent to the impending perils which now threaten the Empire; and, fearing that they will impatiently cast the subject aside and not seek to renew our strength, we call their attention to what Confucius enunciated. The Book of Changes [B.C. 2800] says: "Though threatened by overthrow, we still cling fast to safety." Let us fully realize the magnitude of the danger and then we will put forth our most strenuous efforts to avert it.

Written by
Chang Chih-tung,
of Nan-p'i

CHAPTER I. UNITED HEARTS

When Fan Wen-chang was a mere youth he was so patriotic as to feel that the responsibility of the government rested upon himself. The philosopher Ch'eng said: "If real altruism existed in the heart of only one official, some amount of good would be sure to follow." Another sage has it: "Every man in the Empire, however humble and despised he may be, has some duty to perform to his government." How circumscribed would be the responsibility of one graduate, the altruism of one official, or the duty of a single individual! But if by one determined purpose the hearts of *all* the graduates, the officials and the men of China were united, our country would rest upon a great rock and we could defy the world to overthrow us. To attain this object it is necessary first that every man should fulfil his duty to his parents and elders. The country would then be at peace. And if every Chinese would but exercise his wisdom and courage the Empire would become strong.

Generally speaking, our government institutions are used in times of peace and prosperity for the encouragement of learning, and our officials are employed for the maintenance of power. Thus by favor of the Court the capabilities of the people are enlarged. But when danger and distress threaten to overwhelm the country, the mandarins maintain a rigid chastity and the people stand ready for her defence. Great plainness of speech is employed by the counsellors of the sovereign, and the best wisdom of the Empire is called forth to meet the issue. There is one great purpose in the hearts of all: to save the country from corruption; and the strength of the land is concentrated in order to guard against the impending evil. Thus the resources of the people are exhibited and the Court is freed from anxious care.

We would here state that there are now three things necessary to be done in order to save China from revolution. The first is to *maintain the reigning Dynasty;* the second is to *conserve the Holy Religion;* and the third is to *protect the Chinese Race.* These are inseparably connected; in fact they together constitute one; for in order to protect the Chinese Race we must first conserve the Religion, and if the Religion is to be conserved we are bound to maintain the Dynasty. But, it may be asked, how can we protect the Race? We reply, by knowledge; and knowledge is religion; and religion is propagated by strength; and strength lies in the troops. Consequently, in countries of no prestige and power the native religion is not followed, and in kingdoms that are not prosperous the native race is held in light esteem by their more fortunate neighbors. Mohammedanism is unreasonable, but Turkey is fierce and warlike, so Mohammedanism survives. Buddhism is near the truth, but India is stupid and foolish, and Buddhism perishes. Nestorianism waned because Persia grew weak, and the old Greek religion is dying out for the same reason. Roman Catholicism and Protestantism have been propagated over three-fifths of the globe by military power.

Our Holy Religion has flourished in China several thousand years without change. The early Emperors and Kings embellished our tenets by their noble examples and bequeathed to us the rich legacy which we now possess. The sovereigns were the teachers. The Han, the T'ang and all the Chinese Dynasties to the Ming [embracing a period of 1800 years], honored and revered the religion of Confucius. Religion is the government, and the Emperors of our Dynasty honor Confucianism with a still greater reverence. It was the sages who purged the heresy from the Classics and handed them down to us in compiled form. The Emperors themselves follow the truth and then instruct all in the Empire, so that every one that has breath knows how to honor and how to love. For government and religion are inseparably linked together and constitute the warp of the past and present, the woof of intercommunication between China and the West.

The foundations of our State are deep and durable. Protected by Heaven, the superstructure will certainly stand secure! But supposing this absurd gossip about the partition of China by Europeans were true and the country were cut up, be it ever so exalted and excellent, would foreigners respect the Holy Doctrine of Confucius? Far from it. The Classics of the Four Philosophers would be thrown out as refuse, and the Confucian cap and gown would never more cherish the hope of an official career. Our clever scholars would figure as clergymen, compradores, and clerks, whilst the common people would be required to pay a poll-tax and be used as soldiers, artisans, underlings, and servants. That is what would happen. And the more menial our people became, the more stupid they would be; until being both menial and stupid, they would become reduced to wretched poverty and at last perish miserably. Our Holy Religion would meet the same fate that Brahmanism in India did. Its adherents would be found skulking away, or crouching among the cavernous hills, but clinging fast the while to some tattered remnants of the truth! The Flowery People would become like the black Kwun Lun of the Southern Ocean, the life-long slaves of men, vainly seeking an escape from the curses and blows of their masters.

Under the present circumstances there is nothing for it but to arouse ourselves to the situation. Let us display our loyalty and love and embrace every opportunity to become wealthy and strong; let our first object be the veneration of the Imperial Court which vouchsafes its protection to the commonwealth, and let those who hold the reins of government consider the general good. At this critical time the confidential advisers of the Emperor should be candid and truthful men, who will make it their business to give warning on the slightest approach of danger. The high officers on the frontier should see that the sinews of war are adequate to meet the occasion. The generals and commanders should make clear what the feeling of shame is and teach their troops the art of war. The soldiers and people should all cherish an affection for their superiors and lay down their lives for their elders. The *literati* should become conversant with the things of the times. Thus, if the Emperor and the ministers of China become united in heart, and the people combined in strength, will not the Records of the Chu and Sü [Confucianism] and the descendants of the gods [Chinese] have something on which to depend? There are many patriots in these gloomy times who believe that the mere reverence of Confucian *belles lettres* will protect our religion. Others hold that concerted action alone can conserve the race. These lose sight of the fact that our safety lies in maintaining all three together: the State, the Religion, and the Race; the State first, for this is fundamental. The *Tso Chuan* [A *vade mecum* of the Chinese *literati*] aptly says: "If the skin perishes, where is the good of minding about the hair?" And Mencius says: "If the sovereign possess the power to rule the commonwealth justly, who would dare insult him?" And Mencius is right.

6

Constitutional Principles

1908

On August 27, 1908, the Empress Dowager proclaimed the following statement of constitutional principles which would be given effect within the following nine years. The declared purpose of the document was to "conserve the power of the sovereign and protect the officials and the people."

THE POWERS OF THE SOVEREIGN

1. The Ta Ch'ing Emperor will rule supreme over the Ta Ch'ing Empire for one thousand generations in succession and be honored forever.

2. The sacred majesty of the sovereign may not be offended against.

3. Laws shall be made and promulgated by the sovereign, and he has the power to determine what may be assigned to others for deliberation. (Laws which have been passed by the parliament shall not become operative until approved and promulgated by the sovereign.)

4. The sovereign has the power to convoke, to open and to close, to suspend and to extend the time of, and to dissolve parliament. (On the dissolution of parliament the people shall be called upon to elect a new parliament. The members of the old parliament shall be classed with the common people. If any of them commit offenses they shall be punished by the proper court according to circumstances.)

5. The sovereign has power to appoint all officials and fix their salaries, and to degrade or promote them. (The power to use men rests with the Emperor. The parliament may not interfere with this.)

6. The sovereign has supreme command over the army and navy,

From United States Department of State, *Papers Relating to the Foreign Relations of the United States, with the Annual Message of the President Transmitted to Congress December 8, 1908* (Washington, D.C.: Government Printing Office, 1912), pp. 194–196.

with power to make all regulations concerning them. (The sovereign may dispatch armies and fix the number of soldiers. In this his power is absolute. The parliament may not interfere in military affairs.)

7. The sovereign has power to declare war and to make peace, to make treaties, to appoint and receive ambassadors. (Foreign relations will be controlled by the sovereign, without the advice of the parliament.)

8. The sovereign has power to take repressive measures, and in times of emergency to deprive officials and people of their personal liberty.

9. The sovereign has the power to confer distinctions and to issue pardons. (Mercy is from above. Officials, below, may not arrogate it to themselves.)

10. The sovereign has supreme power over the administration of the laws and the appointment of judges, but he will act in accordance with the imperially sanctioned laws, and not make changes arbitrarily. (Power to administer the law rests with the sovereign. Judges are appointed by the sovereign to act for him in the administration of the laws. Changes will not be made by the sovereign arbitrarily, because the interests at stake in law cases are important, so that imperially settled laws must be treated as final to avoid confusion.)

11. The sovereign has powers to issue "imperial orders" or to cause them to be issued, but in the matter of laws which have already received the imperial sanction he will not change or abrogate laws which have already received the imperial sanction without first obtaining the advice of parliament and acting on its memorial. (Statutes proceed from the power of the sovereign to administer the laws. Imperial orders proceed from the power of the sovereign to carry on government. The two powers are distinguished. Therefore "imperial orders" may not be used to abrogate statutes of law.)

12. When parliament is not in session, in case of urgent necessity, the sovereign may issue emergency orders to raise funds which may be necessary. But the next year when parliament meets he shall refer such matters to the parliament.

13. The expenses of the imperial household shall be fixed by the sovereign and taken from the national treasury without reference to parliament.

14. In the great ceremonies of the imperial household the sovereign shall have supreme authority over the imperial clan and shall appoint ministers to settle such affairs. The parliament may not interfere.

POWERS, PRIVILEGES, AND DUTIES OF THE OFFICERS AND PEOPLE

1. All officers and people who have the qualifications prescribed by law are eligible for appointment as civil or military officials and members of parliament.

2. Officers and people who keep within the law will have freedom of speech, of the press, and of assembly.

3. Officers and people shall not be liable to arrest, restrictions, or punishments except as prescribed by law.

4. Officers and people may appeal to the judiciary officials to judge their cases.

5. Officers and people can be judged by those specially appointed to act as judges.

6. Officers and people shall not be disturbed without cause in their possession of property, nor interfered with in their dwellings.

7. Officers and people have the obligation to pay taxes and render military service as the law may prescribe.

8. Officers and people shall continue to pay taxes at the rate now assessed until the law has been changed.

9. Officers and people have the duty of obedience to the law of the land.

GENERAL LAWS CONCERNING PARLIAMENT

1. The Parliament has only deliberative powers. It has no executive power. Measures which have been decided upon by parliament shall not be carried out by the Government until after the imperial sanction has been obtained.

2. Measures brought up for discussion in parliament must be such as relate to the welfare of the whole nation and not local matters affecting one Province only.

3. Regular annual expenditures which have been determined by imperial fiat, or which are required by law, shall not be abolished by parliament except in consultation with the Government. (The exact figures must be arrived at by proper accounting methods.)

4. Parliament shall assist in estimating the annual budget of revenue and expenditure.

5. If any higher officer of the Government is guilty of violating the law, parliament may impeach him only. The power to retain or dismiss rests with the sovereign. Parliament must not interfere with the right of the Throne to promote and degrade officials.

6. After measures have been agreed upon by the upper and lower houses of parliament they may memorialize the Throne and the measures will be put in force after they have received the imperial sanction.

7. When parliament memorializes the Throne it shall be done through the presiding officer of the parliament.

8. Members of parliament shall not speak disrespectfully of the court or slander others. Violation of this law will be punished.

9. When parliament is in session, the presiding officer shall have the power of directing, conducting judicial examinations, and keeping order.

When any member offends against parliamentary rules the presiding officer may silence or expel him.

10. If any member of parliament does not have the proper qualifications when the presiding officer shall have clearly established the fact, the name of the member shall be immediately expunged.

11. Societies for the study of parliamentary methods which may be organized in the Provinces shall respect the laws for societies and assemblies, and shall not take advantage (of their organization) to collect money and practice extortion. The local officials shall punish any violation of this rule.

GENERAL LAWS CONCERNING ELECTIONS

1. Elections for members of parliament shall be presided over by the prefects, subprefects, and department and district magistrates.

2. Those who lack the legal qualifications shall not vote nor stand as candidates. (These are, men of bad character, bullies, men who have been convicted of crimes, men whose professions are not respectable, men who have been involved in dishonorable business transactions, men regularly accused of crime whose cases have not yet been adjudicated, users of opium, those having mental infirmity, those whose family record is not unblemished, and the illiterate.)

3. On election days inspectors shall be appointed, who shall strictly scrutinize the casting and counting of ballots, to prevent fraud.

4. Special penalties will be decided upon for election frauds (such as casting illegal ballots or falsifying the election returns) and fines will be imposed according to the gravity of the offense.

5. Election by ballot will be by plurality of the votes cast. (Formerly the choice of head men has been called election, but whether the officials have handed down the decision or the influential gentry have recommended, there has been fear of giving offense, and no confidence that the wish of the people had been gained. Now the ballot system has been adopted and will be carried out strictly, in the hope that all these abuses may be done away with.)

6. Those who have not been residents of their native places for one year or more before the time of election shall not have the right to vote or to stand as candidates.

7

The Manifesto of the *T'ung-Meng Hui*

1905

There were more Chinese students in Japan than anywhere else outside of China. These young people were keenly dissatisfied with China's weakness and backwardness and very conscious of the need for radical change. In 1905, under the leadership of the veteran revolutionaries Sun Yat-sen and Huang Hsing, they organized the *T'ung-meng Hui* (United League) in Tokyo and published the following manifesto.

By order of the Military Government on the ——— day, ——— month, ——— year of T'ien-yun,[1] the Commander-in-Chief of the Chinese National Army proclaims the purposes and platform of the Military Government to the people of the nation:

Now the National Army has established the Military Government, which aims to cleanse away two hundred and sixty years of barbarous filth, restore our four-thousand-year-old fatherland, and plan for the welfare of the four hundred million people. Not only is this an unavoidable obligation of the Military Government, but all our fellow-nationals should also take it as their own responsibility. We recall that, since the beginning of our nation the Chinese have always ruled China; although at times alien peoples have usurped the rule, yet our ancestors were able to drive them out and restore Chinese sovereignty so that they could hand down the nation to posterity. Now the men of Han [i.e., the Chinese] have raised a righteous [or patriotic] army to exterminate the northern barbarians. This is a continuation of heroic deeds bequeathed to us by our predecessors, and a great righteous cause lies behind it; there is none among us

Reprinted by permission of the publishers from Ssu-yu Teng & John K. Fairbank *China's Response to the West* Cambridge, Mass.: Harvard University Press, Copyright, 1954, by the President and Fellows of Harvard College.

[1] T'ien-yun (lit., "Heavenly rotation") was the reign title used by Chang Pu-wei at the end of the Ming Dynasty (1637). It was repeatedly used in the documents issued by the *T'ung-Meng Hui*, indicating the revolutionists' repudiation of Manchu rule by their refusal to adopt its reign style.

Chinese who does not understand this. But the revolutions in former generations, such as the Ming Dynasty and the Taiping Heavenly Kingdom, were concerned only with the driving out of barbarians and the restoration of Chinese rule. Aside from these they sought no other change. We today are different from people of former times. Besides the driving out of the barbarian dynasty and the restoration of China, it is necessary also to change the national polity and the people's livelihood. And though there are a myriad ways and means to achieve this goal, the essential spirit that runs through them all is freedom, equality, and fraternity. Therefore in former days there were heroes' revolutions, but today we have a national revolution [*Kuo-min ko-ming*, lit., revolution of the people of the country]. "National revolution" means that all people in the nation will have the spirit of freedom, equality, and fraternity; that is, they will all bear the responsibility of revolution. The Military Government is but their agent. From now on the people's responsibility will be the responsibility of the Military Government, and the achievements of the Military Government will be those of the people. With a coöperative mind and concerted effort, the Military Government and the people will thus perform their duty. Therefore we proclaim to the world in utmost sincerity the outline of the present revolution and the fundamental plan for the future administration of the nation.

1. *Drive out the Tartars:* The Manchus of today were originally the eastern barbarians beyond the Great Wall. They frequently caused border troubles during the Ming dynasty; then when China was in a disturbed state they came inside Shanhaikuan, conquered China, and enslaved our Chinese people. Those who opposed them were killed by the hundreds of thousands, and our Chinese have been a people without a nation for two hundred and sixty years. The extreme cruelties and tyrannies of the Manchu government have now reached their limit. With the righteous army poised against them, we will overthrow that government, and restore our sovereign rights. Those Manchu and Chinese military men who have a change of heart and come over to us will be granted amnesty, while those who dare to resist will be slaughtered without mercy. Chinese who act as Chinese traitors in the cause of the Manchus will be treated in the same way.

2. *Restore China:* China is the China of the Chinese. The government of China should be in the hands of the Chinese. After driving out the Tartars we must restore our national state. Those who dare to act like Shih Ching-t'ang or Wu San-kuei [both were traitors] will be attacked by the whole country.

3. *Establish the Republic:* Now our revolution is based on equality, in order to establish a republican government. All our people are equal and all enjoy political rights. The president will be publicly chosen by the people of the country. The parliament will be made up of members pub-

licly chosen by the people of the country. A constitution of the Chinese Republic will be enacted, and every person must abide by it. Whoever dares to make himself a monarch shall be attacked by the whole country.

4. *Equalize land ownership:* The good fortune of civilization is to be shared equally by all the people of the nation. We should improve our social and economic organization, and assess the value of all the land in the country. Its present price shall be received by the owner, but all increases in value resulting from reform and social improvements after the revolution shall belong to the state, to be shared by all the people, in order to create a socialist state, where each family within the empire can be well supported, each person satisfied, and no one fail to secure employment. Those who dare to control the livelihood of the people through monopoly shall be ostracized.

The above four points will be carried out in three steps in due order. The first period is government by military law. When the righteous army has arisen, various places will join the cause. The common people of each locality will escape from the Manchu fetters. Those who come upon the enemy must unite in hatred of him, must join harmoniously with the compatriots within their ranks and suppress the enemy bandits. Both the armies and the people will be under the rule of military law. The armies will do their best in defeating the enemy on behalf of the people, and the people will supply the needs of the armies, and not do harm to their security. The local administration, in areas where the enemy has been either already defeated or not yet defeated, will be controlled in general by the Military Government, so that step by step the accumulated evils can be swept away. Evils like the oppression of the government, the greed and graft of officials, the squeeze of government clerks and runners, the cruelty of tortures and penalties, the tyranny of tax collections, the humiliation of the queue—shall all be exterminated together with the Manchu rule. Evils in social customs, such as the keeping of slaves, the cruelty of foot-binding, the spread of the poison of opium, the obstructions of geomancy (*feng-shui*), should also be prohibited. The time limit for each district (*hsien*) is three years. In those *hsien* where real results are achieved before the end of three years, the military law shall be lifted and a provisional constitution shall be enacted.

The second period is that of government by a provisional constitution. When military law is lifted in each *hsien*, the Military Government shall return the right of self-government to the local people. The members of local councils and local officials shall all be elected by the people. All rights and duties of the Military Government toward the people and those of the people toward the government shall be regulated by the provisional constitution, which shall be observed by the Military Government, the local councils, and the people. Those who violate the law shall be held responsible. Six years after the securing of peace in the nation the provisional constitution shall be annulled and the constitution shall be promulgated.

The third period will be government under the constitution. Six years after the provisional constitution has been enforced a constitution shall be made. The military and administrative powers of the Military Government shall be annulled; the people shall elect the president, and elect the members of parliament to organize the parliament. The administrative matters of the nation shall proceed according to the provisions of the constitution.

Of these three periods the first is the period in which the Military Government leads the people in eradicating all traditional evils and abuses; the second is the period in which the Military Government gives the power of local self-government to the people while retaining general control over national affairs; the third is the period in which the Military Government is divested of its powers, and the government will by itself manage the national affairs under the constitution. It is hoped that our people will proceed in due order and cultivate their free and equal status; the foundation of the Chinese Republic will be entirely based on this.

[The last paragraph of the manifesto consists of an exhortation to the Chinese people to rise to the occasion, support the ever-faithful Military Government, and shoulder the responsibility of protecting the country and preserving their own ancient and superior race.]

8

Abdication Edict

February 12, 1912

The Hsüan-t'ung Emperor was only five years old when he abdicated in 1912, and his career was far from finished. (See Chapter XI, Selection 66.) The Manchu dynasty had served as a unifying force in the multinational empire of China. The Chinese Republic was to have great difficulty in retaining the allegiance of the peoples of Tibet, Chinese Turkestan, Manchuria, and Mongolia.

We (the Emperor) have respectfully received the following Imperial Edict from Her Imperial Majesty the Empress Dowager Lung Yu:—

Reprinted by permission of Dodd, Mead & Company from *The Fight for the Republic in China* by B. L. Putnam Weale and by permission of Mrs. Lenox-Simpson and Hurst & Blackett Ltd.

As a consequence of the uprising of the Republican Army, to which the different provinces immediately responded, the Empire seethed like a boiling cauldron and the people were plunged into utter misery. Yuan Shih-kai was, therefore, especially commanded some time ago to dispatch commissioners to confer with the representatives of the Republican Army on the general situation and to discuss matters pertaining to the convening of a National Assembly for the decision of the suitable mode of settlement has been discovered. Separated as the South and the North are by great distances, the unwillingness of either side to yield to the other can result only in the continued interruption of trade and the prolongation of hostilities, for, so long as the form of government is undecided, the Nation can have no peace. It is now evident that the hearts of the majority of the people are in favour of a republican form of government: the provinces of the South were the first to espouse the cause, and the generals of the North have since pledged their support. From the preference of the people's hearts, the Will of Heaven can be discerned. How could We then bear to oppose the will of the millions for the glory of one Family! Therefore, observing the tendencies of the age on the one hand and studying the opinions of the people on the other, We and His Majesty the Emperor hereby vest the sovereignty in the People and decide in favour of a republican form of constitutional government. Thus we would gratify on the one hand the desires of the whole nation who, tired of anarchy, are desirous of peace, and on the other hand would follow in the footsteps of the Ancient Sages, who regarded the Throne as the sacred trust of the Nation.

Now Yuan Shih-kai was elected by the Tucheng-yuan to be the Premier. During this period of transference of government from the old to the new, there should be some means of uniting the South and the North. Let Yuan Shih-kai organize with full powers a provisional republican government and confer with the Republican Army as to the methods of union, thus assuring peace to the people and tranquillity to the Empire, and forming the one Great Republic of China by the union as heretofore, of the five peoples, namely, Manchus, Chinese, Mongols, Mohammedans, and Tibetans together with their territory in its integrity. We and His Majesty the Emperor, thus enabled to live in retirement, free from responsibilities, and cares and passing the time in ease and comfort, shall enjoy without interruption the courteous treatment of the Nation and see with Our own eyes the consummation of an illustrious government. Is not this highly advisable?

25th day of the 12th moon of the 3rd year of *Hsuan Tung*
Bearing the Imperial Seal and Signed by *Yuan Shih-kai,* the Premier
Hoo Wei-teh, Acting Minister of Foreign Affairs
Chao Ping-chun, Minister of the Interior

Tan Hsuch-heng, Acting Minister of Navy
Hsi Yen, Acting Minister of Agriculture, Works and Commerce
Liang Shih-yi, Acting Minister of Communications
Ta Shou, Acting Minister of the Dependencies

9

Letter to President Yüan Shih-k'ai

1915

Liang Ch'i-ch'ao

Liang Ch'i-ch'ao, who had formerly advocated the reform of the
Manchu monarchy and opposed republicanism, served in the cabinet of President Yüan Shih-k'ai. However, when Yüan made preparations to reestablish the monarchy with himself as Emperor,
Liang left the capital and published this famous attack on Yüan's
ambitions. Faced with defection and rebellion in the southern provinces, Yüan renounced any intention to become Emperor.

For the Kind Perusal of the Great President:

A respectful reading of your kind instructions reveals to me your
modesty and the brotherly love which you cherish for your humble servant, who is so moved by your heart-touching sympathy that he does not
know how to return your kindness. A desire then seized him to submit
his humble views for your wise consideration; though on the one hand
he has thought that he might fail to express what he wishes to say if he
were to do so in a set of brief words, while on the other hand he has no
desire to trouble the busy mind of one on whose shoulders fall myriads
of affairs, with views expressed in many words. Furthermore, what Ch'i-
chao desires to say relates to what can be likened to the anxiety of one
who, fearing that the heavens may some day fall on him, strives to ward
off the catastrophe. If his words should be misunderstood, it would only
increase his offence. Time and again he has essayed to write; but each
time he has stopped short. Now he is going South to visit his parents; and
looking at the Palace-Gate from afar, he realizes that he is leaving the

Reprinted by permission of Dodd, Mead & Company from *The Fight for the
Republic in China* by B. L. Putnam Weale and by permission of Mrs. Lenox-
Simpson and Hurst & Blackett Ltd.

Capital indefinitely. The thought that he has been a protégé of the Great President and that dangers loom ahead before the nation as well as his sense of duty and friendly obligations, charge him with the responsibility of saying something. He therefore begs to take the liberty of presenting his humble but extravagant views for the kind consideration of the Great President.

The problem of *Kuo-ti* (form of State) appears to have gone too far for reconsideration: the position is like unto a man riding on the back of a wild tiger. . . . Ch'i-chao therefore at one moment thought he would say no more about it, since added comment thereon might make him all the more open to suspicion. But a sober study of the general situation and a quiet consideration of the possible future make him tremble like an autumn leaf; for the more he meditates, the more dangerous the situation appears. It is true that the minor trouble of "foreign advice" and rebel plotting can be settled and guarded against; but what Ch'i-chao bitterly deplores is that the original intention of the Great President to devote his life and energy to the interest of the country—an intention he has fulfilled during the past four years—will be difficult to explain to the world in future. The trust of the world in the Great President would be shattered with the result that the foundation of the country will be unsettled. Do not the Sages say: "In dealing with the people aim at faithfulness?" If faithfulness to promises be observed by those in authority, then the people will naturally surrender themselves. Once, however, a promise is broken, it will be as hard to win back the people's trust as to ascend to the very Heavens. Several times have oaths of office been uttered; yet even before the lips are dry, action hath falsified the words of promise. In these circumstances, how can one hope to send forth his orders to the country in the future, and expect them to be obeyed? The people will say "he started in righteousness but ended in self-seeking: how can we trust our lives in his hands, if he should choose to pursue even further his love of self-enrichment?" It is possible for Ch'i-chao to believe that the Great President has no desire to make profit for himself by the sacrifice of the country, but how can the mass of the people—who believe only what they are told—understand what Ch'i-chao may, perchance, believe?

The Great President sees no one but those who are always near him; and these are the people who have tried to win his favour and gain rewards by concocting the alleged unanimous petitions of the whole country urging his accession to the Throne. In reality, however, the will of the people is precisely the opposite. Even the high officials in the Capital talk about the matter in a jeering and sarcastic way. As for the tone of the newspapers outside Peking, that is better left unmentioned. And as for the "small people" who crowd the streets and the market-places, they go about as if something untoward might happen at any moment. If a kingdom can be maintained by mere force, then the disturbance at the

time of Ch'in Chih-huang and Sui Yang Ti could not have been successful. If, on the other hand, it is necessary to secure the co-operation and
the willing submission of the hearts of the people, then is it not time
that our Great President bethinks himself and boldly takes his own stand?

Some argue that to hesitate in the middle of a course after indulging
in much pomp and pageantry at the beginning will result in ridicule and
derision and that the dignity of the Chief Executive will be lowered. But
do they even know whether the Great President has taken the least part
in connection with the phantasies of the past four months? Do they know
that the Great President has, on many occasions, sworn fidelity before
high Heaven and the noon-day sun? Now if he carries out his sacrosanct
promise and is deaf to the unrighteous advice of evil counsellors, his high
virtue will be made even more manifest than ever before. Wherein then
is there need of doubt or fear?

Others may even suggest that since the proposal was initiated by
military men, the tie that has hitherto bound the latter to the Great President may be snapped in case the pear fails to ripen. But in the humble
opinion of Ch'i-chao, the troops are now all fully inspired with a sense
of obedience to the Chief Executive. Who then can claim the right to
drag our Great President into unrighteousness for the sake of vanity and
vainglory? Who will dare disobey the behests of the Great President if
he should elect to open his heart and follow the path of honour and unbroken vows? If today, as Head of the nation, he is powerless to silence
the riotous clamour of the soldiery as happened at Chen-chiao in ancient
time, then be sure in the capacity of an Emperor he will not be able to
suppress an outbreak of troops even as it happened once at Yuyang in the
Tang dynasty.[1] To give them the handle of the sword is simply courting
trouble for the future. But can we suspect the troops—so long trained
under the Great President—of such unworthy conduct?

The ancients say "However a thing is done, do not hurt the feelings
of those who love you, or let your enemy have a chance to rejoice." Recently calamities in the forms of drought and flood have repeatedly vis-

---

[1] The incident of Chen-chiao is very celebrated in Chinese annals. A yellow
robe, the symbol of Imperial authority, was thrown around General Chao Kuang-
ying, at a place called Chen-chiao, by his soldiers and officers when he commanded
a force ordered to the front. Chao returned to the Capital immediately to assume
the Imperial Throne, and was thus "compelled" to become the founder of the famous
Sung dynasty.

The "incident of Yuyang" refers to the execution of Yang Kuei-fei, the favourite
concubine of Emperor Hsüan Tsung of the Tang dynasty. The Emperor for a long
time was under the alluring influence of Yang Kuei-fei, who had a paramour named
An Lo-hsan. The latter finally rebelled against the Emperor. The Emperor left the
capital and proceeded to another place together with his favourite concubine,
guarded by a large force of troops. Midway, however, the soldiers threatened to
rebel unless the concubine was killed on the spot. The clamour was such that the
Emperor was forced to sacrifice the favourite of his harem, putting her to death in
the presence of his soldiers.

ited China; and the ancients warn us that in such ways does Heaven manifest its Will regarding great movements in our country. In addition to these we must remember the prevailing evils of a corrupt officialdom, the incessant ravages of robbers, excesses in punishment, the unusually heavy burdens of taxation, as well as the irregularity of weather and rain, which all go to increase the murmurs and complaints of the people. Internally, the rebels are accumulating strength against an opportune time to rise; externally, powerful neighbouring countries are waiting for an opportunity to harass us. Why then should our Great President risk his precious person and become a target of public criticism; or "abandon the rock of peace in search of the tiger's tail"; or discourage the loyalty of faithful ones and encourage the sinister ambitions of the unscrupulous? Ch'i-chao sincerely hopes that the Great President will devote himself to the establishment of a new era which shall be an inspiration to heroism and thus escape the fate of those who are stigmatized in our annals with the name of Traitor. He hopes that the renown of the Great President will long be remembered in the land of *Chung Hua* (China) and he prays that the fate of China may not end with any abrupt ending that may befall the Great President. He therefore submits his views with a bleeding heart. He realizes that his words may not win the approval of one who is wise and clever; but Ch'i-chao feels that unless he unburdens what is in his heart, he will be false to the duty which bids him speak and be true to the kindness that has been showered on him by the Great President. Whether his loyalty to the Imperative Word will be rewarded with approval or with reproof, the order of the Great President will say.

There are other words of which Ch'i-chao wishes to tender to the Great President. To be an independent nation today, we must need follow the ways of the present age. One who opposes the current of the world and protects himself against the enriching influence of the world-spirit must eventually share the fate of the unselected. It is sincerely hoped that the Great President will refrain to some extent from restoring the old and withal work for real reform. Law can only be made a living force by both the ruler and the people obeying it with sincerity. When the law loses its strength, the people will not know how to act; and then the dignity of Government will disappear. It is hoped that the Great President will keep himself within the bounds of law and not lead the officials and the people to juggle with words. Participation in politics and patriotism are closely related. Bear well in mind that it is impossible to expect the people to share the responsibilities of the country, unless they are given a voice in the transaction of public business. The hope is expressed that the Great President will establish a real organ representing the true will of the people and encourage the natural growth of the free expression of public opinion. Let us not become so arrogant and oppressive that the people will have no chance to express their views, as this may inspire hatred on the part of the people. The relation between the Central Government and the provincial centres is like that between the trunk and branches of a tree. If the branches are all withered, how can the trunk continue to grow? It is hoped that the Great President, while giving due consideration to the maintenance of the dignity of the Central Government, will at the same time allow the local life of the provinces to develop. Ethics, Righteousness, Purity and Conscientiousness are four great principles. When these four principles are neglected, a country dies. If the whole country should come in spirit to be like "concubines and women," weak and open to be coerced and forced along with whomsoever be on the stronger side, how can a State be established? May the Great President encourage principle, and virtue, stimulate purity of character, reject men of covetous and mean character, and grant wise tolerance to those who know no fear in defending the right. Only then will the vitality of the country be retained in some degree; and in time of emergency, there will be a reserve of strength to be drawn upon in support of the State. All these considerations are of the order of obvious truths and it must be assumed that the Great President, who is greatly wise, is not unaware of the same. The reason why Ch'i-chao ventures to repeat them is this. He holds it true that a duty is laid on him to submit whatever humble thoughts are his, and at the same time he believes that the Great President will not condemn a proper physic even though it may be cheap and simple. How fortunate will Ch'i-chao be if advice so tendered shall meet with approval. He is proceeding farther and farther away from the Palace every day and he does not know how soon he will be able to seek an audience again. He writes these words with tears dropping into the ink-slab and he trusts that his words may receive the attention of the Great President.

SUGGESTED READING

Bodde, Derk. *China's Cultural Tradition: What and Wither?* New York: Holt, Rinehart and Winston, 1957, paperback.

Chan, Wing-tsit. *A Source Book in Chinese Philosophy*. Princeton: Princeton University Press, 1963.

Ch'en, Jerome. *Yuan Shih-k'ai, 1859–1916*. Stanford: Stanford University Press, 1961.

Chen, Stephen, and Payne, Robert. *Sun Yat-sen: A Portrait*. New York: John Day, 1946.

Creel, Herrlee G. *Chinese Thought from Confucius to Mao Tse-tung*. Chicago: University of Chicago Press, 1953. (Paperback edition: Mentor Books)

De Bary, William Theodore; Chan, Wing-tsit; and Watson, Burton, comps. *Sources of the Chinese Tradition*. New York: Columbia University Press, 1960.

Fairbank, John King; Reischauer, Edwin O.; and Craig, Albert M. *East Asia: The Modern Transformation*. Boston: Houghton Mifflin, 1965.

Fitzgerald, Charles Patrick. *China: A Short Cultural History*, 3rd rev. ed. New York: Frederick A. Praeger, 1962, paperback.

Goodrich, L. Carrington. *A Short History of the Chinese People*, 3rd ed. New York: Harper & Row, 1959, paperback.

Griswold, A. Whitney. *The Far Eastern Policy of the United States*. New York: Harcourt, Brace & World, 1938, paperback.

Houn, F. W. *The Central Government of China, 1912–1928: An Institutional Study*. Madison: University of Wisconsin Press, 1957.

Hsüeh, Chün-tu. *Huang Hsing and the Chinese Revolution*. Stanford: Stanford University Press, 1961.

Hucker, Charles O. *Chinese History: A Bibliographic Review*. Washington, D.C.: Service Center for Teachers of History, American Historical Association, 1958, paperback.

Jansen, Marius. *The Japanese and Sun Yat-sen*. Cambridge: Harvard University Press, 1954.

Latourette, Kenneth S. *The Chinese: Their History and Culture*, 4th ed. New York: Macmillan, 1964.

Levenson, Joseph R. *Confucian China and Its Modern Fate*. Berkeley: University of California Press, 1958. (Paperback edition under different title: *Modern China and Its Confucian Past: The Problem of Intellectual Continuity*. Anchor Books)

Levenson, Joseph R. *Liang Ch'i-ch'ao and the Mind of Modern China*. Cambridge: Harvard University Press, 1953.

Li, Dun J. *The Ageless Chinese: A History*. New York: Scribner, 1965.

Lin Yutang. *My Country and My People*. New York: John Day, 1937.

Lin Yutang, ed. *The Wisdom of China and India*. New York: Random House, 1942.

McNair, Harley Farnsworth. *Modern Chinese History: Selected Readings*. Shanghai: Commercial Press, Limited, 1927.

Menzel, Johanna M., ed. *The Chinese Civil Service: Career Open to Talent?* Boston: Heath, 1963, paperback.

Needham, Joseph. *Science and Civilization in China*. 7 vols. Cambridge: Cambridge University Press, 1954.

Pan, Wei-tung. *The Chinese Constitution: A Study of Forty Years of Constitution Making in China*. Washington: Institute of Chinese Culture, 1946.

Purcell, Victor. *The Boxer Uprising: A Background Study*. Cambridge: Cambridge University Press, 1963.

Swisher, Earl. *China's Management of the American Barbarians: A Study in Sino-American Relations*. Locust Valley, N.Y.: Augustin, 1951.

Teng, Ssu-yu, and Fairbank, J. K. *China's Response to the West: A Documentary Survey, 1839–1923*. Cambridge: Harvard University Press, 1954. (Paperback edition: Atheneum)

Vinacke, Harold M. *Modern Constitutional Development in China*. Princeton: Princeton University Press, 1920.

Sharman, Lyon. *Sun Yat-sen: His Life and Its Meaning*. New York: John Day, 1934.

Waley, Arthur. *Three Ways of Thought in Ancient China*. London: G. Allen, 1939.

Weale, B. L. Putnam. *The Fight for the Republic in China*. New York: Dodd, Mead, 1917.

Wittfogel, Karl A. *Oriental Despotism: A Comparative View of Total Power*. New York: Yale University Press, 1957, paperback.

Yu, George T. *Party Politics in Republican China: The Kuomintang, 1912–1924*. Berkeley: University of California Press, 1966.

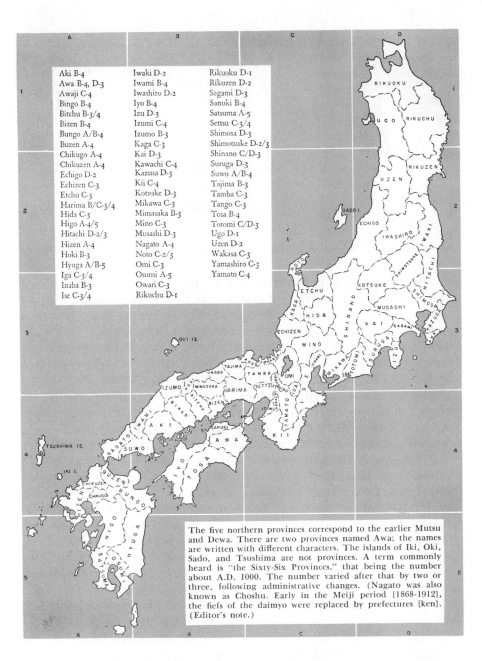

Aki B-4	Iwaki D-2	Rikuoku D-1
Awa B-4, D-3	Iwami B-4	Rikuzen D-2
Awaji C-4	Iwashiro D-2	Sagami D-3
Bingo B-4	Iyo B-4	Sanuki B-4
Bitchu B-3/4	Izu D-3	Satsuma A-5
Bizen B-4	Izumi C-4	Settsu C-3/4
Bungo A/B-4	Izumo B-3	Shimosa D-3
Buzen A-4	Kaga C-3	Shimotsuke D-2/3
Chikugo A-4	Kai D-3	Shinano C/D-3
Chikuzen A-4	Kawachi C-4	Suruga D-3
Echigo D-2	Kazusa D-3	Suwo A/B-4
Echizen C-3	Kii C-4	Tajima B-3
Etchu C-3	Kotsuke D-3	Tamba C-3
Harima B/C-3/4	Mikawa C-3	Tango C-3
Hida C-3	Mimasaka B-3	Tosa B-4
Higo A-4/5	Mino C-3	Totomi C/D-3
Hitachi D-2/3	Musashi D-3	Ugo D-1
Hizen A-4	Nagato A-4	Uzen D-2
Hoki B-3	Noto C-2/3	Wakasa C-3
Hyuga A/B-5	Omi C-3	Yamashiro C-3
Iga C-3/4	Osumi A-5	Yamato C-4
Inaba B-3	Owari C-3	
Ise C-3/4	Rikuchu D-1	

The five northern provinces correspond to the earlier Mutsu and Dewa. There are two provinces named Awa; the names are written with different characters. The islands of Iki, Oki, Sado, and Tsushima are not provinces. A term commonly heard is "the Sixty-Six Provinces," that being the number about A.D. 1000. The number varied after that by two or three, following administrative changes. (Nagato was also known as Choshu. Early in the Meiji period [1868-1912], the fiefs of the daimyo were replaced by prefectures [ken]. (Editor's note.)

The Provinces of Japan

II

The Emergence of the
Japanese Empire

Japan's political traditions are distinct from those of China although there are important common elements. The first Japanese were Mongoloid migrants from northern Asia and possibly Southeast Asia who began to settle in the Japanese Islands several thousand years ago. These early Japanese were divided into clans and hereditary guilds. In the sixth century A.D. Buddhism and Confucianism entered Japan from China by way of Korea. The Japanese called their pantheistic nature cult the Way of the Gods (Shinto) in order to distinguish it from Buddhism. The Shinto Sun Goddess was said to be the ancestress of the Japanese emperor. Despite the spread of Buddhism, Shinto has persisted to modern times, and from 1868 to 1945 it was the established religion of Japan.

The power and prestige of the T'ang dynasty in China (618–907) greatly impressed the Japanese. In 646 an imperial prince carried out the famous Great Reform in order to establish in Japan a copy of the centralized Chinese monarchy. The Japanese, however, did not accept the Confucian theory of the right of revolution against a tyrannical monarch. The power of the local nobility was reduced in order to enhance the strength and wealth of the nobles of the Japanese imperial court. In 710 a permanent capital was established at Nara, modeled after the capital city of China. Apparently to evade the influence of ambitious Buddhist priests, the capital was transferred to Kyoto in 794, where it remained until 1868. The emperors ordinarily did not themselves rule. Regents, drawn from the Fujiwara clan, ruled the country on behalf of the emperors, and emperors were required to marry Fujiwara ladies.

The imperial court would from time to time grant tax-free estates to favorites and great officials. The growth in the size and number of these estates [1] gradually weakened the authority of the capital in the provinces,

---

[1] Often small proprietors would commend their lands to the holders of tax-immune estates in order to avoid the payment of taxes.

and by 1192 a feudal system had come into being. The feudal period in Japan lasted until 1867. The great territorial barons (daimyo) and their retainers (samurai) were governed according to feudal contracts and a code of ethics in modern days idealized as *Bushidō*, the Way of the Warrior (Selection 10). The most powerful of the barons was the shogun, or barbarian-subduing-generalissimo, who held his post as a hereditary commission from the emperor. In 1274 and 1281 the Japanese succeeded in repulsing the Mongols, who, with the help of Chinese and Korean navies, attempted to conquer the land of the rising sun. In 1281 the samurai defenders were aided by a typhoon (*kamikaze*, or wind of the gods) which destroyed or drove away the ships of the invaders. Partly as a result of this experience, until 1945 the Japanese held firmly to the belief that their land enjoyed divine protection and was invincible. The period of the Ashikaga Shoguns (1338–1573) was characterized by incessant civil war. Finally, Toyotomi Hideyoshi, a captain of low origin, emerged as ruler of all Japan. He launched two invasions on Korea in the 1590's, but died before he realized his aim of conquering China.

The last dynasty of Shoguns, the Tokugawa, ruled the country almost as a monarchy from 1603 to 1868. The Shogun's capital was Edo, in eastern Japan, almost 300 miles from the imperial court in Kyoto. Christianity, which flourished in the late sixteenth and early seventeenth centuries, was banned as dangerous to national unity and independence. In 1638 the Christian rebellion at Shimabara was put down with great severity. After that, the only foreigners permitted to trade in Japan were the Chinese and Dutch, who swore not to propagate the forbidden religion. No Japanese were permitted to leave the country. The daimyo were required to reside in Edo at regular intervals, and when they returned to their domains had to leave their families behind in the capital as hostages. The Shogun maintained an effective spy network throughout the country to prevent subversive conspiracies by the daimyo or the imperial court. The long period of peace and national isolation, marred only by occasional violence on the part of masterless samurai and peasant uprisings, led to the development of a flourishing commercial economy.

During the Tokugawa period the rise of a money economy, which replaced the traditional rice economy, worked hardships on many members of the feudal and agrarian classes. Over two hundred years of peace enriched the commercial middle class, but impoverished the warrior aristocracy, which became redundant. Discontented samurai were highly receptive to the influence of nationalist scholars of Japanese history and literature who held that the shogun was a usurper wielding power which rightfully belonged to the emperor. The western clans, Satsuma, Chōshū, Tosa, and Hizen, traditional rivals of the Tokugawa, provided the leadership to overthrow the Shogunate. To exploit the embarrassment of the Shogun when he was unable to resist Commodore Perry's demand for a treaty, they raised the slogan, "Revere the Emperor and expel the barbarian!" In 1867, faced with difficulties on all sides, the Tokugawa Sho-gun abdicated. When it became clear that he was to be completely ignored by the new regime, rather than retain much of his former influence, his followers rebelled unsuccessfully.

Prince Mutsuhito (known as the Meiji Emperor) ascended the imperial throne in 1868. In his famous five-article Charter Oath,[2] he swore to base his policies on public opinion and to seek knowledge from abroad. To symbolize his take-over of administrative authority from the Shogun, the Emperor moved his court from Kyoto to the Shogun's capital, Edo, which was renamed Tokyo (Eastern Capital). The great feudal barons transferred their registers of land and people to the Emperor, bringing feudalism to an end. When the samurai lost their privileges, a number of samurai rebellions broke out against the new government, the most notable being that in Satsuma in 1877. The importance of a strong military establishment to the new regime in enforcing its domestic and foreign policies was emphasized in the Emperor's Precepts to Soldiers and Sailors in 1882 (Selection 11).

Dissident samurai began agitation for a parliament styled after European or British models. Their demands were met by repression and delay until the promulgation in 1889 of the Constitution of the Empire of Japan. The Imperial Constitution was drafted under the direction of Itō Hirobumi. It was largely inspired by the Prussian model, which permitted the executive to administer the state with a minimum of interference by the legislative branch (Selection 12). The most powerful element in the governmental system, not mentioned in the Constitution, was the elder statesmen (genro), who advised the emperor on the selection of the prime minister and on basic policies. The ideology of the new bureaucratic monarchy combined emperor-worship with Neo-Confucianism, particularly as enunciated in the Imperial Rescript on Education (Selection 13).

With few exceptions, the posts of genro and of prime minister were held by the leaders of the Chōshū and Satsuma clans. The most powerful genro during the Meiji era were General Yamagata Aritomo, of Chōshū, who served twice as Prime Minister, and Itō Hirobumi, of the same clan, who was named Prime Minister four times. The Chōshū clan controlled the army and the Satsuma clan the navy. The hegemony of these two great clans was challenged by Ōkuma Shigenobu, of Hizen, and Itagaki Taisuke, of Tosa. These former samurai founded the Progressive Party and the Liberal Party, respectively. On the basis of their party strength in the lower house of the Imperial Diet, Ōkuma and Itagaki were able to form a short-lived government in 1898. Until 1900 the ruling oligarchs sought to ignore the political parties. They were determined to maintain

[2] Quoted in Chapter VII, Selection 45.

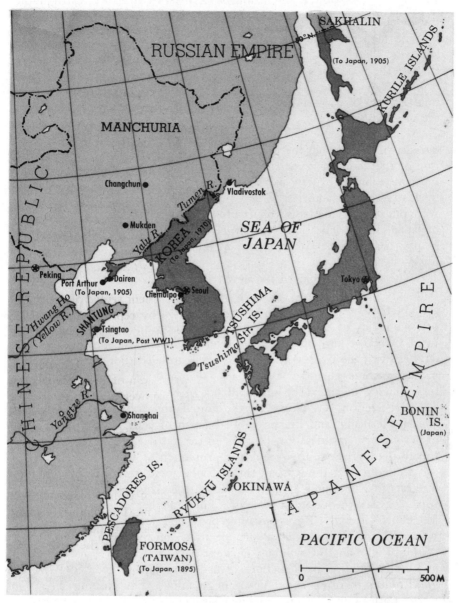

Hugh Borton—*Japan's Modern Century* Copyright 1955 The Ronald Press Company, New York.

Japanese Empire, 1915

the independence of the executive vis-à-vis the parliament; they held that the ministers of the government were answerable only to the emperor and were therefore not responsible to the Diet. In 1900, however, Prince Itō felt the need for party support and assumed the presidency of the Seiyukai (the former Liberal Party). Nevertheless, it was not until 1918 that the grip of the clan oligarchs was relaxed and a commoner assumed the premiership.

The Meiji Emperor reigned from 1868 to 1912. During the early decades of this period, the government gave priority to the industrialization of the nation as a means to increase its military power and wealth. Foreign technical experts were invited to Japan to assist in the establishment of modern factories. When these government-financed enterprises were put on a paying basis, they were sold to private capitalists. The costs of Japan's industrialization were largely borne by agriculturalists who had to pay heavy taxes. Labor remained unorganized and was poorly paid by Western standards.

The foreign policies of the new regime met with remarkable success. Not only did the Empire gradually eliminate the unequal treaties which the Western powers had imposed on her, but she also carried out an aggressive policy of her own, especially in relation to China. Japan incorporated Okinawa into her territory over futile Chinese protests in 1879. Rivalry with the Central Kingdom over Korea led to a Japanese victory in the first Sino-Japanese War (1894–1895) and the Treaty of Shimonoseki, which proclaimed the independence of Korea and granted Taiwan to Japan (Selection 14). However, the humiliating "triple intervention" of Russia, Germany, and France robbed Japan of some of the other fruits of her victory. Japanese involvement in the murder of the Korean Queen forced the Korean court to seek the protection of Russia (Selection 15).

Concern over the Russian threat to Japanese strategic and economic interests in Korea and Manchuria led to the Anglo-Japanese alliance in 1902. Russia's meddling in Korean affairs and her delays in evacuating Manchuria after the Boxer uprising provoked Japan in 1904 to declare war on Russia after making a surprise attack on the Russian fleet at Port Arthur. Following the stunning Japanese naval victory in Tsushima Straits and costly fighting in Manchuria, Russia and Japan accepted American good offices to bring about peace negotiations. The ensuing Treaty of Portsmouth (1905) recognized Japan's preeminent interests in Korea and provided for cession to Japan of Russian rights in the Port Arthur leasehold, the South Manchurian Railway, and the southern half of Sakhalin Island (Selection 16). Japan annexed Korea in 1910.

When the illustrious Meiji Emperor died in 1912, feudalism had been abolished, a strong centralized monarchy had been set up, a powerful army and navy had been built up, modern industry had been established, and Taiwan and Korea had been added to the Empire. The population had increased from 33 million to 50 million. Japan, once a remote and obscure land, had emerged as a great power.

10

Bushidō, The Way of the Warrior

Nitobe Inazo

The code of the samurai (*Bushidō*) in Japan's feudal period was idealized in modern times and invoked to instill patriotism and bravery in the Japanese army. Professor Nitobe, a Japanese Quaker (d. 1933) who devoted his life to the cause of international understanding, was the world's most famous authority on *Bushidō*.

This age [1] naturally brought into strong relief the figure of the warrior, the samurai. We speak of it as one of constant fighting and of horrible bloodshed; but warfare itself developed a cast of character, daring in deed, patient in endurance, subdued by a sense of the vanity of life and of the mutability of earthly things—a sense that Buddhism helped in large measure to encourage. To know the sadness of things was a characteristic of the true samurai. Hence the consummate product of this age is not a fierce fighter, but a strong personality, with the tenderest of emotions; a man who has under control all violent passions, whose tears are kept back by sheer force of will.

Have you not seen a picture of a Japanese warrior on his steed, pausing under a blooming cherry tree? Every Japanese child is familiar with the leader of a great army, who, in the course of his march, had to advance over a path strewn with the wind-blown petals of the cherry. Here he halted, deeming it desecration to trample upon the carpet of blossoms.

The samurai of those days looked upon the profession of arms, not as a matter of slaughter but as a means of mental and spiritual training. He went to battle, and he prepared for combat, not so much to gain a victory

Reprinted by permission of G. P. Putnam's Sons from *The Japanese Nation: Its Land, Its People, Its Life* by Inazo Nitobe. © 1912 by G. P. Putnam's Sons.
[1] The feudal era. [Editor's note.]

as to try his skill with his peer. Fair play and the square deal were the chief attractions of warfare.

We read of a young warrior of the sixteenth century, Kato by name, engaged in a duel with Suwoden. When the latter's sword broke, the former threw away his own weapon; for it was not fair to take advantage of the misfortune of one's enemy. In the grapple that followed, Suwoden got the better of Kato, but as Suwoden had his hand upon his enemy's throat, he said;—"It is not samurai-like for me, sir, to strangle you, who did not slash me when my sword was broken. Now I pay you back; we are on equal terms. This is only a skirmish, let us meet each other again in full battle array." They parted, and in a few days they confronted each other again at the head of their armies. While the battle was raging and the forces of both were in disorder, the two heroes came forth and were soon engaged in single combat. They both knew that Suwoden's was a losing cause. He himself felt that he came to die at the hand of one who had once saved his life; Kato on his part had come to the field with the determination to give a ray of hope by his own death, to his falling enemy, who likewise had spared his life. It was a strange conflict. Neither party seemed to make the right stroke. Both showed ridiculous weakness, as though they were ready to fall at the first thrust. And when through a mishap a slight touch of Kato's sword inflicted on Suwoden a shallow wound, he fell, exclaiming, "I am beaten, sir! Take my head to thy general as an addition to thy many trophies." Then Kato raised him up quickly, assuring him that the cut was not fatal; but the wounded warrior begged that his head be taken by one so worthy of it. According to the etiquette of war, this was done, and after his triumphal return, Kato interred, with due ceremony and with many hot tears, the mortal remains of his friend and opponent.

What do you think of a mode of warfare during the hottest engagements of which poetical tournaments took place or repartee was exchanged between the belligerent parties? The same ideals held sway even in the siege of Port Arthur. It so often happened in that siege that, when Japanese soldiers had occupied a trench, they left behind them a sad or comical letter in broken Russian or else a droll picture, for the Russians who might next take possession of it. Then the Russians would leave behind them some well-meaning memento for the next Japanese party that might retake the trench.

"War is hell";—but in mediæval warfare the sense of honour often robbed it of its horrors, its stigmata, and its subterfuges.

Women, too, imbibed in those militant times those virtues which we still admire in Spartan and Roman matrons. They did not as a rule advance to the front. It was their duty to stay at home, and attend to the training of their children. *Naijo*, the inner or interior help, was their avocation. So, to keep one's family intact and in good order, while the master was in the field, was what was expected of woman. But if for some reason or other she found that she was a hindrance, how unflinchingly she sacrificed herself! We read of a young man infatuated by a girl. When she found that her beauty kept him from marching to the front, she disfigured her face with a red-hot iron. We read of another young warrior who, soon after he left the threshold of his home, where he reluctantly bade his last farewell to his wife, received a note, a few lines of which will show her decision;—"Since we were joined in ties of eternal wedlock, now two short years ago, my heart has followed thee, even as its shadow follows an object, inseparably bound soul to soul, loving and being loved." Then she goes on to say, "Why should I, to whom earth no longer offers hope or joy, why should I detain thee or thy thoughts by living? Why should I not rather await thee on the road which all mortal kind must sometime tread?"

This again is only the prototype of what repeatedly happened during the Russo-Japanese War, when aged mothers were known to stab themselves in order to encourage their sons to go forth and not to have their thoughts drawn backward.

11

Imperial Precepts to the Soldiers and Sailors

January 4, 1882

The hostilities attending the overthrow of the feudal system, the samurai rebellions, and the gunboat diplomacy of the Western powers made plain the need for effective discipline in the military forces to maintain internal unity and national independence. Note the emphasis on the authority of the Emperor and the Confucian principles of obedience and loyalty in this document.

The forces of Our Empire are in all ages under the command of the Emperor. It is more than twenty-five centuries since the Emperor Jimmu, leading in person the soldiers of the Otomo and Mononobé clans, subjected the unruly tribes of the land and ascended the Imperial Throne to rule over the whole country. During this period the military system has undergone frequent changes in accordance with those in the state of society. In ancient times the rule was that the Emperor should take personal command of the forces; and although the military authority was some-

times delegated to the Empress or to the Prince Imperial, it was scarcely
ever entrusted to a subject. In the middle ages, when the civil and military
institutions were framed after the Chinese model, the Six Guards were
founded, the Right and Left Horse Bureaux established, and other organizations, such as that of the Coast Guards, created.

The military system was thus completed, but, habituated to a prolonged state of peace, the Imperial Court gradually lost its administrative
vigour; in course of time soldiers and farmers became distinct classes, and
the early conscription system was replaced by an organization of volunteers, which finally produced the military class. The military power
passed over entirely to the leaders of this class; through disturbances in
the Empire the political power also fell into their hands; and for about
seven centuries the military families held sway. Although these results
followed from changes in the state of society and were beyond human
control, they were deeply to be deplored, since they were contrary to the
fundamental character of Our Empire and to the law of Our Imperial
Ancestors.

Later on, in the eras of Kokwa and Kaéi, the decline of the Tokugawa Shogunate and the new aspect of foreign relations even threatened
to impair our national dignity, causing no small anxiety to Our August
Grandfather, the Emperor Ninko, and Our August Father, the Emperor
Koméi, a fact which We recall with awe and gratitude. When in youth
We succeeded to the Imperial Throne, the Shogun returned into Our
hands the administrative power, and all the feudal lords their fiefs; thus,
in a few years, Our entire realm was unified and the ancient régime restored. Due as this was to the meritorious services of Our loyal officers
and wise councillors, civil and military, and to the abiding influence of
Our Ancestors' benevolence towards the people, yet it must also be attrib-
uted to Our subjects' true sense of loyalty and their conviction of the
importance of "Great Righteousness."

In consideration of these things, being desirous of reconstructing Our
military system and of enhancing the glory of Our Empire, We have in
the course of the last fifteen years established the present system of the
Army and Navy. The supreme command of Our forces is in Our hands,
and although We may entrust subordinate commands to Our subjects, yet
the ultimate authority We Ourself shall hold and never delegate to any
subject. It is Our will that this principle be carefully handed down to
posterity and that the Emperor always retain the supreme civil and military power, so that the disgrace of the middle and succeeding ages may
never be repeated. Soldiers and Sailors, We are your supreme Commander-in-Chief. Our relations with you will be most intimate when We
rely upon you as Our limbs and you look up to Us as your head.

Whether We are able to guard the Empire, and so prove Ourself
worthy of Heaven's blessings and repay the benevolence of Our An-

cestors, depends upon the faithful discharge of your duties as soldiers and sailors. If the majesty and power of Our Empire be impaired, do you share with Us the sorrow; if the glory of Our arms shine resplendent, We will share with you the honour. If you all do your duty, and being one with Us in spirit do your utmost for the protection of the state, Our people will long enjoy the blessings of peace, and the might and dignity of our Empire will shine in the world. As We thus expect much of you, Soldiers and Sailors, We give you the following precepts: —

1. The soldier and sailor should consider loyalty their essential duty. Who that is born in this land can be wanting in the spirit of grateful service to it? No soldier or sailor, especially, can be considered efficient unless this spirit be strong within him. A soldier or a sailor in whom the spirit is not strong, however skilled in art or proficient in science, is a mere puppet; and a body of soldiers or sailors wanting in loyalty, however well ordered and disciplined it may be, is in an emergency no better than a rabble. Remember that, as the protection of the state and the maintenance of its power depend upon the strength of its arms, the growth or decline of this strength must affect the nation's destiny for good or for evil; therefore neither be led astray by current opinions nor meddle in politics, but with single heart fulfil your essential duty of loyalty, and bear in mind that duty is weightier than a mountain, while death is lighter than a feather. Never by failing in moral principle fall into disgrace and bring dishonour upon your name.

2. The soldier and the sailor should be strict in observing propriety. Soldiers and sailors are organized in grades, from the Marshal and the Admiral of the Fleet down to the private soldier or ordinary seaman; and even within the same rank and grade there are differences in seniority of service according to which juniors should submit to their seniors. Inferiors should regard the orders of their superiors as issuing directly from Us. Always pay due respect not only to your superiors but also to your seniors, even though not serving under them. On the other hand, superiors should never treat their inferiors with contempt or arrogance. Except when official duty requires them to be strict and severe, superiors should treat their inferiors with consideration, making kindness their chief aim, so that all grades may unite in their service to the Emperor. If you, Soldiers and Sailors, neglect to observe propriety, treating your superiors with disrespect and your inferiors with harshness, and thus cause harmonious co-operation to be lost, you will not only be a blight upon the forces but also be unpardonable offenders against the state.

3. The soldier and the sailor should esteem valour. Ever since the ancient times valour has in our country been held in high esteem, and without it Our subjects would be unworthy of their name. How then may the soldier and the sailor, whose profession it is to confront the enemy in battle, forget even for one instant to be valiant? But there is

true valour and false. To be incited by mere impetuosity to violent action cannot be called true valour. The soldier and the sailor should have sound discrimination of right and wrong, cultivate self-possession, and form their plans with deliberation. Never to despise an inferior enemy or fear a superior, but to do one's duty as soldier or sailor—this is true valour. Those who thus appreciate true valour should in their daily intercourse set gentleness first and aim to win the love and esteem of others. If you affect valour and act with violence, the world will in the end detest you and look upon you as wild beasts. Of this you should take heed.

4. The soldier and the sailor should highly value faithfulness and righteousness. Faithfulness and righteousness are the ordinary duties of man, but the soldier and the sailor, in particular, cannot be without them and remain in the ranks even for a day. Faithfulness implies the keeping of one's word and righteousness the fulfilment of one's duty. If then you wish to be faithful and righteous in any thing, you must carefully consider at the outset whether you can accomplish it or not. If you thoughtlessly agree to do something that is vague in its nature and bind yourself to unwise obligations, and then try to prove yourself faithful and righteous, you may find yourself in great straits from which there is no escape. In such cases your regrets will be of no avail. Hence you must first make sure whether the thing is righteous and reasonable or not. If you are convinced that you cannot possibly keep your word and maintain righteousness, you had better abandon your engagement at once. Ever since the ancient times there have been repeated instances of great men and heroes who, overwhelmed by misfortune, have perished and left a tarnished name to posterity, simply because in their effort to be faithful in small matters they failed to discern right and wrong with reference to fundamental principles, or because, losing sight of the true path of public duty, they kept faith in private relations. You should, then, take serious warning by these examples.

5. The soldier and the sailor should make simplicity their aim. If you do not make simplicity your aim, you will become effeminate and frivolous and acquire fondness for luxurious and extravagant ways; you will finally grow selfish and sordid and sink to the last degree of baseness, so that neither loyalty nor valour will avail to save you from the contempt of the world. It is not too much to say that you will thus fall into a lifelong misfortune. If such an evil once makes its appearance among soldiers and sailors, it will certainly spread like an epidemic, and martial spirit and morale will instantly decline. Although, being greatly concerned on this point, We lately issued the Disciplinary Regulations and warned you against this evil, nevertheless, being harassed with anxiety lest it should break out, We hereby reiterate Our warning. Never do you, Soldiers and Sailors, make light of this injunction.

These five articles should not be disregarded even for a moment by soldiers and sailors. Now for putting them into practice, the all important is sincerity. These five articles are the soul of Our soldiers and sailors, and sincerity is the soul of these articles. If the heart be not sincere, words and deeds, however good, are all mere outward show and can avail nothing. If only the heart be sincere, anything can be accomplished. Moreover, these five articles are the Grand Way of Heaven and Earth and the universal law of humanity, easy to observe and to practice. If you, Soldiers and Sailors, in obedience to Our instruction, will observe and practice these principles and fulfil your duty of grateful service to the country, it will be a source of joy, not to Ourself alone, but to all people of Japan.

The 4th day of the 1st month of the 15th Year of Meiji.

12

The Constitution of the Empire of Japan

Promulgated February 11, 1889

The Preamble and Chapters I and VII of this Constitution make it clear that a single dynasty reigned and governed by divine right. For a detailed critique, see SWNCC–228 (Chapter VII, Selection 46).

PREAMBLE

Having, by virtue of the glories of Our Ancestors, ascended the Throne of a lineal succession unbroken for ages eternal; desiring to promote the welfare of, and to give development to the moral and intellectual faculties of Our beloved subjects, the very same that have been favored with the benevolent care and affectionate vigilance of Our Ancestors; and hoping to maintain the prosperity of the State, in concert with Our people and with their support, We hereby promulgate, in pursuance of Our Imperial Rescript of the 12th day of the 10th month of the 14th year of Meiji, a fundamental law of State, to exhibit the principles, by which We are to be guided in Our conduct, and to point out to what Our descendants and Our subjects and their descendants are forever to conform.

The rights of sovereignty of the State, We have inherited from Our Ancestors, and We shall bequeath them to Our descendants. Neither We nor they shall in future fail to wield them, in accordance with the provisions of the Constitution hereby granted.

We now declare to respect and protect the security of the rights and of the property of Our people, and to secure to them the complete enjoyment of the same, within the extent of the provisions of the present Constitution and of the law.

The Imperial Diet shall first be convoked for the 23rd year of Meiji and the time of its opening shall be the date when the present Constitution comes into force.

When in the future it may become necessary to amend any of the provisions of the present Constitution, We or Our successors shall assume the initiative right, and submit a project for the same to the Imperial Diet. The Imperial Diet shall pass its vote upon it, according to the conditions imposed by the present Constitution, and in no otherwise shall Our descendants or Our subjects be permitted to attempt any alteration thereof.

Our Ministers of State, on Our behalf, shall be held responsible for the carrying out of the present Constitution, and Our present and future subjects shall forever assume the duty of allegiance to the present Constitution.

CHAPTER I. THE EMPEROR

Article I. The Empire of Japan shall be reigned over and governed by a line of Emperors unbroken for ages eternal.

Article II. The Imperial Throne shall be succeeded to by Imperial male descendants, according to the provisions of the Imperial House Law.

Article III. The Emperor is sacred and inviolable.

Article IV. The Emperor is the head of the Empire, combining in Himself the rights of sovereignty, and exercises them, according to the provisions of the present Constitution.

Article V. The Emperor exercises the legislative power with the consent of the Imperial Diet.

Article VI. The Emperor gives sanction to laws and orders them to be promulgated and executed.

Article VII. The Emperor convokes the Imperial Diet, opens, closes and prorogues it, and dissolves the House of Representatives.

Article VIII. The Emperor, in consequence of an urgent necessity to maintain public safety or to avert public calamities, issues, when the Imperial Diet is not sitting, Imperial Ordinances in the place of law.

Such Imperial Ordinances are to be laid before the Imperial Diet at its next session, and when the Diet does not approve the said Ordinances, the Government shall declare them to be invalid for the future.

Article IX. The Emperor issues or causes to be issued, the Ordinances necessary for the carrying out of the laws, or for the maintenance of the public peace and order, and for the promotion of the welfare of the subjects. But no Ordinance shall in any way alter any of the existing laws.

Article X. The Emperor determines the organization of the different branches of the administration, and salaries of all civil and military officers, and appoints and dismisses the same. Exceptions especially provided for in the present Constitution or in other laws, shall be in accordance with the respective provisions (bearing thereon).

Article XI. The Emperor has the supreme command of the Army and Navy.

Article XII. The Emperor determines the organization and peace standing of the Army and Navy.

Article XIII. The Emperor declares war, makes peace, and concludes treaties.

Article XIV. The Emperor declares a state of siege. The conditions and effects of a state of siege shall be determined by law.

Article XV. The Emperor confers titles of nobility, rank, orders and other marks of honor.

Article XVI. The Emperor orders amnesty, pardon, commutation of punishments and rehabilitation.

Article XVII. A Regency shall be instituted in conformity with the provisions of the Imperial House Law.

The Regent shall exercise the powers appertaining to the Emperor in His name.

CHAPTER II. RIGHTS AND DUTIES OF SUBJECTS

Article XVIII. The conditions necessary for being a Japanese subject shall be determined by law.

Article XIX. Japanese subjects may, according to qualifications determined in laws or ordinances, be appointed to civil or military or any other public offices equally.

Article XX. Japanese subjects are amenable to service in the Army or Navy, according to the provisions of law.

Article XXI. Japanese subjects are amenable to the duty of paying taxes, according to the provisions of law.

Article XXII. Japanese subjects shall have the liberty of abode and of changing the same within the limits of law.

Article XXIII. No Japanese subject shall be arrested, detained, tried or punished, unless according to law.

Article XXIV. No Japanese subject shall be deprived of his right of being tried by the judges determined by law.

Article XXV. Except in the cases provided for in the law, the house of no Japanese subject shall be entered or searched without his consent.

Article XXVI. Except in the cases mentioned in the law, the secrecy of the letters of every Japanese subject shall remain inviolate.

Article XXVII. The right of property of every Japanese subject shall remain inviolate.

Measures necessary to be taken for the public benefit shall be provided for by law.

Article XXVIII. Japanese subjects shall, within limits not prejudicial to peace and order, and not antagonistic to their duties as subjects, enjoy freedom of religious belief.

Article XXIX. Japanese subjects shall, within the limits of law, enjoy the liberty of speech, writing, publication, public meetings and associations.

Article XXX. Japanese subjects may present petitions, by observing the proper forms of respect, and by complying with the rules specially provided for the same.

Article XXXI. The provisions contained in the present Chapter shall not affect the exercise of the powers appertaining to the Emperor, in times of war or in cases of a national emergency.

Article XXXII. Each and every one of the provisions contained in the preceding Articles of the present Chapter, that are not in conflict with the laws or the rules and discipline of the Army and Navy, shall apply to the officers and men of the Army and of the Navy.

CHAPTER III. THE IMPERIAL DIET

Article XXXIII. The Imperial Diet shall consist of two Houses, a House of Peers and a House of Representatives.

Article XXXIV. The House of Peers shall, in accordance with the Ordinance concerning the House of Peers, be composed of the members of the Imperial Family, of the orders of nobility, and of those persons who have been nominated thereto by the Emperor.

Article XXXV. The House of Representatives shall be composed of Members elected by the people, according to the provisions of the Law of Election.

Article XXXVI. No one can at one and the same time be a Member of both Houses.

Article XXXVII. Every law requires the consent of the Imperial Diet.

Article XXXVIII. Both Houses shall vote upon projects of law submitted to it by the Government, and may respectively initiate projects of law.

Article XXXIX. A bill, which has been rejected by either the one or the other of the two Houses, shall not be again brought in during the same session.

Article XL. Both Houses can make representations to the Government, as to laws or upon any other subject. When, however, such representations are not accepted, they cannot be made a second time during the same session.

Article XLI. The Imperial Diet shall be convoked every year.

Article XLII. A session of the Imperial Diet shall last during three months. In case of necessity, the duration of a session may be prolonged by Imperial Order.

Article XLIII. When urgent necessity arises, an extraordinary session may be convoked, in addition to the ordinary one.

The duration of an extraordinary session shall be determined by Imperial Order.

Article XLIV. The opening, closing, prolongation of session and prorogation of the Imperial Diet, shall be effected simultaneously for both Houses.

In case the House of Representatives has been ordered to dissolve, the House of Peers shall at the same time be prorogued.

Article XLV. When the House of Representatives has been ordered to dissolve, Members shall be caused by Imperial Order to be newly elected, and the new House shall be convoked within five months from the day of dissolution.

Article XLVI. No debate can be opened and no vote can be taken in either House of the Imperial Diet, unless not less than one third of the whole number of the Members thereof is present.

Article XLVII. Votes shall be taken in both Houses by absolute majority. In the case of a tie vote, the President shall have the casting vote.

Article XLVIII. The deliberations of both Houses shall be held in public. The deliberations may, however, upon demand of the Government or by resolution of the House, be held in secret sitting.

Article XLIX. Both Houses of the Imperial Diet may respectively present addresses to the Emperor.

Article L. Both Houses may receive petitions presented by subjects.

Article LI. Both Houses may enact, besides what is provided for in the present Constitution and in the Law of the Houses, rules necessary for the management of their internal affairs.

Article LII. No Member of either House shall be held responsible outside the respective Houses, for any opinion uttered or for any vote given in the House. When, however, a Member himself has given publicity to his opinions by public speech, by documents in print or in writing, or by any other similar means, he shall, in the matter, be amenable to the general law.

Article LIII. The Members of both Houses shall, during the session, be free from arrest, unless with the consent of the House, except in cases of flagrant delicts, or of offences connected with a state of internal commotion or with a foreign trouble.

Article LIV. The Ministers of State and the Delegates of the Government may, at any time, take seats and speak in either House.

CHAPTER IV. THE MINISTERS OF STATE
AND THE PRIVY COUNCIL

Article LV. The respective Ministers of State shall give their advice to the Emperor, and be responsible for it.

All Laws, Imperial Ordinances and Imperial Rescripts of whatever kind, that relate to the affairs of the State, require the countersignature of a Minister of State.

Article LVI. The Privy Councillors shall, in accordance with the provisions for the organization of the Privy Council, deliberate upon important matters of State, when they have been consulted by the Emperor.

CHAPTER V. THE JUDICATURE

Article LVII. The Judicature shall be exercised by the Courts of Law according to law, in the name of the Emperor.

The organization of the Courts of Law shall be determined by law.

Article LVIII. The judges shall be appointed from among those who possess proper qualifications according to law.

No judge shall be deprived of his position, unless by way of criminal sentence or disciplinary punishment.

Rules for disciplinary punishment shall be determined by law.

Article LIX. Trials and judgments of a Court shall be conducted publicly. When, however, there exists any fear that such publicity may be prejudicial to peace and order, or to the maintenance of public morality, the public trial may be suspended by provision of law or by the decision of the Court of Law.

Article LX. All matters that fall within the competency of a special Court shall be specially provided for by law.

Article LXI. No suit at law, which relates to rights alleged to have been infringed by the illegal measures of the administrative authorities and which shall come within the competency of the Court of Administrative Litigation specially established by law, shall be taken cognizance of by a Court of Law.

CHAPTER VI. FINANCE

Article LXII. The imposition of a new tax or the modification of the rates (of an existing one) shall be determined by law.

However, all such administrative fees or other revenue having the nature of compensation shall not fall within the category of the above clause.

The raising of national loans and the contracting of other liabilities to the charge of the National Treasury, except those that are provided in the Budget, shall require the consent of the Imperial Diet.

Article LXIII. The taxes levied at present shall, in so far as they are not remodelled by a new law, be collected according to the old system.

Article LXIV. The expenditure and revenue of the State require the consent of the Imperial Diet by means of an annual Budget.

Any and all expenditures overpassing the appropriations set forth in the Titles and Paragraphs of the Budget, or that are not provided for in the Budget, shall subsequently require the approbation of the Imperial Diet.

Article LXV. The Budget shall be first laid before the House of Representatives.

Article LXVI. The expenditures of the Imperial House shall be defrayed every year out of the National Treasury, according to the present fixed amount for the same, and shall not require the consent thereto of the Imperial Diet, except in case an increase thereof is found necessary.

Article LXVII. Those already fixed expenditures based by the Constitution upon the powers appertaining to the Emperor, and such expenditures as may have arisen by the effect of law, or that appertain to the legal obligations of the Government, shall be neither rejected nor reduced by the Imperial Diet, without the concurrence of the Government.

Article LXVIII. In order to meet special requirements, the Government may ask the consent of the Imperial Diet to a certain amount as a Continuing Expenditure Fund, for a previously fixed number of years.

Article LXIX. In order to supply deficiences, which are unavoidable, in the Budget, and to meet requirements unprovided for in the same, a Reserve Fund shall be provided in the Budget.

Article LXX. When the Imperial Diet cannot be convoked, owing to the external or internal condition of the country, in case of urgent need for the maintenance of public safety, the Government may take all necessary financial measures, by means of an Imperial Ordinance.

In the case mentioned in the preceding clause, the matter shall be submitted to the Imperial Diet at its next session, and its approbation shall be obtained thereto.

Article LXXI. When the Imperial Diet has not voted on the Budget, or when the Budget has not been brought into actual existence, the Government shall carry out the Budget of the preceding year.

Article LXXII. The final account of the expenditures and revenue of the State shall be verified and confirmed by the Board of Audit, and it shall be submitted by the Government to the Imperial Diet, together with the report of verification of the said Board.

The organization and competency of the Board of Audit shall be determined by law separately.

CHAPTER VII. SUPPLEMENTARY RULES

Article LXXIII. When it has become necessary in future to amend the provisions of the present Constitution, a project to the effect shall be submitted to the Imperial Diet by Imperial Order.

In the above case, neither House can open the debate, unless not less than two-thirds of the whole number of Members are present, and no amendment can be passed, unless a majority of not less than two-thirds of the Members present is obtained.

Article LXXIV. No modification of the Imperial House Law shall be required to be submitted to the deliberation of the Imperial Diet.

No provision of the present Constitution can be modified by the Imperial House Law.

Article LXXV. No modification can be introduced into the Constitution, or into the Imperial House Law, during the time of a Regency.

Article LXXVI. Existing legal enactments, such as laws, regulations, Ordinances, or by whatever names they may be called, shall, so far as they do not conflict with the present Constitution, continue in force.

All existing contracts or orders, that entail obligations upon the Government, and that are connected with expenditure, shall come within the scope of *Article LXVII.*

13

Imperial Rescript on Education

October 30, 1890

Despite the introduction of Western military and industrial techniques, Confucian principles and respect for the emperor, rather than Christianity and Western individualistic liberalism, served as the moral basis of modern Japan. (After World War II, during the Allied Occupation, this rescript was rescinded by the Japanese Diet because of its undemocratic implications. See Chapter VII, Selection 43.)

Know ye, Our Subjects!

Our Imperial Ancestors have founded Our Empire on a basis broad and everlasting and have deeply and firmly implanted virtue; Our subjects, ever united in loyalty and filial piety, have from generation to generation illustrated the beauty thereof. This is the glory of the fundamental character of Our Empire, and herein also lies the source of Our education. Ye, Our subjects, be filial to your parents, affectionate to your brothers and sisters; as husbands and wives be harmonious, as friends true; bear yourselves in modesty and moderation; extend your benevolence to all; pursue learning and cultivate arts, and thereby develop your intellectual faculties and perfect your moral powers; furthermore, advance the public good and promote common interests; always respect the Constitution and observe the laws; should any emergency arise, offer yourselves courageously to the State; and thus guard and maintain the prosperity of Our Imperial Throne, coeval with heaven and earth. So shall ye not only be Our good and faithful subjects, but render illustrious the best traditions of your forefathers.

The way here set forth is indeed the teaching bequeathed by Our Imperial Ancestors, to be observed alike by Their Descendants and subjects, infallible for all ages and true in all places. It is Our wish to lay it to heart in all reverence, in common with you, Our subjects, that we may all thus attain to the same virtue.

The 30th day of the 10th month of the 23rd year of Meiji
(Imperial Sign Manual)   (Imperial Seal)

14

The Treaty of Shimonoseki
April 17, 1895

When Li Hung-chang arrived in Shimonoseki to negotiate an end to the first Sino-Japanese War, he was shot by a Japanese fanatic and wounded under one eye. This incident embarrassed the Japanese, who agreed to a somewhat less harsh treaty than might otherwise have been the case.

The ink on the treaty was scarcely dry when the Russian, French, and German governments advised the Japanese to renounce their claim to the Liaotung Peninsula (in southern Manchuria, described in Article II [a] of the treaty), on the ground that the cession of this territory to Japan would endanger the independence

From United States Department of State, *Papers Relating to the Foreign Relations of the United States, with the Annual Message of the President, Transmitted to Congress December 2, 1895*, Part I (Washington, D.C.: Government Printing Office, 1896), pp. 200–203.

of China and Korea. The Japanese government, unwilling to challenge the three European powers, accepted the humiliation of bowing to their demand. Within three years, the Russians obtained a leasehold on the peninsula from China. Japan had her revenge against Russia in 1905 (Selection 16). For the future changes in the status of Taiwan and Korea, see the Cairo Declaration (Chapter VI, Selection 37) and the Japanese Peace Treaty (Chapter VIII, Selection 47).

His Majesty the Emperor of China and His Majesty the Emperor of Japan, desiring to restore the blessings of peace to their countries and subjects and to remove all cause for future complications, have named as their plenipotentiaries for the purpose of concluding a treaty of peace; that is to say, His Majesty the Emperor of China, Li Hung Chang, senior tutor to the heir apparent, senior grand secretary of state, minister superintendent of trade for the northern parts of China, viceroy of the province of Chili, and earl of the first rank, and Li Ching Fong, ex-minister of the diplomatic service, of the second official rank, and His Majesty the Emperor of Japan, Count Ito Hirobumi, Junii, grand cross of the imperial order of Paullownia, minister president of state, and Viscount Mutsu Munemitsu, Junii, first class of the imperial order of the second treasure, minister of state for foreign affairs, who, after having exchanged their full powers, which were found to be in good and proper form have agreed to the following articles:

ARTICLE I

China recognizes definitely the full and complete independence and autonomy of Corea, and in consequence the payment of tribute and the performance of ceremonies and formalities by Corea to China, in derogation of such independence and autonomy, shall wholly cease for the future.

ARTICLE II

China cedes to Japan in perpetuity and full sovereignty the following territories, together with all fortifications thereon:

a. The southern portion of the province of Feng Tien within the following boundaries:

The line of demarcation begins at the mouth of the River Yalu and ascends that stream to the mouth of the River An-ping; from thence the line runs to Feng Huang; from thence to Haicheng; from thence to Ying Kow, forming a line which describes the southern portion of the territory.

The places above named are included in the ceded territory. When the line reaches the River Liao at Feng Kow, it follows the course of that stream to its mouth, where it terminates. The mid-channel of the River Liao shall be taken as the line of demarcation.

This cession also includes all islands appertaining or belonging to the province of Feng Tien, situated in the eastern portion of the Bay of Liao Tung and in the northern part of the Yellow Sea.

b. The island of Formosa, together with all the islands appertaining or belonging to said island of Formosa.

c. The Pescadores Group—that is to say, all islands lying between the 119 and 120th degrees of longitude east of Greenwich and the 23rd and 24th degrees of north latitude.

ARTICLE III

The alignments of the portions described in the preceding article and shown on the annexed map shall be subject to verification and demarcation on the spot, by a joint commission of delimitation consisting of two or more Chinese and two or more Japanese delegates to be appointed immediately after the exchange of the ratifications of this act. In case the boundaries laid down in this act are found to be defective at any point, either on account of topography or in consideration of good administration, it shall also be the duty of the delimitation commission to rectify the same.

The delimitation commission will enter upon its duties as soon as possible and will bring its labors to a conclusion within the period of one year after appointment.

The alignments laid down in this act shall, however, be maintained until the rectifications of the delimitation commission, if any are made, shall have received the approval of the Governments of China and Japan.

ARTICLE IV

China agrees to pay to Japan as a war indemnity the sum of 200,000,000 Kuping taels. The said sum is to be paid in eight installments; the first installment of 50,000,000 taels to be paid within six months and the second installment of 50,000,000 taels to be paid within twelve months after the exchange of the ratifications of this act; the remaining sum to be paid in six equal annual installments, as follows:

The first of such equal annual installments to be paid within two years; the second, within three years; the third, within four years; the fourth, within five years; the fifth, within six years; and the sixth, within seven years; after the exchange of the ratifications of this act. Interest at

the rate of 5 per centum per annum shall begin to run on all unpaid portions of the said indemnity from the date the first installment falls due.

China shall, however, have the right to pay by anticipation at any
time any or all of said installments. In case the whole amount of the
said indemnity is paid within three years after the exchange of the ratifications of the present act, all interest shall be waived, and the interest for
two years and a half or for any less period, if then already paid, shall be
included as part of the principal amount of the indemnity.

ARTICLE V

The inhabitants of the territory ceded to Japan, who wish to take up
their residence outside the ceded districts, shall be at liberty to sell their
real property and retire.

For this purpose a period of two years from the date of the exchange
of the ratifications of the present act shall be granted. At the expiration
of that period those of the inhabitants who shall not have left said territories shall, at the option of Japan, be deemed Japanese subjects.

Each of the two Governments shall immediately upon the exchange
of the ratifications of the present act send one or more commissioners to
Formosa to effect a final transfer of that province, and within the space
of two months after the exchange of the ratifications of this act such
transfer shall be completed.

ARTICLE VI

All treaties between China and Japan having come to an end, in
consequence of war, China engages immediately upon the exchange of
the ratifications of this act, to appoint plenipotentiaries to conclude with
the Japanese plenipotentiaries, a treaty of commerce and navigation and
a convention to regulate frontier intercourse and trade.

The treaties, conventions, and regulations now subsisting between
China and European powers shall serve as a basis for the said treaty and
convention between China and Japan. From the date of the exchange of
the ratifications of this act until the said treaty and convention are brought
into actual operation, the Japanese Government, its officials, commerce,
navigation, frontier intercourse and trade, industries, ships, and subjects,
shall, in every respect, be accorded, by China, most-favored-nation treatment.

China makes, in addition, the following concessions, to take effect
six months after the date of the present act:

First. The following cities, towns, and ports, in addition to those
already opened, shall be opened to the trade, residence, industries, and
manufactures of Japanese subjects, under the same conditions and with

the same privileges and facilities as exist at the present open cities, towns, and ports of China.

1. Shashih, in the province of Hupeh.
2. Chungking, in the province in Szechuan.
3. Suchow, in the province of Kian Su.
4. Hang Chow, in the province of Chekiang.

The Japanese Government shall have the right to station consuls at any or all of the above-named places.

Second. Steam navigation for vessels under the Japanese flag for the conveyance of passengers and cargo shall be extended to the following places:

1. On the upper Yangtze River, from Ichang to Chungking.
2. On the Woosung River and the canal, from Shanghai to Suchow and Hangchow.

The rules and regulations which now govern the navigation of the inland waters of China by foreign vessels shall, so far as applicable, be enforced in respect of the above-named routes until new rules and regulations are conjointly agreed to.

Third. Japanese subjects purchasing goods or produce in the interior of China or transporting imported merchandise into the interior of China shall have the right temporarily to rent or hire warehouses for the storage of the articles so purchased or transported without the payment of any taxes or exactions whatever.

Fourth. Japanese subjects shall be free to engage in all kinds of manufacturing industries in all the open cities, towns, and ports of China, and shall be at liberty to import into China all kinds of machinery, paying only the stipulated duties thereon.

All articles manufactured by Japanese subjects in China shall, in respect of inland transit and internal taxes, duties, charges, and exaction of all kinds, and also in respect of warehousing and storage facilities in the interior of China, stand upon the same footing and enjoy the same privileges and exemptions as merchandise imported by Japanese subjects into China.

In the event additional rules and regulations are necessary in connection with these concessions, they shall be embodied in the treaty of commerce and navigation provided for by this article.

ARTICLE VII

Subject to the provisions of the next succeeding article, the evacuation of China by the armies of Japan shall be completely effected within three months after the exchange of the ratifications of the present act.

ARTICLE VIII

As a guarantee of the faithful performance of the stipulations of this act, China consents to the temporary occupation by the military forces of Japan of Wei-hai-wei in the province of Shantung.

Upon the payment of the first two installments of the war indemnity herein stipulated for and the exchange of the ratifications of the treaty of commerce and navigation the said place shall be evacuated by the Japanese forces, provided the Chinese Government consent to pledge, under suitable and sufficient arrangements, the customs revenue of China as a security for the payment of the principal and interest of the remaining installments of said indemnity.

It is, however, expressly understood, that no such evacuation shall take place until after the exchange of the ratifications of the treaty of commerce and navigation.

ARTICLE IX

Immediately upon the exchange of the ratifications of this act all prisoners of war then held shall be restored, and China undertakes not to illtreat or punish prisoners of war so restored to her by Japan. China also engages to at once release all Japanese subjects accused of being military spies or charged with any other military offenses. China further engages not to punish in any manner nor to allow to be punished those Chinese subjects who have in any manner been compromised in their relations with the Japanese army during the war.

ARTICLE X

All offensive military operations shall cease upon the exchange of the ratifications of this act.

ARTICLE XI

The present act shall be ratified by their majesties the Emperor of China and the Emperor of Japan, and the ratifications shall be exchanged at Chefoo, on the 14th day of the 4th month of the 28th year of Kwang Hsü, corresponding to the 8th day of the 5th month of the 28th year of Meiji.

In witness whereof the respective plenipotentiaries have signed the same and have affixed thereto the seal of their arms.

Done at Shimonoseki, in duplicate, this 23rd day of the 3rd month of the 21st year of Kwang Hsü, corresponding to the 17th day of the 4th month of the 28th year of Meiji.

Li Hung Chang [L.S.]

Plenipotentiary of His Majesty the Emperor of China, Senior Tutor of the Heir Apparent, Senior Grand Secretary of State, Minister Superintendent of Trade for the North Ports of China, Viceroy of the Province of Chili, and Earl of the First Rank.

Count Ito Hirobumi [L. S.]

Junii, Grand Cross of the Imperial Order of Paullownia, Minister President of State, Plenipotentiary of His Majesty the Emperor of Japan.

Viscount Mutsu Munemitsu [L.S.]

Junii, First Class of the Imperial Order of the Sacred Treasure, Minister of State for Foreign Affairs, Plenipotentiary of His Majesty the Emperor of Japan.

Separate Articles

ARTICLE I

The Japanese military forces which are, under Article VIII of the treaty of peace signed this day, to temporarily occupy Wei-hai-wei, shall not exceed one brigade, and from the date of the exchange of the ratifications of the said treaty of peace China shall pay annually one-fourth of the amount of the expenses of such temporary occupation, that is to say, at the rate of 500,000 Kuping taels per annum.

ARTICLE II

The territory temporarily occupied at Wei-hai-wei shall comprise the island of Liu Kung and belt of land 5 Japanese Ri wide along the entire coast line of the Bay of Wei-hai-wei. No Chinese troops shall be permitted to approach or occupy any places within a zone of 5 Japanese Ri wide beyond the boundaries of the occupied territory.

ARTICLE III

The civil administration of the occupied territory shall remain in the hands of the Chinese authorities. But such authorities shall at all times be obliged to conform to the orders which the commander of the Japanese army of occupation may deem it necessary to give in the interest of the health, maintenance, safety, distribution, or discipline of the troops.

All military offences committed within the occupied territory shall be subject for the jurisdiction of the Japanese military authorities.

The foregoing separate articles shall have the same force, value, and effect as if they had been, word for word, inserted in the treaty of peace signed this day.

(Signed as above.)

Convention

ARTICLE I

The convention of armistice concluded on the 5th day of the 3rd month of the 21st year of Kwang Hsü, corresponding to the 30th day of the 3rd month of the 28th year of Meiji, from this date.

ARTICLE II

The armistice, which is prolonged by this convention, shall terminate, without notice on either side, at midnight on the 14th day of the 4th month of the 21st year of Kwang Hsü, corresponding to the 8th day of the 5th month of the 28th year of Meiji. The rejection in the meantime, however, of the said treaty of peace, by either high contracting party, shall have the effect of at once terminating this armistice without previous notice.

(Signed as above.)

15

The Murder of Queen Min

L. H. Underwood

Mrs. L. H. Underwood, an American medical missionary who was well acquainted with leading members of the Korean court, here relates how on October 8, 1895, the Taewŏngun (Lord of the

From L. H. Underwood, *Fifteen Years among the Top-Knots; Or Life in Korea* (New York: American Tract Society, 1904), pp. 147–150.

Great Court, who was father of the king) brought about the assassination of the Korean Queen with the aid of Japanese agents. Following this terrifying event, the King, in fear for his life, obtained refuge in the Russian legation. The subsequent growth of Russian influence in Korea was partly the result of the crudeness of Japanese methods.

. . . The Tai Won Kun [Taewŏngun] was at that time under guard, in exile from the court, at his country house, for conspiracy against the king in favor of his grandson, and he of course readily consented to become the leader of the plotters against the queen, to enter the palace at the head of their troops and take possession of the persons of their majesties (and the government incidentally), necessarily, of course, doing away with the queen. The troops therefore marched with the old man in his chair to the palace gates, where all had been made ready. Ammunition had been secretly removed, native troops trained by Americans had been mostly exchanged for those trained by Japanese, and after a few shots, and scarcely a pretence of resistance, the attacking party entered. It was some distance to the royal apartments, and the rumor of disturbance reached there some time before the attacking party. Her majesty was alarmed. She was a brave woman, but she knew she had bitter, powerful and treacherous foes, and that, like Damocles, a sword suspended by only too slight a thread hung over her life.

The king's second son, Prince Oui-wha, begged her to escape with him by a little gate which yet remained unguarded, through which they might pass disguised to friends in the city. The dowager queen, however, was too old to go, and her majesty nobly refused to leave her alone to the terror which occupation of the palace by foreigners would insure, trusting no doubt to the positive assurances of protection that had been made to her through Count Inoye, and the more so, as one of the courtiers in waiting, a man by the name of Chung Pung Ha, had assured her that whatever happened she might rest confident that the persons of their majesties would be perfectly safe. This man was a creature of low origin, whom the queen had raised and bestowed many favors upon, and in whom she placed great reliance. He advised her not to hide, and kept himself informed of all her movements. With no code of honor wider or higher than his pocket, he of course became a ready tool of the assassins, and there is much evidence to show he was a party to the conspiracy.

The queen therefore remained in a good deal of uneasiness and anxiety, but only when the Tai Won Kun and the hired assassins rushed in, calling for the queen, did she attempt, alas! too late, to hide.

There was some confusion, in the numerous verbal reports which reached us, but two foreigners, a Russian, Mr. Sabbatin, and an American,

General Dye, who were eye-witnesses of nearly all that occurred, both agreed in the statement, that Japanese troops under Japanese officers surrounded the courtyard and buildings where the royal party were, and that the Japanese officers were in the courtyard, and saw the outrages which were committed, and knew all that was done by the Japanese *soshi* or professional cutthroats. About thirty of these assassins rushed into the royal apartments crying, "The queen, the queen, where is the queen?"

Then began a mad and brutal hunt for their prey, more like wild beasts than men, seizing the palace women,[1] dragging them about by their hair and beating them, trying to force them to tell where the queen was. Mr. Sabbatin was himself questioned and threatened with death. The *soshi* and officers who wore the Japanese uniform passed through the room where his majesty stood trying to divert attention from the queen. "One of the Japanese caught him by the shoulder and pulled him about, and Yi Kiung Chick, the minister of the royal household, was killed by the Japanese in his majesty's presence. His royal highness, the crown prince, was seized, his hat torn off and broken, and he was pulled about by the hair, the *soshi* threatening him with their swords while demanding where the queen was." [2] At length they hunted the poor queen down, and killed her with their swords. They then covered her body, and bringing in various palace women, suddenly displaying the corpse, when the women shrieked with horror, "The queen, the queen!" This was enough; by this ruse the assassins made sure they had felled the right victim.

Soon after, the remains were taken to a grove of trees not far off, kerosene oil poured over them, and they were burned, only a few bones remaining.

[1] "Korean Repository," 1894.
[2] From official report of "Korean Repository."

16

The Treaty of Portsmouth

September 5, 1905

The skill and courage of Japan's soldiery in Manchuria and her naval victory in the Straits of Tsushima astonished the world. However, Japan's financial resources neared exhaustion. Revolutionary

From John V. A. MacMurray, comp. and ed., *Treaties and Agreements with and Concerning China, 1894–1919* (New York: Oxford University Press, 1921), I, 522–526. Reprinted by permission of the Carnegie Endowment for International Peace.

disturbances broke out in Russia and the Czar's government desired peace. The belligerent powers accepted President Theodore Roosevelt's tender of good offices and their representatives met in Portsmouth, New Hampshire, to make peace. The negotiations nearly broke down because of Japan's demands for an indemnity and Sakhalin Island. President Roosevelt helped to arrange a compromise: Russia would pay no indemnity, but would cede the southern half of Sakhalin to Japan. In 1945, when Russia defeated Japan, she won back all that she had lost in the Treaty of Portsmouth. See the Yalta Agreement (Chapter VI, Selection 38) and the Japanese Peace Treaty (Chapter VIII, Selection 47).

His Majesty the Emperor of Japan on the one part, and His Majesty the Emperor of all the Russias on the other part, animated by the desire to restore the blessings of peace to Their countries and peoples, have resolved to conclude a Treaty of Peace, and have, for this purpose, named Their Plenipotentiaries, that is to say:

His Majesty the Emperor of Japan:

His Excellency Baron Komura Jutaro, Jusammi, Grand Cordon of the Imperial Order of the Rising Sun, His Minister for Foreign Affairs, and

His Excellency M. Takahira Kogoro, Jusammi, Grand Cordon of the Imperial Order of the Sacred Treasure, His Envoy Extraordinary and Minister Plenipotentiary to the United States of America;

and His Majesty the Emperor of all the Russias:

His Excellency M. Serge Witte, His Secretary of State and President of the Committee of Ministers of the Empire of Russia, and

His Excellency Baron Roman Rosen, Master of the Imperial Court of Russia and His Ambassador Extraordinary and Plenipotentiary to the United States of America;

Who, after having exchanged their full powers which were found to be in good and due form, have concluded the following Articles:

ARTICLE I

There shall henceforth be peace and amity between Their Majesties the Emperor of Japan and the Emperor of all the Russias and between Their respective States and subjects.

ARTICLE II

The Imperial Russian Government, acknowledging that Japan possesses in Corea paramount political, military and economical interests, engage neither to obstruct nor interfere with the measures of guidance, protection and control which the Imperial Government of Japan may find it necessary to take in Corea.

It is understood that Russian subjects in Corea shall be treated exactly in the same manner as the subjects or citizens of other foreign Powers, that is to say, they shall be placed on the same footing as the subjects or citizens of the most favoured nation.

It is also agreed that, in order to avoid all cause of misunderstanding, the two High Contracting Parties will abstain, on the Russo-Corean frontier, from taking any military measure which may menace the security of Russian or Corean territory.

ARTICLE III

Japan and Russia mutually engage:

1. To evacuate completely and simultaneously Manchuria except the territory affected by the lease of the Liao-tung Peninsula, in conformity with the provisions of additional Article I. annexed to this Treaty; and

2. To restore entirely and completely to the exclusive administration of China all portions of Manchuria now in the occupation or under the control of the Japanese or Russian troops, with the exception of the territory above mentioned.

The Imperial Government of Russia declare that they have not in Manchuria any territorial advantages or preferential or exclusive concessions in impairment of Chinese sovereignty or inconsistent with the principle of equal opportunity.

ARTICLE IV

Japan and Russia reciprocally engage not to obstruct any general measures common to all countries, which China may take for the development of the commerce and industry of Manchuria.

ARTICLE V

The Imperial Russian Government transfer and assign to the Imperial Government of Japan, with the consent of the Government of China, the lease of Port Arthur, Talien and adjacent territory and territorial waters and all rights, privileges and concessions connected with or forming part of such lease and they also transfer and assign to the Imperial Government of Japan all public works and properties in the territory affected by the above mentioned lease.

The two High Contracting Parties mutually engage to obtain the consent of the Chinese Government mentioned in the foregoing stipulation.

The Imperial Government of Japan on their part undertake that the proprietary rights of Russian subjects in the territory above referred to shall be perfectly respected.

ARTICLE VI

The Imperial Russian Government engage to transfer and assign to the Imperial Government of Japan, without compensation and with the consent of the Chinese Government, the railway between Chang-chun (Kuancheng-tzu) and Port Arthur and all its branches, together with all rights, privileges and properties appertaining thereto in that region, as well as all coal mines in the said region belonging to or worked for the benefit of the railway.

The two High Contracting Parties mutually engage to obtain the consent of the Government of China mentioned in the foregoing stipulation.

ARTICLE VII

Japan and Russia engage to exploit their respective railways in Manchuria exclusively for commercial and industrial purposes and in no wise for strategic purposes.

It is understood that that restriction does not apply to the railway in the territory affected by the lease of the Liao-tung Peninsula.

ARTICLE VIII

The Imperial Governments of Japan and Russia, with a view to promote and facilitate intercourse and traffic, will, as soon as possible, conclude a separate convention for the regulation of their connecting railway services in Manchuria.[1]

ARTICLE IX

The Imperial Russian Government cede to the Imperial Government of Japan in perpetuity and full sovereignty, the southern portion of the Island of Saghalien and all islands adjacent thereto, and all public works and properties thereon. The fiftieth degree of north latitude is adopted as the northern boundary of the ceded territory. The exact alignment of such territory shall be determined in accordance with the provisions of additional Article II. annexed to this Treaty.

Japan and Russia mutually agree not to construct in their respective possessions on the Island of Saghalien or the adjacent islands, any fortifi-

[1] Such a convention was concluded June 13, 1907.

cations or other similar military works. They also respectively engage not to take any military measures which may impede the free navigation of the Straits of La Perouse and Tartary.

ARTICLE X

It is reserved to the Russian subjects inhabitants of the territory ceded to Japan, to sell their real property and retire to their country; but, if they prefer to remain in the ceded territory, they will be maintained and protected in the full exercise of their industries and rights of property, on condition of submitting to Japanese laws and jurisdiction. Japan shall have full liberty to withdraw the right of residence in, or to deport from, such territory, any inhabitants who labour under political or administrative disability. She engages, however, that the proprietary rights of such inhabitants shall be fully respected.

ARTICLE XI [2]

Russia engages to arrange with Japan for granting to Japanese subjects rights of fishery along the coasts of the Russian possessions in the Japan, Okhotsk and Behring Seas.

It is agreed that the foregoing engagement shall not affect rights already belonging to Russian or foreign subjects in those regions.

ARTICLE XII [3]

The Treaty of Commerce and Navigation between Japan and Russia having been annulled by the war, the Imperial Governments of Japan and Russia engage to adopt as the basis of their commercial relations, pending the conclusion of a new treaty of commerce and navigation on the basis of the Treaty which was in force previous to the present war, the system of reciprocal treatment on the footing of the most favoured nation, in which are included import and export duties, customs formalities, transit and tonnage dues, and the admission and treatment of the agents, subjects and vessels of one country in the territories of the other.

ARTICLE XIII

As soon as possible after the present Treaty comes into force, all prisoners of war shall be reciprocally restored. The Imperial Governments

[2] A fisheries convention was concluded between Japan and Russia on July 28, 1907.

[3] A treaty of commerce and navigation, with separate articles, protocol and exchange of notes attached thereto, and a protocol relating to certain Japanese and Russian consulates, were concluded between Japan and Russia on July 28, 1907. See also the political convention of July 30, 1907.

of Japan and Russia shall each appoint a special Commissioner to take charge of prisoners. All prisoners in the hands of one Government shall be delivered to and received by the Commissioner of the other Government or by his duly authorized representative, in such convenient numbers and at such convenient ports of the delivering State as such delivering State shall notify in advance to the Commissioner of the receiving State.

The Governments of Japan and Russia shall present to each other, as soon as possible after the delivery of prisoners has been completed, a statement of the direct expenditures respectively incurred by them for the care and maintenance of prisoners from the date of capture or surrender up to the time of death or delivery. Russia engages to repay to Japan, as soon as possible after the exchange of the statements as above provided, the difference between the actual amount so expended by Japan and the actual amount similarly disbursed by Russia.

ARTICLE XIV

The present Treaty shall be ratified by Their Majesties the Emperor of Japan and the Emperor of all the Russias. Such ratification shall, with as little delay as possible and in any case not later than fifty days from the date of the signature of the Treaty, be announced to the Imperial Governments of Japan and Russia respectively through the French Minister in Tokio and the Ambassador of the United States in Saint Petersburg and from the date of the later of such announcements this Treaty shall in all its parts come into full force.

The formal exchange of the ratifications shall take place at Washington as soon as possible.[4]

ARTICLE XV

The present treaty shall be signed in duplicate in both the English and French languages. The texts are in absolute conformity, but in case of discrepancy in interpretation, the French text shall prevail.

In witness whereof, the respective Plenipotentiaries have signed and affixed their seals to the present Treaty of Peace.

Done at Portsmouth (New Hampshire) this fifth day of the ninth month of the thirty-eighth year of Meiji, corresponding to the twenty-third day of August (fifth September) one thousand nine hundred and five.

(Signed) *Jutaro Komura* [L.S.]
K. Takahira [L.S.]
Serge Witte [L.S.]
Rosen [L.S.]

[4] Ratifications were exchanged at Washington, November 25, 1905.

Additional Articles

In conformity with the provisions of Articles III. and IX. of the Treaty of Peace between Japan and Russia of this date, the undersigned Plenipotentiaries have concluded the following additional Articles:—

I. TO ARTICLE III

The Imperial Governments of Japan and Russia mutually engage to commence the withdrawal of their military forces from the territory of Manchuria simultaneously and immediately after the Treaty of Peace comes into operation, and within a period of eighteen months from that date, the Armies of the two countries shall be completely withdrawn from Manchuria, except from the leased territory of the Liao-tung Peninsula.

The forces of the two countries occupying the front positions shall be first withdrawn.

The High Contracting Parties reserve to themselves the right to maintain guards to protect their respective railway lines in Manchuria. The number of such guards shall not exceed fifteen per kilomètre and within that maximum number, the Commanders of the Japanese and Russian Armies shall, by common accord, fix the number of such guards to be employed, as small as possible having in view the actual requirements.

The Commanders of the Japanese and Russian forces in Manchuria shall agree upon the details of the evacuation in conformity with the above principles, and shall take by common accord the measures necessary to carry out the evacuation as soon as possible and in any case not later than the period of eighteen months.

II. TO ARTICLE IX

As soon as possible after the present Treaty comes into force, a Commission of Delimitation, composed of an equal number of members to be appointed respectively by the two High Contracting Parties, shall on the spot, mark in a permanent manner the exact boundary between the Japanese and Russian possessions on the Island of Saghalien. The Commission shall be bound, so far as topographical considerations permit, to follow the fiftieth parallel of north latitude as the boundary line, and in case any deflections from that line at any points are found to be necessary, compensation will be made by correlative deflections at other points. It shall also be the duty of the said Commission to prepare a list and description of the adjacent islands included in the cession and finally the Commission shall prepare and sign maps showing the boundaries of the ceded territory. The work of the Commission shall be subject to the approval of the High Contracting Parties.

The foregoing additional Articles are to be considered as ratified with the ratification of the Treaty of Peace to which they are annexed.

Portsmouth, the 5th day, 9th month, 38th year of Meiji, correspond-
      23rd August,
ing to the ——————— 1905.
      5th September,

(Signed) *Jutaro Komura*
K. Takahira
Serge Witte
Rosen

SUGGESTED READING

Akita, George. *The Foundations of Constitutional Government in Modern Japan, 1868–1900*. Cambridge: Harvard University Press, 1965.

Beasley, W. G. *Select Documents on Japanese Foreign Policy, 1853–1868*. London: Oxford University Press, 1955.

Beckmann, George M. *The Making of the Meiji Constitution: The Oligarchs and the Constitutional Development of Japan, 1868–1891*. Lawrence: University of Kansas Press, 1957.

Bellah, Robert. *Tokugawa Religion: The Values of Preindustrial Japan*. New York: Free Press, 1957.

Benedict, Ruth. *The Chrysanthemum and the Sword: Patterns of Japanese Culture*. Boston: Houghton Mifflin, 1946.

Blacker, Carmen. *The Japanese Enlightment*. New York: Cambridge University Press, 1964.

Borton, Hugh. *Japan's Modern Century*. New York: Ronald, 1955.

Brown, Delmer M. *Nationalism in Japan: An Introductory Historical Analysis*. Berkeley and Los Angeles: University of California Press, 1955.

Centenary Culture Council, ed. *Japanese Culture in the Meiji Era*, 10 vols. Tokyo: Pan-Pacific Press, 1955–1958.

Conroy, Hilary. *The Japanese Seizure of Korea: 1868–1910*. Philadelphia: University of Pennsylvania Press, 1960.

Craig, Albert. *Choshu and the Meiji Restoration*. Cambridge: Harvard University Press, 1961.

Earl, David M. *Emperor and Nation in Japan: Political Thinkers of the Tokugawa Period*. Seattle: Washington University Press, 1964.

Fukuzawa Yukichi. *The Biography of Fukuzawa Yukichi (1835–1901)*, 3rd and rev. ed. Translated by Kiyooka Eiichi. Tokyo: Hokuseido, 1947.

Hall, John W. *Japanese History: New Dimensions of Approach and Understanding*. Washington, D.C.: Service Center for Teachers of History, American Historical Association, 1961.

Hall, John W. and Beardsley, Richard K. *Twelve Doors to Japan*. New York: McGraw-Hill, 1965.

Harrington, Fred Harvey. *God, Mammon, and the Japanese: Dr. Horace N. Allen and Korean-American Relations, 1884–1905*. Madison: University of Wisconsin Press, 1944.

Hearn, Lafcadio. *Japan: An Attempt at Interpretation*. New York: Macmillan, 1904.

Holtom, D.C. *National Faith of Japan: A Study in Modern Shinto*. London: Kegan Paul, 1938.

Hozumi Nobushige. *Ancestor Worship and Japanese Law*, 4th rev. ed. Tokyo: Maruzen, 1938.

Ike, Nobutaka. *The Beginnings of Political Democracy in Japan*. Baltimore: Johns Hopkins University Press, 1950.

Ishii Ryosuke, ed. *Japanese Legislation in the Meiji Era*. Translated and adapted by William J. Chambliss. Tokyo: Pan-Pacific Press, 1958.

Ito Hirobumi. *Commentaries on the Constitution of the Empire of Japan*. Translated by Ito Miyoji. Tokyo: Insatsu Kyoku, 1889.

Jansen, Marius B., ed. *Changing Japanese Attitudes Toward Modernization*. Princeton: Princeton University Press, 1965.

Jansen, Marius B. *Sakamoto Ryōma and the Meiji Restoration*. Princeton: Princeton University Press, 1961.

Lensen, George A. *The Russian Push towards Japan*. Princeton: Princeton University Press, 1959.

Lockwood, William. *The Economic Development of Japan: Growth and Structural Change, 1868–1938*. Princeton: Princeton University Press, 1954.

Nitobe Inazo. *Bushido: The Soul of Japan*, 16th ed. Tokyo: Teibi Publishing Co., 1919.

Norman, E. Herbert. *Japan's Emergence as a Modern State: Political and Economic Problems of the Meiji Period*. New York: Institute of Pacific Relation, 1940.

Reischauer, Edwin O. *Japan: Past and Present*. New York: Knopf, 1956.

Reischauer, Edwin O., and Fairbank, John K. *East Asia: The Great Tradition*. Boston: Houghton Mifflin, 1960.

Sansom, George Bailey, *The Western World and Japan: A Study of the Interaction of European and Asiatic Cultures*. New York: Knopf, 1950.

Sansom, George Bailey. *Japan: A Short Cultural History*, rev. ed. New York: Appleton-Century-Crofts, 1962.

Scalapino, Robert A. *Democracy and the Party Movement in Prewar Japan: The Failure of the First Attempt*. Berkeley: University of California Press, 1953.

Tiedemann, Arthur. *Modern Japan: A Brief History*, 2nd ed. Princeton: Van Nostrand, 1962, paperback.

Tsunoda, Ryusaku; de Bary, William Theodore; and Keene, Donald, comps. *Sources of the Japanese Tradition*. New York: Columbia University Press, 1958.

Ward, Robert E., and Rustow, Dankwart, eds. *Political Modernization in Japan and Turkey*. Princeton: Princeton University Press, 1964.

Webb, Herschel. *An Introduction to Japan*, 2nd ed. New York: Columbia University Press, 1957.

Yanaga, Chitoshi. *Japan since Perry*. New York: McGraw-Hill, 1949.

III

World War I and the Far East

In terms of both diplomatic and military strategy, the Far East was a relatively minor theater of World War I. Nevertheless, the war gravely affected the politics of East Asia. From the beginning, Japan hoped to capitalize on the preoccupation of the other powers with their war in Europe to expand her influence in China. Using her alliance with Britain as a pretext, Japan issued an ultimatum to Germany to transfer to Japan the German leasehold in Shantung province. The Germans refused, and within a few weeks the Japanese defeated the German troops and captured the base at Tsingtao. In the course of the fighting, the Japanese, over Chinese protests, violated Chinese territory. Following the seizure of the Shantung leasehold, Japan demanded of President Yüan Shih-k'ai that China accept Japanese political advisers, recognize Japanese claims to special privileges in Shantung, southern Manchuria, and eastern Inner Mongolia, and grant 100-year extensions of the Kwantung leasehold and railroad rights. If China had completely acceded to these Twenty-One Demands, she would have been reduced to the position of a protectorate of Japan. By divulging the nature of the demands to the other powers—especially the United States—the Chinese were able to soften the Japanese pressure, but nevertheless had to make important concessions. In addition, the unsuccessful effort of President Yüan to become Emperor and his death in 1916 further weakened China.

In response to pressure from the Allied Powers, China declared war on Germany in August, 1917, but only after a very bitter dispute between Premier Tuan Ch'i-jui, who favored war, and President Li Yüan-hung and the parliament, who opposed it (Selection 17).[1] Chinese served in labor

---

[1] For Sun Yat-sen's attitude, see Chapter IV, Selection 22.

battalions in the European war. The warlord rulers in Peking negotiated the Nishihara loans from Japan and fell under Japanese influence.

President Woodrow Wilson's wartime Fourteen Points for a peace settlement emphasized the principle of national self-determination. Hopes rose in China and Korea that the Western democracies would liberate them from imperialism. At the Paris Peace Conference, however, Wilson was concerned that Japan might refuse to join the League of Nations if her claims in China were not recognized. The Versailles Treaty, therefore, left the former German concessions in China to the Japanese rather than returning them to China. The failure of the Western democracies to support the Chinese demands for an end to foreign privileges disillusioned many Chinese and placed Russia and Marxism in a favorable light. The May 4 (1919) student movement protesting the Versailles Treaty received wide support throughout China and resulted in the refusal of the Chinese delegates at the peace conference to sign the treaty.

Many Koreans hoped that the self-determination principle would result in Korean independence from Japan. On March 1, 1919, Korean patriots, meeting at a public park in Seoul, formally signed a declaration of independence, and throughout Korea peaceful demonstrations were held (Selections 18, 19). Japanese authorities ruthlessly suppressed the movement. A Korean delegation was sent to the Paris Peace Conference, but it received no official recognition. Many of the Korean leaders had studied under American missionaries and vainly hoped that the United States would support their movement. Korea did not achieve her independence until after World War II.

The Versailles Treaty left Japan the dominant power in East Asia. In addition to recognizing Japan's claims to the Shantung leasehold, the peace settlement assigned the German Islands in the Pacific Ocean north of the equator to Japan, which would administer them as a class C mandate under the League of Nations. The islands, the Marshall, the Mariana, and the Caroline groups, lay athwart the sea routes between the United States and the Philippine Islands. Their occupation by Japan later created grave problems for American naval strategists.

The revolution, Allied intervention, and civil war in Russia had repercussions in the Far East. Allied forces—mostly Japanese, but including Americans, British, and French—entered Siberia in 1918. All left in 1920 save the Japanese, who were evidently intent on annexing much of Siberia. Protests by the pro-Soviet Far Eastern Republic (established in 1920) against the Japanese occupation led to American diplomatic efforts to persuade the Japanese to withdraw, which they did in 1922. The Far Eastern Republic was then incorporated into the Soviet Union. In 1921, Outer Mongolia became a Soviet satellite, although it continued to recognize Chinese suzerainty until 1945.

The Washington Conference of 1921–1922 was concerned with the closely related questions of naval disarmament and the Far East settlement. No other disarmament conference has ever been so successful: as a result of limitations imposed, some ships already in existence and others under construction were actually destroyed. The ratio of tonnage for battleships was set at United States: 5; Great Britain: 5; Japan: 3; France: 1.75; and Italy: 1.75. Provisions to preserve the *status quo* in fortifications in the Pacific Ocean and the Japanese mandate over former German islands contributed to the overwhelming Japanese strength in northeast Asian waters. The Nine-Power Open Door Treaty committed the signatories to the principles of equality of commercial and investment opportunity for all nations and of Chinese independence (Selection 20).

World War I, the Versailles settlement, and the Washington Conference left Japan the dominant power politically, economically, and militarily in the Far East. China, on the other hand, was divided among rival warlord regimes which made a mockery of constitutional principles, important points in Chinese territory remained under foreign occupation, and the unequal treaties were still in force. The Russian Far East was for a while under foreign, especially Japanese, occupation. The Bolshevik regime was not recognized by the United States and Britain and was not consulted on Far Eastern questions. The elimination of Germany from the Pacific removed an important buffer between Japan and America, and in subsequent years the naval and economic rivalry between these two powers rapidly intensified.

17

On the Proposed War with Germany

K'ang Yu-wei

K'ang Yu-wei, the famous reformer, expressed the views of many thoughtful persons in China when he opposed the proposal for a Chinese declaration of war on Germany in the spring of 1917.

MEMORANDUM

. . . The breach between the United States and Germany is no concern of ours. But the Government suddenly severed diplomatic rela-

Reprinted by permission of Dodd, Mead & Company from *The Fight for the Republic in China* by B. L. Putnam Weale and by permission of Mrs. Lenox-Simpson and Hurst & Blackett Ltd.

tions with Germany and is now contemplating entry into the war. This is to advance beyond the action of the United States which continues to observe neutrality. And if we analyse the public opinion of the country, we find that all peoples—high and low, well-informed and ignorant—betray great alarm when informed of the rupture and the proposal to declare war on Germany, fearing that such a development may cause grave peril to the country. This war-policy is being urged by a handful of politicians, including a few members of Parliament and several party men with the view of creating a diplomatic situation to serve their political ends and to reap great profits.

Their arguments are that China—by siding with the Entente—may obtain large loans, the revision of the Customs Tariff and the suspension of the Boxer indemnity to Germany, as well as the recovery of the German concessions, mining and railroad rights and the seizure of German commerce. Pray, how large is Germany's share of the Boxer indemnity? Seeing that German commerce is protected by international law, will China be able to seize it; and does she not know that the Kaiser may in the future exact restitution?

PERILS OF WAR

News from Holland tells of a rumoured secret understanding between Germany, Japan and Russia. The Japanese Government is pursuing a policy of friendship toward Germany. This is very disquieting news to us. As to foreign loans and the revision of the Customs Tariff, we can raise these matters at any time. Why then should we traffic for these things at the risk of grave dangers to the nation? My view is that what we are to obtain from the transaction is far less than what we are to give. If it be argued that the policy aims at securing for China her right to live as an unfettered nation, then we ought to ask for the cancellation of the entire Boxer Indemnities, the abolition of exterritoriality, the retrocession of the foreign concessions and the repeal or amendment of all unjust treaties after the war. But none of these have we demanded. If we ourselves cannot improve our internal administration in order to become a strong country, it is absurd to expect our admission to the ranks of the first-class Powers simply by being allowed a seat at the Peace Conference and by taking a side with the Entente!

Which side will win the war? I shall not attempt to predict here. But it is undoubted that all the arms of Europe—and the industrial and financial strength of the United States and Japan—have proved unavailing against Germany. On the other hand France has lost her Northern provinces and Belgium, Serbia and Rumania are blotted off the map. Should Germany be victorious, the whole of Europe—not to speak of a weak country like China—would be in great peril of extinction. Should she be defeated, Germany still can—after the conclusion of peace—send a fleet to war against us. And as the Powers will be afraid of a second world-war, who will come to our aid? Have we not seen the example of Korea? There is no such thing as an army of righteousness which will come to the assistance of weak nations. I cannot bear to think of hearing the angry voice of German guns along our coasts!

If we allow the Entente to recruit labour in our country without restriction, thousands upon thousands of our fellow countrymen will die for no worthy cause; and if we allow free exportation of foodstuff, in a short time the price of daily necessaries will mount ten to a hundredfold. This is calculated to cause internal troubles. Yea, all gains from this policy will go to the politicians but the people will suffer the evil consequences through no fault of theirs.

DIPLOMACY OF CONFUCIUS

In the matter of diplomacy, we do not need to go to the West for the apt learning on the point at issue. Confucius had said: "Be truthful and cultivate friendship—this is the foundation of human happiness." Our country being weak and undeveloped, if we strive to be truthful and cultivate friendship, we can still be a civilized nation, albeit hoary with age. But we are now advised to take advantage of the difficulties of Germany and abandon honesty in order that we may profit thereby. Discarding treaties is to be unfaithful, grasping for gains is not the way of a gentleman, taking advantage of another's difficulties is to be mean and joining the larger in numbers is cowardice. How can we be a nation, if we throw away all these fundamental qualities.

Even in the press of England and the United States, there is opposition to America entering the war. If we observe neutrality, we are not bound to any side; and when the time comes for peace—as a friend to both sides—we may be able to bring about the ends of the war. Is this not a service to humanity and the true spirit of civilization?

Now it is proposed to take the existence of this great nation of five thousand years and four hundred million people in order to serve the interests of politicians in their party struggles. We are now to be bound to foreign nations, without freedom to act for ourselves and running great risks of national destruction. Can you gentlemen bear to see this come to pass? China has severed relations with Germany but the decision for war has not yet been reached. The whole country is telegraphing opposition to the Government's policy and wants to know whether Germany will not in the future take revenge on account of our rupture with her; and if we are not secured against this eventuality, what are the preparations to meet with a contingency? The Government must not stake the fate of the nation as if it be a child's toy, and the people must not be cast into the whirlpool of slaughter. The people are the backbone of a country, and if the people are all opposed to war on Germany, the Government—in spite of the support of Parliament—must call a great citizens' convention to decide the question. We must persist in our neutrality. You gentlemen are patriotic sons of this country and must know that the existence of China as a nation depends upon what she does now in this matter. In tears, I appeal to you.

Kang Yu-wei

18

Independence Manifesto of the Korean National Congress

March 1, 1919

Encouraged by the Allied victory in World War I and Wilson's Fourteen Points, Korean patriots hoped that world opinion would support their bid for independence from Japan. The Japanese tried to counter the independence movement by inducing Korean leaders to sign a statement that the Korean people were happy under Japanese rule. The deposed Korean Emperor refused to sign the statement and died shortly under suspicious circumstances. This event was seized upon as the occasion for a Korean declaration of independence. Copies of the following manifesto were posted along the main street of Seoul on March 1, 1919.

How miserable are our 20,000,000 compatriots. Do you know the reason for the sudden demise of His Majesty the Emperor? He has been always healthy and there was no news of his illness. But he has suddenly expired at midnight in his sleeping chamber. Would this be ordinary? As we advocated the national independence in the Paris Peace Conference, the cunning Japanese produced a certificate stating that "The Korean people are happy with Japanese rule and do not wish to separate from the Japanese," in order to cover the eyes and ears of the world. Yi Wan-yong signed it as the representative of the nobility; Kim Yun-sik signed it as the representative of the scholars; Yun T'aek-yong signed it as the repre-

From Chong-sik Lee, *The Politics of Korean Nationalism* (Berkeley and Los Angeles: University of California Press, 1963), pp. 111–112. Reprinted by permission.

sentative of the royal relatives; Cho Chung-ŭng and Song Pyŏng-jun signed it as social representatives; Shin Hŭng-u signed it as the representative of educational and religious fields. It was then submitted to His Majesty for his royal seal—the worst crime possible. His Majesty was most enraged and reprimanded them. They did not know what to do, and fearing other incidents in the future, they finally decided to assassinate His Majesty. Yun Tŏk-yong and Han Sang-hak, two traitors, were made to serve His Majesty's dinner, and poison was secretly added to his food at night through the two waiting women.

The Royal Body was immediately torn by agony and soon the Emperor took his last breath. There is no way to describe the pain and agony in our hearts. The two women were also put to death by poison, immediately, so that the intrigue might not be leaked out. The hands of the brigands are becoming more obvious, and cruelty is running to extremes. We have not yet revenged the humiliation of the past (the murder of the queen). And yet another calamity is brought upon us. Ask the blue sky who is incurring these misfortunes. If our people still exist, how could we neglect to cleanse these humiliations? Since the American President proclaimed the Fourteen Points, the voice of national self-determination has swept the world, and twelve nations, including Poland, Ireland, and Czechoslovakia, have obtained independence. How could we, the people of the great Korean nation, miss this opportunity? Our compatriots abroad are utilizing this opportunity to appeal for the recovery of national sovereignty, but the compatriots within our country are still unmoved. Support is not very strong, and opinions are not decided. Think, our compatriots! Now is the great opportunity to reform the world and recover us the ruined nation. If the entire nation rises in unity, we may recover our lost national rights and save the already ruined nation.

Also, in order to revenge the mortal foe of His Majesty and Her Highness, our 20,000,000 compatriots, arise!

January, thirteenth year of Yung-hi (1919)

Kungmin Taehoe (Seal)

19

Korean Proclamation of Independence

March 1, 1919

The Korean leaders at first decided to declare independence on March 3, 1919, the date of mourning for their late Emperor. However, Japanese police, aware of strong Korean sentiments, were mobilizing their forces. It seemed advisable to advance the declaration to March 1. At 2:00 P.M. on March 1, the thirty-three signers solemnly read their independence proclamation in downtown Seoul and then gave themselves up to the Japanese police. Peaceful demonstrations simultaneously broke out all over Korea, taking the Japanese by surprise. The Japanese brutally suppressed the movement, and thousands of Korean patriots were killed, tortured, or imprisoned. The independence leaders, many of whom were Christians, expected that the United States would support their cause. But despite President Woodrow Wilson's advocacy of the principle of national self-determination, American policy was indifferent towards the cause of Korean independence and remained so until World War II.

We herewith proclaim the independence of Korea and the liberty of the Korean people. We tell it to the world in witness of the equality of all nations, and we pass it on to our posterity as their inherent right.

We make this proclamation, having back of us a history of forty-three centuries and 20,000,000 united, loyal people. We take this step to insure to our children for all time to come, life and liberty in accord with the awakening conscience of this new era. This is the clear leading of God, the moving principle of the present age, the just claim of the whole human race. It is something that cannot be stamped out, or stifled, or gagged, or suppressed by any means.

Victims of an older age, when brute force and the spirit of plunder ruled, we have come after these long thousands of years to experience the agony of ten years of foreign oppression, with every loss of the right to live, every restriction of the freedom of thought, every damage done to the dignity of life, every opportunity lost for a share in the intelligent advance of the age in which we live.

Reprinted by permission of Dodd, Mead & Company from *Syngman Rhee: The Man Behind the Myth* by Robert T. Oliver. Copyright 1954 by Robert T. Oliver

Assuredly, if the defects of the past are to be rectified, if the wrongs of the present are to be righted, if future oppression is to be avoided, if thought is to be set free, if right of action is to be given a place, if we are to attain to any way of progress, if we are to deliver our children from the painful heritage of shame, if we are to leave blessing and happiness intact for those who succeed us, the first of all necessary things is the complete independence of our people. What cannot our twenty millions do, with hearts consecrated to liberty, in this day when human nature and conscience are making a stand for truth and right? What barrier can we not break, what purpose can we not accomplish?

We have no desire to accuse Japan of breaking many solemn treaties since 1876, nor to single out specially the teachers in the schools or the Government officials who treat the heritage of our ancestors as a colony of their own, and our people and our civilization as a nation of savages, and who delight only in beating us down and bringing us under their heel.

We have no wish to find special fault with Japan's lack of fairness or her contempt for our civilization and the principles on which her state rests; we, who have greater cause to reprimand ourselves, need not spend time in finding fault with others; neither need we, who require so urgently to build for the future, spend useless hours over what is past and gone. Our urgent need today is the rebuilding of this house of ours and not the discussion of who has broken it down, or what has caused its ruin. Our work is to clear the future of defects in accord with the earnest dictates of conscience. Let us not be filled with bitterness or resentment over past agonies or past occasions for anger.

Our part is to influence the Japanese government, dominated as it is by the old idea of brute force which thinks to run counter to reason and universal law, so that it will change and act honestly and in accord with the principles of right and truth.

The result of annexation, brought about against the will of the Korean people, is that the Japanese are concerned only for their own gain, and by a false set of figures show a profit and loss account between us two peoples most untrue, digging a trench of everlasting resentment deeper and deeper the farther they go.

Ought not the way of enlightened courage to be to correct the evils of the past by ways that are sincere, and by true sympathy and friendly feelings make a new world in which the two peoples will be equally blessed?

To bind by force twenty millions of resentful Koreans will mean not only loss of peace forever for this part of the Far East, but also will increase the ever-growing suspicions of four hundred millions of Chinese—upon whom depends the safety of the Far East—besides strengthening the hatred of Japan. From this all the rest of the East will suffer. Today Korean independence will mean not only life and happiness for us, but also Japan's departure from an evil path and her exaltation to the place of true protector of the East, so that China too would put all fear of Japan aside. This thought comes from no minor resentment, but from a large hope for the future welfare and blessings of mankind.

A new era wakes before our eyes, the old world of force is gone, and the new world of righteousness and truth is here. Out of the experience and travail of the old world arises this light on the affairs of life. Insects stifled by their foe, the snows of winter, are also awakened at this time of the year by the breezes of spring and the warm light of the snow upon them.

It is the day of the restoration of all things, on the full tide of which we set forth without delay or fear. We desire a full measure of satisfaction in the way of life, liberty and the pursuit of happiness, and an opportunity to develop what is in us for the glory of our people. In this hope we go forward.

1. This work of ours is in behalf of truth, justice, and life, undertaken at the request of our people, in order to make known their desire for liberty. Let no violence be done to anyone.

2. Let those who follow us show every hour with gladness this same spirit.

3. Let all things be done with singleness of purpose, so that our behavior to the very end may be honorable and upright.

Dated the 4252d Year of the Kingdom of Korea, 3d Month, 1st Day.

20

Terms of the Nine-Power Open Door Treaty

Washington, February 6, 1922

ARTICLE I

The Contracting Powers, other than China, agree:

1. To respect the sovereignty, the independence, and the territorial and administrative integrity of China;

2. To provide the fullest and most unembarrassed opportunity to

Signed by the diplomatic representatives of the United States, Belgium, British Empire, China, France, Italy, Japan, the Netherlands, and Portugal. From United States Department of State, *United States Relations with China with Special Reference to the Period 1944-1949* (Washington, D.C.: Government Printing Office, 1949), pp. 438-443.

China to develop and maintain for herself an effective and stable government;

3. To use their influence for the purpose of effectually establishing and maintaining the principle of equal opportunity for the commerce and industry of all nations throughout the territory of China;

4. To refrain from taking advantage of conditions in China in order to seek special rights or privileges which would abridge the rights of subjects or citizens of friendly States, and from countenancing action inimical to the security of such States.

ARTICLE II

The Contracting Powers agree not to enter into any treaty, agreement, arrangement, or understanding, either with one another, or, individually or collectively, with any Power or Powers, which would infringe or impair the principles stated in Article I.

ARTICLE III

With a view to applying more effectually the principles of the Open Door or equality of opportunity in China for the trade and industry of all nations, the Contracting Powers, other than China, agree that they will not seek, nor support their respective nationals in seeking—

a. any arrangement which might purport to establish in favour of their interests any general superiority of rights with respect to commercial or economic development in any designated region of China;

b. any such monopoly or preference as would deprive the nationals of any other Power of the right of undertaking any legitimate trade or industry in China, or of participating with the Chinese Government, or with any local authority, in any category of public enterprise, or which by reason of its scope, duration or geographical extent is calculated to frustrate the practical application of the principle of equal opportunity.

It is understood that the foregoing stipulations of this Article are not to be so construed as to prohibit the acquisition of such properties or rights as may be necessary to the conduct of a particular commercial, industrial, or financial undertaking or to the encouragement of invention and research.

China undertakes to be guided by the principles stated in the foregoing stipulations of this Article in dealing with applications for economic rights and privileges from Governments and nationals of all foreign countries, whether parties to the present Treaty or not.

ARTICLE IV

The Contracting Powers agree not to support any agreements by their respective nationals with each other designed to create Spheres of

Influence or to provide for the enjoyment of mutually exclusive opportunities in designated parts of Chinese territory.

ARTICLE V

China agrees that, throughout the whole of the railways in China, she will not exercise or permit unfair discrimination of any kind. In particular there shall be no discrimination whatever, direct or indirect, in respect of charges or of facilities on the ground of the nationality of passengers or the countries from which or to which they are proceeding, or the origin or ownership of goods or the country from which or to which they are consigned, or the nationality or ownership of the ship or other means of conveying such passengers or goods before or after their transport on the Chinese Railways.

The Contracting Powers, other than China, assume a corresponding obligation in respect of any of the aforesaid railways over which they or their nationals are in a position to exercise any control in virtue of any concession, special agreement or otherwise.

ARTICLE VI

The Contracting Powers, other than China, agree fully to respect China's rights as a neutral in time of war to which China is not a party; and China declares that when she is a neutral she will observe the obligations of neutrality.

ARTICLE VII

The Contracting Powers agree that, whenever a situation arises which in the opinion of any one of them involves the application of the stipulations of the present Treaty, and renders desirable discussion of such application, there shall be full and frank communication between the Contracting Powers concerned.

ARTICLE VIII

Powers not signatory to the present Treaty, which have Governments recognized by the Signatory Powers and which have treaty relations with China, shall be invited to adhere to the present Treaty. To this end the Government of the United States will make the necessary communications to nonsignatory Powers and will inform the Contracting Powers of the replies received. Adherence by any Power shall become effective on receipt of notice thereof by the Government of the United States.

ARTICLE IX

The present Treaty shall be ratified by the Contracting Powers in accordance with their respective constitutional methods and shall take effect on the date of the deposit of all the ratifications, which shall take place at Washington as soon as possible. The Government of the United States will transmit to the other Contracting Powers a certified copy of the *procès-verbal* of the deposit of ratifications.

The present Treaty, of which the French and English texts are both authentic, shall remain deposited in the archives of the Government of the United States, and duly certified copies thereof shall be transmitted by that Government to the other Contracting Powers.

SUGGESTED READING

Chow, Tse-tsung. *The May Fourth Movement: Intellectual Revolution in Modern China.* Cambridge: Harvard University Press, 1960.

Beers, Burton F. *Vain Endeavor: Robert Lansing's Attempts to End the American-Japanese Rivalry.* Durham: Duke University Press, 1962.

Buell, R. L. *The Washington Conference.* New York: Appleton-Century-Crofts, 1922.

Curry, Roy Watson. *Woodrow Wilson and Far Eastern Policy, 1913–1921.* New York: Bookman Associates, 1957.

Fifield, Russell H. *Woodrow Wilson and the Far East: The Diplomacy of the Shantung Question.* New York: Crowell, 1952.

Hornbeck, Stanley K. *Contemporary Politics in the Far East.* New York: Appleton-Century-Crofts, 1916.

Hu Shih. *The Chinese Renaissance.* Chicago: University of Chicago Press, 1934.

LaFargue, Thomas E. *China and the World War.* Stanford: Stanford University Press, 1937.

Lee, Chong-sik. *The Politics of Korean Nationalism.* Berkeley: University of California Press, 1963.

Morley, James W. *The Japanese Thrust into Siberia, 1918.* New York: Columbia University Press, 1957.

Reinsch, Paul S. *An American Diplomat in China.* Garden City, N.Y.: Doubleday, 1922.

Tang, Peter S. H. *Russian and Soviet Policy in Manchuria and Outer Mongolia, 1913–1931.* Durham: Duke University Press, 1959.

Weale, B. L. Putnam. *The Fight for the Republic in China.* New York: Dodd, Mead, 1917.

Yim, Louise. *My Forty Year Fight for Korea.* New York: Wyn, 1951.

IV

The United Front in China

Sun Yat-sen, whose fortunes were at a low ebb, sought help from the Western powers in his efforts to establish a united, democratic China. They ignored him. In 1923 he met Adolf Joffe, Moscow's special envoy to China, in Shanghai, and they issued a joint statement which would constitute the basis for cooperation between Russia and the Chinese Nationalists (Selection 21). They agreed that China was not yet ready for communism and that the primary task was to achieve national unification and independence. Chinese Communists, on instruction from Moscow, joined Sun's Nationalist Party (Kuomintang) individually to help carry out the nationalist revolution. A leading agent of the Communist International, Michael Borodin, became Sun's adviser. Borodin reorganized the Nationalist Party in imitation of the Communist Party of Russia, with tight discipline, a hierarchical structure, and democratic centralism. The Russian general V. K. Blücher (Galen) was dispatched to China by the Comintern to help train an army for the Nationalist Party, so that the party would no longer have to depend on unreliable warlords for military support. Chiang Kai-shek, one of Sun's disciples, went to Moscow to study military organization and returned to head the Nationalists' Whampoa Military Academy.

Despite the influence of the Comintern, Sun, who was a convert to Christianity, did not adopt Marxism. He lectured on his own ideology, known as the Three Principles of the People: nationalism, democracy, and the people's livelihood (Selection 22). His program was summarized in his Fundamentals of National Reconstruction, which outlined the three stages, including a period of tutelage, through which China should pass in order to achieve democracy (Selection 23). Sun, the Father of the Chinese Republic, died in 1925 and became a legend. His will was later read every Monday at memorial meetings of the party branches, government offices, schools, and factories (Selection 24), and his writings came

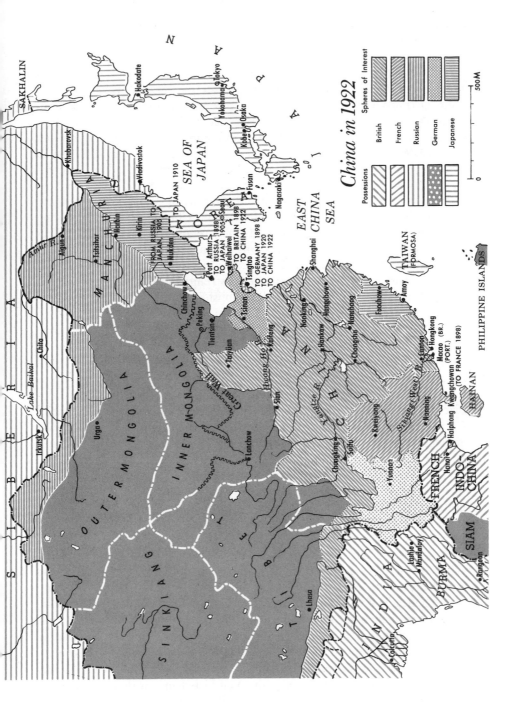

China in 1922

Possessions | Spheres of Interest

British
French
Russian
German
Japanese

0 | 500 M

to be cited by both the Nationalists and the Communists to legitimize their policies.

Equipped with arms from Russia, the Nationalist forces launched the successful Northern Expedition against the Yangtze valley warlords in 1926. After the defeat of the warlords, the left-wing leaders of the Kuomintang transferred the party headquarters and the governmental administration from Canton to the industrial city of Hankow. In April, 1927, Chiang Kai-shek turned against the Communists, liquidated leftists and labor leaders in Shanghai, and set up a non-Communist administration in Nanking. In Hankow a split occurred between some of the left Kuomintang elements on the one hand and the Communists on the other, leading, in July, to the expulsion of Borodin and the exile of Madame Sun Yat-sen. Madame Sun, who was the sister of Madame Chiang, issued a blistering condemnation of Chiang's betrayal of Sun's revolutionary policies (Selection 25). The United Front had come to an end. Communist efforts to organize proletarian uprisings in the cities met with failure, and by 1932 the only center of significant Communist strength was Juichin, in Kiangsi, where Mao Tse-tung and Chu Teh established a territorial base with the support of the local peasantry and a newly organized Red Army.

In 1928 one of Chiang's allies captured Peking from the Manchurian warlord, Marshal Chang Tso-lin. While fleeing from Peking, Marshal Chang was assassinated by Japanese officers, and his son Chang Hsüeh-liang recognized the Nationalist regime. Peking (Northern Capital) was now renamed Peiping (Northern Peace), and the foreign powers recognized the Nationalist regime at Nanking as the legitimate government of China. The military unification of China was deemed accomplished—actually it was not—and the political tutelage which had been envisioned by Sun Yat-sen commenced in 1928.

During the period of tutelage, the Kuomintang exercised the powers of government on behalf of the Chinese people. The national government consisted of five Yuan, or branches (Executive, Legislative, Judicial, Control, and Examination), the personnel of which was appointed by and responsible to the Political Committee of the Nationalist Party. In effect the government during tutelage was a dictatorship under Chiang Kai-shek, who concurrently held the highest offices in the party, the government, and the army.

The leadership of Chiang and the unity of China under the Kuomintang were challenged from three sources: rival warlords (some of them nominally Kuomintang members), the Communists, and the Japanese. In 1929 a revolt in Hunan by supporters of Wang Ching-wei, a leftist Kuomintang leader, was suppressed, and in 1930 an alliance of Wang Ching-wei and Generals Feng Yü-hsiang and Yen Hsi-shan was defeated in a war involving a million men. From 1931 to 1934, Chiang Kai-shek, with the help of German officers, directed a series of five Communist-extermination campaigns, which ended in the historic retreat, or Long March, of the Communists from Kiangsi to Shensi. In the meantime, the Japanese seized Manchuria, setting up a puppet state there in 1932.

The constantly recurring warfare in China meant that military considerations took priority over economic development and social reform. Nationalist leaders made ambitious plans, but the task of modernizing China was too formidable and the political situation too unstable. Sun Yat-sen's plans for agrarian reform were not carried out, and the welfare of the peasantry, who made up 80 percent of the population, was neglected. When the long war with Japan began in 1937, many critical social and economic problems were still crying for solutions.

21

The Sun-Joffe Statement

January 26, 1923

The Sun-Joffe agreement provided the basis for collaboration between the nationalist movement in China and the international Communist movement. The result was the establishment of a united front of the Chinese Nationalist and Chinese Communist Parties and the open participation of Comintern agents in Chinese affairs.

Dr. Sun Yat-sen holds that the communistic order, or even the Soviet system, cannot actually be introduced into China because there do not exist the conditions for the successful establishment of either communism or Sovietism. This view is entirely shared by Mr. Joffe, who is further of the opinion that China's paramount and most pressing problem is to achieve national unification and attain full national independence; and regarding this great task he has assured Dr. Sun Yat-sen that China has the warmest sympathy of the Russian people and can count on the support of Russia.

On the basis of the proposals mentioned in Russia's message dated September 27th 1920, Mr. Joffe assured Dr. Sun Yat-sen that the Soviet Government was prepared to annul all the treaties concluded by Tsarist Russia with China (including the treaties concerning the Trans-Siberian

Stephen Chen and Robert Payne, *Sun Yat-sen: a Portrait*. New York, John Day, 1946 railway) and to negotiate anew with China. Mr. Joffe gave the formal undertaking that the Soviet Government would not attempt to enforce an imperialistic policy in Outer Mongolia or to sever it from Chinese authority.

22

Nationalism and Cosmopolitanism
Lecture Four

Delivered on February 17, 1924

Sun Yat-sen

In this lecture, Dr. Sun points out that the Chinese people need to be nationalistic in order to resist European imperialism, that Communist Russia would aid China in the struggle against imperialism, and that the Chinese people are traditionally peace-loving. These themes have been echoed by subsequent Chinese leaders.

NATIONALISM IN EUROPE

The entire population of the earth is one billion five hundred millions, one fourth of which is Chinese. Thus among every four persons in the world, there is one Chinese. The white people in Europe amount to four hundred millions. The white race which is the most progressive race in the world is divided into four different stocks. Central and Northern Europe is the home of the Teutons, who have established many nations, including Germany, Austria, Sweden, Norway, Holland, and Denmark. In Eastern Europe are the Slavs, the greater number of whom live in Russia. After the war, two new Slavic states were born, namely, Czechoslovakia and Jugoslovakia. The Anglo-Saxons occupy the western part of Europe and have also founded the United States and Canada in North America. The United States and England are the two most powerful Anglo-Saxon states. The Latin people who occupy the southern part of Europe have established France, Italy, Spain, and many other smaller states. The Latin people have also established many states in South America.

From Sun Yat-sen, *The Three Principles of the People,* in Leonard Shihlien Hsü, comp. and trans., *Sun Yat-sen: His Political and Social Ideals* (Los Angeles: University of Southern California Press, 1933), pp. 217–231. Reprinted by permission.

Since the spirit of nationalism has been highly developed among the white nations of Europe, they have established many powerful states though their number is only four hundred millions, and they are divided into so many different stocks. When Europe became overcrowded, they extended their possessions to the Western Hemisphere as well as to Africa and to Australia. The Anglo-Saxon people have the largest colonial possessions in the world; they originated in Europe, but their possessions in Europe are only two small islands, the so-called British Isles. These islands occupy a very strategic position in the Atlantic Ocean similar to Japan's position in the Pacific. The Anglo-Saxons not only have the largest colonial possessions in the world, but are also the wealthiest and most powerful people among all races.

Before the war the Teutons and the Slavs were the most powerful peoples on earth, and the Teutons were specially noted for their intelligence and ability. For instance, Germany was able to unite twenty or more separate kingdoms into one great Empire. When the German Empire was founded, it was principally an agricultural state, and became highly industrialized later on. Gradually Germany developed a powerful army and navy.

CAUSE OF THE WORLD WAR

What we call "imperialism" is the policy of invading other nations by political force. The European peoples have been imbued with imperialistic ideas, and the result has been that there have frequently been international wars. It is said that there is a small war in Europe every ten years and a great war every hundred years. The biggest war they have ever had was the World War which took place just a few years ago. It was called the "World War" because it affected the entire world; and because all nations of the world, with a few exceptions, participated in the struggle.

The first cause of the World War was the struggle between the Teutonic people and the Anglo-Saxon people for supremacy of the sea, for of course Great Britain could not bear to see Germany rise up as the supreme maritime Power. The second cause of the World War was competition among the Powers to acquire colonial possessions. There was a weak nation in eastern Europe called Turkey, known as "the sick man of the Near East." Since that country was very backward and weak, the European Powers had long desired to partition it, but they could not agree among themselves. The question was in dispute for over a hundred years and at length the Powers resorted to arms. We may, then, conclude that the World War was a result of two factors: first, the competition among the European people for power and wealth; and secondly, the attempt to reach a solution of the "world problem."

In regard to the World War, if Germany had been victorious, the supremacy of the sea would have been handed over to Germany; and the British Empire, like the Roman Empire, would have broken into parts. But the war turned out differently, and the military power of imperialist Germany was completely crushed. This war in Europe was indeed the biggest war that ever happened in history. Forty to fifty million men were actually in the field, and the war lasted for four years.

When the war ended, neither side had won a decisive victory. On one side was the Entente which included Germany and Austria, and later on Turkey and Bulgaria; and on the other side, the Allies, which included Servia, France, Russia, Britain, and Japan, and later on Italy and the United States. The United States entered the war purely for nationalistic and racial reasons. During the first two years of the war, the Entente forces almost captured Paris, and blockaded all British waters. The Teutons thought that the British Empire would surely fall. England was much disturbed, and sought rescue from America, persuading the latter to enter into the war on the ground that both countries belonged to the Anglo-Saxon race, and that either one would be weakened if the other was destroyed. Lest she herself should not be strong enough to fight Germany, the United States induced many other neutral states to enter into the war on the side of the Allies.

SELF-DETERMINATION OF NATIONALISM

During the war a great doctrine was formulated which almost everybody approved—the Wilsonian doctrine of the self-determination of nationalities. Since Germany was using force in the attempt to suppress the allied nations of Europe, President Wilson declared that all the oppressed peoples in the world should unite with the Allies to defeat German militarism, and that if the war was won, the smaller nations would have an opportunity to determine their own destiny. The smaller nations believed in Wilson, and hoped fervently that they would be liberated from oppression at the end of the war. The Hindus and Annammites enthusiastically helped even their own enemies, Britain and France respectively, "to win the war" and "to make the world safe for democracy." Other oppressed states in Europe, such as Poland, Czechoslovakia, and Rumania also entered the war because of Woodrow Wilson's promise. China joined in the war for the same reason. Although we did not send troops to Europe, we sent several hundred thousands of labor battalions to the front. Because of this one good principle; namely, self-determination of nationalities, the Powers persuaded practically all the oppressed nations in Europe and Asia to assist them in fighting against the Central Powers.

In order to preserve peace and good will among the nations after the great disaster, Wilson put forth the "Fourteen Points" which included the principle of self-determination of nationalities. When the war was in progress, England and France agreed wholeheartedly with the Fourteen Points. As soon as the war was won, England, France, and Italy tried to frustrate Wilson's program because it was in conflict with their imperialist policies. As a consequence, the Peace Treaty was one of the most unequal treaties ever negotiated in history. The smaller nationalities were not only refused self-determination, but were brought under worse oppression.

The mighty Powers held the supremacy and had control over the resources of all the smaller nations. In order to maintain their monopolistic positions forever, the Powers have prevented the rise of the small states by teaching them the doctrine of cosmopolitanism. They have criticized the doctrine of nationalism as being too narrow and detrimental to humanity. Their doctrine of cosmopolitanism is in fact the doctrine of imperialism in disguise.

In spite of the difficulties and disappointments at the Peace Conference and in the years following, Wilson's doctrine of self-determination has borne fruit. Annam, Burma, Java, India, Malaysia, Afghanistan, and many other small nations in Europe are finding that they have been deceived by the imperialist Powers, and they are trying to liberate themselves.

THE RUSSIAN REVOLUTION

The European War could not destroy imperialism because it was a struggle of the imperialism of one nation against that of another. It was neither a war between savagery and civilization nor one between "might" and "right." The outcome of the war, therefore, was only the overthrow of one system of imperialism by another, and what was left was still imperialism.

The first Revolution in Russia broke forth in 1905, but was not successful. Only after the awakening of the Russian people from their dark, painful experience of the World War was the revolution a success. Russia, being an Ally, sent more than ten millions of soldiers to fight against Germany. Her service to the Allies during the war was not a little, for by keeping part of the German forces in the East fighting the Russians she prevented the Germans from breaking through the Western front and thereby saved France and England from destruction. Suddenly the Russian soldiers and common people realized that the war would do no good to them because they were simply helping one group of imperialist Powers to defeat another group of imperialist Powers.

Furthermore, the Russians as a people had no point of conflict with the Germans; the conflict came from their respective imperialistic policies. When the Russian people learned that imperialism was historically wrong, they set up a revolution in 1917 and overthrew imperialism at home. They then negotiated for peace separately with Germany.

After the Allied nations had negotiated the peace with Germany, the imperialistic Powers intervened in Russia, because Russia, whose policies were contrary to those of the imperialist Powers, was a menace to them. Russia endeavored to unite the small nations to fight against imperialism and capitalism. Such a policy is fundamentally in harmony with the Wilsonian doctrine of self-determination of nationalities. Judging from the experience of the European War, imperialism renders no great benefit to any nation, whereas liberty for all nationalities is the only principle by which humanity will ever be saved.

EMANCIPATION OF THE OPPRESSED

The four hundred millions of white people in Europe and America constitute the strongest race on earth. The Red Indians in America have been almost destroyed by them. The black people in Africa and the brown people in Southern Asia are in danger of extermination. The yellow people in Asia have also been brought under the oppression of the white people, and may soon be destined to the same fate as the red race. But 150,000,000 of Russians, since their Revolution, have parted from the white imperialists and have joined the small nations in the struggle against European militarism. That leaves only 250,000,000 on the side of the imperialists. Hitherto the struggle of mankind has been one between the 1,250,000,000 and the 250,000,000. The latter group, though smaller in number, occupies a very influential place in the world. They use both their powerful political and economic forces to suppress the small nations.

Contrary to the expectation of the imperialists, the 150,000,000 Slavs have risen to speak a word of justice for the oppressed nations, and to oppose imperialism and militarism. The Powers attacked Lenin, as my Russian friend said, because he declared that 1,250,000,000 people were being overridden by the 250,000,000 people and because Lenin, furthermore, engaged in the actual work of liberation and of self-determination. Throughout his life he wrought to emancipate the small nations from the tyranny of the Powers. In spite of the attacks upon Lenin by the capitalist Powers, the world is realizing that it should no longer be bound by hypocrisy and deceit. Since the war, political consciousness of the peoples of the world has evidently progressed to a higher level than ever before.

OUR DUTY—NATIONALISM OR COSMOPOLITANISM?

It is our duty to revive the spirit of Chinese nationalism and to use the strength of our four hundred millions to uphold justice and humanity. The Powers have feared the realization of such a duty on our part, and so they have propagated the doctrine of cosmopolitanism. Their argument is that narrow nationalism is not suited to a progressive civilization, and that we should be broadminded. Unfortunately, the youths of China who advocate the so-called "new culture" are betrayed by such sophistry and are opposed to the doctrine of nationalism without reckoning with our peculiar conditions.

It is evident that unless our country has achieved freedom and independence, we are not in the position to preach cosmopolitanism. If we give up nationalism in order to preach cosmopolitanism, we are like the coolie in Hongkong who threw his bamboo pole into the sea with the winning lottery ticket in it. Cosmopolitanism may be likened to the lottery ticket and nationalism to the bamboo pole. We should know that cosmopolitanism is developed from nationalism. Unless the spirit of nationalism is well developed, the spirit of cosmopolitanism is perilous.

In other words, cosmopolitanism is wrapped up in nationalism just as the lottery ticket was sealed in the bamboo pole. Our giving up nationalism for cosmopolitanism would naturally lead to the destruction of both the pole and the ticket! As already said, our present position is inferior to that of the Annammites and the Koreans. They are men without country and they are slaves; but we are inferior even to slaves! Dear friends, inferior as we are, should we preach nationalism or cosmopolitanism?

The history of the Chinese people springs from imperialism, and our ancestors often used political force to invade the territory of other nations. Our civilization was well developed several thousands of years before European civilization began. European civilization reached its zenith in the time of Rome, yet the Roman Empire was only a contemporary of the Han dynasty. Chinese political thought was far advanced during the Han dynasty, and many Han writers were anti-imperialists. There was abundant anti-imperialist literature, and *The Plea for the Abandonment of the Pearl District* [1] is a notable example. The author of this essay was opposed to the expansion of the Chinese Empire to the South against the wish of the original settlers. You will see, then, that our people were already opposed to imperialism and were advocates of peace as early as the Han dynasty.

During the Sung dynasty when our people would not invade others, the foreigners invaded China, and the Sung régime was replaced by the Mongol rule. When China's independence was restored by the Ming, the latter also, like the Sung, adopted a policy of non-invasion. The small nations in the South Pacific paid tribute to the Ming, not as a result of conquest, but because they admired China, and so they became tributary states to China of their own free will. They considered it an honor to be tributary states of China, and they would have felt offended if the Ming had refused to accept their tribute.

[1] In Chinese, *Ch'i Chu Ai Yi.*

PRESTIGE OF IMPERIALIST CHINA UNEQUALED

A nation with such a prestige that small nations come to her and of their own free will demand to be annexed is very unusual. Contrast with this the relation between the United States and the Philippine Islands: the Philippines are allowed autonomy and are also permitted to send a representative to the Congress in Washington, D.C. Instead of the Philippine government paying a tribute to the American government, America is spending a large amount of money every year for the development of transportation and education in the Islands. Although the American government is so very generous toward the Philippines, the latter still demand independence from America and consider their being a dependency of America as a disgrace.

On the north of the Indian Empire there is a country among the Himalaya Mountains called Nepal. The dominant people in Nepal belong to the Kalmuk stock. Since the Kalmuks are good fighters, the British are afraid of them even though they have taken India into their possession. The British treat the Kalmuks very generously, and every year they give to the Kalmuks a large amount of money, just as the Chinese gave money to the Tartars as tribute during the Sung dynasty. The British, however, do not call it a tribute, but a subsidy. In spite of these favors from the British, the Kalmuks paid at the same time a tribute to China as late as the first year of the Republic.

When I was in Siam about ten years ago I had a conference with the Vice-Minister of Foreign Affairs of Siam at the Foreign Office and we talked over the Far Eastern problem. In the course of conversation, the Siamese Vice-Minister of Foreign Affairs remarked to me: "When your Revolution has succeeded and your nation becomes powerful, we Siamese shall be only too happy to be annexed to China and become a Chinese province." I feel that this statement is representative of the Siamese nation because it was made by their Vice-Minister of Foreign Affairs at the Foreign Office. In recent years, however, the Siamese have been able to get rid of their unequal treaties and to achieve national independence. The position of Siam among the nations has been elevated; and naturally she no longer desires to be annexed to China.

WHO IS THE NEAREST AND BIGGEST ENEMY?

May I relate to you another story? During the European War I established the Constitutional Government in Canton. One day the British Consul-General called on me at the Generalissimo's office to talk over the possibility of the Southern Government's entrance into the War. I asked:

"Why should we enter into the War?"

"Fight Germany," the Consul-General replied, "because she has robbed you of Tsingtao, and you should get it back."

"Tsingtao," I said, "is far away from Canton. How about Hongkong, Burma, Nepal, and Bhutan which were once either our own territory or tributary states, and which are much closer to Canton than Tsingtao? At the present time you have an eye on Tibet. Ordinary logic suggests that if China is strong enough to get back her lost territories, she should proceed first to get back the closer and bigger ones. Tsingtao is but a small place, and Burma is bigger than Tsingtao, and Tibet is still bigger."

"I came to talk business!" remarked the irritated Consul-General.

"I am talking business too!" I answered.

We stared at each other for a long time. Then I broke the silence by saying:

"Our civilization is two thousand years ahead of yours. While we are only too happy to help you to advance yours to our stage, we cannot be pulled backward by you. Two thousand years ago we abandoned imperialism and militarism. We have been peace-lovers ever since. We would of course welcome the War if its purpose were peace, justice, and equality; but as a matter of fact you always prefer war to peace, might to right. We consider the brutalities of your might as nothing short of barbarism. So we shall let you alone until you are tired of war. Perhaps the day of real peace will come, and then you and I will work together for the common good of mankind."

THE PEACE-LOVING QUALITY OF THE CHINESE

"I have another reason, a very strong reason," I continued, "for my refusal to enter the War. It is this: I do not want to see our nation transformed into a militaristic nation, a nation defying justice and right as is the case with your nation. Your suggestion is that after China has entered the War, you will send to China experienced army officers to train good Chinese soldiers and supply China with the best sort of munitions and arms, and within six months you will be able to turn out 300,000 to 500,000 well-trained men and send them to the front; but I say that China's entrance into the War would then be a disastrous thing."

"Why would it be disastrous?" the British Consul-General interrupted.

"In the future," I continued, "this trained army of several hundred thousand men would become the nucleus of Chinese militarism. Our military forces would develop from a few hundred thousands into several millions. Japan's ascendency has been detrimental to your country's expansion; China's ascendency to power would be even more detrimental than that of Japan. If we followed your suggestion, China would become ten times more powerful than Japan, for China is richer and bigger than Japan. Then the whole world, including your country, would probably fall prey to China's arms. All this might happen if we were to do what you suggest, but we have already cast off the shell of barbarism, and we are workers for peace. I sincerely hope that China will always preserve this beautiful quality of peace-loving. I, therefore, oppose our entrance into the War."

After I finished my conversation, the British Consul-General was moved by the philosophy expounded. He said:

"If I were a Chinese, I would have the same idea!"

OUR IDEALS AND POLITICAL PHILOSOPHY
TWO THOUSAND YEARS IN ADVANCE

Gentlemen, revolution is usually a bloody affair. Our Revolution of 1911 did not shed much blood because our people are a peace-loving people. This peace-loving quality is the greatest virtue of the Chinese. I have always tried to persuade other peoples of the world to follow the lead of China and try to build a world upon peace and good will. At present, the Russian Slavs are following China in being peace-loving, and so the 150,000,000 are seeking co-operation with their 400,000,000 brethren in the Middle Kingdom.

Our people are not only peace-loving, but very advanced in civilization. Anarchism and communism which are new political theories in Europe were expounded by our scholars thousands of years ago. For instance, Lao Tzu is the father of anarchistic philosophy. Lao Tzu's description of "The Kingdom of Hua Hsü" where people live in natural order without government and law is typical Utopian literature of anarchistic type. Our youths are constantly trying to learn everything the West has to teach, but what is newest in the West has existed in China for thousands of years. The Soviet system in Russia is not pure communism but Marxism—and Marxism is not communism; the real communism comes from Proudhon and Bakunin. While no country in the West has practiced communism, China during the days of Hung Hsiu-ch'uan [2] gave the theory a trial. The economic system of Hung Hsiu-ch'uan's government was a real communistic experiment which I regret cannot be interpreted in detail on account of lack of time.

CHINA'S NEED OF SCIENCE

Where Europe surpasses China, is not in political philosophy, but in material civilization. The so-called modern living, as well as powerful armies and navies, comes from the development of science. Science is young; it was brought into existence during the seventeenth and eighteenth centuries by great experimentalists like Bacon and Newton. Europe of two hundred years ago was not equal to China. What we should learn from the West is not political philosophy, but science. Really good political philosophy Europe has to learn from China. You know that Germany

[2] Hung Hsiu-ch'üan was the leader of the Taiping Rebellion. [Editor's note.]

is the most advanced nation in the world so far as learning is concerned. But the German scholars are studying Chinese philosophy; they also study Buddhism from India in order to avoid the dogmatism of science.

Cosmopolitanism, which has only recently developed in Europe, has prospered in China for two thousand years. Of course, the Europeans at present cannot understand the beauty of our civilization. Furthermore, the loss of our nationalist spirit has hindered the development of our good racial qualities, our philosophy, and our moral ideals. On the other hand, the European idea of cosmopolitanism is but the doctrine of "might is right" in disguise. The Europeans always say "Let's fight for it" and the Chinese say "Let's reason about it." Reason should be the foundation of cosmopolitanism, and we must preserve it by all means. The way to preserve it is through nationalism. Just as the 150,000,000 Russians laid the foundation of cosmopolitanism in Europe, the 400,000,000 Chinese will lay its foundation in Asia. Once established, the influence of cosmopolitanism will be carried far. I, therefore, conclude that we must preach nationalism before cosmopolitanism; for preaching cosmopolitanism without first preaching nationalism is not practical. True is the saying: "In order to make the world tranquil and happy, the nation must first be well governed!"

23

Fundamentals of National Reconstruction

1924

Sun Yat-sen

Here Sun defines the three principles of the people, describes the three periods in the program of national reconstruction, and outlines the Quintuple-Power Constitution. The Constitution enacted by the Nationalist regime in December, 1946, is largely based on Sun's model. (See also Chapter I, Selection 7.)

1. The National Government shall reconstruct the Republic of China on the basis of the revolutionary *San Min Chu I* (the Three People's Principles) and the Quintuple-Power Constitution.

As given in *China Handbook, 1937–1943: A Comprehensive Survey of Major Developments*. Compiled by the Chinese Ministry of Information (New York: Macmillan, 1943), pp. 55–56. Reprinted by permission.

2. The primary task of reconstruction is the people's livelihood. Consequently, concerning the four great necessities of the people—food, clothing, shelter and means of travel—the Government should, in cooperation with the people, strive together to develop agriculture to feed them; to develop the textile industry to meet their clothing demands; to work out a large-scale housing project to furnish them with better living quarters; to improve and construct roads and canals to facilitate their travelling.

3. Second in importance is the people's sovereignty. The Government should train and direct the people in their acquisition of political knowledge and ability thereby enabling them to exercise the powers of election, recall, initiative, and referendum.

4. Third comes nationalism. The Government should help and guide the weak and small racial groups within its national boundaries toward self-determination and self-government. It should offer resistance to foreign aggression, and simultaneously it should revise foreign treaties in order to restore our equality and independence among the nations.

5. The program of national reconstruction shall be divided into three periods: first, the military period; second, the period of political tutelage; third, the constitutional period.

6. In the military period, the whole administrative system shall be placed under military rule. The Government on the one hand should employ its armed force to eradicate all internal obstacles and, on the other, disseminate its doctrines to enlighten the people as well as to promote national unity.

7. As soon as a province is completely restored to order, the period of political tutelage will commence and the military period will come to an end.

8. In the period of political tutelage the Government should send persons, qualified through training and examination, to various *hsien* (counties) to assist the people in the preparation of self-government. A *hsien* may elect a magistrate for the execution of its administrative affairs and elect representatives for the deliberation and making of its laws in order to become a completely self-governed *hsien*, when a census of the whole *hsien* has been properly taken; a survey of its land has been completed; its police and local defense forces have been satisfactorily maintained; roadbuilding and repairing within its boundaries have been successfully carried out; and its people have received training in the exercise of the four powers, fulfilled their duties as citizens, and pledged themselves to carry out the revolutionary principles.

9. Citizens in a completely self-governed *hsien* shall directly have the power of election, the power of recall, the power of initiative, and the power of referendum.

10. Every *hsien*, at the commencement of self-government, shall first

assess the value of private land in the whole *hsien,* which value is to be declared by the landowner. The local government shall tax private land on the basis of the value assessed, and at any time may buy it on the same basis. If after this assessment the land increases in value as a result of political advancement or social progress, such unearned increment should be shared by the people in the whole *hsien* and should not be kept by the landowners as private benefit.

11. Annual receipts from land tax, unearned increment, products of public land, yields from mountains, forests, rivers and lakes, proceeds from mineral deposits and water power, all belong to the local government, and shall be used for the operation of local public enterprises of the people, for the care of the young and the aged, the poor and the sick, for famine relief, as well as to meet various public demands.

12. In various *hsien,* natural resources and large-scale industrial and commercial enterprises, the opening and development of which lie beyond the means of these *hsien* and require external capital, should be opened and developed with the help of the Central Government. Net profits so realized shall be divided equally between the Central and the local governments.

13. With regard to its obligation to the Central Government every *hsien* shall give a certain percentage of its annual revenue towards the Central Government's annual expenditure. Such percentage shall be determined each year by citizens' delegates, but it shall not be lower than 10 per cent or more than 50 per cent of the *hsien* revenue.

14. Every *hsien,* upon its adoption of self-government, may elect one delegate for the formation of a representative body to participate in political affairs of the Central Government.

15. All candidates and appointed officials, whether belonging to the Central or the local government, shall be persons found qualified in the examinations held by the Central Government or adjudged qualified by the personnel registration organ of the Central Government.

16. The constitutional period shall commence in a province when all the *hsien* of the province have attained complete self-government. The body of citizens' delegates may elect a Governor to supervise self-government of the province. In matters involving national administration the Governor shall be subject to the direction of the Central Government.

17. In this period the authority of the Central Government and that of the provincial government shall be kept in equilibrium. Matters which by nature require uniform action on the part of the nation shall be assigned to the Central Government; matters which by nature should be dealt with locally shall be assigned to the local government. There shall be no tendency either to the centralization or to the decentralization of power.

18. The *hsien* is a unit of local self-government. The province stands between the Central Government and the *hsien* to bring about closer relationship between them.

19. As soon as the constitutional period begins, the Central Government should complete the formation of the five Yuan to experiment on a quintuple-power government. The five Yuan are named in the following order: The Executive Yuan, the Legislative Yuan, the Judicial Yuan, the Examination Yuan, and the Control Yuan.

20. The Executive Yuan shall tentatively have the following ministries: (1) The Ministry of Interior; (2) The Ministry of Foreign Affairs; (3) The Ministry of Military Affairs; (4) The Ministry of Finance; (5) The Ministry of Agriculture and Mining; (6) the Ministry of Industry and Commerce; (7) The Ministry of Education; (8) The Ministry of Communications.

21. Before the promulgation of a Constitution, the presidents of the five Yuan shall be appointed or removed and directed by the President (of the National Government).

22. The draft of the Constitution should be prepared by the Legislative Yuan in accordance with the *Fundamentals of National Reconstruction* and the achievements in the period of political tutelage and the constitutional period. It should, from time to time, be made public to the people in order to facilitate its adoption when the proper time comes.

23. When more than one-half of the provinces have reached the constitutional period, that is when they have completely adopted local self-government, the People's Congress (National Assembly) shall be convened to decide on and promulgate the Constitution.

24. After the promulgation of the Constitution the governing power of the Central Government shall be returned to the People's Congress for execution. That is, the People's Congress shall exercise the powers of election and recall in regard to officials of the Central Government, as well as the powers of initiative and referendum in regard to the laws of the Central Government.

25. The day of the promulgation of the Constitution marks the culmination of constitutional government. All citizens of the nation shall, in accordance with the Constitution, hold a general election. The National Government shall be dissolved within three months after the completion of the election and shall be succeeded by the new popularly-elected government. Whereupon the great task of national reconstruction will be regarded as accomplished.

24

The Will of Dr. Sun Yat-sen

For forty years I have devoted myself to the cause of the people's revolution with but one end in view, the elevation of China to a position of freedom and equality in the family of nations. My experiences during these forty years have firmly convinced me that to attain this goal we must bring about a thorough awakening of our own people and ally ourselves in a common struggle with those peoples of the world who treat us on the basis of equality.

The work of the Revolution is not yet accomplished. Let all our comrades follow my *Plans for National Reconstruction, Fundamentals of National Reconstruction, Three People's Principles* and the Manifesto issued by the First National Congress of our Party, and strive on earnestly for their consummation. Above all, our recent declarations in favor of the convocation of a National Convention and the abolition of unequal treaties should be carried into effect with the least possible delay. This is my heartfelt charge to you.

Written on February 20, 1925   *Sun Wen*, March 11, 1925

As given in *China Handbook, 1937-1943: A Comprehensive Survey of Major Developments*. Compiled by the Chinese Ministry of Information (New York: Macmillan, 1943), p. 45. Reprinted by permission.

25

Statement Before Leaving for Moscow

August 22, 1927

Soong Ching Ling (Madame Sun Yat-sen)

When the first united front of the Nationalists and Communists broke up in 1927, Madame Sun Yat-sen accused Chiang Kai-shek and his supporters of betraying Sun Yat-sen's principles and policies. She is today one of the two Vice-Chairmen of the Communist regime in Peking. She is a sister of Madame Chiang Kai-shek.

If China is to survive as an independent country in the modern struggle of nations, her semi-feudal conditions of life must be fundamentally changed and a modern state created to replace the mediaeval system which has existed for more than a thousand years. This task must needs be done by the method of revolution, if only because the alternative method of gradualness postulates a period of time which is denied the nation by both the cancerous force of Chinese militarism eating from inside and foreign imperialism ravaging from outside.

To forge a fit instrument of revolution, Sun Yat-sen reorganized the Kuomintang on a revolutionary basis in the winter of 1924, and reinforced the Three People's Principles by formulating the Three Great Policies of action. The first of these policies calls for the inclusion and support of the nation's workers and peasants in the work of the revolution. These two massive elements of the national population—one carrying on and sustaining the life of organized society and the other producing food on which man lives—represent nearly 90 per cent of the nation. And, in view of their numerical strength and the fact that the masses ought to be the chief beneficiaries of the revolution, they must be drawn into it if there is to be life and reality in the movement.

The second of the policies laid down by Sun recognizes the necessity of cooperation between the Kuomintang and members of the Chinese Communist Party during the period of revolutionary struggle with Chinese militarism and foreign imperialism. The Chinese Communist Party is

From Soong Ching Ling, *The Struggle for New China* (Peking: Foreign Languages Press, 1952), pp. 7–11.

indubitably the most dynamic of all internal revolutionary forces in China; and its influence over the masses and power of propaganda enabled the Kuomintang to control its military elements and subordinate them to the civil authorities.

The third of Sun Yat-sen's policies deals with the profoundly important question of the connection of the Soviet Union with the Kuomintang. The connection is sometimes justified on the ground that the Soviet Union has no unequal treaties with China. This, however, was a minor consideration in Sun's view of the matter. In formulating the third policy, he was moved by larger reasons. Just as he regarded the Chinese Communist Party as the most active revolutionary force in China, so he envisaged the Soviet Union as the most powerful revolutionary force in the world; and he believed that a right correlation by the Kuomintang of these two outstanding revolutionary forces would signally assist the revolution to realize national independence for China. Sun was not afraid or ashamed to avow this revolutionary thesis, since he knew the revolutionary role played by France, in the person of Lafayette, in the American revolution was repeated in many a chapter in the history of freedom.

It was a statesmanlike application of these three policies of Sun and the correlation of the forces deriving from them that enabled the Kuomintang power to put an end to ten years of disorder and confusion in Canton, and to create and finance revolutionary armies that conquered their way to the historic line of the Yangtze and—after shattering the main force of the Fengtien army [1] in Honan—penetrated to the bank of the Yellow River. Besides its striking administrative work at Canton and the great military achievement of the Northern Expedition, the Kuomintang scored memorable successes in a field in which China has always known defeat and humiliation. It raised the international status of China to a point never attained before, compelling the representatives of great powers to meet the foreign minister of Nationalist China as an equal in council, and causing men in high as well as in the scattered places of the earth to heed his statements on Nationalist aims and aspirations. In those days—it is but three months since—the Kuomintang may have been hated and even feared, but none dared to despise it.

Today it is otherwise. The famous name of the Nationalist Government is now sunk to the level of other semi-feudal remnants in the North; and those who have been entrusted by the revolution with leadership are allowing the new militarist clique in the Yangtze to capture and utilize the Kuomintang; and they themselves are now becoming or are about to become, the secretaries and clerks of the new Caesar. No one fears and no one respects the Kuomintang, which is now despised even by foes who used to blench and flee at the sound of its armies on the march.

---

[1] Manchurian warlord army under Chang Tso-lin.

What is the cause for this startling change in values and in men's opinions? The answer is to be found in the work of the reaction in Canton, in Nanking and Shanghai, in Changsha, and lastly in Wuhan. Peasants and their leaders, workers and their leaders, Communists and their leaders, who labored in order that the Kuomintang power might reach the Yangtze, have been ruthlessly and wantonly killed; and Soviet workers who gave of their best to the Kuomintang and whom men, in later and juster days, will adjudge to have deserved well of Nationalist China, have been forced to leave, because so-called "leaders" of the Kuomintang—petty politicians reverting to type—believe that they can violate Sun Yat-sen's Three Policies and rely on the new militarism to carry out the stupendous task of the revolution.

They will fail and go the way of those before them who have sought to rule in like fashion. But they must not be permitted to involve in their own ultimate ruin the heritage left to us by Sun. His true followers must seek to rescue the real Kuomintang from the degradation of becoming a mere secretariat of the new militarist clique emerging out of the intrigues and disloyalties now afoot.

My own course is clear. Accepting the thesis that the Three Policies are an essential part of the thought and technique of the revolution, I draw the conclusion that real Nationalist success in the struggle with Chinese militarism and foreign imperialism is possible only by a right correlation, under Kuomintang leadership, of the revolutionary forces issuing from the Three Policies. As the reaction led by pseudo-leaders of the Kuomintang endangers the Third Policy, it is necessary for the revolutionary wing of the Kuomintang—the group with which Sun would today be identified had he been alive—to leave no doubt in the Soviet mind that, though some have crossed over to reaction and counter-revolution, there are others who will continue true and steadfast to the Three Policies enunciated by him for the guidance and advancement of the work of the revolution.

I go, therefore, to Moscow to explain this in person.

SUGGESTED READING

Brandt, Conrad. *Stalin's Failure in China, 1924–1927.* Cambridge: Harvard University Press, 1958.

Chang, H. H. *Chiang Kai-shek.* Garden City, N.Y.: Doubleday, 1944.

Ch'ien, T. S. *The Government and Politics of China.* Cambridge: Harvard University Press, 1950.

Hahn, Emily. *Chiang Kai-shek: An Unauthorized Biography.* Garden City, N.Y.: Doubleday, 1930.

Holcombe, Arthur S. *The Chinese Revolution.* Cambridge: Harvard University Press, 1930.

Isaacs, Harold R. *The Tragedy of the Chinese Revolution*, 2nd rev. ed. Stanford: Stanford University Press, 1961.

Leng, Shao-chuan and Palmer, N. D. *Sun Yat-sen and Communism*. New York: Frederick A. Praeger, 1961.

Linebarger, Paul M. A. *Government in Republican China*. New York: McGraw-Hill, 1938.

Linebarger, Paul M. A. *The China of Chiang Kai-shek: A Political Study*. Boston: World Peace Foundation, 1940.

McNair, H. F. *China in Revolution: An Analysis of Politics and Militarism under the Republic*. Chicago: University of Chicago Press, 1932.

North, Robert C. *Moscow and the Chinese Communists*, 2nd ed. Stanford: Stanford University Press, 1963.

North, Robert C., and Eudin, Xenia J. *M. N. Roy's Mission to China*. Berkeley, University of California Press, 1963.

Pan, Wei-tung. *The Chinese Constitution: A Study of Forty Years of Constitution-Making in China*. Washington, D.C.: Institute of Chinese Culture, 1946.

Remer, C. F. *Foreign Investments in China*. New York: Macmillan, 1930.

Roy, M. N. *Revolution and Counter-Revolution in China*. Calcutta: Renaissance Publishers, 1946.

Selle, Earl Albert. *Donald of China*. New York: Harper & Row, 1948.

Sharman, Lyon. *Sun Yat-sen: His Life and Its Meaning*. New York: John Day, 1934.

Sun Yat-sen. *San Min Chu I: The Three Principles of the People*. Translated by Frank Price. Shanghai: China Committee, Institute of Pacific Relations, 1927.

Tang, Leang-li. *The Inner History of the Chinese Revolution*. London: Routledge, 1930.

Tong, Hollington K. *Chiang Kai-shek: Soldier and Statesman*. Shanghai: The China Publishing Company, 1937.

Trotsky, Leon. *Problems of the Chinese Revolution*. New York: Paragon Reprint Corporation, 1966.

Whiting, A. S. *Soviet Policies in China, 1917–1924*. New York: Columbia University Press, 1954.

Wilbur, C. Martin, and How, Julie Lien-ying, eds. *Documents on Communism, Nationalism, and Soviet Advisers in China, 1918–1927: Papers Seized in the 1927 Peking Raid*. New York: Columbia University Press, 1956.

Japanese Militarism

In 1918, during World War I, the rise in prices led to rice riots in a number of Japanese cities. The cabinet of General Terauchi resigned and the genro were unable to find an aristocrat capable of solving the economic and political crisis. They appointed as Premier a man who could command a majority in the lower house of the Diet. Thus Hara Kei, the leader of the Seiyukai party, became the first commoner ever to serve as Prime Minister of Japan. The domination of the clan oligarchs appeared to be broken, and political parties now became a principal factor in determining the make-up of cabinets and the policies of the state. Prince Saionji Kimmochi, after 1924 the sole surviving genro, looked with favor on parliamentary government. The cabinets from 1918 to 1922 and from 1924 to 1932 were headed by leaders of the majority party or majority coalitions in the lower house of the Diet, and the cabinet was regarded as responsible to that house. The army and navy ministries, however, were always held by generals and admirals, and from 1922 to 1924, three successive cabinets were headed by men without party membership. In 1925 the Diet passed a universal manhood suffrage law, but in the same year it also enacted a stringent peace preservation law, which made illegal the advocacy of socialism or of the alteration of the "national structure," in which sovereignty resided with the emperor.

The rise of nationalism in China created problems for the Japanese. The Minseito party, affiliated with the Mitsubishi commercial interests, advocated a conciliatory policy towards China and friendly cooperation with Great Britain and the United States. On the other hand, the Seiyukai party, affiliated with Mitsui heavy industry, advocated a positive policy towards China. In 1928, during the premiership of General Baron Tanaka of the Seiyukai, a clash between Japanese and Chinese Nationalist troops occurred near Tsinan, China. Japanese officers were correctly believed to be implicated in the subsequent murder of Marshal Chang Tso-lin, the warlord of Manchuria and erstwhile cooperator with the Japanese. A boycott of Japanese goods by Chinese merchants led to a temporary softening of Japanese policy and the resignation of Prime Minister Tanaka.

The world depression, which began in 1929, brought a severe decline in international trade. The collapse of the market for Japanese silk in the United States contributed to the impoverishment of the Japanese peasants. Junior officers in the army, most of them of rural origin, sympathized with the poor farmers and blamed the "selfish" capitalists and their tools, the politicians, for the plight of the people. Extremist officers were involved in several assassinations and attempted coups d'état in the 1930's with the aim of ending parliamentary government and bringing about a restoration of direct imperial rule—the Showa Restoration (Selections 26, 27).

Moderate statesmen lived in fear for their lives. The need for maintaining discipline in the army served as an argument for increasing the proportion of military men in the cabinet. An imperial ordinance of 1898 required that the posts of Minister of the Army and Minister of the Navy could be held only by generals (or lieutenant-generals) and admirals (or vice-admirals) on the active list. The armed services could therefore exercise a veto over appointments to the premiership and over governmental policies by refusing to permit one of their officers to serve in the cabinet. The emperor's prerogative of military command, Article XI in the Meiji Constitution, was interpreted to justify the independence of the military branch from the civilian branch of the government. The service ministers had the right of direct access to the emperor on military matters without first reporting to the prime minister.

Bushidō, Shinto, the Emperor cult, and Neo-Confucianism were invoked to rationalize twentieth-century militarism, ultranationalism, and imperialism. General Araki Sadao, a leading militarist, became Minister of Education in 1938 and used his post to propagate chauvinistic doctrines.

The Kwantung Army in the Japanese leasehold in Manchuria, using a bombing incident on the South Manchurian Railway as a pretext, began the seizure of the Manchurian provinces of China on September 18, 1931. The Japanese Foreign Ministry had not given its consent to such a move, but Japanese public opinion tended to support the aggressive policy of the militarists. China appealed to the League of Nations for help, and the United States declared its policy of nonrecognition (Selection 28). A League commission, headed by the British Lord Lytton, was sent to the Far East to investigate the situation.

In the meantime, the Japanese sponsored an independence movement in Manchuria, which was renamed Manchoukuo. The former Manchu Emperor of China, Pu Yi, became chief executive of the puppet government of Manchoukuo, which was established in March, 1932. When the League Assembly adopted a report calling for the restoration of Chinese sovereignty in Manchuria, Japan announced her intention to withdraw from the League of Nations (Selection 29). Pu Yi was proclaimed Emperor of Manchoukuo in 1934.

In 1933 a military truce between China and Japan left the Japanese in occupation of Manchuria and parts of northern China and discouraged further Chinese efforts to recover the northeastern provinces. Chiang Kai-shek was preoccupied with the suppression of the Chinese Communists and did not feel in a position to make war on the Japanese at the same time. The Japanese established puppet regimes in parts of northern China with the evident intention of setting up a single regime for all of northern China after the pattern of Manchoukuo. In areas under their control, the Japanese established commercial monopolies. American protests against the progressive closing of the Open Door in China were without avail.

The failure of the League of Nations and of the United States to take effective measures to halt Japan's aggressive moves appears to have encouraged not only Japan but also Italy and Germany to pursue expansionist policies. By the end of 1937 the three fascist states had all left the League and had joined together in the Anti-Comintern Pact. Japan's disregard of the principles of the Open Door in China and her continuous encroachments on American economic and strategic interests in the Far East made a collision between the two Pacific powers difficult to avert.

26

Plan for the Reorganization of Japan

Kita Ikki

Kita Ikki was a leading advocate of a Showa restoration, which would be carried out by means of a coup d'état. The book by Kita from which the following passage is excerpted was first printed and distributed secretly in 1919 and was banned by the authorities. Kita was involved in the February 26, 1936, attempted coup (see Selection 27) and was executed in 1937.

At present the Japanese empire is faced with a national crisis unparalleled in its history; it faces dilemmas at home and abroad. The vast majority of the people feel insecure in their livelihood and they are on

From Ryusaku Tsunoda, William Theodore de Bary, and Donald Keene, eds., *Sources of the Japanese Tradition* (New York: Columbia University Press, 1958), pp. 775–784. Reprinted by permission.

the point of taking a lesson from the collapse of European societies, while those who monopolize political, military, and economic power simply hide themselves and, quaking with fear, try to maintain their unjust position. Abroad, neither England, America, Germany, nor Russia has kept its word, and even our neighbor China, which long benefited from the protection we provided through the Russo-Japanese War, not only has failed to repay us but instead despises us. Truly we are a small island, completely isolated in the Eastern Sea. One false step and our nation will again fall into the desperate state of crisis—dilemmas at home and abroad—that marked the period before and after the Meiji Restoration.

The only thing that brightens the picture is the sixty million fellow countrymen with whom we are blessed. The Japanese people must develop a profound awareness of the great cause of national existence and of the people's equal rights, and they need an unerring, discriminating grasp of the complexities of domestic and foreign thought. The Great War in Europe was, like Noah's flood, Heaven's punishment on them for arrogant and rebellious ways. It is of course natural that we cannot look to the Europeans, who are out of their minds because of the great destruction, for a completely detailed set of plans. But in contrast Japan, during those five years of destruction, was blessed with five years of fulfillment. Europe needs to talk about reconstruction, while Japan must move on to reorganization. The entire Japanese people, thinking calmly from this perspective which is the result of Heaven's rewards and punishments, should, in planning how the great Japanese empire should be reorganized, petition for a manifestation of the imperial prerogative establishing "a national opinion in which no dissenting voice is heard, by the organization of a great union of the Japanese people." Thus, by homage to the emperor, a basis for national reorganization can be set up.

Truly, our seven hundred million brothers in China and India have no path to independence other than that offered by our guidance and protection. And for our Japan, whose population has doubled within the past fifty years, great areas adequate to support a population of at least two hundred and forty or fifty millions will be absolutely necessary a hundred years from now. For a nation, one hundred years are like a hundred days for an individual. How can those who are anxious about these inevitable developments, or who grieve over the desperate conditions of neighboring countries, find their solace in the effeminate pacifism of doctrinaire socialism? I do not necessarily rule out social progress by means of the class struggle. But still, just what kind of so-called science is it that can close its eyes to the competition between peoples and nations which has taken place throughout the entire history of mankind? At a time when the authorities in the European and American revolutionary creeds have found it completely impossible to arrive at an understanding of the "gospel of the sword" because of their superficial philosophy, the noble Greece of Asian culture must complete her national reorganization on the basis of her own national polity. At the same time, let her lift the virtuous banner of an Asian league and take the leadership in a world federation which must come. In so doing let her proclaim to the world the Way of Heaven in which all are children of Buddha, and let her set the example which the world must follow. So the ideas of people like those who oppose arming the nation are after all simply childish.

SECTION ONE: THE PEOPLE'S EMPEROR

Suspension of the Constitution. In order for the emperor and the entire Japanese people to establish a secure base for the national reorganization, the emperor will, by a show of his imperial prerogative, suspend the Constitution for a period of three years, dissolve both houses of the Diet, and place the entire nation under martial law.

(Note 1: In extraordinary times the authorities should of course ignore harmful opinions and votes. To regard any sort of constitution or parliament as an absolute authority is to act in direct imitation of the English and American semisacred "democracy." Those who do so are the obstinate conservatives who hide the real meaning of "democracy"; they are as ridiculous as those who try to argue national polity on the basis of the [Shintō mythological] High Plain of Heaven. It cannot be held that in the discussion of plans for naval expansion Admiral Tōgō's vote was not worth more than the three cast by miserable members of the Diet, or that in voting on social programs a vote by Karl Marx is less just than seven cast by Ōkura Kihachirō. The effect of government by votes which has prevailed hitherto is really nothing more than a maintenance of the traditional order; its puts absolute emphasis on numbers and ignores those who would put a premium on quality.)

(Note 2: Those who look upon a *coup d'état* as an abuse of power on behalf of a conservative autocracy ignore history. Napoleon's *coup d'état* in refusing to cooperate with reactionary elements offered the only out for the Revolution at a time when the parliament and the press were alive with royalist elements. And even though one sees in the Russian Revolution an incident in which Lenin dissolved with machine guns a parliament filled with obstructionists, the popular view is still that a *coup d'état* is a reactionary act.)

(Note 3: A *coup d'état* should be looked upon as a direct manifestation of the authority of the nation; that is, of the will of society. The progressive leaders have all arisen from popular groups. They arise because of political leaders like Napoleon and Lenin. In the reorganization of Japan there must be a manifestation of the power inherent in a coalition of the people and sovereign.)

(Note 4: The reason why the Diet must be dissolved is that the nobility and the wealthy upon whom it depends are incapable of standing with the emperor and the people in the cause of reorganization. The necessity for suspension of the Constitution is that these people seek protection in the law codes enacted under it. The reason martial law must be proclaimed is that it is essential for the freedom of the nation that there be no restraint in suppressing the opposition which will come from the above groups.

However, it will also be necessary to suppress those who propagate a senseless and half-understood translation of outside revolutionary creeds as the agents of reorganization.)

The True Significance of the Emperor. The fundamental doctrine of the emperor as representative of the people and as pillar of the nation must be made clear.

In order to clarify this a sweeping reform of the imperial court in the spirit of the Emperor Jimmu in founding the state and in the spirit of the great Meiji emperor will be carried out. The present Privy Councillors and other officials will be dismissed from their posts, and in their place will come talent, sought throughout the realm, capable of assisting the emperor.

A Consultative Council (*Kōmonin*) will be established to assist the emperor. Its members, fifty in number, will be appointed by the emperor.

A member of the Consultative Council must tender his resignation to the emperor whenever the cabinet takes action against him or whenever the Diet passes a vote of nonconfidence against him. However, the Council members are by no means responsible to either the cabinet or to the Diet.

(Note 1: Japan's national polity has evolved through three stages, and the meaning of "emperor" has also evolved through three stages. The first stage, from the Fujiwara to the Taira, was one of absolute monarchy. During this stage the emperor possessed all land and people as his private property in theory, and he had the power of life and death over the people. The second stage, from the Minamoto to the Tokugawa, was one of aristocracy. During this period military leaders and nobility in each area brought land and people of their locality under their personal control; they fought wars and made alliances among themselves as rulers of small nations. Consequently the emperor's significance was different from what it had been. He now, like the Roman pope, conferred honor upon the *Bakufu,* the leader of the petty princes, and showed himself the traditional center of the national faith. Such a development can be compared with the role of the Roman pope in crowning the Holy Roman Emperor, leader of the various lords in the Middle Ages in Europe. The third stage, one of a democratic state, began with the Meiji Revolution, which emancipated the samurai and commoners, newly awakened, from their status as private property of their shōgun and feudal lords. Since then the emperor has a new significance as the true center of government and politics. Ever since, as the commanding figure in the national movement and as complete representative of the modern democratic country, he has become representative of the nation. In other words, since the Meiji Revolution Japan has become a modern democratic state with the emperor as political nucleus. Is there any need whatever for us to import a direct translation of the "democracy" of others as though we lacked something? The struggle between those who stubbornly talk about national polity and those who are infatuated with Europe and America, both without a grasp of the background of the present, is a very ominous portent which may cause an explosion between the emperor and the people. Both sides must be warned of their folly.)

(Note 2: There is no scientific basis whatever for the belief of the democracies that a state which is governed by representatives voted in by the electorate is superior to a state which has a system of government by a particular person. Every nation has its own national spirit and history. It cannot be maintained, as advocates of this theory would have it, that China during the first eight years of the republic was more rational than Belgium, which retained rule by a single person. The "democracy" of the Americans derives from the very unsophisticated theory of the time which held that society came into being through a voluntary contract based upon the free will of individuals; these people, emigrating from each European country as individuals, established communities and built a country. But their theory of the divine right of voters is a half-witted philosophy which arose in opposition to the theory of the divine right of kings at that time. Now Japan certainly was not founded in this way, and there has never been a period in which Japan was dominated by a half-witted philosophy. Suffice it to say that the system whereby the head of state has to struggle for election by a long-winded self-advertisement and by exposing himself to ridicule like a low-class actor seems a very strange custom to the Japanese people, who have been brought up in the belief that silence is golden and that modesty is a virtue.)

(Note 3: The imperial court today has restored corrupt customs of the Middle Ages and has moreover added others which survived in European courts; truly it has drifted far from the spirit of the founder of the nation—a supreme commander above an equal people. The revolution under the great Meiji emperor restored and modernized this spirit. Accordingly at that time a purification of the imperial court was carried out. The necessity for doing this a second time is that when the whole national structure is being reorganized fundamentally we cannot simply leave the structure of the Court in its present state of disrepair.)

(Note 4: The provision for censure of members of the Consultative Council by cabinet and Diet is required in view of the present situation in which many men do as they wish on the excuse that they are duty-bound to help the Emperor. The obstinacy and arrogance of the members

of the Privy Council is not very different from that of the court officials
in Russia before the revolution. The men who cause trouble for the
emperor are men of this kind.)

The Abolition of the Peerage System. The peerage system will be
abolished, and the spirit of the Meiji Restoration will be clarified by removal of this barrier which has come between the emperor and the
people.

The House of Peers will be abolished and replaced by a Council of
Deliberation (*Shingiin*), which shall consider action taken by the House of
Representatives.

The Council of Deliberation will be empowered to reject decisions
taken by the House of Representatives a single time. The members of the
Council of Deliberation will consist of distinguished men in many fields
of activity, elected by each other and appointed by the emperor.

(Note 1: The Restoration Revolution, which destroyed government
by the aristocracy, was carried out determinedly, for it also confiscated
the estates of the aristocracy. It went much farther than did European
countries, for with the single exception of France they were unable to dis-
pose of the medieval estates of earlier days. But with the death of men
like the great Saigō, who embodied the revolutionary spirit, men like Itō
Hirobumi, with no understanding of our advancement, and men who
simply acted as attendants in the Revolution, imitated and transplanted
backward aristocratic and medieval privileges which had survived in
Western countries. To abolish the peerage system is to abandon a system
translated directly from Europe and to return to the earlier Meiji Revolution. Do not jump to the conclusion that this is a shortcoming we are
seeking to correct. We have already advanced farther than some other
countries as a democratic country.)

(Note 2: The reason a bicameral system is subject to fewer errors
than a unicameral system is that in very many cases public opinion is emo-
tional, uncritical and changeable. For this reason the upper house will be
made up of distinguished persons in many fields of activity instead of
medieval relics.)

Universal Suffrage. All men twenty-five years of age, by their rights
as people of Great Japan, will have the right, freely and equally, to stand
for election to and to vote for the House of Representatives. The same
will hold for local self-government assemblies.

Women will not have the right to participate in politics.

(Note 1: Although a tax qualification has determined suffrage in
other countries and this system was first initiated in England, where the
Parliament was originally set up to supervise the use of tax money collected by the Crown, in Japan we must establish it as a fundamental principle that suffrage is the innate right of the people. This universal suffrage
must not be interpreted as a lowering of the tax qualification on grounds

that all men pay at least indirect taxes. Rather, suffrage is a "duty of the people" in the same sense that military service is a "duty of the people.")

(Note 2: The duty of the people to defend the country cannot be separated from their duty to participate in its government. As this is a fundamental human right of the Japanese people, there is no reason why the Japanese should be like the slaves in the Roman Empire or like the menials driven from the imperial gate during the monarchical age—simply ruled, having to live and die under orders from a ruling class. Nothing can infringe upon the right and duty of suffrage under any circumstances. Therefore officers and soldiers on active service, even if they are overseas, should elect and be elected without any restrictions.)

(Note 3: The reason for the clear statement that "Women will not have the right to participate in politics" is not that Japanese women today have not yet awakened. Whereas the code of chivalry for knights in medieval Europe called for honoring women and gaining their favor, in medieval Japan the samurai esteemed and valued the person of woman on approximately the same level as they did themselves, while it became the accepted code for women to honor the men and gain their favor. This complete contrast in developments has penetrated into all society and live-lihood, and continues into modern history—there has been agitation by women for suffrage abroad while here women have continued devoted to the task of being good wives and wise mothers. Politics is a small part of human activity. The question of the place of women in Japan will be satisfactorily solved if we make an institutional reorganization which will guarantee the protection of woman's right to be "mother of the na-tion and wife of the nation." To make women accustomed to verbal warfare is to do violence to their natural aptitude; it is more terrible than using them in the line of battle. Anyone who has observed the stupid talkativeness of Western women or the piercing quarrels among Chinese women will be thankful that Japanese women have continued on the right path. Those who have developed good trends should let others who have developed bad trends learn from them. For this reason, one speaks today of a time of fusion of Eastern and Western civilization. But the ugliness of direct and uncritical borrowing can be seen very well in the matter of woman suffrage.)

The Restoration of the People's Freedom. The various laws which have restricted the freedom of the people and impaired the spirit of the constitution in the past—the Civil Service Appointment Ordinance, the Peace Preservation police law, the Press Act, the Publication Law, and similar measures—will be abolished.

(Note: This is obviously right. These laws work only to maintain all sorts of cliques.)

The National Reorganization Cabinet. A Reorganization Cabinet will be organized while martial law is in effect; in addition to the present ministries, it will have ministries for industries and several Ministers of State without Portfolio. Members of the Reorganization Cabinet will not be chosen from the present military, bureaucratic, financial, and party cliques, but this task will be given to outstanding individuals selected throughout the whole country.

All the present prefectural governors will be dismissed from their offices, and National Reorganization Governors will be appointed by the same method of selection as given above.

(Note: This is necessary for the same reasons that the Meiji Revolution could not have been carried out by the Tokugawa shogun and his vassals. But a revolution cannot necessarily be evaluated according to the amount of bloodshed. It is just as impossible to say of a surgical operation that it was not thorough because of the small amount of blood that was lost. It all depends on the skill of the surgeon and the constitution of the patient undergoing the operation. Japan today is like a man in his prime and in good health. Countries like Russia and China are like old patients whose bodies are in total decay. Therefore, if there is a technician who takes a far-sighted view of the past and present, and who draws judiciously on East and West, the reorganization of Japan can be accomplished during a pleasant talk.)

The National Reorganization Diet. The National Reorganization Diet, elected in a general election and convened during the period of martial law, will deliberate on measures for reorganization.

The National Reorganization Diet will not have the right to deliberate on the basic policy of national reorganization proclaimed by the emperor.

(Note 1: Since in this way the people will become the main force and the emperor the commander, this *coup d'état* will not be an abuse of power but the expression of the national determination by the emperor and the people.)

(Note 2: This is not a problem of legal philosophy but a question of realism; it is not an academic argument as to whether or not the emperors of Russia and Germany were also empowered with such authority, but it is a divine confidence which the people place only in the Emperor of Japan.)

(Note 3: If a general election were to be held in our present society of omnipotent capital and absolutist bureaucracy the majority of the men elected to the Diet would either be opposed to the reorganization or would receive their election expenses from men opposed to the reorganization. But, since the general election will be held and the Diet convened under martial law, it will of course be possible to curb the rights of harmful candidates and representatives.)

(Note 4: It is only because there was such a divine emperor that, despite the fact that the Restoration Revolution was carried out with greater thoroughness than the French Revolution, there was no misery and disorder. And thanks to the existence of such a godlike emperor, Japan's national reorganization will be accomplished a second time in an orderly manner, avoiding both the massacres and violence of the Russian Revolution and the snail's pace of the German revolution.)

The Renunciation of the Imperial Estate. The emperor will personally show the way by granting the lands, forests, shares, and similar property owned by the Imperial House to the nation.

The expenses of the Imperial Household will be limited to approximately thirty million yen per year, to be supplied by the national treasury.

However, this amount can be increased with consent of the Diet if the situation warrants such action.

(Note: The present imperial estate began with holdings taken over from the Tokugawa family, and however the true meaning of the emperor might shine forth, it is inconsistent to operate such medieval finances. It is self evident that every expense of the people's emperor should be born by the nation.)

27

The February 26, 1936, Incident

Joseph C. Grew

Here the United States Ambassador to Japan, Joseph C. Grew, describes the attempted coup d'état in 1936.

THE AMBASSADOR IN JAPAN (GREW) TO THE SECRETARY OF STATE

TOKYO, *February 26, 1936—noon*
[Received February 26—4:52 A.M.[1]]

37. Embassy's 36, February 26, 10 A.M.

1. It now appears fairly certain that former Premier Admiral Saito, former Lord Keeper of the Privy Seal Count Makino, Grand Chamberlain Admiral Suzuki, and General Watanabe, Inspector General of Military

From United States Department of State, *Foreign Relations of the United States: Diplomatic Papers, 1936* (Washington, D.C.: Government Printing Office, 1954), IV, 719–720.

[1] Telegram in four sections.

Education, have been assassinated. It is also reported that Finance Minister Takahashi and the Chief of the Metropolitan Police Board have been wounded.

2. The Military have established a cordon around the district containing the Government Administration Offices and the Imperial Palace and do not permit ingress without army passes. Telephonic communication with the administrative offices has also been stopped. The stock exchange has been closed.

3. It has been reported that Premier Okada, Home Minister Goto and former War Minister Hayashi were also assassinated and that Finance Minister Takahashi has died of his wounds. The Embassy cannot confirm any of these rumors.

4. So far there has been no disorder and no street fighting as far as the Embassy is aware. The troops taking part in the uprising appear to be under perfect discipline and are not interfering with normal affairs of the people. Until the nature and probable results of the uprising are better understood by the Embassy however the Embassy is advising those who ask to remain at home. There appears to be absolutely no anti-foreign feeling involved in the affair.

5. A mimeographed statement was left by groups of soldiers at each of the principal newspaper offices this morning. The statement alleged that the present Government had been drifting away from the true spirit of Japan and that it had usurped the prerogatives of the Emperor. As evidence of this statement cited the signing of the London Naval Treaty [2] and the dismissal of General Masaki. It continued rather vaguely with an expression translated by the United Press about as follows: "If this condition is permitted to continue, the relations of Japan to China, Russia, Britain and the United States will become 'explosive in nature'." The statement was signed by Captain Nonaka and Captain Ando, both of the Third Infantry Regiment stationed in Tokyo. According to the soldiers who delivered the statement, another announcement will be made at 5 o'clock this evening and at that time "a new law of state" will be promulgated. The Embassy's informant believes that certain constitutional prerogatives will be suspended. He likened the existing situation to the Batista *coup d'état* in Cuba.[3]

6. As far as the Embassy has yet been able to ascertain, the uprising is in the nature of a *coup d'état* engineered by the young Fascist element in the army and intended to destroy the entire group of elder statesmen who have been advisers to the Throne and thereby to effect the so-called "Showa restoration." The Emperor himself is apparently being held incommunicado in the Palace presumably to prevent anyone from obtaining access to him and securing an Imperial mandate which would interfere

[2] Signed April 22, 1930, *Foreign Relations*, 1930, vol. i, p. 107.
[3] See *ibid.*, 1933, vol. v, pp. 361 ff.

with the plans of the army group. The immediate causes of the uprising appear to have been the recent election which returned an unexpectedly large number of the more liberal candidates and the trial of Aizawa, murderer of General Nagata, which has excited the feelings of the Fascist element in the army.

Latest reports indicate that General Masaki is the leading spirit in the affair and that Admiral Osumi, Minister of the Navy, has assumed the position of Acting Prime Minister. The movement appears to have been thoroughly organized in advance down to the last detail.

7. The Embassy has just learned from a fairly reliable source that Count Makino is safe.

Grew

28

The United States Policy of Nonrecognition

Henry L. Stimson

SECRETARY STIMSON TO THE AMBASSADOR
IN JAPAN (FORBES)

WASHINGTON, *January 7, 1932—noon*

7. Please deliver to the Foreign Office on behalf of your Government as soon as possible the following note:

"With the recent military operations about Chinchow, the last remaining administrative authority of the Government of the Chinese Republic in South Manchuria, as it existed prior to September 18th, 1931, has been destroyed. The American Government continues confident that the work of the neutral commission recently authorized by the Council of the League of Nations will facilitate an ultimate solution of the difficulties now existing between China and Japan. But in view of the present situation and of its own rights and obligations therein, the American Government deems it to be its duty to notify both the Imperial Japanese Government and the Government of the Chinese Republic that it cannot admit the legality of any situation *de facto* nor does it intend to recognize any treaty or agreement entered into between those Governments, or agents

From *United States Relations with China: With Special Reference to the Period 1944–1949* (Washington, D.C.: Government Printing Office, 1949), pp. 446–447.

thereof, which may impair the treaty rights of the United States or its citizens in China, including those which relate to the sovereignty, the independence, or the territorial and administrative integrity of the Republic of China, or to the international policy relative to China, commonly known as the open door policy; and that it does not intend to recognize any situation, treaty or agreement which may be brought about by means contrary to the covenants and obligations of the Pact of Paris of August 27, 1928, to which Treaty both China and Japan, as well as the United States, are parties."

State that an identical note is being sent to the Chinese government.

Stimson

29

Notification by the Japanese Government of Its Intention to Withdraw from the League of Nations

On February 23, 1933, Matsuoka Yōsuke delivered an impassioned defense of his country's policies to the League of Nations General Assembly and then, with the rest of the Japanese delegation, dramatically walked out. The following month, Japan withdrew from the League, making clear to everyone her willingness to defy world public opinion in order to carry out her program in East Asia.

TELEGRAM FROM THE MINISTER FOR FOREIGN AFFAIRS OF JAPAN TO THE SECRETARY-GENERAL

Tokio, *March 27th, 1933*

The Japanese Government believe that the national policy of Japan, which has for its aim to ensure the peace of the Orient and thereby to contribute to the cause of peace throughout the world, is identical in spirit with the mission of the League of Nations, which is to achieve international peace and security. It has always been with pleasure, therefore, that this country has for thirteen years past, as an original Member of the

League of Nations, *Official Journal*, 14th Year, No. 5, May, 1933, pp. 657–658.

League and a permanent Member of its Council, extended a full measure of co-operation with her fellow-Members towards the attainment of its high purpose. It is, indeed, a matter of historical fact that Japan has continuously participated in the various activities of the League with a zeal not inferior to that exhibited by any other nation. At the same time, it is and has always been the conviction of the Japanese Government that, in order to render possible the maintenance of peace in various regions of the world, it is necessary in existing circumstances to allow the operation of the Covenant of the League to vary in accordance with the actual conditions prevailing in each of those regions. Only by acting on this just and equitable principle can the League fulfill its mission and increase its influence.

Acting on this conviction, the Japanese Government, ever since the Sino-Japanese dispute was, in September, 1931, submitted to the League, have, at meetings of the League and on other occasions, continually set forward a consistent view. This was that, if the League was to settle the issue fairly and equitably, and to make a real contribution to the promotion of peace in the Orient, and thus enhance its prestige, it should acquire a complete grasp of the actual conditions in this quarter of the globe and apply the Covenant of the League in accordance with these conditions. They have repeatedly emphasized and insisted upon the absolute necessity of taking into consideration the fact that China is not an organized State; that its internal conditions and external relations are characterized by extreme confusion and complexity and by many abnormal and exceptional features; and that, accordingly, the general principles and usages of international law which govern the ordinary relations between nations are found to be considerably modified in their operation so far as China is concerned, resulting in the quite abnormal and unique international practices which actually prevail in that country.

However, the majority of the Members of the League evinced, in the course of its deliberations during the past seventeen months, a failure either to grasp these realities or else to face them and take them into proper account. Moreover, it has frequently been made manifest in these deliberations that there exist serious differences of opinion between Japan and these Powers concerning the application and even the interpretation of various international engagements and obligations, including the Covenant of the League and the principles of international law. As a result, the report adopted by the Assembly at the special session of February 24th last, entirely misapprehending the spirit of Japan, pervaded as it is by no other desire than the maintenance of peace in the Orient, contains gross errors both in the ascertainment of facts and in the conclusions deduced. In asserting that the action of the Japanese army at the time of the incident of September 18th and subsequently did not fall within the just limits of self-defence, the report assigned no reasons and came to an arbi-

trary conclusion, and in ignoring alike the state of tension which preceded, and the various aggravations which succeeded, the incident—for all
of which the full responsibility is incumbent upon China—the report
creates a source of fresh conflict in the political arena of the Orient. By
refusing to acknowledge the actual circumstances that led to the foundation of Manchukuo, and by attempting to challenge the position taken up
by Japan in recognizing the new State, it cuts away the ground for the
stabilization of the Far-Eastern situation. Nor can the terms laid down in
its recommendations—as was fully explained in the statement issued by
this Government on February 25th last—ever be of any possible service
in securing enduring peace in these regions.

The conclusion must be that, in seeking a solution of the question,
the majority of the League have attached greater importance to upholding
inapplicable formulas than to the real task of assuring peace, and higher
value to the vindication of academic theses than to the eradication of the
sources of future conflict. For these reasons, and because of the profound
differences of opinion existing between Japan and the majority of the
League in their interpretation of the Covenant and of other treaties, the
Japanese Government have been led to realize the existence of an ir-
reconcilable divergence of views, dividing Japan and the League on
policies of peace, and especially as regards the fundamental principles to
be followed in the establishment of a durable peace in the Far East. The
Japanese Government, believing that, in these circumstances, there remains
no room for further co-operation, hereby gives notice, in accordance
with the provisions of Article I, paragraph 3, of the Covenant, of the
intention of Japan to withdraw from the League of Nations.

(Signed) *Count Yasuya Uchida*
Minister for Foreign Affairs
of Japan

SUGGESTED READING

Borg, Dorothy. *The United States and the Far Eastern Crisis of 1933–1938.*
    Cambridge: Harvard University Press, 1964.
Borton, Hugh. *Japan since 1931: Its Political and Social Development.* New
    York: Institute of Pacific Relations, 1940.
Butow, Robert. *Tojo and the Coming of the War.* Princeton: Princeton Uni-
    versity Press, 1961.
Byas, Hugh. *Government by Assassination.* New York: Knopf, 1942.
Crowley, James B. *Japan's Quest for Autonomy: National Security and For-
    eign Policy, 1930–1938.* Princeton: Princeton University Press, 1966.
Embree, John F. *Suye Mura: A Japanese Village.* Chicago: University of
    Chicago Press, 1939.
Grew, Joseph C. *Ten Years in Japan.* New York: Simon and Schuster, 1944.

Holtom, D. C. *Modern Japan and Shinto Nationalism: A Study of Present-Day Trends in Japanese Religions*, 2nd ed. Chicago: University of Chicago Press, 1947.

Irie, Akira. *After Imperialism: The Search for a New Order in the Far East, 1921-1931*. Cambridge: Harvard University Press, 1965.

Maruyama Masao. *Thought and Behavior in Modern Japanese Politics*. London: Oxford University Press, 1963.

Maxon, Y. C. *Control of Japanese Foreign Policy: A Study of Civil-Military Rivalry, 1930-1945*. Berkeley: University of California Press, 1957.

Miller, Frank O. *Minobe Tatsukichi: Interpreter of Constitutionalism in Japan*. Berkeley: University of California Press, 1965.

Morris, Ivan, ed. *Japan, 1931-1945: Militarism, Fascism, Japanism?* Boston: Heath, 1963, paperback.

Ogata, Sadako. *Defiance in Manchuria*. Berkeley: University of California Press, 1964.

Reischauer, Robert Karl. *Japan: Government-Politics*. New York: Ronald, 1939.

Scalapino, Robert. *Democracy and the Party Movement in Pre-War Japan: The Failure of the First Attempt*. Berkeley: University of California Press, 1953.

Stimson, Henry L. *The Far Eastern Crisis*. New York: Harper & Row, 1935.

Storry, Richard. *The Double Patriots*. London: Chatto & Windus, 1957.

Takeuchi Tatsuji. *War and Diplomacy in the Japanese Empire*. Garden City, N.Y.: Doubleday, 1935.

Tanin, O. and Yohan, E. *Militarism and Fascism in Japan*. New York: International Publishers, 1934.

Totten, George O., ed. *Democracy in Prewar Japan: Groundwork or Façade?* Boston: Heath, 1965, paperback.

Totten, George O. *The Social Democratic Movement in Prewar Japan*. New Haven: Yale University Press, 1966.

Toynbee, Arnold J. *Survey of International Affairs, 1920-1938*. London: Royal Institute of International Affairs, 1925-1941.

Yoshihashi, Takehiko. *Conspiracy at Mukden: The Rise of the Japanese Military*. New Haven: Yale University Press, 1964.

Willoughby, W. W. *The Sino-Japanese Controversy and the League of Nations*. Baltimore: Johns Hopkins University Press, 1935.

Young, A. Morgan. *Imperial Japan (1926-1938)*. New York: Morrow, 1938.

VI

World War II in the Far East

In 1933, after Japan's take-over in Manchuria, the Chinese Nationalists made a truce with the Japanese. The Nationalist forces then intensified their attacks on the Chinese Communist Army, compelling it to make its famous retreat (Long March) to northwestern China in 1934–35. In the meantime, the Japanese established puppet regimes in northern China, and the Chinese people became increasingly concerned about the Japanese threat. The National Salvation movement of students and labor unionists demanded an end to the civil war in China and the formation of an anti-Japanese united front.

In December, 1936, Chiang Kai-shek flew to Sian to encourage the Northeast Army of Chang Hsüeh-liang to make more strenuous efforts against the Communists. However, Chang's forces preferred to make common cause with the Communists to expel the Japanese from Manchuria. They placed Chiang Kai-shek under arrest.[1] His life seemed to be in danger, but he was subsequently released and became the leader of a second united front of Nationalists and Communists, whose aim now was to expel the Japanese (Selection 30).

The Chinese people demonstrated their united determination to resist the Japanese following a clash with Japanese forces at Marco Polo bridge, near Pieping, on July 7, 1937. Nevertheless, China's appeals for help to the League of Nations and the signatories of the Nine-Power Pact failed to elicit anything more than sympathy. In 1938 Japanese pressure forced the Nationalist government to move from Nanking to Hankow, and then to Chungking. By the end of the year, much of northern China and the entire coast were under Japanese control. The Chinese continued their stubborn resistance, receiving substantial aid in credits and military equip-

---

[1] The kidnapping of Chiang Kai-shek came to be known as "the Sian incident."

ment from the Soviet Union and, to a lesser extent, from the United States.

Faced with the refusal of Chiang's government to accede to their demands, the Japanese sponsored the establishment of a series of puppet regimes in northern China, climaxed by the formation of a reformed National Government in Nanking, headed by Chiang's rival, Wang Ching-wei, in March, 1940. This Nanking regime, which was recognized only by the Axis Powers, yielded to Japanese demands for special rights in China.

War had broken out in Europe in September, 1939. In September, 1940, the Axis Powers (Germany, Italy, and Japan) signed a tripartite pact which provided that if any of the three states found itself at war with a country not then fighting in Europe or Asia, the other two parties to the pact would enter the war on the side of their ally. Since the USSR had already made a nonaggression pact with Germany and was negotiating to join the Axis, the Tripartite Pact appeared to be aimed against the United States rather than the Soviet Union. In April, 1941, Japan and the Soviet Union concluded a neutrality treaty. The United States was increasingly committed to support Great Britain against the Axis and became concerned about the security of the strategic raw materials in the British, French, and Dutch empires in the Far East.

In response to the large-scale movement of Japanese troops into southern French Indochina in July, 1941, the United States froze Japanese assets in America, thus preventing Japan from importing oil and other necessities for her war machine. The Americans hoped that economic pressure would force Japan to halt her aggression in Asia. At the Imperial Conference of September 6, 1941, attended by Japanese government and military leaders and the Emperor, Japan's minimum demands vis-à-vis America were defined, and it was decided that if these demands could not be obtained by diplomatic negotiation within a month, Japan would go to war with the United States, Great Britain, and France (Selection 31).

Premier Konoe proposed a Pacific conference between himself and President Roosevelt to settle outstanding differences between the United States and Japan. He apparently believed that he could make substantial concessions to the United States and, by having the resultant treaty sanctioned by the Emperor, impose it on the Japanese militarists. Although the American Ambassador to Japan favored the proposed Roosevelt-Konoe meeting, the United States State Department feared that the proposed negotiations would only serve as a cover for more Japanese aggression, and did not agree to the meeting (Selection 32). On October 16, Konoe resigned the premiership in favor of General Tōjō Hideki, who doubted that Japan's objectives could be achieved by diplomacy.

On November 26, Secretary of State Cordell Hull presented to the Japanese proposals for a settlement: the United States would resume full commercial relations with Japan if the latter would withdraw her troops from China and Indochina (Selections 33, 34). The Hull proposals (sometimes referred to as an ultimatum) were unacceptable to the Japanese militarists, who would have lost face if forced to withdraw from China. The gravity of the situation was fully understood in Washington, and on December 6, 1941, President Roosevelt sent a telegram to the Emperor urging that the Japanese withdraw from Indochina in order to avert war (Selection 35). On December 7, Japanese forces launched surprise attacks on Pearl Harbor (the American naval base in Hawaii), the Philippines, Hongkong, and Malaya. Japan's declaration of war followed the attack (Selection 36).

The blow at Pearl Harbor wiped out most of America's Pacific fleet, excepting aircraft carriers. In both its diplomacy and strategic planning, the United States had grossly underestimated Japan's determination and daring. Within seven months the Japanese conquered virtually all of Southeast Asia, including Malaya, Singapore, Burma, the Philippines, and the Dutch East Indies, and were not checked until the battle of Midway in June, 1942. Although the Allies gave priority to the war in Europe, they were able to assume the offensive against the Japanese in the Solomon Islands (east of New Guinea) in August.

At the Cairo Conference (December, 1943), Roosevelt, Churchill, and Chiang Kai-shek published a declaration providing that Japan would have to give up her conquests and that in "due course" after the war Korea would receive her independence (Selection 37). At Yalta, in February, 1945, Roosevelt and Churchill secretly promised Stalin that, in exchange for entering the war against Japan, the Soviet Union would receive the Kurile Islands (Japan's since 1875) as well as southern Sakhalin and the railway and harbor rights in Manchuria which Russia had lost to Japan in 1905 (Selection 38).

Throughout the war, the Allied strategists held the view that the key to victory over the Axis was the defeat of Hitler's Germany. So long as Germany remained in the war, the outcome was problematical, but once Germany was beaten, the other Axis nations would soon have to surrender. The priority given the European theater meant that supplies sent to China and Southeast Asia were meager and slow in arriving. After Germany had been beaten and it appeared that Japan could be defeated by a strategy of island-hopping and blockade, the China-Burma-India theater seemed even less important. The Chinese Nationalists under Chiang Kai-shek suffered not only from shortages of supplies but also from the tendency of rival generals and the Communists to use the war situation to improve their military posture vis-à-vis Chiang. The wartime strain on the Chinese economy and morale facilitated a Communist takeover of China after the war. At the same time, throughout Southeast Asia, the Japanese conquests and the collapse of European prestige greatly stimulated the local nationalist movements. Thus, the grand strategy of the Allies in the Second World War ironically contributed to the postwar Communist conquest of China and the independence of the Southeast Asian nations.

30

Manifesto on the Seizure of Chiang Kai-shek

December 12, 1936

The following telegram to the nation was issued by General Chang Hsüeh-liang and his associates to explain their patriotic motive in holding Chiang Kai-shek captive in Sian.

Ever since the loss of the North-Eastern Provinces five years ago, our national sovereignty has been steadily weakened, and our territory has dwindled day by day. We suffered national humiliation at the time of the Shanghai Truce, and again with the Tangku Truce and the Ho-Umetsu Agreement. There is not a single citizen who does not feel sick at heart because of this.

Recently there have been startling changes in the international situation. Certain Powers are intriguing with one another, and using our nation and our people as a sacrifice. When hostilities began in East Suiyuan, popular resentment reached its height, and our soldiers everywhere were very indignant.

At this juncture, our Central Leader ought to encourage both military and civilians to organize the whole people in a united war of national defence. But while those soldiers at the front endure death and bloodshed in the defence of our national territories, the diplomatic authorities are still seeking compromises.

Ever since the unjust imprisonment of the patriotic leaders in Shanghai, the whole world has been startled; the whole of our people has been filled with anger and distress. To love one's country is an offence! This is a terrifying prospect.

Generalissimo Chiang Kai-shek, surrounded by a group of unworthy advisers, has forfeited the support of the masses of our people. He is deeply guilty for the harm his policies have done the country. We, Chang Hsueh-liang and the others undersigned, advised him with tears to take another way; but we were repeatedly rejected and rebuked.

Not long ago, the students in Sian were demonstrating in their National Salvation movement, and General Chiang set the police to killing these patriotic children. How could anyone with a human conscience bear to do this? We, his colleagues of many years' standing, could not bear to sit still and witness it.

Therefore we have tendered our last advice to Marshal Chiang, while guaranteeing his safety, in order to stimulate his awakening.

The Military and Civilians in the North-West unanimously make the following demands:

1. Reorganize the Nanking Government, and admit all parties to share the joint responsibility of saving the nation.

2. Stop all kinds of civil wars.

3. Immediately release the patriotic leaders arrested in Shanghai.

4. Release all political prisoners throughout the country.

5. Emancipate the patriotic movement of the people.

6. Safeguard the political freedom of the people to organize and call meetings.

7. Actually carry out the Will of Dr. Sun Yat-sen.

8. Immediately call a National Salvation Conference.

The eight items above are the points of National Salvation unanimously maintained by us and by all the Military and Civilians throughout the North-West.

We, therefore, hope that you gentlemen will stoop to meet public sentiment and sincerely adopt these demands, so as to open one line of life for the future, and remedy past mistakes that have been the ruin of the country. The great cause is before us: it does not permit glancing backward. We hope to carry out the policies here maintained only for the liberation and benefit of the country. As to our merit or guilt, we leave this to the judgment of our fellow-countrymen.

In sending this telegram, we urgently await your order.

Sian, December 12, 1936

31

Plans for the Prosecution of the Policy
of the Imperial Government
(Agenda for a Council in the Imperial Presence)

September 6, 1941

> The decisions made at this conference in the presence of the Emperor meant that Japan would probably go to war if she could not obtain her demands by diplomacy.

In view of the increasingly critical situation, especially the aggressive plans being carried out by America, England, Holland and other countries, the situation in Soviet Russia and the Empire's latent potentialities, the Japanese Government will proceed as follows in carrying out its plans for the southern territories as laid in "An Outline of the Policy of the Imperial Government in View of Present Developments."

1. Determined not to be deterred by the possibility of being involved in a war with America (and England and Holland) in order to secure our national existence, we will proceed with war preparations so that they be completed approximately toward the end of October.

2. At the same time, we will endeavor by every possible diplomatic means to have our demands agreed to by America and England. Japan's minimum demands in these negotiations with America (and England), together with the Empire's maximum concessions are embodied in the attached document.

3. If by the early part of October there is no reasonable hope of having our demands agreed to in the diplomatic negotiations mentioned above, we will immediately make up our minds to get ready for war against America (and England and Holland).

Policies with reference to countries other than those in the southern

From United States Congress, *Pearl Harbor Attack: Hearings before the Joint Committee on the Investigation of the Pearl Harbor Attack*, 79th Congress, 2nd Session. Public Document 79716. (Washington, D.C.: Government Printing Office, 1946), XX, 4022–4023.

territories will be carried out in harmony with the plans already laid. Special effort will be made to prevent America and Soviet Russia from forming a united front against Japan.

ANNEX DOCUMENT. A LIST OF JAPAN'S MINIMUM DEMANDS AND HER MAXIMUM CONCESSIONS IN HER NEGOTIATIONS WITH AMERICA AND ENGLAND

I. JAPAN'S MINIMUM DEMANDS IN HER NEGOTIATIONS WITH AMERICA (AND ENGLAND)

1. America and England shall not intervene in or obstruct a settlement by Japan of the China Incident.

a. They will not interfere with Japan's plan to settle the China Incident in harmony with the Sino-Japanese Basic Agreement and the Japan-China-Manchoukuo Tri-Partite Declaration.

b. America and England will close the Burma Route and offer the Chiang Regime neither military, political nor economic assistance.

Note: The above do not run counter to Japan's previous declarations in the "N" plan for the settlement of the China Incident. In particular, the plan embodied in the new Sino-Japanese Agreement for the stationing of Japanese troops in the specified areas will be rigidly adhered to. However, the withdrawal of troops other than those mentioned above may be guaranteed in principle upon the settlement of the China Incident.

Commercial operations in China on the part of America and England may also be guaranteed, in so far as they are purely commercial.

2. America and England will take no action in the Far East which offers a threat to the defense of the Empire.

a. America and England will not establish military bases in Thai, the Netherlands East Indies, China or Far Eastern Soviet Russia.

b. Their Far Eastern military forces will not be increased over their present strength.

Note: Any demands for the liquidation of Japan's special relations with French Indo-China based on the Japanese-French Agreement will not be considered.

3. America and England will cooperate with Japan in her attempt to obtain needed raw materials.

a. America and England will restore trade relations with Japan and furnish her with the raw materials she needs from the British and American territories in the Southwest Pacific.

b. America and England will assist Japan to establish close economic relations with Thai and the Netherlands East Indies.

II. MAXIMUM CONCESSIONS BY JAPAN

It is first understood that our minimum demands as listed under I above will be agreed to.

1. Japan will not use French Indo-China as a base for operations against any neighboring countries with the exception of China.

Note: In case any questions are asked concerning Japan's attitude towards Soviet Russia, the answer is to be that as long as Soviet Russia faithfully carries out the Neutrality Pact and does not violate the spirit of the agreement by, for instance, threatening Japan or Manchuria, Japan will not take any military action.

2. Japan is prepared to withdraw her troops from French Indo-China as soon as a just peace is established in the Far East.

3. Japan is prepared to guarantee the neutrality of the Philippine Islands.

32

What the Embassy Believed

Joseph C. Grew

The American Ambassador to Japan from 1932 to 1941 here expresses the view that if President Roosevelt had consented to the summit conference proposed by Premier Konoe (Konoye), the war between Japan and the United States might have been averted.

We in the Embassy believed that the proposed meeting between the President and Prince Konoye should have taken place in spite of the failure of the exploratory conversations to yield all that we desired of them; we believed that at that meeting the Administration might have placed our cards face-up on the table along the general lines of the 10-point draft program of November 26 while at the same time emphasizing the benefits which Japan would unquestionably derive from an acceptance of that program, benefits which might helpfully have been stressed in an earlier speech by the President. We believed that at the same time sympathetic

From *Turbulent Era: A Diplomatic Record of Forty Years 1904–1945*. Vol. 2 by Joseph C. Grew. Used by permission of Houghton Mifflin Company.

study might have been accorded to the problems facing the Japanese
Government which Prince Konoye would then have presented, and that
the latter might have been informed that the Government of the United
States recognized the inherent difficulties which would confront the
Japanese Government in meeting completely and immediately such commitments as Prince Konoye had already professed himself willing to
undertake, but that the relaxation of our economic sanctions could take
place only gradually and *pari passu* with the implementation of those
commitments. In the meantime, as a gauge of our own good faith and
with a view to affording Prince Konoye some concrete achievement to
take home to the Japanese people, our Government might well have
offered to commence negotiations at an early date for a new treaty of
commerce and navigation with Japan, on the distinct understanding that
the signature of such a treaty and its ultimate ratification must depend
upon the effectiveness of the measures taken by the Japanese Government
toward implementing such commitments as might have been undertaken
at the conference.

The crux of this whole situation, as it existed in the early autumn of
1941, was clearly expressed to me by a former Japanese Prime Minister,
Mr. Hirota, having important influence in the highest political circles. He
said, on October 1, that the proposal of Prince Konoye to meet the President of the United States on American soil was generally approved, even
among the military, in view of the absolute necessity of arriving at a
settlement with the United States because of the economic situation; that
delegations representing important political groups had met with Prince
Konoye and had given him assurances that his endeavors to attain an
agreement with the United States would be supported by the Japanese
nation as a whole; *and since, if the proposed conference were held, it
would be unthinkable for Prince Konoye to return to Japan from a mission which had ended in failure, the American terms would perforce have
to be accepted by the Prime Minister who would and could carry the
entire Japanese nation, including the military, with him.*

We believed that the American embargoes and freezing order had
created precisely the situation in Japan which they were intended to
create, but that our Government failed to profit by the situation thus
produced by its own carefully calculated measures. We believed that
in the perpetual tug-of-war between the military extremists and the moderate elements in Japan, those moderate elements, as represented by Prince
Konoye and his Government, which desired and aimed to avoid at almost
any cost a war with the United States, for the first time in ten years pre-
dominated, and that the American Government should have accorded to
Prince Konoye all reasonable support and assistance in achieving his difficult but enlightened task. We believed that had the proposed conference
between Prince Konoye and the President been held it would have led,

without sacrificing any point of principle or interest whatsoever, to a rehabilitation of the relations between the United States and Japan, and to an ultimate settlement of the whole problem of the Pacific.

33

Document Handed by the United States Secretary of State to the Japanese Ambassador (Nomura)

Compare these American proposals for an American-Japanese agreement with the Japanese demands decided upon at the Imperial Council of September 6, 1941 (Selection 31). Why were the American proposals unacceptable to the Japanese?

WASHINGTON, *November 26, 1941*

OUTLINE OF PROPOSED BASIS FOR AGREEMENT BETWEEN THE UNITED STATES AND JAPAN

SECTION I. DRAFT MUTUAL DECLARATION OF POLICY

The Government of the United States and the Government of Japan both being solicitous for the peace of the Pacific affirm that their national policies are directed toward lasting and extensive peace throughout the Pacific area, that they have no territorial designs in that area, that they have no intention of threatening other countries or of using military force aggressively against any neighboring nation, and that, accordingly, in their national policies they will actively support and give practical application to the following fundamental principles upon which their relations with each other and with all other governments are based:

1. The principle of inviolability of territorial integrity and sovereignty of each and all nations.
2. The principle of non-interference in the internal affairs of other countries.
3. The principle of equality, including equality of commercial opportunity and treatment.

From United States Department of State, *Peace and War: United States Foreign Policy, 1931–1941* (Washington, D.C.: Government Printing Office, 1943), pp. 810–812.

4. The principle of reliance upon international cooperation and conciliation for the prevention and pacific settlement of controversies and for improvement of international conditions by peaceful methods and processes.

The Government of Japan and the Government of the United States have agreed that toward eliminating chronic political instability, preventing recurrent economic collapse, and providing a basis for peace, they will actively support and practically apply the following principles in their economic relations with each other and with other nations and peoples:

1. The principle of non-discrimination in international commercial relations.
2. The principle of international economic cooperation and abolition of extreme nationalism as expressed in excessive trade restrictions.
3. The principle of non-discriminatory access by all nations to raw material supplies.
4. The principle of full protection of the interests of consuming countries and populations as regards the operation of international commodity agreements.
5. The principle of establishment of such institutions and arrangements of international finance as may lend aid to the essential enterprises and the continuous development of all countries and may permit payments through processes of trade consonant with the welfare of all countries.

SECTION II. STEPS TO BE TAKEN BY THE GOVERNMENT OF THE UNITED STATES AND BY THE GOVERNMENT OF JAPAN

The Government of the United States and the Government of Japan propose to take steps as follows:

1. The Government of the United States and the Government of Japan will endeavor to conclude a multilateral non-aggression pact among the British Empire, China, Japan, the Netherlands, the Soviet Union, Thailand and the United States.

2. Both Governments will endeavor to conclude among the American, British, Chinese, Japanese, the Netherland and Thai Governments an agreement whereunder each of the Governments would pledge itself to respect the territorial integrity of French Indochina and, in the event that there should develop a threat to the territorial integrity of Indochina, to enter into immediate consultation with a view to taking such measures as may be deemed necessary and advisable to meet the threat in question. Such agreement would provide also that each of the Governments party to the agreement would not seek or accept preferential treatment in its trade or economic relations with Indochina and would use its influence to obtain for each of the signatories equality of treatment in trade and commerce with French Indochina.

3. The Government of Japan will withdraw all military, naval, air and police forces from China and from Indochina.

4. The Government of the United States and the Government of Japan will not support—militarily, politically, economically—any government or regime in China other than the National Government of the Republic of China with capital temporarily at Chungking.

5. Both Governments will give up all extraterritorial rights in China, including rights and interests in and with regard to international settlements and concessions, and rights under the Boxer Protocol of 1901.

Both Governments will endeavor to obtain the agreement of the British and other governments to give up extraterritorial rights in China, including rights in international settlements and in concessions and under the Boxer Protocol of 1901.

6. The Government of the United States and the Government of Japan will enter into negotiations for the conclusion between the United States and Japan of a trade agreement, based upon reciprocal most-favored-nation treatment and reduction of trade barriers by both countries, including an undertaking by the United States to bind raw silk on the free list.

7. The Government of the United States and the Government of Japan will, respectively, remove the freezing restrictions on Japanese funds in the United States and on American funds in Japan.

8. Both Governments will agree upon a plan for the stabilization of the dollar-yen rate, with the allocation of funds adequate for this purpose, half to be supplied by Japan and half by the United States.

9. Both Governments will agree that no agreement which either has concluded with any third power or powers shall be interpreted by it in such a way as to conflict with the fundamental purpose of this agreement, the establishment and preservation of peace throughout the Pacific area.

10. Both Governments will use their influence to cause other governments to adhere to and to give practical application to the basic political and economic principles set forth in this agreement.

34

Oral Statement Handed by the United States Secretary of State to the Japanese Ambassador (Nomura)

WASHINGTON, *November 26, 1941*

The representatives of the Government of the United States and of the Government of Japan have been carrying on during the past several months informal and exploratory conversations for the purpose of arriving at a settlement if possible of questions relating to the entire Pacific area based upon the principles of peace, law and order and fair dealing among nations. These principles include the principle of inviolability of territorial integrity and sovereignty of each and all nations; the principle of non-interference in the internal affairs of other countries; the principle of equality, including equality of commercial opportunity and treatment; and the principle of reliance upon international cooperation and conciliation for the prevention and pacific settlement of controversies and for improvement of international conditions by peaceful methods and processes.

It is believed that in our discussions some progress has been made in reference to the general principles which constitute the basis of a peaceful settlement covering the entire Pacific area. Recently the Japanese Ambassador has stated that the Japanese Government is desirous of continuing the conversations directed toward a comprehensive and peaceful settlement in the Pacific area; that it would be helpful toward creating an atmosphere favorable to the successful outcome of the conversations if a temporary *modus vivendi* could be agreed upon to be in effect while the conversations looking to a peaceful settlement in the Pacific were continuing. On November 20 the Japanese Ambassador communicated to the Secretary of State proposals in regard to temporary measures to be taken respectively by the Government of Japan and by the Government of the United States, which measures are understood to have been designed to accomplish the purpose above indicated.

The Government of the United States most earnestly desires to con-

From United States Department of State, *Peace and War: United States Foreign Policy, 1931–1941* (Washington, D.C.: Government Printing Office, 1943), pp. 812–814.

tribute to the promotion and maintenance of peace and stability in the Pacific area, and to afford every opportunity for the continuance of discussions with the Japanese Government directed toward working out a broad-gauge program of peace throughout the Pacific area. The proposals which were presented by the Japanese Ambassador on November 20 contain some features which, in the opinion of this Government, conflict with the fundamental principles which form a part of the general settlement under consideration and to which each Government has declared that it is committed. The Government of the United States believes that the adoption of such proposals would not be likely to contribute to the ultimate objectives of ensuring peace under law, order and justice in the Pacific area, and it suggests that further effort be made to resolve our divergences of views in regard to the practical application of the fundamental principles already mentioned.

With this object in view the Government of the United States offers for the consideration of the Japanese Government a plan of a broad but simple settlement covering the entire Pacific area as one practical exemplification of a program which this Government envisages as something to be worked out during our further conversations.

The plan therein suggested represents an effort to bridge the gap between our draft of June 21, 1941 and the Japanese draft of September 25 by making a new approach to the essential problems underlying a comprehensive Pacific settlement. This plan contains provisions dealing with the practical application of the fundamental principles which we have agreed in our conversations constitute the only sound basis for worthwhile international relations. We hope that in this way progress toward reaching a meeting of minds between our two Governments may be expedited.

35

Message from President Roosevelt to Emperor Hirohito

It has been said that if the delivery of this telegram had not been delayed for over ten hours in the Tokyo central telegraph office, the war between the United States and Japan would have been averted.

WASHINGTON, *December 6, 1941*

Almost a century ago the President of the United States addressed to the Emperor of Japan a message extending an offer of friendship of the people of the United States to the people of Japan. That offer was accepted, and in the long period of unbroken peace and friendship which has followed, our respective nations, through the virtues of their peoples and the wisdom of their rulers have prospered and have substantially helped humanity.

Only in situations of extraordinary importance to our two countries need I address to Your Majesty messages on matters of state. I feel I should now so address you because of the deep and far-reaching emergency which appears to be in formation.

Developments are occurring in the Pacific area which threaten to deprive each of our nations and all humanity of the beneficial influence of the long peace between our two countries. These developments contain tragic possibilities.

The people of the United States, believing in peace and in the right of nations to live and let live, have eagerly watched the conversations between our two Governments during these past months. We have hoped

This message was transmitted in telegram 818, Dec. 6, 1941, 9 p.m., to the Ambassador in Japan (Grew), under instructions to communicate the President's message to the Japanese Emperor in such manner as deemed most appropriate by the Ambassador and at the earliest possible moment, addressed to "His Imperial Majesty, the Emperor of Japan." The telegram added that the press was being informed that the President was dispatching a message to the Emperor.

From United States Department of State, *Peace and War: United States Foreign Policy, 1931–1941* (Washington, D.C.: Government Printing Office, 1943), pp. 829–831.

for a termination of the present conflict between Japan and China. We have hoped that a peace of the Pacific could be consummated in such a way that nationalities of many diverse peoples could exist side by side without fear of invasion; that unbearable burdens of armaments could be lifted for them all; and that all peoples would resume commerce without discrimination against or in favor of any nation.

I am certain that it will be clear to Your Majesty, as it is to me, that in seeking these great objectives both Japan and the United States should agree to eliminate any form of military threat. This seemed essential to the attainment of the high objectives.

More than a year ago Your Majesty's Government concluded an agreement with the Vichy Government by which five or six thousand Japanese troops were permitted to enter into Northern French Indochina for the protection of Japanese troops which were operating against China further north. And this Spring and Summer the Vichy Government permitted further Japanese military forces to enter into Southern French Indochina for the common defense of French Indochina. I think I am correct in saying that no attack has been made upon Indochina, nor that any has been contemplated.

During the past few weeks it has become clear to the world that Japanese military, naval and air forces have been sent to Southern Indochina in such large numbers as to create a reasonable doubt on the part of other nations that this continuing concentration in Indochina is not defensive in its character.

Because these continuing concentrations in Indochina have reached such large proportions and because they extend now to the southeast and the southwest corners of that Peninsula, it is only reasonable that the people of the Philippines, of the hundreds of Islands of the East Indies, of Malaya and of Thailand itself are asking themselves whether these forces of Japan are preparing or intending to make attack in one or more of these many directions.

I am sure that Your Majesty will understand that the fear of all these peoples is a legitimate fear in as much as it involves their peace and their national existence. I am sure that Your Majesty will understand why the people of the United States in such large numbers look askance at the establishment of military, naval and air bases manned and equipped so greatly as to constitute armed forces capable of measures of offense.

It is clear that a continuance of such a situation is unthinkable.

None of the peoples whom I have spoken of above can sit either indefinitely or permanently on a keg of dynamite.

There is absolutely no thought on the part of the United States of invading Indochina if every Japanese soldier or sailor were to be withdrawn therefrom.

I think that we can obtain the same assurance from the Governments of the East Indies, the Governments of Malaya and the Government of Thailand. I would even undertake to ask for the same assurance on the part of the Government of China. Thus a withdrawal of the Japanese forces from Indochina would result in the assurance of peace throughout the whole of the South Pacific area.

I address myself to Your Majesty at this moment in the fervent hope that Your Majesty may, as I am doing, give thought in this definite emergency to ways of dispelling the dark clouds. I am confident that both of us, for the sake of the peoples not only of our own great countries but for the sake of humanity in neighboring territories, have a sacred duty to restore traditional amity and prevent further death and destruction in the world.

Franklin D. Roosevelt

36

Imperial Rescript: Japanese Declaration of War on the United States and the British Empire

We, by grace of heaven, Emperor of Japan, seated on the Throne of a line unbroken for ages eternal, enjoin upon ye, Our loyal and brave subjects:

We hereby declare war on the United States of America and the British Empire. The men and officers of Our army and navy shall do their utmost in prosecuting the war. Our public servants of various departments shall perform faithfully and diligently their appointed tasks, and all other subjects of Ours shall pursue their respective duties; the entire nation with a united will shall mobilize their total strength so that nothing will miscarry in the attainment of our war aims.

To insure the stability of East Asia and to contribute to world peace is the farsighted policy which was formulated by Our Great Illustrious Imperial Grandsire and Our Great Imperial Sire succeeding Him, and which We lay constantly to heart.

To cultivate friendship among nations and to enjoy prosperity in common with all nations has always been the guiding principle of Our

Released by the Japanese Government Board of Information, December 8, 1941.

Empire's foreign policy. It has been truly unavoidable and far from Our wishes that Our Empire has now been brought to cross swords with America and Britain.[1]

More than four years have passed since China, failing to comprehend the true intentions of Our Empire, and recklessly courting trouble, disturbed the peace of East Asia and compelled Our Empire to take up arms. Although there has been re-established the National Government of China, with which Japan had effected neighborly intercourse and co-operation, the regime which has survived at Chungking, relying upon American and British protection, still continues its fratricidal opposition.

Eager for the realization of their inordinate ambition to dominate the Orient, both America and Britain, giving support to the Chungking regime, have aggravated the disturbances in East Asia.

Moreover, these two Powers, inducing other countries to follow suit, increased military preparations on all sides of Our Empire to challenge us. They have obstructed by every means our peaceful commerce, and finally resorted to a direct severance of economic relations, menacing gravely the existence of Our Empire.

Patiently have We waited and long have We endured in the hope that Our Government might retrieve the situation in peace, but Our adversaries showing not the least spirit of conciliation, have unduly delayed a settlement; and in the meantime, they have intensified the economic and political pressure to compel thereby Our Empire to submission.

This trend of affairs would, if left unchecked, not only nullify Our Empire's efforts of many years for the sake of the stabilization of East Asia, but also endanger the very existence of Our nation. The situation being such as it is, Our Empire for its existence and self-defense has no other recourse but to appeal to arms and to crush every obstacle in its path.

The hallowed spirits of Our Imperial Ancestors guarding Us from above, We rely upon the loyalty and courage of Our subjects in Our confident expectation that the task bequeathed by Our Forefathers will be carried forward, and that the source of evil will be speedily eradicated and an enduring peace immutably established in East Asia, preserving thereby the glory of Our Empire.

---

[1] This sentence is said to have been inserted on the personal request of the Emperor. [Editor's note.]

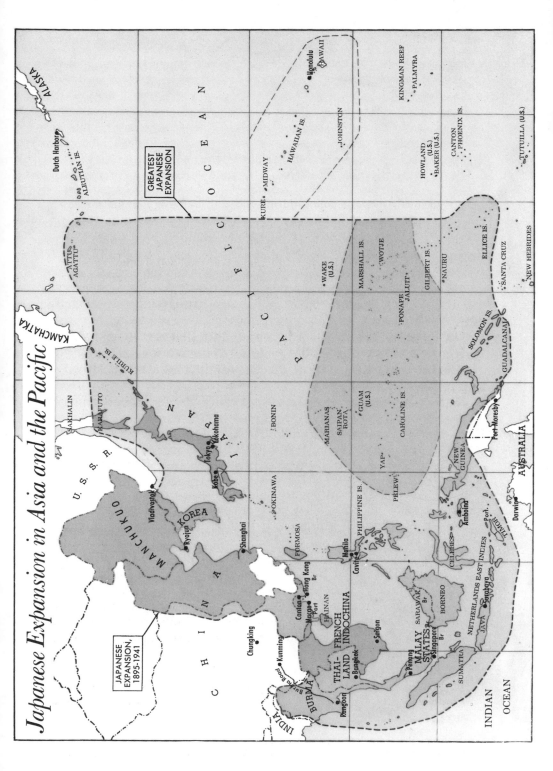

Japanese Expansion in Asia and the Pacific

GREATEST JAPANESE EXPANSION

JAPANESE EXPANSION, 1895-1941

ALASKA

Dutch Harbor
ALEUTIAN IS.
ATTU
AGATTU

PACIFIC OCEAN

Honolulu
HAWAII
HAWAIIAN IS.
KINGMAN REEF
PALMYRA

JOHNSTON

CANTON
PHOENIX IS.
HOWLAND (U.S.)
BAKER (U.S.)

TUTUILLA (U.S.)

KURE • MIDWAY

WAKE (U.S.)

MARSHALL IS.
WOTJE
JALUIT
GILBERT IS.
NAURU
ELLICE IS.
SANTA CRUZ
NEW HEBRIDES

PONAPE

MARIANAS
SAIPAN, ROTA
GUAM (U.S.)
CAROLINE IS.
YAP
PELEW

SOLOMON IS.
GUADALCANAL

BONIN

KAMCHATKA

SAKHALIN

KURILE IS.

KARAFUTO

U.S.S.R.

Vladivostok
Ryojun
KOREA

MANCHUKUO

Shanghai

C H I N A

Chungking

Kunming

Burma Road

BURMA

Rangoon

INDIA

Tokyo
Yokohama
Kobe

J A P A N

FORMOSA

OKINAWA

PHILIPPINE IS.
Manila
Cavite

NEW GUINEA
Port Moresby

AUSTRALIA
Darwin

Canton
Macao
Port
HAINAN
Hong Kong Br

THAI-
LAND
Bangkok

FRENCH
INDOCHINA
Saigon

MALAY
STATES
Penang
Singapore Br

SARAWAK
Br
BORNEO

SUMATRA

NETHERLANDS EAST INDIES
JAVA
Sourabaya

CELEBES

Amboina

TIMOR
Port.

INDIAN OCEAN

153

37

The Cairo Conference

It was American policy during the war to recognize the Great Power status of China notwithstanding the latter's military weakness. The priority given to the war in Europe meant that many of the generous promises made to China were not kept. The promise of the return of Manchuria to China was modified by the restoration of Russian interests in Manchurian railroads and ports, provided in the Yalta agreement (Selection 38).

UNITED STATES OF AMERICA: PRESIDENT ROOSEVELT
CHINA: GENERALISSIMO CHIANG KAI-SHEK
UNITED KINGDOM: PRIME MINISTER CHURCHILL

Statement released December 1, 1943

The several military missions have agreed upon future military operations against Japan. The Three Great Allies expressed their resolve to bring unrelenting pressure against their brutal enemies by sea, land, and air. This pressure is already rising.

The Three Great Allies are fighting this war to restrain and punish the aggression of Japan. They covet no gain for themselves and have no thought of territorial expansion. It is their purpose that Japan shall be stripped of all the islands in the Pacific which she has seized or occupied since the beginning of the first World War in 1914, and that all the territories Japan has stolen from the Chinese, such as Manchuria, Formosa, and the Pescadores, shall be restored to the Republic of China. Japan will also be expelled from all other territories which she has taken by violence and greed. The aforesaid three great powers, mindful of the enslavement of the people of Korea, are determined that in due course Korea shall become free and independent.

With these objects in view the three Allies, in harmony with those of the United Nations at war with Japan, will continue to persevere in the serious and prolonged operations necessary to procure the unconditional surrender of Japan.

From the United States Department of State, *Occupation of Japan: Policy and Progress* (Washington, D.C.: Government Printing Office, n.d. [1946?]), pp. 51–52.

38

Agreement Regarding Entry of the Soviet Union into the War Against Japan

February 11, 1945

For obvious strategic reasons, this understanding among the Allies, signed at Yalta, was kept secret at the time. It was released to the press by the United States Department of State on February 11, 1946. It is often asserted that the provisions concerning Manchuria and Outer Mongolia are largely to blame for the Communist conquest of China after the war, but it is not clear what would have happened in the absence of the agreement. Russia regained at Yalta what she had lost at Portsmouth in 1905 (See Chapter II, Selection 16).

TOP SECRET

AGREEMENT

The leaders of the three Great Powers—the Soviet Union, the United States of America and Great Britain—have agreed that in two or three months after Germany has surrendered and the war in Europe has terminated the Soviet Union shall enter into the war against Japan on the side of the Allies on condition that:

1. The *status quo* in Outer-Mongolia (The Mongolian People's Republic) shall be preserved;

2. The former rights of Russia violated by the treacherous attack of Japan in 1904 shall be restored, viz:

a. the southern part of Sakhalin as well as all the islands adjacent to it shall be returned to the Soviet Union,

b. the commercial port of Dairen shall be internationalized, the preeminent interests of the Soviet Union in this port being safeguarded and the lease of Port Arthur as a naval base of the USSR restored,

c. the Chinese-Eastern Railroad and the South-Manchurian Railroad

From United States Department of State, *Foreign Relations of the United States Diplomatic Papers: The Conferences at Malta and Yalta, 1945* (Washington, D.C.: Government Printing Office, 1955), p. 984.

which provides an outlet to Dairen shall be jointly operated by the establishment of a joint Soviet-Chinese Company it being understood that the preeminent interests of the Soviet Union shall be safeguarded and that China shall retain full sovereignty in Manchuria;

3. The Kuril islands shall be handed over to the Soviet Union.

It is understood, that the agreement concerning Outer-Mongolia and the ports and railroads referred to above will require concurrence of Generalissimo Chiang Kai-Shek. The President will take measures in order to obtain this concurrence on advice from Marshal Stalin.

The Heads of the three Great Powers have agreed that these claims of the Soviet Union shall be unquestionably fulfilled after Japan has been defeated.

For its part the Soviet Union expresses its readiness to conclude with the National Government of China a pact of friendship and alliance between the USSR and China in order to render assistance to China with its armed forces for the purpose of liberating China from the Japanese yoke.

February 11, 1945

Joseph Stalin
Franklin D. Roosevelt
Winston Churchill

SUGGESTED READING

Butow, Robert J. C. *Tojo and the Coming of the War*. Princeton: Princeton University Press, 1961.

Chiang Kai-shek and Madame Chiang Kai-shek. *General Chiang Kai-shek: The Account of the Fortnight in Sian When the Fate of China Hung in Balance*. New York: The Book League of America, 1937.

Feis, Herbert. *The Road to Pearl Harbor*. Princeton: Princeton University Press, 1949. (Paperback edition: Atheneum)

Grew, Joseph C. *Ten Years in Japan*. New York: Simon and Schuster, 1944.

Grew, Joseph C. *Turbulent Era: A Diplomatic Record of Forty Years, 1904–1945*. 2 vols. Boston: Houghton Mifflin, 1952.

Hull, Cordell. *The Memoirs of Cordell Hull*. 2 vols. New York: Macmillan, 1948.

Ike, Nobutaka. *Japan's Decision for War: Records of the 1941 Policy Conferences*. Stanford: Stanford University Press, 1967.

Johnson, Chalmers. *An Instance of Treason: Ozaki Hotsumi and the Sorge Spy Ring*. Stanford: Stanford University Press, 1964.

Jones, F. C. *Japan's New Order in East Asia, 1937–1945*. London: Oxford University Press, 1954.

Jones, F. C.; Borton, Hugh; and Pearn, B. R. *The Far East, 1942–1946*. London: Oxford University Press, 1955.

Kase, Toshikazu. *Journey to the Missouri*. New Haven: Yale University Press, 1950.

Kato, Masuo. *The Lost War*. New York: Knopf, 1946.

Lin Yutang. *The Vigil of a Nation*. New York: John Day, 1945.

MacArthur, Douglas. *Reminiscences*. New York: McGraw-Hill, 1964. Paperback: Fawcett Crest Book.

Maxon, Yale Candee. *Control of Japanese Foreign Policy: A Study of Civil Military Rivalry, 1930–1945*. Berkeley: University of California Press, 1957.

Meskill, Johanna Menzel. *Hitler and Japan: The Hollow Alliance*. New York: Atherton, 1966.

Millis, Walter. *This is Pearl!* New York: Morrow, 1947.

Prange, Gordon. *Tora! Tora!* New York: McGraw-Hill, in preparation. (Condensed version in *Readers Digest*, October, November, 1963.)

Presseisen, Ernst L. *Germany and Japan: A Study in Totalitarian Diplomacy, 1933–1941*. The Hague: Martinius Nijhoff, 1958.

Quigley, Harold S. *Far Eastern War, 1937–1941*. Boston: World Peace Foundation, 1942.

Rowe, David Nelson. *China among the Powers*. New York: Harcourt, Brace & World, 1945.

Rosinger, Lawrence K. *China's Crisis*. New York: Knopf, 1945.

Rosinger, Lawrence K. *China's Wartime Politics, 1937–1944*. Princeton: Princeton University Press, 1944.

Shigemitsu, Mamoru. *Japan and Her Destiny: My Struggle for Peace*. New York: Dutton, 1958.

Taylor, George E. *The Struggle for North China*. New York: Institute of Pacific Relations, 1940.

Togo Shigenori. *The Cause of Japan*. New York: Simon and Schuster, 1956.

Tolischus, Otto D. *Through Japanese Eyes*. New York: Reynal & Hitchcock, 1945.

Trefousse, Hans L., ed. *What Happened at Pearl Harbor?* New York: College and University Press, 1958, paperback.

Wohlstetter, Roberta. *Pearl Harbor: Warning and Decision*. Stanford: Stanford University Press, 1962, paperback.

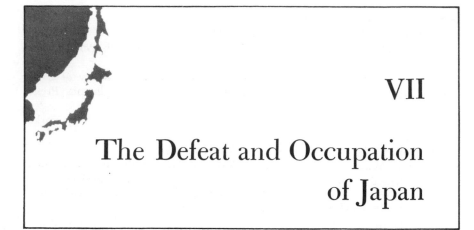

VII

The Defeat and Occupation of Japan

In February, 1945, Prince Konoe, the former Prime Minister, advised the Emperor that Japan's defeat was inevitable and that a prolongation of the war would likely result in a Communist revolution and the abolition of the Emperor system in Japan (Selection 39). The Japanese military, however, was in complete control of the government and mass communications, and was able to forestall any move towards peace. In June Premier Suzuki announced Japan's intention to fight to the bitter end; the people would defend the soil of their homeland against the invaders with bamboo spears, if necessary. Japanese diplomats tried to obtain the mediation of the Soviet Union (still neutral in the Pacific war) to end the war.

On July 26, 1945, the leaders of the Allied Powers, meeting in Potsdam, called upon Japan to surrender unconditionally (Selection 40). In response, Premier Suzuki announced that the Potsdam terms should be ignored; the Americans dropped atom bombs on Hiroshima and Nagasaki on August 6 and 9 respectively, and on August 9, the Soviet Union declared war on Japan, in evident violation of the Soviet-Japanese Neutrality Pact of 1941. On August 10, the Japanese Emperor, siding with the Premier and Foreign Minister against the War Minister, decided in favor of acceptance of the Potsdam terms on condition that the prerogatives of the emperor as sovereign ruler would not be prejudiced. Secretary of State James Byrnes replied that the Emperor and government of Japan would be subject to the authority of the Allied commander and that the ultimate form of the Japanese government would be determined by the free will of the Japanese people. The Emperor again resolved a cabinet deadlock in favor of accepting the Allied peace terms. An attempted military coup d'état almost prevented the Emperor's recorded message announcing the surrender to the Japanese people from being broadcast (Selection 41). On September 2, 1945, the instrument of surrender was signed by representatives of both the Japanese government and the Japanese general headquarters aboard the U.S.S. *Missouri*, anchored in Tokyo Bay.

The purpose of the Allied Occupation was to enforce the provisions of the Potsdam Declaration and to ensure that Japan would never again become a menace to world peace. An eleven-nation Far Eastern Commission (FEC), meeting in Washington, was established to make policy for the Occupation, to be enforced by the Supreme Commander for the Allied Powers (SCAP) with the advice of a four-power Allied Council for Japan, meeting in Tokyo. The Occupation, however, was essentially an American undertaking because SCAP and most of his staff were American, and the United States had a veto power in the FEC. Direct military government was not set up in Japan. Instead, SCAP Headquarters issued written and oral directives and suggestions to the Imperial Japanese Government, which in turn carried out the required reforms (Selection 42).

The Japanese army and navy were demobilized, the freedoms of speech, press, and assembly were assured, the unionization of labor was encouraged, land was transferred by sale from absentee landowners to the tillers, and women were given an equal right to vote and run for office. Officials with records of militarism and ultranationalism were purged from public office, war criminals were tried, and the great *zaibatsu* monopolies were partially broken up. The educational and police systems were democratized (Selection 43).

During and immediately following the war, there was a dispute in the Allied countries as to whether or not the Japanese Emperor should be tried as a war criminal and the monarchy abolished. A leading opponent of the Japanese Emperor system was Sun Fo, President of the Legislative Yuan of China, the son of Dr. Sun Yat-sen. Senator Richard Russell proposed a congressional resolution calling for the trial of Emperor Hirohito as a war criminal (Selection 44). In December, 1945, Shinto, which had fostered the cult of the Emperor, was disestablished as Japan's state religion by order of the Occupation. Apparently to make the monarchy more acceptable to the Allies, the Emperor renounced his divinity in his 1946 New Year's Day rescript (Selection 45).

In 1946 the cabinet sponsored and the Diet passed a new Constitution which for the most part had been secretly drafted in SCAP Headquarters. Instructions from Washington had emphasized the need for constitutional reforms which would establish a government responsible to the people and the supremacy of the civilian branch over the military (Selection 46). The new Constitution, effective in 1947, declared that the emperor was "the symbol of the State and of the unity of the people, deriving his power from the will of the people with whom resides sovereign power" (Appendix A). A parliamentary-cabinet type of democracy was set up in which the cabinet was responsible to the lower house of the popularly

Sketch Map adapted from the *National Geographic Magazine - Atlas · Plate 51 · Dec. 1960*

CHINA

U.S.S.R.

SAKHALIN ISLAND
(U.S.S.R. ADMIN.)

SEA OF OKHOTSK

KURIL ISLANDS
(U.S.S.R. ADMIN.)

HOKKAIDŌ

HOKKAIDŌ

Shikotan I.

Habomai Is.
(U.S.S.R. ADMIN.)

Vladivostok

SEA

OF JAPAN

• Sapporo

Aomori
AOMORI

AKITA

• Morioka

Akita

IWATE

Cease-fire line, July 27, 1953

KOREA

• Seoul

YAMAGATA

Yamagata•

MIYAGI

• Sendai

Niigata •

• Fukushima

Toyama

NIIGATA

FUKUSHIMA

• Nagano

TOCHIGI

GUMMA

• Utsunomiya

KOREA STRAIT

TSUSHIMA

Kanazawa•

ISHIKAWA

TOYAMA

Maebashi•

• Mito

NAGANO

SAITAMA

IBARAKI

KYŌTO

FUKUI

Fukui•

GIFU

Kōfu

Urawa•

TŌKYŌ ★

Chiba

━ Tōkyō

Matsue•

TOTTORI

Gifu•

YAMANASHI

• Yokohama

HONSHŪ

SHIMANE

Tottori•

Kyō•

SHIGA

•Ōtsu

SHIZUOKA

KANAGAWA

CHIBA

HYŌGO

OKAYAMA

Okayama•

Nagoya•

Tsu•

Shizuoka•

Yamaguchi•

HIROSHIMA

Hiroshima•

Kōbe•Osaka

ŌSAKA Nara

MIE

AICHI

YAMAGUCHI

KAGAWA

Takamatsu•

Wakayama•

NARA

FUKUOKA

TOKUSHIMA

SAGA

•Fukuoka

Matsuyama•Kōchi

WAKAYAMA

NAGASAKI

Saga•

EHIME

KŌCHI

INLAND

Tokushima•

SEA

•Ōita

Nagasaki•

ŌITA

SHIKOKU

PACIFIC

•Kumamoto

KUMAMOTO

MIYAZAKI

KAGOSHIMA

•Miyazaki

OCEAN

Kagoshima•

KYŪSHŪ

AMAMI Ō SHIMA

RYUKYU ISLANDS

Prefectures and Principal Cities of

JAPAN

★ National Capitals   • Prefectural Capitals

0   50   100   200
STATUTE MILES

BONIN ISLANDS
?(U.S. ADMIN.)

OKINAWA (U.S. ADMIN.)

elected bicameral Diet. The Supreme Court was explicitly empowered to determine the constitutionality of legislation. Article 9 of the Constitution renounced war and the maintenance of armaments.

By mid-1947 the principal political reforms of the Occupation had been accomplished. Attention was now directed to the economic rehabilitation of Japan to relieve the American taxpayer of the burden of subsidizing the prostrate country. As the Cold War became more acute, and as China fell increasingly under Communist control, American policy shifted from the punishment and reform of Japan to the reconstruction of Japan as a bulwark against communism. The war crimes trials were brought to an end following the conviction of Tōjō and his principal accomplices, purged politicians were permitted to resume their careers, and the breakup of the *zaibatsu* was halted.

In 1950, when American troops were shipped to Japan to fight in Korea, a National Police Reserve was created in Japan by MacArthur's orders. This organization of 75,000 men was originally intended to prevent internal subversion, but it served as a nucleus for what within a decade became a Self-Defense Force. Also in 1950, when the Japanese Communists turned from peaceful to violent tactics, General MacArthur ordered the purge of the leading Communists for obstructing the Occupation, although the Communists had certainly not been guilty of leading Japan into war. The so-called reverse course of the Occupation, from democratic reform to anticommunism and rearmament, aroused cynical doubts as to the real motives of the Occupation authorities.

On balance, the Occupation was successful. A peacefully inclined and democratic government was established, and the economy was rehabilitated. Although the Japanese regained their independence with the end of the Occupation in 1952, they have not yet altered a word of their democratic Constitution. No doubt Japan's rapid economic revival and the notable rise in the standard of living go far to explain popular acceptance of the new liberal democratic institutions.

39

The Konoe Memorial

February 14, 1945

The militarists were in complete control of the Japanese government during the war and prevented anyone suspected of advocating
peace from publicly expressing their views or conferring with the
Emperor. Following the American landing on the Philippines, the
Emperor let it be known that he wished to consult with the *jūshin*
(former prime ministers). In February, 1945, they visited him on
the pretext of inquiring about his health. Of the *jūshin*, only Prince
Konoe, whose statement to the Emperor is reproduced here, emphatically urged strong steps to bring about an early peace. When
the Japanese military police learned that Yoshida Shigeru, a former
Ambassador to Great Britain, had assisted Konoe in the preparation
of the statement, Yoshida was placed under arrest. (In 1946, during
the Occupation of Japan, Yoshida became Prime Minister.)

I believe that, regrettable though it is, our defeat in war is imminent
and inevitable.

I respectfully submit the following on the basis of this premise.

Although defeat will be a stain on the national structure,[1] thus far
public opinion in America and Great Britain has not gone so far as to
favor a change of the national structure. (Of course, a part of public
opinion is radical, and it is difficult to predict how opinion will change
in the future.) I believe that, consequently, as far as the defeat itself is
concerned, we need not worry too much about its effect on the national

Translated by Theodore McNelly. Somewhat varying Japanese texts may be
found in Yabe Sadaji, *Konoe Fumimaro* (Tokyo: Kōbundō, 1952), II, 529–533; *Gai-
mushō* (comp.), *Shūsen Shiroku* (Tokyo: Shimbun Gekkan Sha, 1952), pp. 195–198;
and Nihon Gaikō Gakkai (comp.), *Taiheiyō Sensō Shūketsu Ron* (Tokyo: Tokyo
Daigaku Shuppan Kai, 1958), pp. 107–110. English translations appear in United States
Strategic Bombing Survey, *Japan's Struggle to End the War* (1 July, 1946), pp. 21–22;
and Robert J. C. Butow, *Japan's Decision to Surrender* (Stanford: Stanford University
Press, 1954), pp. 47–50.

[1] In order to ensure clarity throughout this translation, *kokutai*, and only *kokutai*,
has consistently been translated as *national structure*. Other translators sometimes render *kokutai* as *national polity*, or *state form*. The central feature of Japan's national
structure was the emperor system. [Editor's note.]

structure. From the standpoint of the preservation of the national structure, what is most to be deplored, even more than defeat, is a communist
revolution which would arise with the defeat.

Upon careful consideration, I believe that conditions both inside and
outside our country are even now rapidly moving in the direction of a
communist revolution. Abroad, the Soviet Union is making unusual ad-
vances. The people of our country have no firm apprehension of the
intentions of the Soviet Union. Since the tactic of the popular front in
1935, that is to say, the adoption of the tactic of the two-stage revolution,
and especially since the recent dissolution of the Comintern, the people
have conspicuously tended to view lightly the danger of communization.
This, I believe, is a superficial and facile point of view. The crude actions
which the Soviet has recently carried out with respect to the countries
in Europe have gradually made it clear that the Soviet Union will never
ultimately give up the policy of world communization.

In Europe, the Soviet Union is progressing step by step with various
projects with the purpose of establishing Soviet-type regimes in its neighboring countries and regimes which are at least friendly and pro-Communist in the other countries, and is now in a position to see the success of
its efforts for the most part. The Tito regime in Yugoslavia is the most
classical concrete expression of this policy. In Poland, the Soviet has had
its own way in establishing a new regime centered about the Poland Patriotic League, previously prepared in the Soviet Union, in disregard of
the exile regime in England. When we look at the truce conditions for
Rumania, Bulgaria, and Finland, although professing the principle of non-
intervention in internal political affairs, the Soviet has demanded the dissolution of organizations supporting Hitler and in actuality has made it
impossible for these countries to exist unless they accept Soviet regimes.
In Iran, on the pretext that their demands for oil rights had been unan-
swered, they compelled the resignation of the cabinet. When Sweden
proposed the beginning of diplomatic relations, the Soviet Union refused
on the grounds that the Swedish government was pro-Axis and compelled
the resignation of the foreign minister. In occupied France, Belgium, and
the Netherlands, the armed revolutionary groups which had been used
against Germany are continuing the war with the governments, and these
countries are all afflicted with political crises. The leaders of these armed
bands are for the most part connected with communists. With respect to
Germany, as with respect to Poland, they plan in so far as possible to
establish a new regime centered about the Free German Committee which
they have set up; this is presumably a source of worry for England and
the United States.

In this way, the Soviet Union on the surface professes the principle of
noninterference in the internal political affairs of European countries, but in
actuality interferes in an extreme degree in their politics and draws their

politics to a pro-Soviet orientation. These plans of the Soviet Union are the same for East Asia as well. The Japanese Emancipation League has been organized under the leadership of Okano,[2] who was sent from Moscow to Yenan, and it, in collaboration with the Korea Independence League, the Korean Volunteer Army, and the Taiwan Vanguard Units, is addressing itself to Japan. In considering such a situation, it is conceivable that there is ample danger that the Soviet Union will before long interfere in Japan's internal political affairs. (Namely, the recognition of the Communist Party, participation of communists in the cabinet just as demanded of the de Gaulle and Badoglio governments, and abolition of the peace-preservation law and of the Anti-Comintern Pact, etc.) And now, when one looks at the internal situation in this country, all of the conditions for the accomplishment of a communist revolution appear day by day to be realized. In particular, there are the poverty of livelihood, the increase in the demands of the workers, the pro-Soviet atmosphere reflecting the growing hostility towards the English and Americans, the reform movement of a group in the army, the movement of the so-called new bureaucrats who take advantage of this, and the secret maneuvers of the leftist elements which are manipulating them from behind the scenes.

What is of special concern in all of this is the reform movement of a group in the military. The majority of young soldiers believe that the country's national structure and communism are mutually compatible, and I believe that such a view is in harmony with the reformist sentiment in the military. I have heard that even among persons in the imperial family there are those who give a hearing to such arguments.[3] The majority of professional soldiers come from lower than middle-class homes and are in circumstances favorable to the reception of communist arguments; furthermore, taking advantage of the fact that in their military training the concept of the national structure was the only thing that was thoroughly dinned into them, the communist elements intend to attract the military with the argument that the national structure and communism can coexist.

I believe that it is now clear the Manchurian affair and the China affair and their enlargement to bring on finally the Great East Asia War were all the conscious plan of this group in the military. It is a notorious fact that at the time of the Manchurian affair, the goal of this affair was declared to be reform in Japan. At the time of the China affair, a principal leader of this band publicly declared, "It will be good if this affair drags out a long time; if it is resolved, internal reform will be impossible."

The reformist aim of this group in the military may not necessarily be communist revolution. However, I believe that elements of the bureaucracy and their civilian sympathizers who surround the military (they

[2] I.e., Nosako Sanzo, a Japanese Communist leader. [Editor's note.]
[3] This sentence, which refers to the imperial family, is not included in some Japanese versions. [Editor's note.]

may be called either right-wingers or left-wingers; the so-called right-wingers are communists clothed in the garb of the national structure) consciously entertain hopes to bring about a communist revolution. I believe it is safe to assume that the ignorant and simple-minded soldiers have been manipulated by them.

Your unworthy servant, who for the past fifty years has had friends in many quarters among the military, the bureaucracy, the rightists and leftists, has recently, after quiet reflection, arrived at these conclusions. When I ponder the events of the past ten years, I discover a great many points which seem to bear out these conclusions.

I have twice received the imperial mandate to form the cabinet. I concentrated my efforts to achieve national unity and to avoid internal friction accepted so far as possible the arguments of the reformists. I feel a deep responsibility for my inability to grasp adequately the meaning behind the reformists' arguments, and there is no excuse whatsoever for my lack of foresight.

Today, together with reports of the grave war situation, the voices demanding that one hundred million die heroic deaths [4] grow increasingly louder. Although those who advocate such a thing are the so-called rightists, I believe that the behind-the-scenes agitators of this are the communist elements who by this means would throw the nation in disorder and finally achieve their goal of revolution.

It seems that on the one hand some people advocate the complete destruction of America and England and on the other hand the pro-Soviet atmosphere increasingly thrives. It is said that there are those in the military who even argue that at the price of any sacrifice we should come to terms with the Soviet Union, and some think of making common cause with Yenan. [5] In such manner, all the conditions necessary for the advancement of communism both at home and abroad are growing day by day, and if the present war situation becomes increasingly disadvantageous, these conditions will develop very rapidly. Things would be different if we could say that there was a glimmer of hope for a favorable break in the war situation, but arguing on the premise that defeat is inevitable, to continue longer a war with no prospect of victory would play completely into the hands of the communists. Consequently, from the standpoint of the preservation of the national structure, I firmly believe that we must prepare the way for concluding the war at the earliest possible time. I think that the greatest obstacle to the conclusion of the war is the existence of this group in the military which has driven the country since the

[4] Literally "one hundred million gems shatter." The one hundred million refers to the population of the Japanese Empire; the shattering of gems recalls the Japanese proverb, "Better to become a gem that is shattered than a roof tile intact"; i.e., it is better to be a dead hero than a live coward. [Editor's note.]

[5] The Chinese Communists, whose capital was then in Yenan, China. [Editor's note.]

Manchurian affair until today's situation. Although they have in their hearts lost self confidence to continue the war, they will probably resist to the death in order to save face.

If we try to end the war immediately without eliminating this group, rightist and leftist civilian sympathizers, influenced by this group, would cause great disturbances in the country and I fear, would make it difficult to attain the desired objective. Consequently, if it is planned to end the war, first, as a prerequisite, the elimination of this group is essential. If this group is eliminated, the opportunistic bureaucrats and civilian elements of the right and left will disappear from sight. Because these opportunists probably do not yet have great strength of their own and can attain their goals only by using the military, if the roots are destroyed I believe that the leaves and branches will of themselves wither. Perhaps I am somewhat guilty of wishful thinking, but if these elements are eliminated might not the image of the military be completely changed and the atmosphere in America, England, and Chungking [6] become more moderate?

Originally the declared goal of America, England, and Chungking was to overthrow the Japanese militarist clique, but if the character of the military changes and its policies are revised, might not these powers begin to consider the question of the continuation of the war? Aside from this particular consideration, if the elimination of this group and the reconstruction of the military are the prerequisite condition for saving Japan from a communist revolution, I respectfully believe that Your Majesty's extraordinary bold decision is much to be desired.

[6] I.e., the Nationalist Government of China, the capital of which was then located in Chungking, China. [Editor's note.]

40

The Potsdam Proclamation

July 26, 1945

In the hope of inducing the Japanese to surrender before an invasion of the Japanese main islands and before the use of the atomic bomb, the Allies published this declaration to Japan. It has been asserted subsequently that the declaration should have (1) explicitly mentioned the atomic weapon or (2) contained a promise that the

From United States Department of State, *Foreign Relations of the United States Diplomatic Papers: The Conference of Berlin (The Potsdam Conference), 1945* (Washington, D.C.: Government Printing Office, 1960), II, 1474–1476.

Japanese might retain their Emperor if they wished after surrendering. The first Japanese response to the declaration was that they would ignore it. After two atomic bombings and the Soviet declaration of war, the Japanese agreed to accept the terms of the Potsdam Proclamation. The policies of the Allied Occupation of Japan were based upon the provisions of the Potsdam Proclamation.

PROCLAMATION BY THE HEADS OF GOVERNMENTS, UNITED STATES, CHINA AND THE UNITED KINGDOM

1. We, the President of the United States, the President of the National Government of the Republic of China and the Prime Minister of Great Britain, representing the hundreds of millions of our countrymen, have conferred and agree that Japan shall be given an opportunity to end this war.

2. The prodigious land, sea and air forces of the United States, the British Empire and of China, many times reinforced by their armies and air fleets from the west are poised to strike the final blows upon Japan. This military power is sustained and inspired by the determination of all the Allied nations to prosecute the war against Japan until she ceases to resist.

3. The result of the futile and senseless German resistance to the might of the aroused free peoples of the world stands forth in awful clarity as an example to the people of Japan. The might that now converges on Japan is immeasurably greater than that which, when applied to the resisting Nazis, necessarily laid waste to the lands, the industry and the method of life of the whole German people. The full application of our military power, backed by our resolve, *will* mean the inevitable and complete destruction of the Japanese armed forces and just as inevitably the utter devastation of the Japanese homeland.

4. The time has come for Japan to decide whether she will continue to be controlled by those self-willed milita[r]istic advisers whose unintelligent calculations have brought the Empire of Japan to the threshold of annihilation, or whether she will follow the path of reason.

5. Following are our terms. We will not deviate from them. There are no alternatives. We shall brook no delay.

6. There must be eliminated for all time the authority and influence of those who have deceived and misled the people of Japan into embarking on world conquest, for we insist that a new order of peace, security and justice will be impossible until irresponsible militarism is driven from the world.

7. Until such a new order is established *and* until there is convincing proof that Japan's war-making power is destroyed, points in Japanese territory to be designated by the Allies shall be occupied to secure the achievement of the basic objectives we are here setting forth.

8. The terms of the Cairo Declaration shall be carried out and Japanese sovereignty shall be limited to the islands of Honshu, Hokkaido, Kyushu, Shikoku and such minor islands as we determine.

9. The Japanese military forces, after being completely disarmed, shall be permitted to return to their homes with the opportunity to lead peaceful and productive lives.

10. We do not intend that the Japanese shall be enslaved as a race or destroyed as [a] nation, but stern justice shall be meted out to all war criminals, including those who have visited cruelties upon our prisoners. The Japanese government shall remove all obstacles to the revival and strength[en]ing of democratic tendencies among the Japanese people. Freedom of speech, of religion, and of thought, as well as respect for the fundamental human rights shall be established.

11. Japan shall be permitted to maintain such industries as will sustain her economy and permit the exaction of just reparations in kind, but not those industries which would enable her to re-arm for war. To this end, access to, as distinguished from control of raw materials shall be permitted. Eventual Japanese participation in world trade relations shall be permitted.

12. The occupying forces of the Allies shall be withdrawn from Japan as soon as these objectives have been accomplished and there has been established in accordance with the freely expressed will of the Japanese people a peacefully inclined and responsible government.[1]

13. We call upon the Government of Japan to proclaim now the unconditional surrender of all the Japanese armed forces, and to provide proper and adequate assurances of their good faith in such action. The alternative for Japan is prompt and utter destruction.

Potsdam, July 26, 1945

Harry S. Truman
Winston Churchill
by *H.S.T.*
President of China
by wire

[1] In an important working paper of this proclamation, this paragraph read as follows:

12. The occupying forces of the Allies shall be withdrawn from Japan as soon as these objectives have been accomplished and there has been established beyond doubt a peacefully inclined, responsible government of a character representative of the Japanese people. This may include a constitutional monarchy under the present dynasty if the peace-loving nations can be convinced of the genuine determination of such a government to follow policies of peace which will render impossible the future development of aggressive militarism in Japan.

Cf. United States Department of State, *Foreign Relations of the United States Diplomatic Papers: The Conference of Berlin (The Potsdam Conference), 1945* (Washington, D.C.: Government Printing Office, 1960), I, 899. [Editor's note.]

41

Imperial Rescript on the End of the War

August 14, 1945

The recording of the Emperor's voice which read the surrender rescript nearly fell into the hands of mutineers in the Imperial Guard who were determined to continue the war against the Allies. Fortunately the attempted coup d'état was suppressed and the rescript was broadcast. The wording of the historic statement was partly based upon the Emperor's remarks at the imperial conference in which he broke the deadlock in the cabinet over whether or not to accept the Allied terms. Note the reference to the preservation of the "structure of the Imperial State."

To Our good and loyal subjects:

After pondering deeply the general trends of the world and the actual conditions obtaining in Our Empire today, We have decided to effect a settlement of the present situation by resorting to an extraordinary measure.

We have ordered Our Government to communicate to the Governments of the United States, Great Britain, China and the Soviet Union that Our Empire accepts the provisions of their Joint Declaration [Potsdam Declaration].

To strive for the common prosperity and happiness of all nations as well as the security and well-being of Our subjects is the solemn obligation which has been handed down by Our Imperial Ancestors, and which We lay close to heart. Indeed, We declared war on America and Britain out of Our sincere desire to ensure Japan's self-preservation and the stabilization of East Asia, it being far from Our thought either to infringe upon the sovereignty of other nations or to embark upon territorial aggrandizement. But now the war has lasted for nearly four years. Despite the best that has been done by everyone—the gallant fighting of military and naval forces, the diligence and assiduity of Our servants of the State and the devoted service of Our one hundred million people, the war situation has developed not necessarily to Japan's advantage, while the general trends of the world have all turned against her interest. Moreover, the enemy has begun to employ a new and most cruel bomb, the power of which to do damage is indeed incalculable, taking the toll of many innocent lives. Should We continue to fight, it would not only result in an ultimate collapse and obliteration of the Japanese nation, but also it would lead to the total extinction of human civilization. Such being the case, how are We to save the millions of Our subjects; or to atone Ourselves before the hallowed spirits of Our Imperial Ancestors? This is the reason why We have ordered the acceptance of the provisions of the Joint Declaration of the Powers.

We cannot but express the deepest sense of regret to our Allied nations of East Asia, who have consistently co-operated with the Empire towards the emancipation of East Asia. The thought of those officers and men as well as others who have fallen in the fields of battle, those who died at their posts of duty, or those who met with untimely death and all their bereaved families, pains Our heart night and day. The welfare of the wounded and the war-sufferers, and of those who have lost their home and livelihood, are the objects of Our profound solicitude. The hardships and sufferings to which Our nation is to be subjected hereafter will be certainly great. We are keenly aware of the inmost feelings of all ye, Our subjects. However, it is according to the dictate of time and fate that We have resolved to pave the way for a grand peace for all the generations to come by enduring the unendurable and suffering what is insufferable.

Having been able to safeguard and maintain the structure of the Imperial State, We are always with ye, Our good and loyal subjects, relying upon your sincerity and integrity. Beware most strictly of any outbursts of emotion which may engender needless complications, or any fraternal contention and strife which may create confusion, lead ye astray and cause ye to lose the confidence of the world. Let the entire nation continue as one family from generation to generation, ever firm in its faith of the imperishableness of its divine land, and mindful of its heavy burden of responsibilities, and the long road before it. Unite your total strength to be devoted to the construction for the future. Cultivate the ways of rectitude; foster nobility of spirit; and work with resolution so as ye may enhance the innate glory of the Imperial State and keep pace with the progress of the world.

42

On Being a Good Loser

Yoshida Shigeru

I assumed office as Foreign Minister in the Higashikuni Cabinet on 17 September 1945, on the same day that General MacArthur's GHQ was transferred to the Dai-Ichi Sogo building across the street from the Imperial Palace. A few days later I visited Admiral Kantaro Suzuki, who had been Prime Minister at the time of the surrender. Before accepting that office, the Admiral was for many years Grand Chamberlain to the Emperor, and I had come to know him intimately in this connection through Count Makino, my father-in-law. Admiral Suzuki had been burned out of his home during a war-time raid and was then living in a friend's house. I told him I had been appointed Foreign Minister and said I had come to seek his advice as to how to set about my work: he replied that it was important to be a good winner in a war but equally important to be a good loser, and that he wanted me to remember carefully that cardinal fact. It was good advice, and I decided then and there to follow it throughout in my dealings with GHQ.

Being a good loser does not mean saying yes to everything the other party says; still less does it mean saying yes and going back on one's word later. It was obviously important to co-operate with the Occupation authorities to the best of one's power. But it seemed to me that where the men within GHQ were mistaken, through their ignorance of the actual facts concerned with my country, it was my duty to explain matters to them; and should their decision nevertheless be carried through, to abide by it until they themselves came to see that they had made a mistake. My policy, in other words, was to say whatever I felt needed saying, and to accept what transpired.

This was an attitude which General MacArthur seemed to understand perfectly, but others within GHQ seemed to consider it as one of resistance and obstruction. At least, they showed signs of regarding me as an unmanageable person; and the loss is theirs. Of course, now that the Occupation is a matter of history, we hear people boast of how they resisted the Americans during those years. But it seems to me that one should give words like resisting and resistance a definite meaning and use them according to the sense thus defined. Thus Gandhi resisted the British while they ruled India, and one may legitimately speak of the resistance which the French put up against the Germans while France was occupied during the

From Shigeru Yoshida, *The Yoshida Memoirs: The Story of Japan in Crisis*. Translated by Kenichi Yoshida. (Boston: Houghton Mifflin, 1962; London: Heinemann), pp. 58–60. Reprinted by permission. Title supplied by the editor.

Second World War. But resistance of that sort was not carried on by us during the Occupation of Japan. Our object was to remonstrate, or to explain, whenever that was deemed necessary, because we thought that such a course was for the good of the Occupation authorities and ourselves, and I believe we were justified in so thinking.

At the time of the surrender our greatest fear was that perhaps Japan might remain under Occupation for an indefinite number of years. Actually, we regained our independence after only six years and eight months, and it seems to me that we were able to attain our objective so quickly through being good losers.

When we come to consider individual cases, however, the record connot be said to have been kept up throughout. There were two sorts of Japanese who were particularly obnoxious. One consisted of those who, because they wanted to obtain some advantage through the good graces of GHQ, made extravagant presents to the men in it, or gave them lavish dinner parties, so either incurring their contempt or succeeding in actually spoiling them. Presents and dinners may be the normal outcome of the Japanese love of hospitality, but there are surely limits to such practices, and when it is a question of expecting something in return, it does not bear speaking of further. It was this kind of person who also, during the Occupation years, took whatever GHQ said, in whatever circumstances, as law, whether out of an inordinate respect for foreigners, or from a comic sense of being helplessly Japanese. It was not edifying and I hope there are fewer such people about now.

The second sort were those who, being what are called 'progressives' or radicals, made assiduous pilgrimages to GHQ, particularly at the beginning of the Occupation, to denounce and report on their fellow Japanese, no doubt activated by the desire to rid the country of what they considered were undesirable elements. They played an active part in the purges, particularly purges connected with the press and the publishing world generally. And since, as I have pointed out before, there was a good deal of the Leftist element within GHQ itself at the start of the Occupation, the two groups got together and made use of each other for the greater glory of their peculiar ideals. Our progressives and radicals might now say they were merely co-operating with the Occupation, but the fact remains that their co-operation had as its main object the promotion of those of their own set, to the indiscriminate detriment of other citizens, and, objectively considered, their actions cannot escape the censure of disloyalty and downright treachery. But enough has been said of these people.

There are some now in Japan who point to similarities between the Allied, and predominantly American, Occupation of Japan, and our Occupation of Manchuria, China and other countries of Asia—the idea apparently being that, once an Occupation régime has been established, the relationship between victors and vanquished is usually found to be the same. I regret that I cannot subscribe to this opinion. Japan's Occupation of various Asian countries, carried out by Army officers of no higher rank than colonel and more often by raw subalterns, became an object of hatred and loathing among the peoples of the occupied countries, and there is none to dispute that fact. The Americans came into our country as our enemies, but after an Occupation lasting little less than seven years, an understanding grew up between the two peoples which is remarkable in the history of the modern world.

Criticism of Americans is a right accorded even to Americans. But in the enumeration of their faults we cannot include their Occupation of Japan.

43

Diet Resolution Rescinding the Imperial Rescript on Education

June 19, 1948

In order to democratize Japan, it seemed necessary to renounce explicitly the feudalistic and militaristic ideologies that had been fostered by the government in prewar Japan.

Whereas the Diet has legalized a Basic Law of Education in accordance with the universal human principles of the Japanese Constitution, eliminating thoroughly the error of an education that would put our state and nation at the center of the universe and instead proclaiming solemnly the concepts of democratic education aimed at rearing a humanity that stands for truth and peace,

Whereas the Imperial Rescript on Education,[1] as well as the Imperial Rescript to the Army and Navy, the Imperial Rescript to Students, and the like, have thereby lost their validity.

Whereas we fear that some ill-advised elements may entertain the notion that these documents still retain their validity and wish to make clear the fact that they are no longer valid and to cause the Government to collect all copies of such documents in the possession of universities and schools,

Let it be resolved, therefore, that we shall conscientiously strive to disseminate the new educational concepts manifested by the Basic Law of Education, so that the true dignity of education may be upheld and national morals may be uplifted.

From Supreme Commander for the Allied Powers, Government Section, *Political Reorientation of Japan: September 1945 to September 1948* (Washington, D.C.: Government Printing Office, n.d. [1949?]), II, 585.

[1] See Chapter II, Selection 13.

44

79TH CONGRESS
1ST SESSION
S. J. Res. 94

IN THE SENATE OF THE UNITED STATES

SEPTEMBER 18 (legislative day, SEPTEMBER 10), 1945

Mr. RUSSELL introduced the following joint resolution; which was read twice and referred to the Committee on Military Affairs

---

JOINT RESOLUTION
Declaring that it is the policy of the United States that Emperor Hirohito of Japan be tried as a war criminal.

1   *Resolved by the Senate and House of Representatives*

2   *of the United States of America in Congress assembled,*

3   That it is hereby declared to be the policy of the

4   United States to try Hirohito, Emperor of Japan, as a war

5   criminal.

6   SEC. 2. The Supreme Commander of the Armed Forces

7   of the United States in Japan and the representatives of the

8   United States on any international body established for the

9   prosecution or trial of Japanese war criminals are hereby

10   directed to take all necessary steps toward effectuating the

11   policy announced in section 1 of this joint resolution.

[The above follows the format of the proposed resolution. The editor is grateful to Senator Richard Russell for kindly supplying a copy of this document.]

45

Rescript on the Construction of a New Japan

January 1, 1946

At a time when there was much agitation for the abolition of Japan's divine right monarchy among the Allied Powers, the Emperor renounced his divinity in this rescript. That the statement may have been written largely for foreign consumption is suggested by the fact that part of it was originally written in English and that it was approved by the Occupation before it was published. Note the references to radical tendencies and confusion of thoughts, which suggest that the throne would prove useful in maintaining internal order in Japan.

In greeting the new year we recall to mind that the Emperor Meiji proclaimed as the basis of our national policy the five clauses of the charter at the beginning of the Meiji era. The charter oath signified:

1. Deliberative assemblies shall be established and all measures of government decided in accordance with public opinion.

2. All classes high and low shall unite in vigorously carrying on the affairs of State.

3. All common people, no less than the civil and military officials, shall be allowed to fulfill their just desires so that there may not be any discontent among them.

4. All the absurd usages of old shall be broken through and equity and justice to be found in the workings of nature shall serve as the basis of action.

5. Wisdom and knowledge shall be sought throughout the world for the purpose of promoting the welfare of the Empire.

The proclamation is evident in its significance and high in its ideals. We wish to make this oath anew and restore the country to stand on its own feet again. We have to reaffirm the principles embodied in the charter and proceed unflinchingly toward elimination of misguided practices of the past; and, keeping in close touch with the desires of the people,

From United States Department of State, *Occupation of Japan: Policy and Progress* (Washington, D.C.: Government Printing Office, n.d. [1946?]), pp. 133–135.

we will construct a new Japan through thoroughly being pacific, the officials and the people alike obtaining rich culture and advancing the standard of living of the people.

The devastation of the war inflicted upon our cities the miseries of the destitute, the stagnation of trade, shortage of food and the great and growing number of the unemployed are indeed heartrending; but if the nation is firmly united in its resolve to face the present ordeal and to see civilization consistently in peace, a bright future will undoubtedly be ours, not only for our country but for the whole of humanity.

Love of the family and love of country are especially strong in this country. With more of this devotion should we now work toward love of mankind.

We feel deeply concerned to note that consequent upon the protracted war ending in our defeat our people are liable to grow restless and to fall into the slough of despond. Radical tendencies in excess are gradually spreading and the sense of morality tends to lose its hold on the people with the result that there are signs of confusion of thoughts.

We stand by the people and we wish always to share with them in their moment of joys and sorrows. The ties between us and our people have always stood upon mutual trust and affection. They do not depend upon mere legends and myths. They are not predicated on the false conception that the Emperor is divine and that the Japanese people are superior to other races and fated to rule the world.[1]

Our Government should make every effort to alleviate their trials and tribulations. At the same time, we trust that the people will rise to the occasion and will strive courageously for the solution of their outstanding difficulties and for the development of industry and culture. Acting upon a consciousness of solidarity and of mutual aid and broad tolerance in their civic life, they will prove themselves worthy of their best tradition. By their supreme endeavors in that direction they will be able to render their substantial contribution to the welfare and advancement of mankind.

The resolution for the year should be made at the beginning of the year. We expect our people to join us in all exertions looking to accomplishment of this great undertaking with an indomitable spirit.

[1] The wording of this sentence was suggested by Harold Henderson, an American official in the Civil Information and Education Section of General MacArthur's Headquarters. [Editor's note.]

46

Reform of the Japanese Governmental System
(SWNCC-228)

This document was adopted by the United States State-War-Navy Coordinating Committee (SWNCC) on January 7, 1946, and was used as a guide by the Government Section of General Mac-Arthur's Headquarters in drafting a new constitution for Japan. It is included here because it contains a scholarly analysis of the undesirable features of the Meiji Constitution (Chapter II, Selection 12), which needed to be changed. (The principal author of SWNCC-228 was Dr. Hugh Borton, an authority on Japan then in the State Department and today President of Haverford College.)

THE PROBLEM

1. To determine the constitutional reforms which the occupation authorities should insist be carried out in Japan.

FACTS BEARING ON THE PROBLEM

2. See Appendix "A."

DISCUSSION

3. See Appendix "B."

CONCLUSIONS

4. It is concluded that:

a. The Supreme Commander should indicate to the Japanese authorities that the Japanese governmental system should be reformed to accomplish the following general objectives:

1. A government responsible to an electorate based upon wide representative suffrage;

The complete text of this formerly secret document has not previously been published in the United States. The editor is grateful to the United States Department of State for making it available.

2. An executive branch of government deriving its authority from and responsible to the electorate or to a fully representative legislative body;

3. A legislative body, fully representative of the electorate, with full power to reduce, increase or reject any items in the budget or to suggest new items;

4. No budget shall become effective without the express approval of the legislative body;

5. Guarantee of fundamental civil rights to Japanese subjects and to all persons within Japanese jurisdiction;

6. The popular election or local appointment of as many of the prefectural officials as practicable;

7. The drafting and adoption of constitutional amendments or of a constitution in a manner which will express the free will of the Japanese people.

b. Though the ultimate form of government in Japan is to be established by the freely expressed will of the Japanese people, the retention of the Emperor institution in its present form is not considered consistent with the foregoing general objectives.

c. If the Japanese people decide that the Emperor Institution is not to be retained, constitutional safeguards against the institution will obviously not be required but the Supreme Commander should indicate to the Japanese that the constitution should be amended to conform to the objectives listed in *a* above and to include specific provisions:

1. That any other bodies shall possess only a temporary veto power over legislative measures, including constitutional amendments approved by the representative legislative body, and that such body shall have sole authority over financial measures;

2. That the Ministers of State or the members of a Cabinet should in all cases be civilians;

3. That the legislative body may meet at will.

d. The Japanese should be encouraged to abolish the Emperor Institution or to reform it along more democratic lines. If the Japanese decide to retain the Institution of the Emperor, however, the Supreme Commander should also indicate to the Japanese authorities that the following safeguards in addition to those enumerated in *a* and *c* above would be necessary:

1. That the Ministers of State, chosen with the advice and consent of the representative legislative body, shall form a Cabinet collectively responsible to the legislative body;

2. That when a Cabinet loses the confidence of the representative legislative body, it must either resign or appeal to the electorate;

3. The Emperor shall act in all important matters only on the advice of the Cabinet;

4. The Emperor shall be deprived of all military authority such as that provided in Articles XI, XII, XIII, and XIV of Chapter I of the Constitution;

5. The Cabinet shall advise and assist the Emperor;

6. The entire income of the Imperial Household shall be turned into the public treasury and the expenses of the Imperial Household shall be appropriated by the legislature in the annual budget.

5. Only as a last resort should the Supreme Commander order the Japanese Government to effect the above listed reforms, as the knowledge that they had been imposed by the Allies would materially reduce the possibility of their acceptance and support by the Japanese people for the future.

6. The effectiveness of governmental reforms in preventing the re-surgence of military control in Japan will depend in a large measure upon the acceptance by the Japanese people of the entire program. In the implementation of allied policy on the reform of the Japanese Govern-ment, the Supreme Commander for the Allied Forces must take into ac-count the problems of sequence and timing, as well as measures which might be adopted to prepare the Japanese people to accept the changes, in order to insure that the reforms are lasting in strengthening representa-tive government in Japan.

7. This paper should not be released for publication. The eventual release of a statement of allied policy on the reform of the Japanese Gov-ernment should be coordinated with the Supreme Commander for the Allied Powers in order not to impede the accomplishment of such re-forms in Japan itself.

RECOMMENDATIONS

8. It is recommended that:

a. Upon approval by the State-War-Navy Coordinating Commit-tee of the Conclusions in paragraphs 4, 5, 6, and 7 above:

1. The report, as amended, be forwarded to the State, War and Navy Departments and the Joint Chiefs of Staff for information; and

2. The report, as amended, be forwarded to the American Rep-resentative on the Far Eastern Commission for his guidance in negotiations with other members of the Commission on the formu-lation of an Allied policy on the reform of the Japanese Govern-ment.

b. No part of this report be released to the press at present.

FACTS BEARING ON THE PROBLEM

1. The Potsdam Declaration provides that:

The Japanese Government shall remove all obstacles to the revival and strengthening of democratic tendencies among the Japanese people. Freedom of speech, of religion, and of thought, as well as respect for the fundamental human rights shall be established.

The occupying forces of the Allies shall be withdrawn from Japan as soon as these objectives [as set forth in the Potsdam Declaration] have been accomplished and there has been established in accordance with the freely expressed will of the Japanese people a peacefully inclined and responsible government.

2. The Allied note of August 11 to the Japanese Government stated that:

The ultimate form of government of Japan shall, in accordance with the Potsdam Declaration, be established by the freely expressed will of the Japanese people.

3. One of the ultimate objectives of the United States in regard to Japan is stated in United States Initial Post-Defeat Policy Relating to Japan, to be:

To bring about the eventual establishment of a peaceful and responsible government which will respect the rights of other states and will support the objectives of the United States as reflected in the ideals and principles of the Charter of the United Nations. The United States desires that this government should conform as closely as may be to principles of democratic self-government but it is not the responsibility of the Allied Powers to impose upon Japan any form of government not supported by the freely expressed will of the people.

DISCUSSION

1. The Potsdam Declaration stipulates that the occupying forces shall not be withdrawn from Japan until a "peacefully inclined and responsible government" has been established. Past declarations of the United Nations, and the clear intention of the Allies permanently to eliminate Japanese practices and institutions which have made that country a danger to other nations, clearly indicate that that stipulation refers not merely to the particular Japanese Government which the Allies recognize prior to withdrawal, but also to the nature of Japan's governmental institutions. Although "the ultimate form of government of Japan" is to be determined by the "freely expressed will of the Japanese people," the Allies, in accordance with the above provision and as a part of their over-all program

for the demilitarization of Japan, are fully empowered to insist that Japanese basic law be so altered as to provide that in practice the government is responsible to the people, and that the civil is supreme over the military branch of the government.

2. The existing Japanese governmental system, resting on the Constitution, the Imperial House Law, basic statutes and Imperial Ordinances supplementary to the Constitution, and customs and practices observed virtually as law, has shown itself unsuited to the development of peaceful practices and policies primarily by reason of the defects described in the following paragraphs.

3. *The Absence of an Effective System of Responsibility of the Government to the People.*

a. There are of course several ways in which this responsibility may be effected. In the United States the executive government is directly responsible to the President, who is himself elected by the people and is limited by the judicially enforced Constitution from encroaching upon the rights of the judiciary and the congress. In Great Britain the executive government is nominally responsible to an hereditary monarch, but actually it is responsible to the House of Commons, which is elected by the people. While in theory the power of the Parliament is absolute, in practice it recognizes the independence of the courts and certain rights of the executive.

b. The present Japanese Constitution was drawn up with the dual purpose of, on the one hand, stilling popular clamor for representative institutions, and on the other of fortifying and perpetuating the centralized and autocratic governmental structure which its framers, the Meiji leaders, believed necessary for Japan's continued existence and development in the modern world. Consistent with this latter purpose, power was retained in the hands of a small group of personal advisors around the Throne, and the people's elected representatives in the Diet were given only limited supervisory powers over legislation. When a Cabinet falls the new Prime Minister, who selects his own Cabinet, is appointed by the Emperor not automatically from the leadership of the majority party in the Lower House but on the recommendation of these advisors, originally the Genro and more recently a council of former prime ministers. The nature and composition of a new government, consequently, was determined by the balance of forces around the Throne rather than by the majority view in the Lower House.

c. This lack of responsibility of the Cabinet to the Lower House was also the result of the Diet's limited powers over the budget. The Constitution provides (Article 71) that if a budget is rejected by the Diet, the budget of the preceding year automatically goes into effect. Consequently, even though the Prime Minister failed a vote of confidence in the Lower House he knew that he was assured of a budget equal at least to that of the current year.

d. Although the passing of general laws pertaining to the internal affairs of the nation are within its province, in practice most bills are introduced by members of the Cabinet, in whose selection the Diet has no part. The power to declare war, make peace, and conclude treaties are Imperial prerogatives over which the Parliament can exert only the most indirect influence because of its inability to control the Cabinet and the Privy Council which, together with the Keeper of the Privy Seal, the Minister of the Imperial Household and others close to the Throne, advise the Emperor on these matters. The Diet has no power over dynastic affairs, it cannot initiate amendments to the Constitution, it cannot convene of its own accord, and it may be prorogued for a period up to fifteen days any number of times during a session by the Emperor on the advice of the Prime Minister.

e. Although the Diet possesses indirect means of impressing its views upon the government which have proven more effective in practice than the direct controls, budgetary or otherwise, at its disposal, even these indirect methods have been of limited value. Its power to address the Throne or make representations to the government has little practical significance, because neither is bound to respond to its representations. Its power to establish committees of inquiry on any matters of state is limited by its inability to compel the attendance of witnesses. Interpellations and questions from the floor can embarrass a Cabinet and have been among the Diet's most effective weapons, but ministers are free to make evasive replies or to refuse to answer at all on the ground of "military security" or "diplomatic security" or as "contrary to public interest." Although both Houses are empowered by custom to pass resolutions on matters within their jurisdiction, and resolutions of no confidence by the Lower House prior to 1931 frequently led to the resignation of a cabinet or of the ministers thus censured, such resolutions have also frequently led to the dissolution of the House and a new election which, although it supported the House against the government, was not followed by the latter's resignation. Nevertheless, during the past fifteen years, criticism of the government from the floor or in address or representation resolutions have been virtually the only means by which members could hope to influence policy.

4. *The Dual Nature of Japanese Government which Permits the Military to Act Independently of the Civil Government and of the Parliament.*

a. The supreme command of the army and navy, and the power to determine their peacetime standing, are stated in the Constitution to be among the Emperor's prerogatives. This has been interpreted by the military services to mean that they are responsible solely to the Emperor and may act independently of the Cabinet and the Diet in matters of military concern. Only in matters of major importance have they felt obliged to seek the Emperor's approval, frequently interpreting and expanding that approval to suit their own ends. The right of direct access to the Emperor possessed by the Chiefs of Staff and the Ministers of the Army and Navy, a privilege enjoyed by the Prime Minister but by no other member of the Cabinet, has been an indispensable condition of the services' independence of action.

b. The ability of the military to affect government policy both within and without the area of their assigned responsibilities is further enhanced by the provision, based on an Imperial Ordinance of 1898, that the Minister of War and the Minister of the Navy must be a general or a lieutenant-general or an admiral or vice-admiral respectively on the active list. This provision has been repeatedly used by the military services to overthrow an existing cabinet by requiring the resignation of the Minister of War or the Minister of the Navy or to prevent the formation of a new Cabinet by the refusal to permit eligible officers to fill these posts. Divided responsibility between the military and civil authorities in the Japanese Government, beside giving the services undue weight in the determination of policy, has on numerous occasions prevented the civil government, which of its own accord might have acted in good faith, from fulfilling its international commitments.

5. *The Excessive Power of the House of Peers and the Privy Council.*

a. Except for the fact that financial bills must be initiated in the Lower House, and that the Lower House may be dissolved by the Emperor at any time whereas the Upper House can only be prorogued, the legislative powers of both Houses are the same. Inasmuch as the House of Peers is composed approximately one-half of the nobility, one-fourth of persons elected by and from the highest taxpayers and one-fourth of Imperial appointees, its equal powers with the popularly elected Lower House gives representatives of the propertied and conservative classes in Japan an undue influence on legislation.

b. The Privy Council, composed of a president, a vice-president, twenty-four councilors appointed by the Emperor for life, and the members of the cabinet *ex officio*, serves as the supreme advisory body to the Emperor. The ordinance defining its powers, promulgated in 1890, stipulated that generally speaking its advice was to be solicited by the Emperor only on constitutional questions, international treaties and agreements, and prior to the issuance of emergency Imperial ordinances. Gradually, however the Council has extended its activities and increased its power until in recent decades it has come to resemble a "third chamber," with broad supervisory powers over the executive in both foreign and domestic matters. It has frequently opposed the Cabinet on policy questions, and on several occasions has forced the downfall of Cabinets possessing the confidence of the Diet. Owing no political responsibility to the Diet or to the people for its activities, and yet exerting important influence over the entire affairs of the state, the Privy Council as presently constituted has proved an important barrier to the development of a sound parliamentary system.

6. *Inadequate Provision for the Protection of Civil Rights.*

a. The Japanese people have been deprived in practice, particularly during the past fifteen years, of many of the civil rights guaranteed them in the Constitution. Qualification of the constitutional guarantees by the phrase "except in the cases provided by law" or "unless according to law" has permitted the enactment of statutes involving wholesale infringement of these rights. At the same time Japanese courts have shown themselves subservient to social, even if not to direct governmental, pressures, and have failed signally to administer impartial justice.

b. To rectify this situation, General MacArthur, on October 4, 1945, ordered the Japanese Government to abolish all measures which restricted freedom of speech, of thought and of religion and to report to him by October 15, 1945, on all steps which had been taken to assure civil rights to the people.

c. In one other respect the Japanese Constitution falls short of other constitutions in its guarantee of fundamental rights. Instead of granting those rights to all persons it stipulates that they shall apply only to Japanese subjects, leaving other persons in Japan without their protection.

7. To have lasting value and hence to be most effective, the constitutional and administrative reforms necessary to correct the defects in Japan's governmental system should be initiated and carried into effect by the Japanese Government out of a desire to eliminate elements of the national structure which have brought Japan to its present pass and to comply with the provisions of the Potsdam Declaration. Failing such spontaneous action by the Japanese, the Supreme Commander should indicate the reforms which this Government considers necessary before it can consider a "peacefully inclined and responsible government" to have been established in Japan, a condition of the occupation forces' withdrawal. Only as a last resort should a formal instruction be issued to the Japanese Government specifying in detail the reforms to be effected.

8. The combination of new provisions in the Constitution that (1) the government shall be responsible to an electorate based upon wide representative suffrage, (2) that the executive branch of government shall

derive its authority from and be responsible to the electorate or to a fully representative legislative body and (3) when a Cabinet loses the confidence of the representative legislative body it must resign or appeal to the electorate would ensure the development of a truly representative government responsible to the people. This direct responsibility of the government to the people would be further strengthened by conferring full budgetary powers on the representative legislative body. If the government lost the confidence of the representative legislative body, it would be forced to resign at the end of the fiscal year because of the lack of funds.

9. Explicit provision in the Constitution for the guarantee of fundamental civil rights both to Japanese subjects and to all persons within Japanese jurisdiction would create a healthy condition for the development of democratic ideas and would provide foreigners in Japan with a degree of protection which they have not heretofore enjoyed. The position of a representative legislative body would be further strengthened by granting to the Diet the right to meet at will and allowing any other organ of the government only a temporary veto over legislative measures approved by the legislative body, including amendments to the constitution. The popular election or local appointment of as many of the prefectural officials as practicable would lessen the political power formerly possessed by the Home Minister as a result of his appointment of governors of prefectures. At the same time it would further encourage the development of genuinely representative local government.

10. Although the authority and influence of the military in Japan's governmental structure will presumably disappear with the abolition of the Japanese armed forces, formal action permanently subordinating the military services to the civil government by requiring that the ministers of state or the members of a Cabinet must, in all cases, be civilians would be advisable.

11. While this Government is anxious to encourage the Japanese either to abolish the Imperial Institution or to reform it along more democratic lines, the question of the retention of the Imperial Institution will have to be left to the Japanese to decide for themselves. If the Imperial Institution is retained, many of the changes recommended above, such as the provisions for the direct responsibility of the government to the people through granting full budgetary powers to the representative legislative body and the requirement that only civilians serve as ministers of state or the members of a Cabinet in all cases, will go far towards reducing the power and influence of the Imperial Institution. Further safeguards must be established to prevent the resurgence of "dual government" in Japan and the use of the Emperor by nationalistic and militaristic groups to threaten the future peace in the Pacific. Those safeguards should include provisions that (1) the Emperor act in all important matters only

on the advice of the Cabinet, (2) the Emperor be deprived of all military authority such as that provided in Articles XI, XII, XIII and XIV of Chapter I of the Constitution, (3) the Cabinet shall advise and assist the Emperor, (4) the entire income of the Imperial Household shall be turned into the public treasury and the expense of the Imperial Household shall be appropriated by the legislature in the annual budget.

12. There are a number of desirable reforms in the Japanese governmental system which have not been specified in the conclusions, such as strengthening of the prefectural and municipal assemblies, and revision of the election laws to eliminate dishonest election practices. It is further believed that measures to strengthen the local assemblies and effect a thoroughgoing reform of the election system can be safely left, and would be better left, to be initiated by a genuinely representative national government at Tokyo, whose establishment the reforms specified in this paper should ensure. Elections during the occupation period will, presumably, be adequately supervised by the occupation forces.

SUGGESTED READING

Baerwald, Hans H. *The Purge of Japanese Leaders under the Occupation.* Berkeley: University of California Press, 1959, paperback.

Ball, W. Macmahon. *Japan: Enemy or Ally?* New York: John Day, 1949.

Bisson, T. A. *Prospects of Democracy in Japan.* New York: Macmillan, 1949.

Bisson, T. A., *Zaibatsu Dissolution in Japan.* Berkeley: University of California Press, 1954.

Blakeslee, George H. *A History of the Far Eastern Commission.* Washington, D.C.: Government Printing Office, 1953, paperback.

Borton, Hugh. *Japan's Modern Century.* New York: Ronald, 1955.

Brines, Russell. *MacArthur's Japan.* Philadelphia: Lippincott, 1948.

Butow, Robert J. C. *Japan's Decision to Surrender.* Stanford: Stanford University Press, 1954.

Cohen, Jerome B. *Japan's Economy in War and Reconstruction.* Minneapolis: University of Minnesota Press, 1949.

Colbert, Evelyn. *The Left Wing in Japanese Politics.* New York: Institute of Pacific Relations, 1952.

Dore, Ronald P. *Land Reform in Japan.* New York: Oxford University Press, 1959.

Fearey, Robert. *The Occupation of Japan: The Second Phase, 1948–1950.* New York: Macmillan, 1950.

Feis, Herbert. *Japan Subdued: The Atom Bomb and the End of the War in the Pacific.* Princeton: Princeton University Press, 1961.

Fogelman, Edwin, ed. *Hiroshima: The Decision to Use the A-Bomb.* New York: Scribner, 1964, paperback.

Gayn, Mark. *Japan Diary.* New York: Sloane, 1948.

Gibney, Frank. *Five Gentlemen of Japan: The Portrait of a Nation's Character.* New York: Farrar, Straus & Giroux, 1953, paperback.

Hall, Robert King. *Education for a New Japan*. New Haven: Yale University Press, 1949.

Haring, Douglas G., ed., *Japan's Prospect*. Cambridge: Harvard University Press, 1946.

Hersey, John. *Hiroshima*. New York: Knopf, 1946.

Johnstone, W. C. *The Future of Japan*. New York: Oxford University Press, 1945.

Jones, F. C., Borton, Hugh, and Pearn, B. R. *The Far East: 1946–1949*. London: Oxford University Press, 1955.

Kawai, Kazuo. *Japan's American Interlude*. Chicago: University of Chicago Press, 1960.

Kelley, Frank, and Ryan, Cornelius. *Star Spangled Mikado*. New York: McBride, 1947.

Lattimore, Owen. *Solution in Asia*. Boston: Little, Brown, 1945.

MacArthur, Douglas. *Reminiscences*. New York: McGraw-Hill, 1964.

Martin, Edwin M. *The Allied Occupation of Japan*. New York: The Institute of Pacific Relations, 1948.

Mears, Helen. *Mirror for Americans: Japan*. Boston: Houghton Mifflin, 1948.

Moseley, Leonard. *Hirohito: Emperor of Japan*. Englewood Cliffs, N.J.: Prentice-Hall, 1966.

Roth, Andrew. *Dilemma in Japan*. Boston: Little, Brown, 1945.

Sebald, William. *With MacArthur in Japan: A Personal History of the Occupation*. New York: Norton, 1965.

Supreme Commander for the Allied Powers, Government Section. *The Political Reorientation of Japan: September 1945 to September 1948*. Washington, D.C.: Government Printing Office, n.d. [1949?].

Takagi Yasaka. *Toward International Understanding*. Tokyo: Kenkyusha, 1954.

Textor, Robert B. *Failure in Japan*. New York: John Day, 1951.

Wakefield, Harold. *New Paths for Japan*. New York: Oxford University Press, 1948.

Whitney, Courtney. *MacArthur: His Rendezvous with History*. New York: Knopf, 1956.

Wildes, Harry Emerson. *Typhoon in Tokyo: The Occupation and Its Aftermath*. New York: Macmillan, 1954.

Yoshida Shigeru. *The Yoshida Memoirs: The Story of Japan in Crisis*. Boston: Houghton Mifflin, 1962.

Democracy in Japan

The Cold War made it impossible for the United States and the Soviet Union to agree on peace terms for Japan, and in 1951, when the United States urged Japan to sign a peace treaty which was opposed by the Soviet Union, the Japanese were divided on what to do. The Occupation had lasted for six years, and the American-sponsored treaty would restore sovereignty and independence to Japan. The proposed settlement, however, also included a mutual security pact between Japan and the United States which would allow the continued maintenance of American military bases in Japan. The conservatives (Liberal Party and Democratic Party) favored signing both the peace treaty and the accompanying security treaty. The Socialists opposed the security pact, which they regarded as a provocative military alliance against the Soviet Union, especially dangerous to Japan in view of the war then raging in Korea. The Socialists divided on the question of the peace settlement, those opposing both the peace treaty and the security pact forming the left wing, and those favoring the peace treaty but opposing the security pact becoming the right wing.

The governments of fifty-five states were invited to the peace conference in San Francisco to sign the Japanese peace treaty proposed by Mr. John Foster Dulles (Selection 47). China was not invited because of American opposition to the Communist regime and British rejection of the Nationalist government. The Soviet proposals that Communist China participate, that the disarmament of Japan be guaranteed, and that democratic freedoms be ensured by the treaty were rejected, and the Soviet bloc refused to adhere to the treaty. On September 8, 1951, the representatives of forty-eight Allies and Japan signed the Treaty of San Francisco. At about the same time, the United States negotiated security treaties with Japan, the Philippines, and Australia and New Zealand (ANZUS pact). Although the conference was hailed as a success for American diplomacy, distrust of Japan continued, and Japan remained technically at war with the Soviet Union and China. When the treaty went into effect in April, 1952, the Occupation ended, and Japan was again sovereign and independent, but American troops remained in the country under the terms of the security pact. In 1952 Japan made a peace treaty with Nationalist China. Following the lead of the United States, Japan did not recognize the Peking regime. The Japanese government, however, encouraged the growth of trade with mainland China. In 1956 the USSR and Japan issued a joint peace declaration, but a dispute over the Soviet-occupied Southern Kuriles and neighboring islands has thus far delayed the making of a Soviet-Japanese peace treaty. In the same year, Japan was admitted to membership in the United Nations.

In 1955 the right- and left-wing Socialists united, stimulating the conservative Liberal and Democratic Parties to merge. The new Liberal-Democratic Party has governed Japan from 1955 until today. Even the widespread unpopularity of the 1960 security pact did not cause it to lose lower house seats in the election of that year. The "income-doubling" program of Premier Ikeda and unprecedented economic prosperity help to explain the nearly two-thirds majority which the Liberal Democratic Party has managed to maintain in both houses of the Diet.

Internal disputes over ideology and leadership have continued to afflict the Socialist Party. In 1959 the pro-Communist tendencies of the left wing and the party's subservience to the Sōhyō labor confederation provoked the secession of a group which formed the Democratic-Socialist Party. The Democratic-Socialists have, however, enjoyed very little success at the polls. The Socialist Party has been rent by a dispute over "structural reform," a program for raising living standards by parliamentary methods without necessarily awaiting a socialist take-over of the government. The continuing failure of the Socialists to appeal to other groups besides organized labor suggests that it will be some time before they can even hope to capture a majority in either house of the Diet. The rapidly growing Soka Gakkai, a highly disciplined laymen's organization of Nichiren Buddhists, has recently entered politics. Its political party, the Kōmeitō, sponsors candidates for local assemblies and the upper house of the Diet, where it now holds twenty seats, and its increasing power is a source of concern for the other parties.

Experience with atomic bombs and awareness of the vulnerability of their great cities to air attack explain much of the appeal of neutralism to the Japanese. Many fear that American air bases in Japan could not effectively protect the cities from air attack, but, on the contrary, tend to provoke Chinese and Russian hostility. These sentiments have been capitalized upon by the Socialists and Communists, who oppose the alliance with America and advocate friendlier relations with the Communist bloc. The neutralists were heartened in 1959 by the Tokyo District Court's decision that the establishment of American military bases in

Greeting Mr. Dulles

In January 1951, President Truman's envoy, Mr. John Foster Dulles, came to Japan to make arrangements for a peace treaty. The Socialists favored a peace treaty with all major powers, the Liberal government of Premier Yoshida favored a pro-American treaty, and the Democrats advocated the establishment of a self-defense force. (From left to right: Dulles, Tomabeji [Democrat], Prime Minister Yoshida [Liberal], Suzuki [Socialist].

Japan contravened the disarmament clause (Article 9) of the Constitution. However, the Japanese Supreme Court overruled the lower court and asserted the constitutional right of the government to make such arrangements for the national defense (Selection 48).

The Socialists opposed the revised U.S.-Japan security treaty in 1960. When the Liberal-Democrats in the lower house approved the treaty at midnight, May 19–20, 1960, while the Socialists were boycotting the session, the latter accused the Kishi government of trampling on parliamentary democracy. The opposition parties (Socialists, Democratic-Socialists, and Communists) demanded that Premier Kishi resign, that the lower house be dissolved, and that ratification of the treaty be delayed until after a general election (Selection 49). Mass street demonstrations of labor unionists and students and strikes were staged to reinforce these demands. The anti-Kishi movement began to assume an anti-American color when President Eisenhower announced that he intended to visit Japan in accordance with long-standing plans. After a coed was killed during a clash of students and police at the Diet building in June, Premier

Kishi requested that Mr. Eisenhower postpone his visit. The new security pact was ratified, but the unpopular Kishi had to resign in favor of his intraparty rival, Ikeda Hayato. During the ensuing lower house electoral campaign, the Chairman of the Socialist Party, Asanuma Inejiro, was stabbed to death by a rightist youth. The turbulence of politics in 1960 gradually subsided in subsequent years as leftist groups were increasingly plagued with internal disunity.

Normal diplomatic relations with Korea, Japan's former colony, were difficult to establish because of the existence of two rival governments in that divided country, reparations claimed by the Koreans, and disputes over fishing rights. The United States, which had very friendly relations with both South Korea and Japan, wished to see them cooperate in resisting communism in Asia. Not until 1965 did the Japanese and South Koreans sufficiently overcome their historic resentments to agree on a treaty settling Korean claims and making possible the establishment of permanent diplomatic missions in Seoul and Tokyo.

All Japanese are aware that their present economic prosperity is heavily dependent on foreign trade. The United States is their best customer, but American pressures to restrict Japanese imports and the protectionist policies of the European Common Market have stimulated the Japanese to expand their trade with Latin America, Africa, Southeast Asia, and Communist China. The escalation of the Vietnam conflict in 1965 was regarded with distress by the Japanese. They feared that the United States, which had large air and naval bases in Japan and Okinawa, might somehow involve Japan in the conflict. Indeed, America was urging Japan to assume greater responsibility for her own defense and the economic strengthening of the non-Communist countries of Asia. Japan was willing to play a more active role in world affairs and had already begun a modest foreign aid program, consisting of loans, grants, technical assistance, and a peace corps program. At the same time, the Japanese business community, which dominated the conservative government, hoped for increased trade with Communist China as well as the United States and showed no enthusiasm for military adventures.

47

Treaty of Peace with Japan

September 8, 1951

Whereas the Allied Powers and Japan are resolved that henceforth their relations shall be those of nations which, as sovereign equals, co-operate in friendly association to promote their common welfare and to maintain international peace and security, and are therefore desirous of concluding a Treaty of Peace which will settle questions still outstanding as a result of the existence of a state of war between them;

Whereas Japan for its part declares its intention to apply for membership in the United Nations and in all circumstances to conform to the principles of the Charter of the United Nations; to strive to realize the objectives of the Universal Declaration of Human Rights; to seek to create within Japan conditions of stability and well-being as defined in Articles 55 and 56 of the Charter of the United Nations and already initiated by post-surrender Japanese legislation; and in public and private trade and commerce to conform to internationally accepted fair practices;

Whereas the Allied Powers welcome the intentions of Japan set out in the foregoing paragraph;

The Allied Powers and Japan have therefore determined to conclude the present Treaty of Peace, and have accordingly appointed the under-signed Plenipotentiaries, who, after presentation of their full powers, found in good and due form, have agreed in the following provisions:

CHAPTER I. PEACE

Article 1. (*a*) The state of war between Japan and each of the Allied Powers is terminated as from the date on which the present Treaty comes into force between Japan and the Allied Power concerned as provided for in Article 23.

(*b*) The Allied Powers recognize the full sovereignty of the Japanese people over Japan and its territorial waters.

Excerpts from United States Department of State, *United States Treaties and Other International Agreements* (Washington, D.C.: Government Printing Office, 1955), III, 3169–3191. Chapters IV–VII are not reproduced here.

CHAPTER II. TERRITORY

Article 2. (*a*) Japan, recognizing the independence of Korea, renounces all right, title and claim to Korea, including the islands of Quelpart, Port Hamilton and Dagelet.

(*b*) Japan renounces all right, title and claim to Formosa and the Pescadores.

(*c*) Japan renounces all right, title and claim to the Kurile Islands, and to that portion of Sakhalin and the islands adjacent to it over which Japan acquired sovereignty as a consequence of the Treaty of Portsmouth of September 5, 1905.

(*d*) Japan renounces all right, title and claim in connection with the League of Nations Mandate System, and accepts the action of the United Nations Security Council of April 2, 1947, extending the trusteeship system to the Pacific Islands formerly under mandate to Japan.

(*e*) Japan renounces all claim to any right or title to or interest in connection with any part of the Antarctic area, whether deriving from the activities of Japanese nationals or otherwise.

(*f*) Japan renounces all right, title and claim to the Spratly Islands and to the Paracel Islands.

Article 3. Japan will concur in any proposal of the United States to the United Nations to place under its trusteeship system, with the United States as the sole administering authority, Nansei Shoto south of 29° north latitude (including the Ryukyu Islands and the Daito Islands), Nanpo Shoto south of Sofu Gan (including the Bonin Islands, Rosario Island and the Volcano Islands) and Parece Vela and Marcus Island. Pending the making of such a proposal and affirmative action thereon, the United States will have the right to exercise all and any powers of administration, legislation and jurisdiction over the territory and inhabitants of these islands, including their territorial waters.

Article 4. (*a*) Subject to the provisions of paragraph (*b*) of this Article, the disposition of property of Japan and of its nationals in the areas referred to in Article 2, and their claims, including debts, against the authorities presently administering such areas and the residents (including juridical persons) thereof, and the disposition in Japan of property of such authorities and residents, and of claims, including debts, of such authorities and residents against Japan and its nationals, shall be the subject of special arrangements between Japan and such authorities. The property of any of the Allied Powers or its nationals in the areas referred to in Article 2 shall, insofar as this has not already been done, be returned by the administering authority in the condition in which it now exists. (The term nationals whenever used in the present Treaty includes juridical persons.)

(*b*) Japan recognizes the validity of dispositions of property of Japan and Japanese nationals made by or pursuant to directives of the United States Military Government in any of the areas referred to in Articles 2 and 3.

(*c*) Japanese owned submarine cables connecting Japan with territory removed from Japanese control pursuant to the present Treaty shall be equally divided, Japan retaining the Japanese terminal and adjoining half of the cable, and the detached territory the remainder of the cable and connecting terminal facilities.

CHAPTER III. SECURITY

Article 5. (*a*) Japan accepts the obligations set forth in Article 2 of the Charter of the United Nations, and in particular the obligations

(i) to settle its international disputes by peaceful means in such a manner that international peace and security, and justice, are not endangered;

(ii) to refrain in its international relations from the threat or use of force against the territorial integrity or political independence of any State or in any other manner inconsistent with the Purposes of the United Nations;

(iii) to give the United Nations every assistance in any action it takes in accordance with the Charter and to refrain from giving assistance to any State against which the United Nations may take preventive or enforcement action.

(*b*) The Allied Powers confirm that they will be guided by the principles of Article 2 of the Charter of the United Nations in their relations with Japan.

(*c*) The Allied Powers for their part recognize that Japan as a sovereign nation possesses the inherent right of individual or collective self-defense referred to in Article 51 of the Charter of the United Nations and that Japan may voluntarily enter into collective security arrangements.[1]

Article 6. (*a*) All occupation forces of the Allied Powers shall be withdrawn from Japan as soon as possible after the coming into force of the present Treaty, and in any case not later that 90 days thereafter. Nothing in this provision shall, however, prevent the stationing or retention of foreign armed forces in Japanese territory under or in consequence of any bilateral or multilateral agreements which have been or may be made between one or more of the Allied Powers, on the one hand, and Japan on the other.

[1] This provision is notable because it encouraged Japan to rearm in spite of the renunciation of war and arms in Article 9 of the new Japanese Constitution. See Selection 48. [Editor's note.]

(*b*) The provisions of Article 9 of the Potsdam Proclamation of July 26, 1945, dealing with the return of Japanese military forces to their homes, to the extent not already completed, will be carried out.

(*c*) All Japanese property for which compensation has not already been paid, which was supplied for the use of the occupation forces and which remains in the possession of those forces at the time of the coming into force of the present Treaty, shall be returned to the Japanese Government within the same 90 days unless other arrangements are made by mutual agreement. . . .

48

Japan Supreme Court Decision in the Sunakawa Case

December 16, 1959

The arrest of demonstrators who opposed the enlargement of an American air base at Sunakawa (Tachikawa), near Tokyo, resulted in the sensational decision of the Tokyo District Court that the U.S.-Japan security treaty was invalid because the stationing of American forces in Japan violated Article 9, the disarmament clause, of the Japanese Constitution. (See Appendix A.) When the case was appealed to the Japanese Supreme Court, the decision of the lower court was quashed. The Sunakawa decision is significant not only because of the interpretation of Article 9, which has implications concerning Japanese rearmament, but also because it defines limits on the scope of judicial review.

MAIN TEXT

Judgment of the Original Court shall be quashed.
The case shall be remanded to the Tokyo District Court.

REASONS

Regarding the substance of the appeal submitted by Mr. Satao Nomura, Chief Procurator, Tokyo District Procurator's Office:

From *Judgment upon Case of the So-Called "Sunakawa Case"* (Tokyo: General Secretariat, Supreme Court of Japan, 1960), pp. 2–8. The present excerpt does not include supplementary and individual opinions.

The substance of the original judgment is that Article 2 of the Special Criminal Law Enacted in Consequence of the Administrative Agreement under Article III of the Security Treaty between Japan and the United States of America is null and void, as it contradicts Article 31 of the Constitution on the premise that the stationing of the United States armed forces in Japan contravenes the provisions of the first part of paragraph 2, Article 9 of the Constitution and, therefore, cannot be permitted to stand.

1. The Court will first examine the meaning of the first part of paragraph 2, Article 9 of the Constitution. It may be stated at the beginning that Article 9 of the Constitution was promulgated with a sincere desire for lasting peace by the people of Japan who, in consequence of the acceptance of the Potsdam Declaration as a result of the defeat of our country and reflecting upon the errors of militaristic activities committed by the government in the past, have firmly resolved that never again shall we be visited with the horrors of war through the action of the government. In conjunction with the spirit of international cooperation expressed in the Preamble and paragraph 2, Article 98 of the Constitution, it is an embodiment of the concept of pacifism which characterizes the Japanese Constitution. The Constitution proclaims in paragraph 1 of Article 9 that "the Japanese people sincerely aspire to an international peace based on justice and order," and that "the Japanese people forever renounce war as a sovereign right of the nation and the threat or use of force as means of settling international disputes." Under paragraph 2 of the same Article it is further provided that "In order to accomplish the aim of the preceding paragraph, land, sea, and air forces, as well as other war potential, will never be maintained. The right of belligerency of the state will not be recognized."

Thus, this Article renounces the so-called war and prohibits the maintenance of the so-called war potential, but certainly there is nothing in it which would deny the right of self-defense inherent in our nation as a sovereign power. The pacifism advocated in our Constitution was never intended to mean defenselessness or non-resistance.

As it is clear from the Preamble of the Constitution, we, the people of Japan, desire to occupy an honored place in international society, which is striving for the preservation of peace and the banishment of tyranny and slavery, oppression and intolerance for all time from the earth, and affirm that we have the right, along with and in the same manner as all the people of the world, to live in peace, free from fear and want.

In view of this it is only natural for our country, in the exercise of powers inherent in a state, to maintain peace and security, to take whatever measures may be necessary for self-defense, and to preserve its very existence. We, the people of Japan, do not maintain the so-called war potential provided in paragraph 2, Article 9 of the Constitution, but we have

determined to supplement the shortcomings in our national defense resulting therefrom by trusting in the justice and faith of the peace loving people of the world, and thereby preserve our peace and existence.

This, however, does not necessarily mean that our recourse is limited
to such military security measures as may be undertaken by an organ of
the United Nations, such as the Security Council, as stated in the original
decision. It is needless to say that we are free to choose whatever method
or means deemed appropriate to accomplish our objectives in the light
of the actual international situation, as long as such measures are for the
purpose of preserving the peace and security of our country. Article 9
of the Constitution does not at all prohibit our country from seeking a
guarantee from another country in order to maintain the peace and
security of the country.

Now, therefore, let us consider the legal intent of paragraph 2 in the
light of the purport of Article 9 elucidated above. It is entirely proper
to interpret that the prohibition of the maintenance of war potential contained in this paragraph was intended for the purpose of preventing Japan
from maintaining the so-called war potential of its own, exercising its
own control and command over the same, and thereby instigating a war
of aggression renounced forever in the first paragraph of the Article.
Putting aside the question of whether paragraph 2 prohibits the maintenance of war potential even for self-defense, what has been prohibited
by this paragraph is the possession of war potential of our own over which
we can exercise the right of command and supervision. In final analysis,
it means the war potential of our country; and consequently, it may be
properly construed that the provision of paragraph 2 does not include
foreign armed forces even if they are to be stationed in our country.

2. The next point in issue is whether the stationing of the United
States armed forces in Japan is contrary to the purport of Article 9;
paragraph 2, Article 98; and the Preamble of the Constitution. Inasmuch
as the stationing of the United States troops in Japan is predicated upon
the Security Treaty between Japan and the United States, now under consideration, determination of the constitutionality of this treaty must of
necessity precede the determination of this point.

The Security Treaty was concluded on the same day as the Treaty of
Peace with Japan (Treaty No. 5, 28 April 1952), and it maintains a very
close and inseparable relationship with that treaty. That is to say, under
the proviso contained in Article 6 (a) of the Treaty of Peace, it is stated
that "Nothing in this provision shall, however, prevent the stationing or
retention of foreign armed forces in Japanese territory under or in consequence of any bilateral or multilateral agreements which have been or
may be made between one or more of the Allied Powers," thus, recognizing the stationing of foreign troops within the territorial limits of Japan.
The Security Treaty is a treaty concluded between Japan and the United

States regarding stationing of the United States armed forces, the foreign armed forces recognized in the above provision of the Treaty of Peace. This provision was approved and signed by a majority of forty countries out of sixty United Nations countries.

According to the Preamble of the Japan-United States Security Treaty, the Treaty of Peace recognizes that in consideration of the fact that Japan will not have the effective means to exercise its inherent right of self-defense at the time of coming into force of the Treaty of Peace, and since there is a necessity of coping with the danger of irresponsible militarism, that Japan, as a sovereign nation, has the right to enter into collective security arrangements. Further, the Charter of the United Nations recognizes that all nations possess an inherent right of individual and collective self-defense. It is clear, therefore, that the purpose of the Japan-United States Security Treaty is to provide, as a provisional arrangement, for the defense of Japan, and to stipulate matters necessary to insure the safety and defense of our country, such as granting of the right to the United States to deploy its armed forces in and about Japan to guard against armed attack upon the country. Consequently, it must be stated that the Security Treaty, in its essence, bears a vital relationship with peace and security and also with the very existence of our sovereign country.

In the formulation of the treaty, the Cabinet of the Japanese Government then in power, negotiated with the United States on a number of occasions in accordance with the Constitutional provisions, and finally concluded the same as one of the most important national policies. It is also a well-accepted public knowledge that, subsequent thereto, the question of whether the treaty was in accord with the Constitution was carefully discussed by both Houses and finally ratified by the Diet as being a legal and proper treaty.

The Security Treaty, therefore, as stated before, is featured with an extremely high degree of political consideration, having bearing upon the very existence of our country as a sovereign power, and any legal determination as to whether the content of the treaty is constitutional or not is in many respects inseparably related to the high degree of political consideration or discretionary power on the part of the Cabinet which concluded the treaty and on the part of the Diet which approved it. Consequently, as a rule, there is a certain element of incompatibility in the process of judicial determination of its constitutionality by a court of law which has as its mission the exercise of the purely judicial function. Accordingly, unless the said treaty is obviously unconstitutional and void, it falls outside the purview of the power of judicial review granted to the court. It is proper to construe that the question of the determination of its constitutionality should be left primarily to the Cabinet which has the power to conclude treaties and the Diet which has the power to ratify them; and ultimately to the political consideration of the people with whom rests the sovereign power of the nation.

This is true whether the question of constitutionality of the Security Treaty or the action of the government stemming from the treaty obligation, is directly before the court, or where such a question is to be determined as pre-requisite to determining another problem as it is in this case.

3. Accordingly, the Court in proceeding to deliberate over the Security Treaty relating to the stationing of the United States armed forces and the provisions of the Administrative Agreement based on Article 3 of the said treaty, finds that these Security Forces are foreign troops, and naturally they are not a war potential of our country. All command and supervisory authorities are vested in the United States, and furthermore, it is clear that our country has no right to command or supervise such armed forces as we do over our own armed forces. These armed forces are stationed here in accordance with the principle set forth in the Preamble to the Security Treaty, and as stated in Article 1 of the Treaty, these forces are to be utilized to contribute to the maintenance of international peace and security in the Far East and to the security of Japan against armed attack from without, including assistance given at the express request of the Japanese Government to put down large-scale internal riots and disturbances in Japan caused through instigation of, or intervention by, an outside power or powers. Its objective is to maintain the peace and security of Japan and the Far East, including Japan, and to insure that never again shall we be visited by the horrors of war. It can readily be seen that the reason for permitting the stationing of these forces was none other than to supplement the lack of our own defense power, by trusting in the justice and faith of the peace loving people of the world.

If such be the case, it cannot be acknowledged that the stationing of the United States armed forces is immediately, clearly unconstitutional and void, contravening the purport of Article 9, paragraph 2 of Article 98, and the Preamble of the Constitution. On the contrary, it must be held that it is in accord with the intent and purpose of these constitutional provisions. This is true, regardless of whether the provisions of paragraph 2 of Article 9 were intended to prohibit the maintenance of war potential even for self-defense. (The Administrative Agreement was not specifically ratified by the Diet, but it was signed by the Government on 28 February 1952. The Agreement itself and the Minutes pertaining thereto were prepared at the time of the conclusion of the Agreement and were submitted to the Foreign Affairs Committee of the House of Representatives during the first part of March of the same year; and thereafter, various interpellations were made and answers given in this Committee as well as in the Judicial Affairs Committee of the same House. In respect to the Administrative Agreement there was some discussion to the effect that it should also be ratified by the Diet, but the Government has asserted that since the Security Treaty, which contains the basis for the Administrative Agreement, was ratified by the Diet there was no need for this Agreement to be specifically ratified by the Diet. On the 25th of March, 1952, the Plenary Session of the House of Councillors rejected a resolution which advocated that since the Administrative Agreement is a treaty within the meaning of Article 73 of the Constitution it should also be ratified by the Diet according to its provisions. In the House of Representatives, on the 26th day of the same month of the same year, a resolution that the Administrative Agreement went beyond the scope of the disposition clause pertaining to the United States armed forces delegated to the Government by virtue of Article 3 of the Security Treaty and that it contains substance which requires processing through the Diet under Article 73 of the Constitution was also rejected at its Plenary Session. In view of these facts it must be considered that the Administrative Agreement, which provides for conditions of disposition of the United States armed forces, was already recognized as coming within the scope of the delegation set forth in Article 3 of the Security Treaty, which has already received the sanction of the Diet. Therefore, the contention that it is void and unconstitutional because it had not especially been ratified by the Diet cannot be recognized.)

The original decision, which adjudged that the stationing of the United States armed forces cannot be permitted as it contravenes the first part of paragraph 2, Article 9 of the Constitution, went beyond the scope of the right of judicial review, and constituted an error in interpreting the Preamble of the Constitution and other constitutional provisions cited above. The original court also committed an error when it ruled that Article 2 of the Special Criminal Law was unconstitutional and void, based on the assumption that the stationing of the US troops was illegal. On this point, it is considered that the prosecution's argument, in its final analysis, was well taken. The original judgment cannot escape reversal even without the necessity of arguing other points contained in the appellate brief.

Therefore, this Court renders judgment as set forth in the main text in accordance with the provisions of paragraph 1, Article 410; Item 1, Article 405; and Article 413 of the Code of Criminal Procedure.

This judgment is based on the supplementary opinions of Justices Kotaro Tanaka, Tamotsu Shima, Hachiro Fujita, Toshio Irie, Katsumi Tarumi, Daisuke Kawamura and Shuichi Ishizaka, and a separate opinion of Justices Katsushige Kotani, Kenichi Okuno, and Kiyoshi Takahashi, and on the unanimous opinion of all justices.

49

Statement

June 18, 1960

Japan Democratic-Socialist Party

During the 1960 political crisis, the Democratic-Socialist Party attempted to steer a moderate course between that of the Liberal-Democratic Party and that of the Socialist Party, both of which had violated orderly parliamentary processes. After the postponement of the Eisenhower visit, the Democratic-Socialists issued the following public statement, which may be taken to represent the view of many Japanese observers.

At the House of Representatives on May 19, the Government and the Ministerial Party extended the session by force of the majority, and forcibly passed the new Japan-US Security Pact in the absence of opposition party members. Since then the Security Pact has not been discussed at the Diet, and the Government regards it as automatically approved by the Diet today, which was so abnormal that no opposition party were present.

The exercise of force by the Kishi Cabinet in passing the Security Pact gave rise to the use of violence on the part of the opposing groups, and to consequent social confusions and paralysis in politics, until at last the radical groups took advantage of the people's voice for the immediate resignation of the Kishi Cabinet and the dissolution of the Diet, and openly resorted to violence, so that the Government was compelled to request for the postponement of President Eisenhower's trip to Japan. Moreover, the vicinity of the Diet House is now in utter disorder, and bloody incidents occur in succession. Democratic Parliamentarism is confronted with the gravest crisis in the history of Japan.

Judging from the serious significance of the new Security Pact, the validity or invalidity of the so-called automatic approval of the Pact must not be discussed from the standpoint of mere formalism in legality. We do not recognize the Pact as approval by the will of the Japanese people,

The editor is indebted to the headquarters of the Japan Democratic-Socialist Party for kindly providing this English version of the statement.

since the contents of the treaty, as well as the procedure by which it is said to have been approved, are suspect to be against the national Constitution. We do not think that a political treaty important both to Japan and to America should be based upon such an unstable foundation as this.

We members of the Democratic Socialist Party maintain that the present Security Pact should be dissolved step by step in the future. On one hand, we are opposed to the immediate, unconditional, and unilateral abolition of the present security scheme, while on the other hand we are absolutely opposed to the Government's project of concluding the new Security Pact, which is a sort of military alliance. In order to prevent this, we are unswerving in maintaining that the ultimate decision on the new Security Pact should be made by the will of the Japanese nation by means of general election after dissolving the Diet.

Since the aggravation of the situation following the reckless step taken by the Government on the dawn of May 20, we have laid stress not only on our anti-Security Pact struggles, but also on our struggles to protect democratic parliamentarism from violence of leftists and rightists. We have been strongly insisting to the Kishi Cabinet that Premier Kishi should resign immediately, and that general election should be effected in order to ascertain the will of the people on the issue of the Security Pact. At the same time we have been warning against general strike of the working classes and the fomenting of anti-US activities, while emphasizing the inadvisability of the resignation en masse of the Socialist members of the Diet.

After the extraordinary state of affairs resultant from the bloody incident of June 15, we proposed a three-head talk to prevent a further aggravation of the situation, and also proposed the adjournment of the session by resolution for the purpose of preventing the new treaty from being automatically approved. It is to be regretted, however, that all our efforts have been wasted on account of the failure of the Socialist and the Liberal-Democratic parties to give adequate consideration to the situation.

To sum up our aims are:

a. to oppose the conclusion of the new Security Pact, and to abolish the present Security Pact step by step;

b. to promote the resignation of the Kishi Cabinet, and to effect general election;

c. to protect democratic parliamentarism; and

d. to oppose absolutely the exercise of violence.

Our endeavors inside as well as outside the Diet may be summed up as follows:

1. We demand the dissolution of the Diet in order to appeal through general election to the judgment of the people on the issue of the new Security Pact.

2. We propose the opening of a three-head talk in order to normalize the Diet and to save the situation through the resignation of the Kishi Cabinet, the immediate dissolution of the Diet, and the complete abolition of violence. We particularly insist that the present abnormal session of the Diet should be closed, and that a new extra session should be opened to renew the people's mind.

Convinced that all these beliefs are completely congruous with the opinion of people with good sense on today's problems, we announce herewith that with our renewed conviction and courage we shall make every effort to translate into reality the spirit with which we have organized our Party, that is, to establish a peaceful order and to protect democratic parliamentarism.

June 18, 1960

The Japan Democratic Socialist Party

SUGGESTED READING

Abegglen, James C. *The Japanese Factory: Aspects of Its Social Organization.* New York: Free Press, 1958.

Allen, George C. *Japan's Economic Expansion.* London: Oxford University Press, 1965.

Anderson, Ronald S. *Japan: Three Epochs in Modern Education.* Washington, D.C.: Government Printing Office, 1959.

Ayusawa Iwao. *Organized Labor in Japan.* Tokyo: Foreign Affairs Association of Japan, 1962.

Battistini, Lawrence H. *The Postwar Student Struggle in Japan.* Tokyo, Japan, and Rutland, Vt.: Charles E. Tuttle Company, 1956, paperback.

Beardsley, Richard K.; Hall, John W.; and Ward, Robert E. *Village Japan.* Chicago: University of Chicago Press, 1959.

Borton, Hugh, et al. *Japan between East and West.* New York: Harper & Row, 1957.

Burks, Ardath W. *The Government of Japan.* 2nd ed. New York: Crowell, 1963, paperback.

Cary, James. *Japan: Reluctant Ally.* New York: Frederick A. Praeger, 1962.

Cohen, Jerome B. *Japan's Postwar Economy.* Bloomington: University of Indiana Press, 1958.

Cole, Allen B. *Japanese Society and Politics: The Impact of Social Stratification and Mobility on Politics.* Boston: Boston University Press, 1956.

Cole, Allen B. *Political Tendencies of Japanese Small Enterprises, with Special Reference to the Social Democratic Party.* New York: Institute of Pacific Relations, 1959.

Colton, Kenneth E.; Colton, Hattie K.; and Totten, George O, eds. "Japan since the Recovery of Independence," *The Annals of the American Academy of Political and Social Science,* Vol. 308 (November, 1956).

Dore, Ronald P. *City Life in Japan: A Study of a Tokyo Ward.* Berkeley: University of California Press, 1958, paperback.

Dunn, Frederick S. *Peace-Making and the Settlement with Japan.* Princeton: Princeton University Press, 1963.

Hall, Robert B., Jr. *Japan: Industrial Power of Asia.* Princeton: Van Nostrand, 1963, paperback.

Harris, George L., et al. *U.S. Army Area Handbook for Japan,* 2nd ed. Washington, D.C.: Government Printing Office, 1964, paperback.

Henderson, Dan Fenno. *Conciliation and Japanese Law: Tokugawa and Modern.* Seattle: University of Washington Press, 1965.

Higa Mikio. *Parties and Politics in Postwar Okinawa.* Vancouver: University of British Columbia Press, 1963.

Ike, Nobutaka. *Japanese Politics: An Introductory Survey,* New York: Knopf, 1957.

Japanese National Commission for UNESCO, ed. *Japan: Its People and Culture.* Tokyo: Printing Bureau, Ministry of Finance, 1958.

Kurzman, Dan. *Kishi and Japan: The Search for the Sun.* New York: Ivan Oblensky, 1960.

Langdon, Frank. *Politics in Japan.* Boston: Little, Brown, 1967.

Leng, Shao Chuan. *Japan and Communist China.* Kyoto: Doshisha University Press, 1958.

Levine, Solomon B. *Industrial Relations in Postwar Japan.* Urbana: University of Illinois Press, 1958.

Lockwood, W. W. *The Economic Development of Japan: Growth and Structural Change.* Princeton: Princeton University Press, 1955.

Maki, John M. *Court and Constitution in Japan: Selected Supreme Court Decisions, 1948–60.* Seattle: Washington University Press, 1964.

Maki, John M. *Government and Politics in Japan: The Road to Democracy.* New York: Frederick A. Praeger, 1962, paperback.

Maruyama, Masao. *Thought and Behavior in Modern Japanese Politics.* London: Oxford University Press, 1963.

McNelly, Theodore. *Contemporary Government of Japan.* Boston: Houghton Mifflin, 1963, paperback.

Mendel, Douglas H. *The Japanese People and Foreign Policy: A Study of Public Opinion in Post-Treaty Japan.* Berkeley: University of California Press, 1961.

Morley, James W. *Japan and Korea: America's Allies in the Pacific.* New York: Walker & Company, 1965, paperback.

Morris, Ivan. *Nationalism and the Right Wing in Japan: A Study of Post-War Trends.* London: Oxford University Press, 1960.

Offner, C. B. and van Straelen, H. *Modern Japanese Religions.* New York: Twayne, 1963.

Olson, Lawrence. *Dimensions of Japan.* New York: American Universities Field Staff, 1963.

Passin, Herbert, ed. *The United States and Japan.* Englewood Cliffs, N.J.: Prentice-Hall, 1966, paperback.

Packard, George R., III. *Protest in Tokyo: The Security Treaty Crisis of 1960*. Princeton: Princeton University Press, 1966.

Quigley, Harold S., and Turner, John E. *The New Japan: Government and Politics*. Minneapolis: University of Minnesota Press, 1956.

Reischauer, Edwin O. *The United States and Japan*. 3rd ed. Cambridge: Harvard University Press, 1965. (Paperback: Viking Press, Compass Books)

Scalapino, Robert A. *The Japanese Communist Movement, 1920–1966*. Berkeley: University of California Press, 1967.

Scalapino, Robert A., and Masumi, Junnosuke. *Parties and Politics in Contemporary Japan*. Berkeley: University of California Press, 1962, paperback.

Steiner, Kurt. *Local Government in Japan*. Stanford: Stanford University Press, 1965.

Stoetzel, Jean. *Without the Chrysanthemum and the Sword: A Study of the Attitudes of Youth in Post-War Japan*. New York: Columbia University Press, 1955.

Swearingen, Rodger, and Langer, Paul. *Red Flag in Japan: International Communism in Action, 1919–1951*. Cambridge: Harvard University Press, 1957.

Thomsen, Harry. *The New Religions of Japan*. Rutland, Vt.: and Tokyo, Japan: Charles E. Tuttle Company, 1963.

Tsuneishi, Warren A. *Japanese Political Style: An Introduction to the Government and Politics of Modern Japan*. New York: Harper & Row, 1966, paperback.

Von Mehren, Arthur Thayer, ed. *Law in Japan: The Legal Order in a Changing Society*. Cambridge: Harvard University Press, 1963.

Ward, Robert E., and Macridis, Roy C., eds. *Modern Political Systems: Asia*. Englewood Cliffs, N.J.: Prentice-Hall, 1963.

Whittemore, Edward P. *The Press in Japan Today: A Case Study*. Columbia: University of South Carolina Press, 1961, paperback.

Yanaga, Chitoshi. *Japanese People and Politics*. New York: Wiley, 1956.

IX

The Communist
Victory in China

The first United Front in China ended in April, 1927, when Chiang Kai-shek split with the leftist Wuhan regime. In July the left-wing Nationalists in Wuhan expelled their Communist collaborators. The Communists were without allies, but acting on ambiguous orders from the Kremlin, they tried to maintain the form of the United Front at the same time that they launched coups against the Nationalists. The party's Secretary-General, Ch'en Tu-hsiu, was blamed for the failure of the United Front strategy, accused of right-wing opportunism, and finally expelled from the party as a Trotskyite. The Communists' situation became so precarious in 1928 that it was necessary to hold the party's Sixth National Congress in Moscow. Li Li-san, the party's new leader, directed a series of violent insurrections by the proletariat in the cities, but these were harshly suppressed by the police, and the Communists rapidly lost the last vestiges of their influence among the workers. As a revolutionary force, the Chinese proletariat, weak in numbers and class consciousness, had proven a keen disappointment to China's Marxist-Leninists.

Traditional Marxism had scorned the peasantry as lacking in revolutionary spirit. However, while engaged in political activity among the peasants in his native province, one Communist leader, Mao Tse-tung, made a significant discovery. In his *Report on an Investigation of the Peasant Movement in Hunan*, he pointed out that the peasantry had emerged as the most effective revolutionary class in China (Selection 50). After the breakup of the United Front and the unsuccessful workers' uprisings, the real base of Communist strength in China was no longer the city but the countryside, particularly the mountains on the border of Hunan and Kiangsi provinces. Here Communists led by Mao enforced a land reform program and consolidated their military strength. In 1931

206

Mao was elected Chairman of the Central Soviet Government at the first All-China Congress of Soviets, held at Juichin, Kiangsi. Following the Japanese invasion of Manchuria, the newly founded Chinese Soviet Republic declared war on Japan and called on all groups and classes in China to resist Japanese aggression. Thus the Communists established their claim to be anti-Japanese and patriotic while the Nationalist government bore the difficult responsibility of dealing with the Japanese militarily and diplomatically.

In 1934, following a series of extermination campaigns, the Nationalist army forced the Communists to abandon their base in southern China. They retreated to the Northwest by a circuitous 6000-mile route through the mountains of western China. This was the heroic Long March later celebrated in Communist literature. The Communists established a new capital at Yenan, in the Northwest, but were confronted with a Nationalist blockade, and their future looked bleak.

The patriotic National Salvation movement and the Sian incident in 1936 led to a cessation of the civil war and the formation of a new united front, this time directed against Japan. In 1940 Mao Tse-tung pointed out in his *New Democracy* that a bourgeois-democratic revolution of the new type was then in progress in China; the proletarian-socialist revolution would come later. He stated that the new-type bourgeois-democratic revolution in China would be carried out largely under the leadership of the proletariat, because of the tendency of the Chinese bourgeoisie to compromise with feudal landowners and foreign imperialists (Selection 51).

During the war against Japan, the Communists organized guerrilla resistance and established a *de facto* government in northern China behind the Japanese lines. At the same time, the Communist military forces grew stronger. By 1945 it was estimated that some 90,000,000 people in northern China were under Communist rule. Thus the war with Japan greatly strengthened the Communists vis-à-vis the Nationalists. However, in August, 1945, the Soviet Union negotiated a treaty of friendship and alliance with the Nationalist government of China, thus appearing to support the Nationalist regime and snub the Chinese Communists.

World War II gravely damaged the Chinese economy, and the inflation of the currency threatened to delay a recovery. The United States was willing to extend economic aid in the postwar period, but the prevention of a civil war between the Nationalists and the Communists was a prerequisite to American help. In December, 1945, President Truman sent his wartime Chief of Staff, General George C. Marshall, to mediate the internal conflict in China by bringing about the establishment of a coalition regime which would include all major groups, including the Communists as well as the Nationalists (Selection 52). The Nationalists had promised in 1936 to convene a National Assembly for the purpose of adopting a constitution and ending the "political tutelage" under the Kuomintang, but the war with Japan had made necessary the postponement of this major reform.

In January and February, 1946, General Marshall succeeded in bringing about a truce in the fighting. At the same time, the Political Consultative Conference made arrangements whereby a coalition government would be set up and the Communist armies would gradually merge with the Nationalist armies. However, in Manchuria, which had been occupied by the Soviet Union since the end of the war, the Soviet forces postponed their departure until April, delayed the deployment of Nationalist troops in the area, and permitted the Chinese Communists to acquire weapons surrendered by the Japanese. The control of the Manchurian cities and countryside became a source of keen dispute between the Nationalists and the Communists, and fighting broke out with increasing frequency. By stages, the truce arranged under Marshall's guidance broke down, the fighting spread, and the agreement for a coalition government was repudiated by uncompromising elements among the Nationalists and Communists.

In November the Nationalists, over the protests of the Communists and the Democratic League, convened the National Assembly for the purpose of adopting a new constitution. The Communists and Democratic League boycotted the Assembly, although seats were reserved for them. In December, 1946, the new Constitution was promulgated, to go into effect the following year. The Constitution, however, was not recognized as valid by the Communists, and the possibility of a reconciliation of the opposing groups in China seemed very remote. In January, 1947, General Marshall was recalled to the United States to become Secretary of State. Faced with the increasing unwillingness of both the Communists and Nationalists to settle their differences, the United States gave up any further attempt to mediate.

For a brief period, it appeared that Chiang Kai-shek would be able to defeat the Communists. His troops spread across China and Manchuria and managed in March, 1947, to force the Communists to abandon their capital at Yenan. But the Nationalist successes were temporary. Although able to occupy the principal cities and railroads, the Nationalists were unable to dislodge the Communists from their bases in the countryside or to retain the loyalty of the population. The Nationalist armies were dispersed throughout the country and became engrossed with garrison duty. They failed to mount a coordinated effort to destroy their enemy, and the Communists cut their communications and assumed the initiative. The Communists immobilized the Nationalists with their hit-and-run guerrilla tactics, and in 1948 began to defeat the Nationalists in open battles (Selections 53, 54). At the same time, the postwar economic recovery lagged, as production and transportation failed to revive. Runaway inflation destroyed the value of money, and official corruption led the population to take a cynical attitude towards the Nationalist Party.

In the spring of 1948, the National Assembly elected Chiang Kai-shek President of China, but expressed its dissatisfaction with the government's policies by refusing to elect Chiang's choice for the vice-presidency. The outlawing of the Democratic League and the police suppression of expressions of dissent did not strengthen the popularity or prestige of the Nationalists, and the political deterioration of the Nationalist regime paralleled its declining military fortunes.

By January, 1949, the military and political situation had become so unfavorable to the Nationalists that they requested the Big Four Powers (Great Britain, France, the United States, and the Soviet Union) to mediate, but without success. The United States refused either to aid in negotiating a settlement with the Communists or to extend the massive military and economic aid necessary to stem a Communist victory. The American government believed that a large-scale military intervention by American forces would be too costly in money and lives and, in any event, would probably not defeat the Communists.

In the face of the imminent military collapse of the Nationalists, Chiang Kai-shek retired in favor of Vice-President Li Tseng-jen, who became Acting President. Peiping was surrendered to the Communists without a fight late in January. In February, most government offices were moved from Nanking to Canton. Li Tsung-jen's difficulties were aggravated by the marked tendency of the bureaucracy and military to disregard his authority in favor of instructions from Chiang Kai-shek and a Canton faction, led by Sun Fo. Li sent negotiators to Peiping to negotiate a truce, but the Communists, confident of military victory, insisted on the punishment of a list of war criminals, headed by Chiang Kai-shek, and the establishment of a Communist-dominated government. To accept the Communist demands would have amounted to capitulation, and the Nationalists continued their ineffective resistance.

In August, 1949, after northern China and much of the South had fallen into Communist hands, the United States State Department issued a white paper (*United States Relations with China: With Special Reference to the Period 1944–1949*), which was apparently intended to clear the American government of blame for the decline in the fortunes of the Nationalist regime. In his letter of transmittal to President Truman, Secretary of State Acheson pointed out that the collapse of the Nationalists was not the consequence of inadequate material support from the United States, but was rather a result of the shortcomings of the Nationalists themselves (Selection 55). On the other hand, it has been asserted that the State Department's instructions to General Marshall of December,

1945, were of such a nature that only the Communists could have bene-fited from the American effort to mediate the Chinese civil war (Selec-tion 56).

The publication of the white paper ended any remaining hope of American aid to Chiang's cause. Nationalist leaders who did not defect or surrender to the Communists fled to Formosa or the United States. In September, 1949, the Communists announced the establishment of the People's Republic of China with its capital at Peiping, which they re-named Peking (Northern Capital).[1] The new regime was immediately recognized by the Soviet Union and Great Britain, but not by the United States and France.[2]

In January, 1950, President Truman announced that the United States would not provide military aid or advice to the Nationalist forces in Taiwan and would not pursue a course that would lead to involvement in the Chinese civil war (Selection 57). The American State Department had apparently become reconciled to the Communist take-over of main-land China and to the imminent capture of Formosa by the Communists. However, the outbreak of the Korean War later in 1950 resulted in the dispatch of the United States Seventh Fleet to the Formosan Strait to neutralize the area, thus preventing a Communist invasion of Taiwan. American and Chinese forces clashed in North Korea in December.

In the United States, many people blamed the fall of the Nationalists on the policies of the Roosevelt and Truman administrations. In any event, it is usually agreed that the following contributed in varying degrees to the Communist victory in China: the war weariness of the Chinese people following twenty years of civil war and war with Japan, the runaway inflation of the currency, corruption in the Nationalist regime on both high and low levels, Nationalist mistakes in military strategy and tactics, uncertainties of American policy, the clever use made of truces and armistices by the Communists, the timing of the Soviet withdrawal from Manchuria—permitting Japanese weapons to fall into the hands of the Chinese Communists, poor morale in the Nationalist forces, the willingness of opportunistic Nationalist generals to make deals with the Communists, Communist ideological zeal, the lack of an effective "third force" in Chinese politics which could provide a non-Communist alternative to the declining Nationalist regime, and the failure of the Marshall mission to establish a broadly-based and effective moderate gov-ernment. Finally, the huge area and manpower resources of China tended to discourage American military intervention.

[1] Because this city is not considered the legitimate capital by the Chinese Na-tionalists and the United States State Department, they continue to call it Peiping.
[2] France recognized the Peking regime in 1964.

50

Report on an Investigation of the Peasant Movement in Hunan

February, 1927

Mao Tse-tung

Note how Mao Tse-tung, contrary to orthodox Marxist tradition, here gives the peasantry seven-tenths of the credit for the progress of the Chinese revolution; the urban proletariat is scarcely mentioned.

I. AGRARIAN REVOLUTION

SERIOUSNESS OF THE PEASANT PROBLEM

On a thirty-two-day (January 4–February 5, 1927) inspection tour of five *hsien* [districts or counties] of Hunan–Hsiangtan, Hsianghsiang, Hengshan, Liling, and Changsha–I have collected a considerable body of materials by listening carefully to reports made by experienced peasants and comrades in the peasant movement at informatory meetings held both in county-seats and villages. Many aspects of the peasant movement directly contradict what we have learned from the gentry in Hankow and Changsha. Some unique incidents have never been seen or heard of before. These conditions, I think, prevail in other provinces too; thus various arguments against the peasant movement must be controverted immediately and the erroneous decisions of the revolutionary régime [i.e. the Wuhan government] in regard to the peasant movement must be quickly corrected. Only thus can the revolution benefit in the future. The further development of the peasant movement is a tremendous problem. Within a short time, hundreds of millions of peasants will rise in Central, South, and North China, with the fury of a hurricane; no power, however strong, can restrain them. They will break all the shackles that bind them

Reprinted by permission of the publishers from Conrad Brandt, Benjamin Schwartz, John K. Fairbank *Documentary History of Chinese Communism* Cambridge, Mass.: Harvard University Press, 1952; London: G. Allen & Unwin; pp. 80–89.

and rush towards the road of liberation. *All imperialists, warlords, corrupt officials, and bad gentry will meet their doom at the hands of the peasants* [underlining in original]. All revolutionary parties and comrades will be judged by them. *Are we to get in front of them and lead them or criticize them behind their backs or fight them from the opposite camp?* Among these three alternatives every Chinese can choose freely, but the current situation demands a quick decision. The following are the results of my inspection and my opinions are presented in detail for reference by revolutionary comrades.

Let's Organize. The Hunanese peasant movement, as regards the well-organized counties in central and southern Hunan, can be divided into two stages: the first being that of organization, from January to September 1926. Within this stage, there was a secret period from January to June and an open period from July to September, when the revolutionary armies were engaged in the ousting of Chao [Chao Heng-hsi, then governor of Hunan]. In that stage, the total membership of the Peasant Associations did not exceed 300,000 or 400,000; and the masses under their direct command totalled just a little over 1,000,000. There were few instances of conflict inside the villages; hence there was only a little criticism from the different classes in this regard. Because members of the Peasant Associations served [the revolutionary army] as guides, scouts, and coolies, some officers spoke even favourably of them. The second, or revolutionary, stage lasted from October [1926] to January of this year. The membership of the Peasant Associations jumped up to 2,000,000 and the number of people under their direct command increased to 10,000,000. (When joining a Peasant Association, the peasants usually put down one name for the whole family; thus 2,000,000 members means 10,000,000 people.) About half of the entire peasantry in Hunan is organized. In such places as Hsiangtan, Hsianghsiang, Liuyang, Changsha, Liling, Ninghsiang, Pingkiang, Hsiangying, Hengshan, Hengyang, Leiyang, Chenhsien, Anhwa, etc., almost the entire peasantry has been incorporated into the Peasant Associations and take orders from them. After organizing themselves extensively, the peasants began to take action. Thus, within four months, an unprecedented agrarian revolution broke out.

Down with the Village Bosses (t'u-hao) and Bad Gentry, All Power Belongs to the Peasant Associations. After the peasants organized themselves, action ensued. The major targets of their attack were the *t'u-hao*, bad gentry, and illegitimate landlords, as well as the old patriarchal ideology, corruption of city officials, and undesirable village customs. This attack was like a hurricane: only those could survive who bent to its force. As a result, privileges of the feudal landlord class, thousands of years old, were totally swept away. Their prestige and prerogatives were altogether abolished. After the overthrow of the gentry's power, the Peasant Associations became the only organs of power and [the slogan] "all power to the Peasant Associations" became literally true. Even such trifles as quarrels between married couples were referred to the Peasant Associations for settlement. No problem could be solved independently of the Peasant Association membership, whose every word passed for a command. In the villages the Peasant Associations became the authority for everything [seeing to it that], "whatever was promised, was done." Outsiders could comment only favourably, not critically, on the Peasant Associations. Bad gentry, *t'u-hao*, and illegitimate landlords were deprived of their right of free speech; [so] nobody dared to voice objections. Under the Peasant Association régime, the top-layer *t'u-hao* and bad gentry fled to Shanghai; the second layer fled to Hankow; the third layer to Changsha, and the fourth layer to the county-seats [*hsien* cities], while the small fry of the fifth layer and below surrendered to the Peasant Associations in the villages.

"I contribute ten dollars, so please let me join the Peasant Association," pleaded the small-fry bad gentry.

"Ha! Who cares about your bloody money?" answered the peasants.

Many middle and small landlords, as well as rich and middle peasants who formerly opposed the Peasant Associations, now begged for admission to them. I met a number of those people in the places I visited, and they said: "I beg the commissioner from the capital [Changsha] to endorse me!"

At the time of the Manchu dynasty, when the population census was made, there were two kinds of census, one regular and another subsidiary. Decent people were registered in the regular census and bad elements such as bandits, etc., were registered in the subsidiary census. At present the peasants in some localities have threatened those who opposed the Peasant Associations with the remark: "You will be registered in the subsidiary census!"

Those who were afraid of being registered in the subsidiary census tried by various means to gain admission into the Peasant Associations, not resting till their names were included in the rosters. Often the Peasant Associations refused categorically and threw them out; then they spent their days in suspense, like homeless wanderers. Such a condition is called "*Ta ling*" [lit., a lone wanderer] in the local slang. Thus, the so-called "peasant society" that was despised by most people four months ago has become a thing of glory today. Those who knelt before the gentry now kneel before the power of the peasants. Indisputably, the situation before last October and that after it belong to two [different] worlds.

Very Bad and Very Good. The peasant revolt in the countryside awakened the gentry from their sweet dreams. When the news reached the cities from the villages, the urban gentry protested tumultuously. On first arriving in Changsha, I met people of different backgrounds and heard a lot of gossip. From the middle social strata to the KMT right wing the general comment was: "very bad." Even some revolutionary [-minded] people did not object to this comment, especially when they used their imagination as to the conditions in the countryside. Some progressive elements only remarked apologetically: "Though this is bad, it is inevitable during the process of revolution." All in all, nobody entirely denied the epithet "bad." But as pointed out previously, it is actually the rising up of the vast peasant masses to accomplish their historic mission; it is the rising up of the democratic forces in the countryside to overthrow the feudal forces in the villages, which is the true goal of the national revolution. Sun Yat-sen devoted forty years to the national revolution; what he wanted but failed to achieve has been accomplished by the peasants in a few months. The patriarchal, feudal *t'u-hao* and bad gentry, together with the illegitimate landlords, were not only the foundation of the dictatorial régime of the past several thousand years, [but also] the tools of the imperialists, warlords, and corrupt officials. This is a great achievement unprecedented in the past forty years or several thousand years. This is "very good"—not in the least "bad," and not at all "very bad." To give credits where they are due, if we allot ten points to the accomplishments of the democratic revolution, then the achievements of the urban dwellers and the military units rate only three points, while the remaining seven points should go to the peasants in their rural revolution.[1] The comment "very bad" *is obviously an argument to serve the interests of the landlords and crush the peasants: it is obviously an argument of the landlord class, which tries to preserve the old feudal order by obstructing the establishment of a new democratic order: it is obviously an anti-revolutionary argument.* No revolutionary comrade should blindly repeat such remarks. If you are a person of firm revolutionary ideology and visit the countryside, you will experience a satisfaction never felt before; tens of thousands of slaves—the peasants—are overthrowing their man-eating enemy. The action of the peasants is entirely correct; their action is "very good!" "Very good" is a slogan of the peasants and other revolutionary groups. All revolutionary comrades should realize that the national revolution requires a tremendous change in the villages. The Revolution of 1911 did not achieve such a change, and therefore it failed; now there is such a change, and it is one of the major factors in the accomplishment of the revolution. Every revolutionary comrade should support this movement; otherwise he is against the revolution.

The Problem of "Excesses." Another group of people say: "Peasant Associations should be organized, but their actions are too excessive." This is the argument of the middle-of-the-road group. But what are the facts? The peasants in the villages have indeed been "disorderly." The power of the Peasant Associations being supreme, the landlords have been prohib-

---

[1] This un-Marxistlike statement does not appear in recent Peking editions of the Report. [Editor's note.]

ited from speaking up and their prestige is wiped out. This is like stepping on the landlord after striking him down. The phrase is coined, "All landowners are *t'u-hao* and all gentry are bad." In some places those who owned fifty *mou* of land or more were automatically called *t'u-hao* and those who wore long gowns were all branded as bad gentry. Their "names being recorded in the subsidiary census," *t'u-hao* and bad gentry were fined, required to make contributions, and had their sedan chairs smashed. Some people forced their way into the homes of *t'u-hao* and bad gentry who were hostile to the Peasant Association, and killed their pigs and commandeered their grain. The ivory beds of the daughters and daughters-in-law of the *t'u-hao* and bad gentry were stepped upon by the dirty feet of the peasants. On the slightest provocation men were paraded down the streets, wearing tall paper hats [such as are worn by criminals *en route* to punishment]. "Vile gentry! Now comes our day!" Actions were unrestrained; things were turned upside down, and terror swept some of the villages. This is what some people called "excesses," "going to the other extreme" or "unspeakable." This kind of comment appears superficially correct, but actually it is erroneous.

First, the above-mentioned incidents were the result of oppression by the *t'u-hao,* bad gentry, and illegitimate landlords, who bore down on the peasants with their power and privileges. Thus [the peasants'] tumultuous resistance is only a reaction. Their resistance is most intensive and disorderly when *t'u-hao,* bad gentry and illegitimate landlords have wreaked the worst damage. The peasants' eyes make no mistakes. Who is bad and who is not bad; who should be punished most severely and who should be punished lightly: the peasants judge this most clearly; only very seldom do they hand out undeserved verdicts. So even Mr. T'ang Menghsiao [General T'ang Sheng-chih, militarist supporter of the Wuhan government] once said: "When the peasants attacked the *t'u-hao* and bad gentry in the villages, they were right in nine out of ten cases."

Secondly, revolution is not a dinner-party, nor literary composition, nor painting, nor embroidering. It cannot be done so delicately, so leisurely, so gentlemanly, and so "gently, kindly, politely, plainly, and modestly" [quoted from the *Analects* of Confucius]. Revolution is insurrection, the violent action of one class overthrowing the power of another. An agrarian revolution is a revolution by the peasantry to overthrow the power of the feudal landlord class. If the peasants do not apply great force, the power of the landlords, consolidated over thousands of years, can never be uprooted. There must be a revolutionary tidal wave in the countryside in order to mobilize tens of thousands of peasants and weld them into this great force. The excesses described above result from the tremendous revolutionary enthusiasm of the peasants. In the second [revolutionary] stage of the peasant movement, such acts are very necessary. In this second stage, an absolute peasant power must be established, no criticism of the Peasant Associations should be allowed; the gentry's power must be totally liquidated, the gentry knocked down, even trodden upon. All excesses in the second stage have a revolutionary significance. In fine, every village should be in a state of terror for a brief period; otherwise, counter-revolutionary activities in the villages cannot be suppressed, and the gentry's power cannot be overthrown. To correct wrongs one must go to the other extreme, without which they cannot be righted. The argument of this group [against peasant "excesses"] appears superficially different from that of the former group; but in reality it is based on the same viewpoint, being an argument for the interests of the privileged landlord class. This kind of argument retards the development of the peasant movement and serves to sabotage the revolution. We cannot but oppose it firmly.

II. THE VANGUARD OF REVOLUTION

THE "P'I-TZU" MOVEMENT

[i.e. the movement of rural "undesirables"—paupers, gamblers, loafers, et al.].

The KMT right wing claims: "The peasant movement is a *p'i-tzu* movement—a movement of peasant loafers." This argument was widely circulated in Changsha. When I visited the villages, the gentry told me: "Peasant Associations are all right, but their present leadership is unacceptable and should be replaced." This comment has the same meaning as that of the [KMT] right wing, namely, that the peasant movement is all right (it being already in existence, no one dares to say otherwise), but that the present leaders of the peasant movement are not all right, especially those in the lower units, all of whom are allegedly *p'i-tzu* who used to go around in worn-out shoes, carry broken umbrellas, wear blue gowns, and gamble. In brief, all those who used to be despised and trodden down by the gentry, who had no social standing, and were deprived of their right to speak, are now raising their heads. They are not only raising their heads, but are holding power in their hands. They have become kings of the village Peasant Associations (the lowest units of the Peasant Associations), which they have turned into deadly weapons. They put their muscular, sunburnt hands on the heads of the gentry. They bind the bad gentry with ropes, put tall paper hats on them, and parade them through the villages. Their crude curses are heard every day by the gentry. They give orders to all, standing above all, where previously they stood below. Hence this is called "abnormal."

Revolutionary Vanguard or Revolutionary Heroes. An issue or a person can be viewed from two opposing angles; thus two contradictory arguments can be arrived at. "Very good" and "very bad" is one example; "*p'i-tzu*" and "revolutionary vanguard" is another. As recounted above, the peasants have fulfilled a long unfulfilled revolutionary mission, performing the major task in the national revolution. But is this revolutionary mission, this major revolutionary task, carried out by all the peasantry? No. The peasantry is divided into three sub-classes: rich, middle, and poor peasants. Their conditions differ, and so do their concepts regarding the revolution. During the first stage, rich peasants (those with cash and grain surpluses) picked up the news that [the Nationalist revolutionary army] had been routed in Kiangsi, that Chiang Kai-shek had been wounded in the foot and flown back to Kwangtung, that Yochow had been reoccupied by Wu P'ei-fu, and that the Peasant Associations would not last long nor would the Three People's Principles [*San-min chu-i*] expand, since they had never existed before. When managers of the village Peasant Associations (many of them *p'i-tzu*) approached the rich peasants with the membership list, saying: "Please join," some of the rich peasants replied blandly: "Peasant Association? I have lived and tilled the land here for many decades but have never heard of any Peasant Association; yet I still eat my rice. I advise you not to start such a thing." "To hell with the Peasant Association; heads will roll and troubles flow," sneered other rich peasants. But believe it or not, the Peasant Associations have lasted several months already and even dared to oppose the gentry. Some gentry in the adjacent districts who refused to turn in their opium pipes were arrested and paraded through the villages by the Peasant Associations. Some big gentry in the cities were even killed (such as Yen Yung-ch'iu of Hsiangtan or Yang Chih-tse of Ninghsiang). On the anniversary of the October revolution, at anti-British rallies, and at the general celebration of the victory of the Northern Expedition [of 1926–7], more than 10,000 peasants raised banners of various sizes, amidst poles and hoes, and paraded in great strength. Then the rich peasants began to feel perturbed. At the celebration of the victory of the Northern Expedition, they heard that Kiukiang had fallen, that Chiang Kai-shek had not been wounded in the foot, and that Wu P'ei-fu had finally been defeated. Also the slogans "Long live the Three People's Principles," "Long live the Peasant Associations," and "Long live the peasants" appeared clearly on colourful handbills.

"Long live the peasants; do these men deserve that?" The rich peasants were deeply disturbed. The Peasant Association thus assumed an important role. Its members said to the rich peasants: "Your names will be registered in the subsidiary census!" and "In a month, the membership fee for new-comers will be ten dollars!"

Under such conditions and threats the rich peasants gradually began to join the Peasant Association. Some paid the membership fee of fifty cents or one dollar (the stipulated fee is ten cents), and some were admitted only through the good offices of a third party. Some die-hards still refused to join the Peasant Associations. When rich peasants enrol in the Peasant Associations, they usually put down the name of a sixty- or seventy-year-old family patriarch because they were still afraid of being conscripted. They did not work enthusiastically for the Peasant Associations even after joining, but remained passive. As to the middle peasants (those having no surplus cash or grain, nor debts, but barely maintaining a living), they adopted a wavering attitude, thinking that they would not benefit much from the revolution. They had rice in the pot and were not disturbed by creditors knocking at their door at midnight. On the basis of "precedent" they brooded: "Will the Peasant Associations survive?" "Are the Three People's Principles going to last?" Their consolation was: "Probably not!" They held that everything would be decided by the will of Heaven. "Organizing a Peasant Association—who knows whether the will of Heaven favours it or not?" In the first stage, when members of the Peasant Associations entered the households of the middle peasants with the Peasant Association roster and said: "Please join!" they answered "Do not rush me!" Only when the Peasant Associations became very powerful in the second stage did the middle peasants begin to join up. They are better than rich peasants as Peasant Association members, but rarely become active, and retain their wavering attitude. Only one group in the countryside has fought hard and relentlessly from the very start: the poor peasants. Out of the secret stage into the open stage, it was they who fought, who organized, and who did the revolutionary work. They alone were the deadly enemies of the t'u-hao and bad gentry, whose bastions they attacked unreservedly. They alone were capable of doing the destructive work. They asked the rich and middle peasants: "We joined the Peasant Association long ago, why do you hesitate?" The rich and middle peasants answered sarcastically: "You have not a single tile above you, nor a needle-sized [strip of] land beneath you—naturally you joined the Peasant Association!"

It is true that the poor peasants have nothing to lose. They are the outcasts or semi-outcasts of the village, and some of them are literally "without a single tile above and without a strip of land below." Why shouldn't they join the Peasant Association? According to an investigation made at Changsha, the poor peasants constituted seventy per cent, the middle peasants twenty per cent, and the rich peasants ten per cent [of the total] peasantry. The poor peasants can be further classified as very poor and poor. The very poor—twenty out of the [total] seventy per cent— are entirely without occupation, having neither land nor capital; with nothing to live on, they have to become soldiers, or hired hands, or beggars or bandits. The remaining fifty per cent constitute the poor [peasants] who are partially without occupation, but who have a little land or capital, though not enough to meet their expenses. Thus they suffer all year long—handicraftsmen, tenants (except rich tenants), and owner-tenants. (The percentage of poor peasants may be less in other *hsien* than Changsha, but the difference is slight.)

This multitudinous mass of poor peasants is the core of the Peasant Associations, the vanguard in the overthrowing of feudal forces, accomplishing the not-yet-accomplished revolutionary mission. Without the poor peasant class (in the words of the gentry: without the *p'i-tzu*), no revolutionary conditions would exist as they do now in rural areas; and the *t'u-hao* and bad gentry could never be overthrown to complete the democratic revolution. The poor peasants (especially the very poor) secured the leadership of the Peasant Associations because they were the most revolutionary. During the first and second stages [of the peasant movement], the chairmen and committee members in the lowest units of the Peasant Associations (village Peasant Associations) were almost entirely poor peasants. (In the village Peasant Associations of Hengshan, fifty per cent of the cadres came from the very poor peasant class, forty per cent from the poor peasant class, and ten per cent from poor educated elements.) *This leadership by the poor peasants is very essential. Without the poor peasants, there will be no revolution.* To reject them is to reject the revolution; a blow at them is a blow at the revolution. Their revolutionary course is faultless from beginning to end. They have cost the *t'u-hao* and bad gentry "face." They have thrown the big and small *t'u-hao* and bad gentry to the ground and have trampled on them. Many "excesses" of theirs during the revolutionary period have been a revolutionary necessity.

Some *hsien* magistrates, *hsien* Party headquarters, and the Peasant Associations of certain *hsien* in Hunan have already committed a number of errors. Some even dispatched soldiers to arrest the lower cadres of the Peasant Associations at the request of landlords. In the prisons of Hengshan and Hsianghsiang *hsien*, many chairmen and committee members of the village Peasant Associations are imprisoned. This error is extremely grave. Unintentionally, it strengthens the position of the reactionaries. The mere fact that the illegitimate landlords rejoiced and that the reactionary atmosphere thickened when the chairmen and committee members of the village Peasant Associations were arrested is sufficient to expose the mistaken nature [of the arrests]. We should oppose such anti-revolutionary slogans as "*p'i-tzu* movement" and "lazy peasant movement," while taking special care not to help the *t'u-hao* and bad gentry (even unintentionally) by attacks on the leading class of the poor peasants. As a matter of fact, though some of the poor peasant leaders have indeed been "gamblers without gainful occupation," the majority of them have since reformed. They themselves now prohibit gambling and clean up banditry. Where the power of the Peasant Associations is strong, local gambling is completely prohibited and banditry disappears. In some localities it is safe to leave articles unattended on the roadside and doors unlocked at night.

According to [my] investigation in Hengshan, eighty-five per cent of the poor peasant leaders are now reformed, able, and hardworking people. Only fifteen per cent still retain some of their bad habits. These can only be called "a few undesirable elements," but one should never imitate the slander of the *t'u-hao* and bad gentry by branding them as "*p'i-tzu.*" As regards these "few undesirable elements," Peasant Association discipline should be improved by mass propaganda and individual training among them, under the slogan "strengthen the discipline of the Peasant Associations!" Indiscriminate arrests by soldiers, which cost the faith of the poor peasant class and strengthen the position of the *t'u-hao* and bad gentry, should definitely be avoided. This point deserves the utmost attention.

51

On New Democracy

January, 1940

Mao Tse-tung

In *On New Democracy*, Mao describes the pattern for two-stage revolutions in colonial and semi-colonial areas. Thus Mao's revolutionary theory is applicable to most of the emerging nations and has had great influence on the Communist movement in Asia and Africa. The success of the Chinese Communists in seizing control of all of mainland China is cited in the Preamble of the Chinese Communist Constitution (Appendix B) as proof of the validity of Mao's theory of the new democratic revolution.

. . . The historical feature of the Chinese revolution consists in the two steps to be taken, democracy and socialism, and the first step is now no longer democracy in a general sense, but democracy of the Chinese type, a new and special type—New Democracy. How then is this historical feature formed? Has it been in existence for the past hundred years, or is it only of recent birth?

If we only make a brief study of the historical development of China and of the world we shall understand that this historical feature did not emerge as a consequence of the Opium War, but began to take shape only

From Mao Tse-tung, *On New Democracy* (Peking: Foreign Languages Press, 1954), pp. 7–14.

after the first imperialist world war and the Russian October Revolution. Let us now study the process of its formation.

Evidently, the colonial, semi-colonial and semi-feudal character of present-day Chinese society determines that two steps must be taken in the Chinese revolution. The first step is to change a society that is colonial, semi-colonial and semi-feudal into an independent, democratic society. The second step is to develop the revolution further and build up a socialist society. In the present Chinese revolution we are taking the first step.

The preparatory period for taking the first step began from the Opium War in 1840, *i.e.*, from the time when Chinese society started to change from a feudal into a semi-colonial and semi-feudal society. The movement of the T'aip'ing Heavenly Kingdom,[1] the Sino-French War,[2] the Sino-Japanese War,[3] the Reformist Movement of 1898,[4] the Revolution of 1911,[5] the May 4 Movement, the Northern Expedition, the War

[1] This refers to the revolutionary war the Chinese peasants waged in the middle of the nineteenth century against the feudalist rule and national oppression of the Manchus. In January 1851, Hung Hsiu-ch'uan, Yang Hsiu-ch'ing and others led the peasants to stage an uprising in Chintien village, Kweiping county, Kwangsi, and established the T'aip'ing Heavenly Kingdom. In 1852 the revolutionary forces embarked on an expedition from Kwangsi. They fought through Hunan, Hupeh, Kiangsi, Anhwei, and took Nanking in 1853. After that, a part of the revolutionary forces was dispatched northward till they reached the vicinity of Tientsin. The T'aip'ing Army, however, did not establish consolidated bases in areas under its occupation, and after Nanking was founded as the capital, its leading bloc committed many political and military blunders. In consequence, it failed to repulse the combined assaults of the Manchus and the British, French and American aggressors, and met with final defeat in 1864.

[2] In 1884 the French invaded Indo-China, Kwangsi, Fukien, Taiwan and Chekiang. The Chinese troops, led by Feng Tzu-ts'ai, Liu Yung-fu and others, put up resistance and won a number of battles. In spite of this, the corrupt Manchu regime signed the humiliating Tientsin Treaty with the French government, recognising its occupation of Indo-China and placing South China under its thumb.

[3] The war broke out as a result of Japan's aggression upon Korea and its provocation against China's ground and sea forces. Although her armed forces fought heroically, China was defeated in the next year because of the corruption of the Manchu government and the lack of preparation for a resolute fight against aggression. The result was the conclusion of a humiliating treaty at Shimonoseki (Bakan), whereby the Manchu government agreed to cede Taiwan and the Pescadores to Japan, to pay an indemnity of 200,000,000 taels (a tael being about 1.33 ounces) of silver, to allow the Japanese to establish factories in China, to open Shasi, Chungking, Soochow and Hangchow as treaty ports, and to place Korea in Japan's hands as her vassal state.

[4] Led by K'ang Yu-wei, Liang Ch'i-ch'ao, T'an Szu-t'ung and others, this reformist movement stood for the interests of a section of the liberal bourgeoisie and the enlightened landlords. Although backed by Emperor Kuanghsu, it had no mass basis. When Yuan Shih-k'ai, with armed forces at his disposal, betrayed the reformists to the Empress Dowager, head of the die-hard clique, the Empress regained political power and had Emperor Kuanghsu incarcerated, and T'an Szu-t'ung and five others beheaded. Thus the movement ended in a tragic defeat.

[5] The revolution that ended the autocratic rule of the Manchu dynasty. On October 10, 1911, under the influence of the bourgeois and petty-bourgeois revolutionary groups, a section of the imperial "New Army" staged an uprising in Wuchang, provincial capital of Hupeh. Similar uprisings in other provinces followed in

of the Agrarian Revolution and the present Anti-Japanese War—these stages have altogether taken up a whole century and, from a certain point of view, represent this first step taken by the Chinese people on different occasions and in various degrees to fight against imperialism and the feudal forces, to strive to build up an independent, democratic society and to complete the first revolution. The Revolution of 1911 was the beginning of that revolution in a fuller sense. In its social character, that revolution is bourgeois-democratic rather than proletarian-socialist. That revolution is not yet completed and great efforts are still required because the enemies of the revolution are still very strong. When Dr. Sun Yat-sen said: "The revolution is not yet completed, all my comrades must strive on," he was referring to such a bourgeois-democratic revolution.

A change, however, occurred in the Chinese bourgeois-democratic revolution after the outbreak of the first imperialist world war in 1914 and the founding of a socialist state on one-sixth of the globe through the Russian October Revolution in 1917.

Before these events, the Chinese bourgeois-democratic revolution belonged to the category of the old bourgeois-democratic world revolution, and was part of that revolution.

After these events, the Chinese bourgeois-democratic revolution changes its character and belongs to the category of the new bourgeois-democratic revolution and, so far as the revolutionary front is concerned, forms part of the proletarian-socialist world revolution.

Why? Because the first imperialist world war and the first victorious socialist revolution, the October Revolution, have changed the historical direction of the whole world and marked a new historical era of the whole world.

In an era when the world capitalist front has collapsed in one corner of the globe (a corner which forms one-sixth of the world), while in other parts it has fully revealed its decadence; when the remaining parts of capitalism cannot survive without relying more than ever on the colonies and semi-colonies; when a socialist state has been established and has declared that it is willing to fight in support of the liberation movement of all colonies and semi-colonies; when the proletariat of the capitalist countries is freeing itself day by day from the social-imperialist influence of the Social-Democratic Parties, and has also declared itself in support of the liberation movement of the colonies and semi-colonies—in such an era, any revolution that takes place in a colony or semi-colony against

---

rapid succession and the Manchu regime soon crumbled. On New Year's Day, 1912, the Provisional Government of the Republic of China was inaugurated in Nanking with Sun Yat-sen as President. This revolution at first triumphed through an alliance of the bourgeoisie with the peasants, the workers and the urban petty bourgeoisie, but finally failed because its leading groups took to compromise. Giving the peasants no real benefits and yielding to the pressure of the imperialist and feudal forces, they let political power slip into the hands of Yuan Shih-k'ai, founder of the Northern clique of warlords.

imperialism, *i.e.*, against the international bourgeoisie and international capitalism, belongs no longer to the old category of bourgeois-democratic world revolution, but to a new category, and is no longer part of the old bourgeois or capitalist world revolution, but part of the new world revolution, the proletarian-socialist world revolution. Such revolutionary colonies and semi-colonies should no longer be regarded as allies of the counter-revolutionary front of world capitalism; they have become allies of the revolutionary front of world socialism.

Although in its social character the first stage of, or the first step taken in, this revolution in a colonial and semi-colonial country is still fundamentally bourgeois-democratic, and although its objective demand is to clear the path for the development of capitalism, yet it no longer belongs to the old type of revolution led by the bourgeoisie with the aim of establishing a capitalist society and a state under bourgeois dictatorship, but belongs to the new type of revolution which, led by the proletariat, aims at establishing first a new-democratic society and a state under the joint dictatorship of all revolutionary classes. Thus this revolution exactly serves to clear a path even wider for the development of socialism. In the course of its progress such a revolution further falls into several stages because of changes in the enemy's conditions and in the ranks of its allies; but its fundamental character will remain unchanged.

Such a revolution deals unrelenting blows to imperialism, and hence is disapproved and opposed by imperialism. But it meets the approval of socialism and is supported by the socialist state and the socialist international proletariat.

Therefore, such a revolution cannot but become part of the proletarian-socialist world revolution.

The correct thesis that "the Chinese revolution is part of the world revolution" was propounded as early as 1924–27 during the period of China's First Great Revolution. It was propounded by the Chinese Communists and approved by all who participated in the anti-imperialist and anti-feudal struggle of the time. But at that time the meaning of this theoretical proposition was not yet fully expounded, and consequently it was only vaguely understood.

This "world revolution" refers no longer to the old world revolution—for the old bourgeois world revolution has long become a thing of the past—but to a new world revolution, the socialist world revolution. Similarly, to form "part" of the world revolution means to form no longer a part of the old bourgeois revolution but that of the new socialist revolution. This is an exceedingly great change unparalleled in the history of China and of the world.

This correct thesis propounded by the Chinese Communists is based on Stalin's theory.

As early as 1918, Stalin wrote in an article commemorating the first anniversary of the October Revolution:

The great world-wide significance of the October Revolution chiefly consists in the fact that:

1. It has widened the scope of the national question and converted it from the particular question of combating national oppression in Europe into the general question of emancipating the oppressed peoples, colonies and semi-colonies from imperialism;

2. It has opened up wide possibilities for their emancipation and the right paths towards it, has thereby greatly facilitated the cause of the emancipation of the oppressed peoples of the West and the East, and has drawn them into the common current of the victorious struggle against imperialism;

3. It has thereby erected a bridge between the socialist West and the enslaved East, having created a new front of revolutions against world imperialism extending from the proletarians of the West, through the Russian revolution, to the oppressed peoples of the East.[6]

[6] J. V. Stalin, *Works*, Eng. ed., Vol. IV, pp. 169–170, Moscow [Foreign Languages Publishing House], 1953.

52

President Truman's Instructions to General Marshall

WASHINGTON, *December 15, 1945*

My dear General Marshall: On the eve of your departure for China I want to repeat to you my appreciation of your willingness to undertake this difficult mission.

I have the utmost confidence in your ability to handle the task before you but, to guide you in so far as you may find it helpful, I will give you some of the thoughts, ideas, and objectives which Secretary Byrnes and I have in mind with regard to your mission.

I attach several documents which I desire should be considered as part of this letter. One is a statement of U.S. policy towards China which was, I understand, prepared after consultation with you and with officials of the Department. The second is a memorandum from the Secretary of State to the War Department in regard to China. And the third is a copy of my press release on policy in China. I understand that these documents have been shown to you and received your approval.

The fact that I have asked you to go to China is the clearest evidence

From United States Department of State, *United States Relations with China: With Special Reference to the Period 1944–1949* (Washington, D.C.: Government Printing Office, 1949), pp. 605–607. For a critique see Selection 56.

of my very real concern with regard to the situation there. Secretary Byrnes and I are both anxious that the unification of China by peaceful, democratic methods be achieved as soon as possible. It is my desire that you, as my Special Representative, bring to bear in an appropriate and practicable manner the influence of the United States to this end.

Specifically, I desire that you endeavor to persuade the Chinese Government to call a national conference of representatives of the major political elements to bring about the unification of China and, concurrently, to effect a cessation of hostilities, particularly in north China.

It is my understanding that there is now in session in Chungking a Peoples' Consultative Council made up of representatives of the various political elements, including the Chinese Communists. The meeting of this Council should furnish you with a convenient opportunity for discussions with the various political leaders.

Upon the success of your efforts, as outlined above, will depend largely, of course, the success of our plans for evacuating Japanese troops from China, particularly north China, and for the subsequent withdrawal of our own armed forces from China. I am particularly desirous that both be accomplished as soon as possible.

In your conversations with Chiang Kai-shek and other Chinese leaders you are authorized to speak with the utmost frankness. Particularly, you may state, in connection with the Chinese desire for credits, technical assistance in the economic field, and military assistance (I have in mind the proposed U.S. military advisory group which I have approved in principle), that a China disunited and torn by civil strife could not be considered realistically as a proper place for American assistance along the lines enumerated.

I am anxious that you keep Secretary Byrnes and me currently informed of the progress of your negotiations and of obstacles you may encounter. You will have our full support and we shall endeavor at all times to be as helpful to you as possible.

Sincerely yours,

Harry Truman

[Enclosure]

MEMORANDUM BY SECRETARY BYRNES

Washington, *December 9, 1945*

FOR THE WAR DEPARTMENT

The President and the Secretary of State are both anxious that the unification of China by peaceful democratic methods be achieved as soon as possible.

At a public hearing before the Foreign Relations Committee of the Senate on December 7, the Secretary of State said:

"During the war the immediate goal of the United States in China was to promote a military union of the several political factions in order to bring their combined power to bear upon our common enemy, Japan. Our longer-range goal, then as now, and a goal of at least equal importance, is the development of a strong, united, and democratic China.

"To achieve this longer-range goal, it is essential that the Central Government of China as well as the various dissident elements approach the settlement of their differences with a genuine willingness to compromise. We believe, as we have long believed and consistently demonstrated, that the government of Generalissimo Chiang Kai-shek affords the most satisfactory base for a developing democracy. But we also believe that it must be broadened to include the representatives of those large and well organized groups who are now without any voice in the government of China.

"This problem is not an easy one. It requires tact and discretion, patience and restraint. It will not be solved by the Chinese leaders themselves. To the extent that our influence is a factor, success will depend upon our capacity to exercise that influence in the light of shifting conditions in such a way as to encourage concessions by the Central Government, by the so-called Communists, and by the other factions."

The President has asked General Marshall to go to China as his Special Representative for the purpose of bringing to bear in an appropriate and practicable manner the influence of the United States for the achievement of the ends set forth above. Specifically, General Marshall will endeavor to influence the Chinese Government to call a national conference of representatives of the major political elements to bring about the unification of China and, concurrently, effect a cessation of hostilities, particularly in north China.

In response to General Wedemeyer's recent messages, the State Department requests the War Department to arrange for directions to him stipulating that:

1. He may put into effect the arrangements to assist the Chinese National Government in transporting Chinese troops to Manchurian ports, including the logistical support of such troops;

2. He may also proceed to put into effect the stepped-up arrangements for the evacuation of Japanese troops from the China theater;

3. Pending the outcome of General Marshall's discussions with Chinese leaders in Chungking for the purpose of arranging a national conference of representatives of the major political elements and for a cessation of hostilities, further transportation of Chinese troops to north China, except as north China ports may be necessary for the movement of troops and supplies into Manchuria, will be held in abeyance;

4. Arrangements for transportation of Chinese troops into north China may be immediately perfected, but not communicated to the Chinese Government. Such arrangements will be executed when General Marshall determines either (a) that the movement of Chinese troops to north China can be carried out consistently with his negotiations, or (b) that the negotiations between the Chinese groups have failed or show no prospect of success and that the circumstances are such as to make the movement necessary to effectuate the surrender terms and to secure the long-term interests of the United States in the maintenance of international peace.

53

Ten Major Principles of Operation

Mao Tse-tung

In a report to the Central Committee of the Communist Party of China on December 25, 1947, Mao Tse-tung listed the ten principles of operation employed by the Communist forces against the Nationalists. These tactics largely explain how the Communists finally won the civil war in China even though they began with greatly inferior forces.

1. Attack dispersed, isolated enemy forces first; attack concentrated, strong enemy forces later.
2. Take small and medium cities and extensive rural areas first; take big cities later.
3. Make wiping out the enemy's effective strength our main objective; do not make holding or seizing a city or place our main objective. Holding or seizing a city or place is the outcome of wiping out the enemy's effective strength, and often a city or place can be held or seized for good only after it has changed hands a number of times.
4. In every battle, concentrate an absolutely superior force (two, three, four and sometimes even five or six times the enemy's strength), encircle the enemy forces completely, strive to wipe them out thoroughly and do not let any escape from the net. In special circumstances, use the method of dealing the enemy crushing blows, that is, concentrate all our

Excerpts from "The Present Situation and Our Tasks" in Mao Tse-tung, *The Selected Military Writings of Mao Tse-tung* (Peking: Foreign Languages Press, 1963), pp. 343–350.

strength to make a frontal attack and an attack on one or both of his flanks, with the aim of wiping out one part and routing another so that our army can swiftly move its troops to smash other enemy forces. Strive to avoid battles of attrition in which we lose more than we gain or only break even. In this way, although inferior as a whole (in terms of numbers), we shall be absolutely superior in every part and every specific campaign, and this ensures victory in the campaign. As time goes on, we shall become superior as a whole and eventually wipe out all the enemy.

5. Fight no battle unprepared, fight no battle you are not sure of winning; make every effort to be well prepared for each battle, make every effort to ensure victory in the given set of conditions as between the enemy and ourselves.

6. Give full play to our style of fighting—courage in battle, no fear of sacrifice, no fear of fatigue, and continuous fighting (that is, fighting successive battles in a short time without rest).

7. Strive to wipe out the enemy when he is on the move. At the same time, pay attention to the tactics of positional attack and capture enemy fortified points and cities.

8. With regard to attacking cities, resolutely seize all enemy fortified points and cities which are weakly defended. At opportune moments, seize all enemy fortified points and cities defended with moderate strength, provided circumstances permit. As for strongly defended enemy fortified points and cities, wait till conditions are ripe and then take them.

9. Replenish our strength with all the arms and most of the personnel captured from the enemy. Our army's main sources of manpower and material are at the front.

10. Make good use of the intervals between campaigns to rest, train and consolidate our troops. Periods of rest, training and consolidation should not in general be very long, and the enemy should so far as possible be permitted no breathing space.

54

The Nationalists' Military Collapse

Major General David Barr

General Barr vividly explains the causes of the Nationalist military
failures in 1948, in the following excerpts from a report which he
submitted early the following year. The comments in brackets have
been added by the Department of State.

An early estimate of the situation, prior to the first formal meeting
of the select combined group, convinced me of the futility of continuing
to hold isolated Manchurian cities which were totally dependent upon air
for both civilian and military supply. The combined airlift capacity of
Chinese civilian and military transports fell far short of the enormous tonnage requirements. The cost of air-lift replacement, maintenance and fuel
—in a country bereft of gold credits—could only result in economic disaster, while making only ineffectual contributions to the supply effort.

Early in March, therefore, when the Communists had withdrawn
their main forces from the vicinity of Changchun and Mukden, after their
winter offensive, I strongly urged the Generalissimo to take advantage of
this opportunity to make a progressive withdrawal from Manchuria. He
was aghast at this proposal, stating that no circumstances would induce
him to consider such a plan. Hopeful of a compromise, I suggested the
withdrawal into Mukden of the Changchun, Kirin and Ssupingchieh garrisons. To this the Generalissimo replied that political considerations precluded the abandonment of Changchun, the ancient capital of Manchuria,
but that he would consider a plan for withdrawing the Kirin garrison into
Changchun. The Kirin garrison was accordingly withdrawn at a later
date.

In my next conference with the Generalissimo, and after his reiter-
ated determination not to consider a withdrawal from Manchuria, I proposed that an early offensive be launched to open rail communications

"Report of Operational Advice Given to the Generalissimo, the Minister of National Defense and the Chief of the Supreme Staff by Major General David Barr," as
printed in United States Department of State, *United States Relations with China:
With Special Reference to the Period 1944–1949* (Washington, D.C.: Government
Printing Office, 1949), pp. 325–338.

between Chinchow and Mukden. The Generalissimo enthusiastically concurred, and instructed his staff to prepare a plan in consultation with my assistants.

At a meeting at the Ministry of National Defense War Room on 8 March 1948 General Lo indicated that a general plan for the opening of a corridor to Mukden had been prepared and approved by the Generalissimo. . . . On 5 May 1948, a coordinated attack from Mukden and Chinchow would be mounted to open a corridor along the railroad between those two points.

The lack of a broad strategic plan for operations was so obviously missing that I inquired if such a plan existed. I was told that the Chinese Armed Forces were then operating under a "Six Months' Plan" and that a "Two Year Plan" had been prepared but was not yet approved by the Generalissimo.

During the period between the date of the above meeting and 17 March 1948, the following events occurred:

The Nationalist 69th Army evacuated Kirin on 12 March and withdrew into Changchun.

Ssupingchieh was captured by the Communists on the night of 12 March.

Air lift of 23,000 Nationalist troops from the Kaifeng-Loyang area to Sian was initiated. For this air lift, all available military transport aircraft was employed, the operation extending over several weeks to the detriment of other operations I considered more important. General Hu Tsung-nan, an old friend of the Generalissimo, had prevailed upon him to reinforce his Sian garrison to an extent which was later to prove disastrous to the Nationalists in East Central China. The loss to the Communists of the Kaifeng-Chenghsien-Loyang area was a direct result of this shift of troops to the west. It has been my contention throughout that the strategic importance of Sian was highly overrated. To this day, a large number of Nationalist troops remain at Sian which could have been far more profitably employed elsewhere.

The greater part of two Nationalist divisions were destroyed in the mountains northeast of Sian because of poor reconnaissance and no march security.

A meeting was held at the Ministry of National Defense War Room on 17 March 1948. In discussing the coming offensive to open a corridor to Mukden, the Chinese stated that it would take six months to repair the railroad between Chinchow and Hsinmin.

On being questioned as to the amount of destruction the Nationalists were able to achieve prior to the evacuation of Kirin, the Chinese were vague. I pointed out that a large amount of the arms and ammunition in the hands of the Communists was captured Nationalist equipment and that the practice of permitting such material to fall into the hands of the Communists was prolonging the war. Although I stressed this point many times after that, it was of little avail. The Chinese seemed inherently unable to destroy anything of value.

At a meeting with the Generalissimo on 24 March, I discussed with him the following subjects, among others:

1. The food situation in Mukden and our ability to assist by immediate delivery of 12 United States C–46's out of a total of 20 available in Japan for turnover to the Chinese.

2. That United States ammunition from the Pacific, destined for Mukden, had not yet been moved to that city although it had arrived in Shanghai.

3. The necessity of a definite and detailed plan for the opening of a line of communication to Mukden. In this connection, the Generalissimo again assured me that he intended to hold Mukden at all cost.

4. The Generalissimo stressed the need for .45 caliber ammunition for use in the large number of submachine guns being used in the Nationalist Army.

In connection with paragraphs (1) and (4) above, I was able to forward a memorandum to the Generalissimo on 29 March informing him that 1 million rounds of .45 caliber ammunition were being made available to him and that the transfer of 16 to 20 United States C–46's had been approved.

A meeting was held at the Ministry of National Defense War Room on 16 April. . . . Following the above meeting, I called on General Yu Ta-wei, Minister of Communications, and learned that his office had received no instructions regarding the reconstruction of the Chinchow-Hsinmin railroad. He stated, however, that he had been informed of the plan and was going ahead with his preparations.

On the 29th of April, at a conference with the Supreme G–3, he again assured my staff that the Mukden attack would be launched on 5 May. He stated that the Generalissimo had ordered the attack to jump off not later than the 5th day of May. . . .

On the 30th of April, my staff interviewed an officer of the Combined Service Forces installation in Mukden. He had only been in office 4 days but had been sent to Nanking by Wei Li-huang to plead with the Ministry for food and gasoline and additional air transport to carry it in. He stated that the Army had food for about 3 weeks and that he needed 3 million gallons of gasoline. He stated that he had had a meeting with the Supreme Staff and that he could get no cooperation from the Chinese Air Force but had arranged with the civilian air lines to fly in an additional month's supply of food. (COMMENT: Each day brought new facts to confirm my belief that General Wei Li-huang had no intention of mounting the proposed attack on 5 May.)

On 1 May 1948 my staff, in conference with the Supreme G–3, was informed of a victory northwest of Sian in which parts of the 2d, 4th and 6th Communist columns in that area were destroyed by the 82d Nationalist Division and other troops of General Ma. A dispatch from General Li, Deputy Supreme G–3, then in Mukden, stated that Wei Li-huang wanted reinforcements from North China before staging his attack. General Lo Tseh-Kai, Supreme G–3, did not believe then that the attack would be mounted. He stated that Wei Li-huang was coming to Nanking to confer with the Generalissimo. (COMMENT: I determined then that if the attack did not take place as planned, I would recommend to the Generalissimo that Mukden be evacuated quickly before the Communists could stage their spring offensive, since Mukden and Changchun could not be indefinitely supplied by air.)

Having been notified that General Chiang, Deputy Chief of Staff of the Mukden Headquarters was in Nanking, I arranged a conference with him at the Ministry on 4 May 1948. General Chiang led off with a lengthy description of recent Communist movements from the north towards the Mukden area, of their excellent state of supply and training and of the assistance they were receiving from Russia. It was obvious that he was leading up to the news that the proposed Nationalist attack to open the corridor to Chinchow would not be mounted.

He stated that the morale of the Mukden forces was high and that they wanted to fight and defeat the Communists. When asked "why not then fight now before it is too late?" General Chiang answered that reinforcements from North China were necessary. He stated that a strong defense of the Mukden-Chinchow areas should be made at that time and a coordinated attack to open a corridor be made later. He advised to sit tight until the Communist intentions became clear and then take action. This was undoubtedly the policy Wei Li-huang would pursue in spite of all orders to the contrary from the Generalissimo and the Supreme Staff. The opportunity to take the initiative away from the Communists had been lost. It was extremely doubtful if a later attempt to open a corridor would be successful.

I attended the conference mentioned above, on the afternoon of the 5th of May at the Generalissimo's home. Present were the Generalissimo and Madame Chiang Kai-shek, the three Mukden Generals mentioned above and several members of the Supreme General Staff. After a lengthy discourse by the Mukden Generals as to the reasons the long awaited Manchurian operations could not then be staged, the Generalissimo asked for my opinions. I told him that I had heard nothing but reasons why the attack could not be mounted. That at a later date I was convinced the same excuses would be given plus those that would develop during the interim. I recommended that the attack be mounted then and that if this could not be accomplished then Manchuria should be evacuated while an opportunity still offered itself. I pointed out that Communist strength in

Manchuria was increasing and that if success was uncertain at this time, it was definitely impossible later. I further pointed out that Changchun and Mukden could not be indefinitely supplied by air. The Generalissimo stated that because General Fu Tso-yi could not spare two armies from North China at that time to reinforce the Chinchow garrison, a reinforcement being considered necessary to the success of the operation, he had decided to postpone the attack to 1 August 1948. He further stated that the troops then available in Manchuria would be the only ones that could be counted upon and enjoined the Mukden commanders to use the time available for the intensive training of these troops. (I would like to point out at this time that the Generalissimo had directed General Wei Li-huang as early as the preceding winter to prepare plans and ready himself for an attack early in May to open a corridor from Mukden to Chinchow. That the Supreme G–3 and members of his division had made six separate trips to Mukden in an effort to press preparations for this attack. That both myself and my staff had continuously urged the Chinese towards this effort since early February. That General Wei Li-huang was able to get away with such complete disobedience of orders without punishment or even censure, as far as I know, points out one reason why the Nationalists are losing the present war.)

On 6 May 1948, the Supreme G–3 had a conference with the three visiting Mukden Generals. General Chao had told him that the Communists had learned of the proposed Nationalist attempt to open the corridor and were moving troops to intercept the attack. He insisted that more time was needed to train and organize more troops. His main theme was to *defend* Mukden and Chinchow thus containing large masses of Manchurian Communists which in turn meant the salvation of North China. The G–3 disagreed and pointed out that another such opportunity to wrest the initiative from the Communists and defeat them would not occur again.

At a meeting on 29th May I asked whether there was any intention or thought being given to a withdrawal from Manchuria and was given a negative answer. I stated that if Chinchow fell as a result of inaction at Mukden, then Mukden was surely lost and that this should be made clear to Wei Li-huang. The Chief of Staff informed me that an agreement was reached at the Generalissimo's headquarters that if Wei Li-huang failed to assist the Chinchow garrison, he would be severely punished.

During the month of May 1948, certain political and military developments occurred which are of interest. The National Assembly adjourned on 1 May after electing Chiang Kai-shek and Li Tsung-jen President and Vice President respectively. On 10 May the Executive Yuan resigned en bloc which brought most government efforts to a standstill and made decisions difficult to obtain. A new Cabinet was not appointed until after Inaugural Day, 20 May. General Ku Chutung, Commander of the Ground Forces, was named Supreme Chief of Staff during the week ending 14 May and General Yu Han-mou was named as Commander of the Ground Forces. The selection of these officers to fill these highly important military posts was a disappointment to me. Their military background left much to be desired. They were staunch supporters of the Generalissimo and it was obvious that their appointment was for political expediency rather than ability. I had met them both before and had been impressed by their lack of personality.

[In view of the Chinese determination not to abandon Manchuria and following an inspection of certain areas there by American officers, General Barr on June 2, 1948, submitted new proposals for offensive action in Manchuria.]

During the period from the 20th to the 30th of June, my staff in personal conferences with the Supreme G–2 and G–3, were made acquainted with the following facts:

Because of the serious situation forming in East Central China, the Generalissimo flew to Chienhsien, west of Kaifeng to personally direct operations. On the 24th of June he held an important military commanders' meeting at Sian. In connection with this and other such meetings, the Minister of National Defense, General Ho Ying-chin, complained to me, with some bitterness, that the Generalissimo often issued operational orders direct without informing him or the Supreme General Staff. This is a well known failing of the Generalissimo's. It was reported to my staff that the Chinese Air Force in a weak effort to support the defenders of Kaifeng, strafed Communist columns from elevations well above 2,000 feet. This failing was mentioned to the Chinese on innumerable occasions without apparent result. Not only did they strafe from ineffective heights, but they also bombed from ridiculous elevations. It was also reported that Kaifeng was bombed during the Communist occupation, which was later proven untrue or at least the results were very ineffective.

Decision was made by the Generalissimo to defend isolated Tsinan to the last. (Such decisions have been costly to the Nationalists in troops and supplies.) I pointed out again to the Generalissimo and to the Supreme Staff the futility of attempting to hold cities from within restricted perimeters by purely defensive measures against overpowering enemy forces. Tsinan at this time was isolated from Hsuchow by Communist forces at Yenchow and Taian. Although in considerable strength in this area the main Communist force was still on the Honan plains, southeast of Kaifeng. An opportunity existed to do one of two things. By offensive action north from Hsuchow and south from Tsinan, the Nationalist forces were capable of destroying the Communists and reopening the corridor between Hsuchow and Tsinan. The Nationalists were also capable at this time of evacuating Tsinan and withdrawing into Hsuchow. Having no confidence in the will to fight of the Tsinan garrison after their ineffective attempt to recapture Weihsien, and having heard reports of the questionable loyalty of some of the senior commanders, I recommended that the city be evacuated, and the troops be withdrawn to Hsuchow. Again, as in the case of Changchun, I was told that because of political reasons, Tsinan, the capital of Shantung Province, must be defended.

On July 2, 1948, at the invitation of the American Military Attaché, Brig. Gen. Robert H. Soule, I flew over Kaifeng and the area to the southeast thereof where heavy fighting was reported to be in progress. Reports of destruction in Kaifeng by the Chinese Air Force bombing and fire were proven untrue. With the exception of a few bomb craters outsid the city walls, no effects of the bombing could be seen. We circled at lo altitude all over the reported battle area southeast of the city, but with the exception of a few burning houses in scattered villages, a few mortar shell bursts, some marching troops and two fighter planes flying higher than we were, there was little evidence of the reported clash of half a million men.

At a meeting in the Ministry of National Defense War Room on 14 September 1948, the following observations were made by the Chinese:

The G–3 stated that although completely surrounded and isolated, food was still coming to Tsinan from the countryside. He believed that an additional division could be air lifted into Tsinan to assist in the defense. I recommended strongly against this believing that the city was lost and that it only meant the loss to the Nationalists of an additional division. One had already been air lifted in from Tsingtao. I recommended, that rather than fly in additional troops, the present Tsinan garrison be air lifted to Hsuchow.

On 24 September 1948 I learned that Tsinan had been captured by the Communists. The unexpectedly early fall of the city was the result of a defection to the Communists of an entire Nationalist division which had been entrusted with the defense of the western approaches to the city. This division, former puppet troops, had been suspected and should have previously been relieved.

At a meeting with the Generalissimo on the 29th of September, the following matters, among others, were discussed:

The Generalissimo expressed deep disappointment over the outcome of the battle of Tsinan and stated that its fall was unexpected. He said that it was necessary for a study to be made on Chinese strategy, tactics, training and organization of field units in order that the mistakes committed at Tsinan would not be repeated. He said that the old strategy of holding strong points or key cities at all cost would have to go.

The Generalissimo said that my reasoning was very sound and expressed the hope that I would attend the weekly military operational conference held each Wednesday in the Ministry of Defense War Room. He asked that I give his operational officers the benefit of my experience and advice. I stated that I would be glad to comply with his request.

[In view of Communist activity around Chinchow the Generalissimo had ordered General Wei in Mukden to take aggressive offensive action to relieve the pressure further south. General Barr made the following comment on a meeting held October 1 in the Ministry of National Defense War Room:]

I pointed out that the situation in Chinchow was extremely critical, that five days had passed since General Wei Li-huang had received orders to attack to the west and that there had been no indication of such an attack getting under way. I recommended that the Mukden troops break out to the west of their position at once, ready or not.

At a luncheon meeting on 7 October 1948 the following matters were discussed and recommendations made:

General Ho Ying-chin announced that it had been determined to organize, train and equip an additional 28 strategic reserve divisions (three regiments in each) over and above the nine presently being organized and trained. I pointed out that little progress had been made in the original plan to form nine divisions and asked how he expected to handle 28 more. He replied that there were that many in the south and west that had been depleted in combat, were partially equipped, and could be brought up to strength and equipped with United States aid supplies supplemented by Chinese production. He stated that his representatives would confer shortly with Brigadier General Laurence Keiser, my Ground Division Senior Adviser, on the plan. This was another example of Chinese grandiose planning without thought or regard to the possibility of its implementation.

General Ho stated that the Generalissimo was in Peiping. (The General did not return to Nanking until after the fall of Mukden and Chinchow. He directed this operation from Peiping without the assistance of his Supreme Staff whom he failed to keep informed as to what was taking place. In spite of this unorthodox procedure, the plans made and orders given were sound and had they been obeyed, the results would probably have been favorable.)

At a meeting in the Ministry of National Defense War Room on 13 October 1948, the following matters were discussed:

General Wei Li-huang had used only 11 divisions in his breakout to the west instead of 15 as ordered. He had been directed to employ his 52d Army to reinforce his operations. The attack had commenced on 9 October, 13 days after receipt of orders to attack immediately. Progress had been very slow to date.

In discussing the situation at Changchun, I learned that the garrison commander, General Cheng Tung-kuo, had received instructions from Wei Li-huang to coordinate his breakout with Wei Li-huang's attack, immediately before, during or immediately after. To date there had been no indications of any effort on his part to comply with these confused instructions and the situation at Changchun was obscure.

At a meeting in the Ministry of National Defense War Room on the 20th of October 1948, the following matters were discussed:

A briefing by the Supreme G–2 and G–3 disclosed the loss to the Communists on 20 October of Changchun after the defection of the majority of the garrison and the suicide of the garrison commander, General Cheng Tung-kuo. This report of suicide was later found to be untrue. It was reported also that Chinchow had fallen with four of the victorious Communist columns already moving south towards Hulutao. The efforts of the Nationalists to attack north from the Chinsi-Hulutao area had been completely unsuccessful while the movement southwest from Mukden of General Wei Li-huang's armies was disappointingly slow.

I asked whether or not plans had been prepared for the evacuation of the Chinsi-Hulutao area and upon being answered in the negative, I recommended that plans be made then to include shipping necessary for the evacuation of heavy equipment and supplies, and suggested that the troops fight south down the corridor.

I asked if it was known what General Wei Li-huang intended to do, since Chinchow had fallen, and suggested that he should evacuate Mukden entirely and fight southwest with the idea of entering North China. I pointed out that if he returned into Mukden, the Nationalist Government could not supply him much longer by air and that his position would deteriorate into a second Changchun. General Ho Ying-chin agreed and stated that he had put this question up to the Generalissimo who was still in Peiping, but had received no reply.

In a visit to G–3 on the morning of 28 October 1948, my staff learned of the defeat of General Wei Li-huang's forces west of Mukden on 27 October. I recommended that the 11 Nationalist divisions then in the Chinsi-Hulutao area, be evacuated by sea at once or make a determined effort to fight their way south into north China before the main Communist strength could return to prevent it. I further recommended that the troops in Yinkow, and all that could reach Yinkow from Mukden, also be evacuated by sea at once. I could not refrain from pointing out that if Wei Li-huang had moved southwest promptly after receiving his orders on the 25th of September, instead of delaying until the 9th of October, and then had moved with speed in the attack, he would have saved Chinchow and could have brought all his strength into North China. General Ho admitted that I was correct, but stated that his hands were tied and that the Generalissimo had directed the entire operations alone from Peiping without reference to him or to the Supreme Staff. In this, of course, the Generalissimo was wrong, but the orders he issued to General Wei Li-huang for the conduct of operations in Manchuria were sound. Had they been carried out with determination and speed there was every chance of success. Chinchow, though sorely pressed, held out against the Communists long enough to enable the Mukden and the Hulutao-Chinsi forces to converge to their rescue had they moved promptly and fought with sufficient determination to get there in time. The Nationalist troops, in Manchuria, were the finest soldiers the Government had. The large majority of the units were United States equipped and many soldiers and junior officers still remained who had received United States training during the war with Japan. I am convinced that had these troops had proper leadership from the top the Communists would have suffered a major defeat. The Generalissimo placed General Tu Yu-ming, an officer of little worth, in charge of field operations, properly relegating to General Wei Li-huang over-all supervision from Mukden where he could do little harm. But Tu Yu-ming also fought the battle from Mukden, placing the burden of active command in the field to General Liao Yao-hsiang, Commanding General of the 9th Army Group. Liao was a good general but was killed early in the action. Without top leadership and in the confusion that followed the Communists were able to segment the Nationalist forces and destroy them piecemeal. General Wei Li-huang and General Tu Yu-ming deserted the troops and were safely in Hulutao at the end. The efforts of the troops in the Chinsi-Hulutao area to relieve Chinchow were also futile. Instead of mounting an all-out attack with full force initially, which could have swept aside the Communists who were weakened by withdrawals sent against Wei Li-huang, the attack was developed slowly with troops being thrown in piecemeal. The attack soon bogged down with the troops showing little will to fight. The loss of Manchuria and some 300,000 of its best troops was a stunning blow to the Government. To me, the loss of the troops was the most serious result. It spelled the beginning of the end. There could be no hope for North China with an additional 360,000 Communist troops now free to move against its north flank.

[Following the loss of forces in Manchuria the center of activity shifted to Hsuchow.]

At a meeting in the Ministry of National Defense War Room on the 25th of November 1948, the following matters were discussed:

The Supreme G–2 and G–3 briefed the assembly on the current military situation. The strength of the Hsuchow garrison was given as 270,000. Regarding supplies, it was stated that ammunition was sufficient but a food shortage existed. I strongly recommended that Hsuchow be evacuated at once and that its troops move south against the rear of the Communists forces below Shusien. The G–2 reported that the Mukden-Chinchow railroad had been restored. It had taken the Communists just 25 days to restore this line, a project the Nationalists had insisted would take 6 months when discussions were under way concerning the proposed Nationalist 5 May attack which never materialized.

At a meeting in the Ministry of National Defense War Room on 1 December 1948, the following subjects were discussed:

The usual G–2—G–3 briefing disclosed that four of the nine Nationalist armies at Hsuchow were not being employed in the attack to the south. I recommended that the attack be an all-out one and that all troops be employed with a view toward evacuating the city entirely. I again stressed the necessity for speed. General Ho Ying-chin stated that the orders issued had been to that effect.

[Despite belated efforts of the forces in the Hsuchow area to withdraw to more easily defensible positions these forces were surrounded and destroyed by the Communists as were units moving to their relief. As it became apparent that the remaining military forces of the Government were powerless to stop the Communist armies and that their defeat was inevitable, steps were taken to decrease the size of JUSMAG, for American military personnel associated with it did not have the diplomatic immunity accorded attachés. With the certainty that Nanking would fall in the immediate future and with the disorganized condition of the Chinese armies, its period of usefulness had passed and orders were issued for its removal from China. On December 18 in a telegram to the Department of the Army General Barr stated in part: "Marked by the stigma of defeat and the loss of face resulting from the forced evacuation of China, north of the Yangtze, it is extremely doubtful if the National Government could muster the necessary popular support to mobilize sufficient manpower in this area (South China) with which to rebuild its forces even if time permitted. Only a policy of unlimited United States aid including the immediate employment of United States armed forces to block the southern advance of the Communists, which I emphatically do not recommend, would enable the Nationalist Government to maintain a foothold in southern China against a determined Communist advance. . . . The complete defeat of the Nationalist Army . . . is inevitable."]

[General Barr summarized his views of the causes for the Government's defeat as follows:]

Many pages could be written covering the reasons for the failure of Nationalist strategy. I believe that the Government committed its first politico-military blunder when it concentrated its efforts after V–J Day on the purely military reoccupation of the former Japanese areas, giving little consideration to long established regional sentiments or to creation of efficient local administrations which could attract wide popular support in the liberated areas. Moreover, the Nationalist Army was burdened with an unsound strategy which was conceived by a politically influenced and militarily inept high command. Instead of being content with consolidating North China, the Army was given the concurrent mission of seizing control of Manchuria, a task beyond its logistic capabilities. The Government, attempting to do too much with too little, found its armies scattered along thousands of miles of railroads, the possession of which was vital in view of the fact that these armies were supplied from bases in central

China. In order to hold the railroads, it was also necessary to hold the large cities through which they passed. As time went on, the troops degenerated from field armies, capable of offensive combat, to garrison and lines of communication troops with an inevitable loss of offensive spirit. Communist military strength, popular support, and tactical skill were seriously under-estimated from the start. It became increasingly difficult to maintain effective control over the large sections of predominantly Communist countryside through which the lines of communication passed. Lack of Nationalist forces qualified to take the field against the Communists enabled the latter to become increasingly strong. The Nationalists, with their limited resources, steadily lost ground against an opponent who not only shaped his strategy around available human and material resources, but also capitalized skillfully on the Government's strategic and tactical blunders and economic vulnerability.

Initially, the Communists were content to fight a type of guerrilla warfare, limiting their activities to raids on lines of communication and supply installations. The success of their operations, which were purely offensive, instilled in them the offensive attitude so necessary to success in war. On the other hand, the Nationalist strategy of defense of the areas they held, developed in them the "wall psychology" which has been so disastrous to their armies. As the Communists grew stronger and more confident, they were able, by concentrations of superior strength, to surround, attack, and destroy Nationalist units in the field and Nationalist held cities. It is typical of the Nationalists, in the defense of an area or a city, to dig in or retire within the city walls, and there to fight to the end, hoping for relief which never comes because it cannot be spared from elsewhere. The Chinese have resisted advice that, in the defense of an area or a city, from attack by modern methods of warfare, it is necessary to take up positions away from the walls where fire and maneuver is possible. Further, they have been unable to be convinced of the necessity for withdrawing from cities and prepared areas when faced with overpowering opposition and certain isolation and defeat, while the opportunity still existed for them to do so. In some cases their reasons for failure to withdraw and save their forces were political, but in most cases, they were convinced that by defensive action alone, they could, through attrition, if nothing else, defeat the enemy. Because of this mistaken concept and because of their inability to realize that discretion is usually the better part of valor, large numbers of Nationalist troops were lost to the Government.

It must be understood that all through the structure and machinery of the Nationalist Government there are interlocking ties of interest peculiar to the Chinese—family, financial, political. No man, no matter how efficient, can hope for a position of authority on account of being the man best qualified for the job; he simply must have other backing. In too many cases, this backing was the support and loyalty of the Generalissimo for his old army comrades which kept them in positions of high responsibility regardless of their qualifications. A direct result of this practice is the unsound strategy and faulty tactics so obviously displayed in the fight against the Communists.

Cooperation among and coordination of effort between the Armed Forces leaves much to be desired. The Ground Forces, being the old and dominant arm, is the source from which the large majority of top military positions are filled. These officers, mostly old and loyal contemporaries of the Generalissimo, have little or no knowledge of the newer arms: the Air Force and the Navy. The Chinese Air Force, consisting of $8\frac{1}{3}$ groups, is far in excess of what a country bereft of gold credits can support. Although it has among its personnel over five thousand United States trained pilots, it accomplished little, other than air-lifting troops and operating its transports for personal gains. There was an ever present reluctance to take a chance on losing equipment or personnel, which was clearly reflected in their constant refusal to operate at other than high altitudes. There was an ingrained resentment in the Chinese Air Force against killing Chinese Communists who had no air support. All of these factors are important and unfortunate because the Chinese Air Force, unopposed, could have rendered invaluable support in ground operations had its capabilities been properly employed. From a military viewpoint, the case of the Navy is not so important since its employment, right or wrong, could have had little effect on the final outcome; all operations were land based. From an economic viewpoint, the Navy could have been of inestimable value in suppressing smugglers in Hong Kong-Canton waters had it been willing to suppress and not participate. It was completely relieved of this mission in March 1948, and reputedly millions of dollars in customs revenue continue to be lost to the Government.

It might be expected that the Communists, being Chinese themselves, would also suffer from these faulty Nationalist traits and characteristics, and to a certain extent they do, but they have wisely subordinated them and made their ideology of Communism almost a fetish. By means of total mobilization in the areas they control, propaganda, and the use of political commissars within their armed forces, they maintain loyalty to the established order. Their leaders are men of proven ability who invariably outgeneral the Nationalist commanders. The morale and fighting spirit of the troops is very high because they are winning.

55

Letter of Transmittal, in the
China White Paper

Dean Acheson

The reasons for the failures of the Chinese National Government appear in some detail in the attached record. They do not stem from any inadequacy of American aid. Our military observers on the spot have reported that the Nationalist armies did not lose a single battle during the crucial year of 1948 through lack of arms or ammunition. The fact was that the decay which our observers had detected in Chungking early in the war had fatally sapped the powers of resistance of the Kuomintang. Its leaders had proved incapable of meeting the crisis confronting them, its troops had lost the will to fight, and its Government had lost popular support. The Communists, on the other hand, through a ruthless discipline and fanatical zeal, attempted to sell themselves as guardians and liberators of the people. The Nationalist armies did not have to be defeated; they disintegrated. History has proved again and again that a regime without faith in itself and an army without morale cannot survive the test of battle.

The record obviously can not set forth in equal detail the inner history and development of the Chinese Communist Party during these years. The principal reason is that, while we had regular diplomatic relations with the National Government and had the benefit of voluminous reports from our representatives in their territories, our direct contact with the Communists was limited in the main to the mediation efforts of General Hurley and General Marshall.

Fully recognizing that the heads of the Chinese Communist Party were ideologically affiliated with Moscow, our Government nevertheless took the view, in the light of the existing balance of forces in China, that peace could be established only if certain conditions were met. The Kuomintang would have to set its own house in order and both sides would have to make concessions so that the Government of China might

From United States Department of State, *United States Relations with China: With Special Reference to the Period 1944–1949* (Washington, D.C.: Government Printing Office, 1949), pp. xiv–xvii. Only the concluding portion of the letter is printed here.

become, in fact as well as in name, the Government of all China and so that all parties might function within the constitutional system of the Government. Both internal peace and constitutional development required that the progress should be rapid from one party government with a large opposition party in armed rebellion, to the participation of all parties, including the moderate non-communist elements, in a truly national system of government.

None of these conditions has been realized. The distrust of the leaders of both the Nationalist and Communist Parties for each other proved too deep-seated to permit final agreement, notwithstanding temporary truces and apparently promising negotiations. The Nationalists, furthermore, embarked in 1946 on an over-ambitious military campaign in the face of warnings by General Marshall that it not only would fail but would plunge China into economic chaos and eventually destroy the National Government. General Marshall pointed out that though Nationalist armies could, for a period, capture Communist-held cities, they could not destroy the Communist armies. Thus every Nationalist advance would expose their communications to attack by Communist guerrillas and compel them to retreat or to surrender their armies together with the munitions which the United States has furnished them. No estimate of a military situation has ever been more completely confirmed by the resulting facts.

The historic policy of the United States of friendship and aid toward the people of China was, however, maintained in both peace and war. Since V-J Day, the United States Government has authorized aid to Nationalist China in the form of grants and credits totaling approximately 2 billion dollars, an amount equivalent in value to more than 50 per cent of the monetary expenditures of the Chinese Government and of proportionately greater magnitude in relation to the budget of that Government than the United States has provided to any nation of Western Europe since the end of the war. In addition to these grants and credits, the United States Government has sold the Chinese Government large quantities of military and civilian war surplus property with a total procurement cost of over 1 billion dollars, for which the agreed realization to the United States was 232 million dollars. A large proportion of the military supplies furnished the Chinese armies by the United States since V-J Day has, however, fallen into the hands of the Chinese Communists through the military ineptitude of the Nationalist leaders, their defections and surrenders, and the absence among their forces of the will to fight.

It has been urged that relatively small amounts of additional aid—military and economic—to the National Government would have enabled it to destroy communism in China. The most trustworthy military, economic, and political information available to our Government does not bear out this view.

A realistic appraisal of conditions in China, past and present, leads to the conclusion that the only alternative open to the United States was full-scale intervention in behalf of a Government which had lost the confidence of its own troops and its own people. Such intervention would have required the expenditure of even greater sums than have been fruitlessly spent thus far, the command of Nationalist armies by American officers, and the probable participation of American armed forces—land, sea, and air—in the resulting war. Intervention of such a scope and magnitude would have been resented by the mass of the Chinese people, would have diametrically reversed our historic policy, and would have been condemned by the American people.

It must be admitted frankly that the American policy of assisting the Chinese people in resisting domination by any foreign power or powers is now confronted with the gravest difficulties. The heart of China is in Communist hands. The Communist leaders have foresworn their Chinese heritage and have publicly announced their subservience to a foreign power, Russia, which during the last 50 years, under czars and Communists alike, has been most assiduous in its efforts to extend its control in the Far East. In the recent past, attempts at foreign domination have appeared quite clearly to the Chinese people as external aggression and as such have been bitterly and in the long run successfully resisted. Our aid and encouragement have helped them to resist. In this case, however, the foreign domination has been masked behind the façade of a vast crusading movement which apparently has seemed to many Chinese to be wholly indigenous and national. Under these circumstances, our aid has been unavailing.

The unfortunate but inescapable fact is that the ominous result of the civil war in China was beyond the control of the government of the United States. Nothing that this country did or could have done within the reasonable limits of its capabilities could have changed that result; nothing that was left undone by this country has contributed to it. It was the product of internal Chinese forces, forces which this country tried to influence but could not. A decision was arrived at within China, if only a decision by default.

And now it is abundantly clear that we must face the situation as it exists in fact. We will not help the Chinese or ourselves by basing our policy on wishful thinking. We continue to believe that, however tragic may be the immediate future of China and however ruthlessly a major portion of this great people may be exploited by a party in the interest of a foreign imperialism, ultimately the profound civilization and the democratic individualism of China will reassert themselves and she will throw off the foreign yoke. I consider that we should encourage all developments in China which now and in the future work toward this end.

In the immediate future, however, the implementation of our historic policy of friendship for China must be profoundly affected by current developments. It will necessarily be influenced by the degree to which the Chinese people come to recognize that the Communist regime serves not their interests but those of Soviet Russia and the manner in which, having become aware of the facts, they react to this foreign domination. One point, however, is clear. Should the Communist regime lend itself to the aims of Soviet Russian imperialism and attempt to engage in aggression against China's neighbors, we and the other members of the United Nations would be confronted by a situation violative of the principles of the United Nations Charter and threatening international peace and security.

Meanwhile our policy will continue to be based upon our own respect for the Charter, our friendship for China, and our traditional support for the Open Door and for China's independence and administrative and territorial integrity.

56

On American Policy in China

Hu Shih

Hu Shih, the leader of the literary renaissance in 1918, was China's Ambassador to the United States during the critical years 1938 to 1942 and President of the Academia Sinica in Taiwan at the time of his death in 1962. He was an advocate of scientific method and an outspoken critic of both Marxism and reactionary Confucianism. He was attacked by the Chinese Communists as the symbol of "decadent American bourgeois pragmatism." His frank views on the work of the Marshall mission in China follow.

The objectives of the Marshall Mission were summed up in these directives as "the unification of China by peaceful, democratic methods . . . as soon as possible." Specifically, they were twofold:

First, "the United States is cognizant that the present National Government of China is a 'one-party government' and believes that peace, unity and democratic reform in China will be furthered if the basis of this Government

From the Introduction, by Dr. Hu Shih, to *Fifty Years in China*, by John Leighton Stuart. Copyright, 1954 by John Leighton Stuart. Reprinted by permission of Random House, Inc.

is broadened to include other political elements in the country. Hence, the United States strongly advocates that the national conference of representatives of major political elements in the country agree upon arrangements which will give those elements a fair and effective representation in the Chinese National Government."

And secondly, "the existence of autonomous armies such as that of the Communist army is inconsistent with, and actually makes impossible, political unity in China. With the institution of a broadly representative government, autonomous armies should be eliminated as such and all armed forces in China integrated effectively into the Chinese National Army." [1]

The first objective was to cause the Chinese to form a coalition government with the Chinese Communists fairly and effectively represented; the second was to cause them to "eliminate" the autonomous armies of the Chinese Communist Party and "integrate" them into the National Army.

As Secretary of State Byrnes states in one of the directives:

This problem is not an easy one. . . . *It will not be solved by the Chinese themselves.* To the extent that our influence is a factor, success will depend upon our capacity to exercise that influence in the light of shifting conditions in such a way as to encourage concessions by the Central Government, by the so-called Communists, and by the other factions. The President has asked General Marshall to go to China as his Special Representative for the purpose of bringing to bear in an appropriate and practicable manner the influence of the United States for the achievement of the ends set forth above. (*Italics mine.*) [2]

Such was the inherently impossible dual task of the Marshall Mission. The Chinese Communists wanted to get into a coalition government: that was the Yalta formula deviously devised by Stalin for Poland and for all "Liberated Europe"; that was what Mao Tse-tung openly demanded on April 24, 1945, in his fifty-thousand-word report to the Seventh Congress of the Chinese Communist Party held in Yenan—a report entitled "On Coalition Government." But they had absolutely no intention of having their autonomous armies "eliminated" or "integrated" into the National Army: on the contrary, the Communist Army, which Mao Tse-tung on April 24, 1945, claimed to number 910,000 men in regular units and 2,200,000 men in the "people's militia force," was expanding during the first six months of General Marshall's stay in China into 1,200,000 men in its regular formations.

And what were to be the ways and means by which the Marshall Mission was to "bring to bear the influence of the United States for the

[1] United States Department of State. *United States Relations with China: With Special Reference to the Period 1944–1949* (Washington, D.C.: Government Printing Office, 1949), p. 608. [Editor's note.]

[2] See Selection 52. [Editor's note.]

achievement of the ends set forth above"? President Truman directed General Marshall:

> In your conversations with Chiang Kai-shek and other Chinese leaders you are authorized to speak with the utmost frankness. Particularly, you may state, in connection with the Chinese desire for credits, technical assistance in the economic field, and military assistance, . . . that a China disunited and torn by civil strife could not be considered realistically as a proper place for American assistance.

In plain language, the weapon was to be not military pressure or intervention, but the withholding of American aid to China.

But this weapon could only checkmate the Chinese Government and had no effect whatever on the Chinese Communists, whose armies had been racing by land and by sea to Manchuria where they could obtain unlimited aid from the Soviet Occupation Forces and from the Soviet Union, now the contiguous, strongest base of revolution for the Chinese Communists. So, during the entire period of the Marshall Mission, the Chinese Communist delegation was constantly and successfully pressing General Marshall to stop or suspend American aid to China! And General Marshall and the United States Government did many times stop and suspend all American aid to China because of the loud protests of the Chinese Communists.

So the Marshall Mission failed because of its inherently impossible objectives, which neither Secretary Byrnes, nor President Truman, nor General Marshall, nor Mr. John Carter Vincent (who more than anyone else was largely responsible for drafting the Marshall directives) ever fully understood.

And the ambassadorship of Dr. Stuart failed too, because, in his own words, he was "a tyro in diplomacy"; and because, again in his own words:

> General Marshall had originally brought me into his efforts to form a coalition government because of my reputation as a liberal American, friendly to the Chinese people as a whole, and with no pronounced sympathy for any one faction or school of thought. This included the Communists, several of whose leaders I had known fairly well.

All these seemingly harsh words I have said without the slightest intention of ridiculing the naïveté of those idealistic statesmen of an idealistic age. In fact I, too, was just as naïve a tyro in national and international politics in those days of expansive idealism. So naïve, indeed, was I that shortly after V-J Day I sent a lengthy radiogram to Chungking to be forwarded to my former student Mao Tse-tung, solemnly and earnestly pleading with him that, now that Japan had surrendered, there was no more justification for the Chinese Communists to continue to maintain a huge private army, and that his Party should now emulate the good example of the British Labor Party which, without a single soldier of its own, had just won an overwhelming victory at the recent election and acquired undisputed political power for the next five years. On August 28, 1945, Mao Tse-tung arrived at Chungking accompanied by the American Ambassador, General Patrick Hurley, another tyro in diplomacy, and my Chungking friend radioed me that my message had been duly forwarded to Mr. Mao in person. Of course, to this day I have never received a reply.

In conclusion, I want sincerely to voice my hearty agreement with the reflections of my old friend Dr. Stuart on the China "White Paper" and on what policy his great country should pursue in regard to China. And, since this is an introduction written by an unreconstructed, heathen Chinese to a book of memoirs by a great Christian leader, I would like to conclude with a quotation from his beloved New Testament. When in 1949 I read Secretary Dean Acheson's Letter of Transmittal of the China "White Paper" and came to these sentences: ". . . the ominous result of the civil war in China was beyond the control of the government of the United States. Nothing that this country did or could have done within the reasonable limits of its capabilities could have changed that result; nothing that was left undone by this country has contributed to it." —when I read those sentences, I wrote on the margin: "Matthew 27:24." This is the text:

When Pilate saw that he could prevail nothing, but that a tumult was made, he took water, and washed his hands before the multitude, saying, I am innocent of the blood of this just man: see ye to it.

Because of the betrayal of China at Yalta, because of its withholding of effective aid to China at crucial times, and, above all, because of its great power and undisputed world leadership, the United States was not "innocent of the blood" of fallen China.

And I agree with Dr. Stuart that the least the United States can do to redeem itself is to continue in its refusal to recognize the Communist Government and continue to oppose admission of that government to China's place in the United Nations. That is at least in line with the great tradition of the historic Doctrine of Non-recognition upheld by Henry L. Stimson and Herbert Hoover and written into the Atlantic Charter by President Roosevelt and Prime Minister Churchill.

57

United States Policy Toward Formosa

January 5, 1950

President Harry S. Truman

> Following the Communist victory on the Chinese mainland, the
> United States sought to disengage itself from the Chinese civil war
> by refraining from giving military aid or advice to the Nationalist
> forces in Formosa, as indicated in this statement by the President.
> This policy was reversed when the North Korean Communists
> invaded South Korea in June, 1950 (see Chapter X, Selection 58).

The United States Government has always stood for good faith in
international relations. Traditional United States policy toward China, as
exemplified in the open-door policy, called for international respect for
the territorial integrity of China. This principle was recently reaffirmed
in the United Nations General Assembly resolution of December 8, 1949,
which, in part, calls on all states—

To refrain from (*a*) seeking to acquire spheres of influence or to create
foreign controlled regimes within the territory of China; (*b*) seeking to obtain special rights or privileges within the territory of China.

A specific application of the foregoing principles is seen in the present
situation with respect to Formosa. In the joint declaration at Cairo on
December 1, 1943, the President of the United States, the British Prime
Minister, and the President of China stated that it was their purpose that
territories Japan had stolen from China, such as Formosa, should be restored to the Republic of China. The United States was a signatory to the
Potsdam declaration of July 26, 1945, which declared that the terms of
the Cairo declaration should be carried out. The provisions of this declaration were accepted by Japan at the time of its surrender. In keeping with
these declarations, Formosa was surrendered to Generalissimo Chiang
Kai-shek, and for the past 4 years, the United States and the other Allied
Powers have accepted the exercise of Chinese authority over the Island.

Released to the press, January 5, 1950. From *Department of State Bulletin*, Vol.
XXII, No. 550, Publication 3727, January 16, 1950, p. 79.

The United States has no predatory designs on Formosa or on any other Chinese territory. The United States has no desire to obtain special rights or privileges or to establish military bases on Formosa at this time. Nor does it have any intention of utilizing its armed forces to interfere in the present situation. The United States Government will not pursue a course which will lead to involvement in the civil conflict in China.

Similarly, the United States Government will not provide military aid or advice to Chinese forces on Formosa. In the view of the United States Government, the resources on Formosa are adequate to enable them to obtain the items which they might consider necessary for the defense of the Island. The United States Government proposes to continue under existing legislative authority the present ECA program of economic assistance.

SUGGESTED READING

Barnett, A. Doak. *China on the Eve of Communist Takeover*. New York: Frederick A. Praeger, 1964, paperback.

Brandt, Conrad; Schwartz, Benjamin; and Fairbank, John K. *A Documentary History of Chinese Communism*. Cambridge: Harvard University Press, 1952.

Chassin, Lionel Max. *The Communist Conquest of China*. Cambridge: Harvard University Press, 1965.

Ch'en, Jerome. *Mao and the Chinese Revolution*. New York: Oxford University Press, 1965.

Chiang Kai-shek. *Soviet Russia and China: A Summing Up at Seventy*, rev. abridged ed. New York: Farrar, Strauss & Giroux, 1965, paperback.

Ch'ien Tuan-sheng. *The Government and Politics of China*. Cambridge: Harvard University Press, 1950.

Clubb, O. Edmund. *Twentieth Century China*. New York: Columbia University Press, 1964, paperback.

Fairbank, John K. *The United States and China*, 2nd ed. Cambridge: Harvard University Press, 1958.

Fei Hsiao-tung. *Peasant Life in China*. London: Oxford University Press, 1946.

Feis, Herbert. *The China Tangle*. Princeton: Princeton University Press, 1953. (Paperback: Atheneum)

Fitzgerald, Charles Patrick. *The Birth of Communist China*. Harmondsworth: Penguin Books, 1964, paperback.

Hsüeh, Chün-tu. *The Chinese Communist Movement: An Annotated Bibliography*. 2 vols. Stanford: Hoover Institution, 1960–1962.

Johnson, Chalmers. *Peasant Nationalism and Communist Power: The Emergence of Revolutionary China, 1937–1945*. Stanford: Stanford University Press, 1962, paperback.

Kiang, Wen-han. *The Chinese Student Movement*. New York: King's Crown, 1948.

Kubek, Anthony. *How the Far East Was Lost: American Policy and the Creation of Communist China, 1941–1949*. Chicago: Regnery, 1963.

Latourette, K. S. *The American Record in the Far East, 1945–1951*. New York: Macmillan, 1951.

Liu, F. F. *A Military History of Modern China, 1924–1949*. Princeton: Princeton University Press, 1956.

Loh, Pinchon P. Y. *The Kuomintang Debacle of 1949—Collapse or Conquest*. Boston: Heath, 1965, paperback.

Mao Tse-tung. *Selected Military Writings of Mao Tse-tung*. Peking: Foreign Languages Press, 1963.

Mao Tse-tung. *Selected Works of Mao Tse-tung*. 4 vols. Peking: Foreign Languages Press, 1961.

North, Robert C. *Chinese Communism*. New York: McGraw-Hill, 1966, paperback.

North, Robert C. *Moscow and the Chinese Communists*. Stanford: Stanford University Press, 1953.

Payne, Robert. *Mao Tse-tung: Ruler of Red China*. New York: Abelard-Schuman, 1950.

Powell, R. L. *The Rise of Chinese Military Power*. Princeton: Princeton University Press, 1955.

Quigley, Harold S. *China's Politics in Perspective*. Minneapolis: University of Minnesota Press, 1962.

Riggs, F. *Formosa under Chinese Nationalist Rule*. New York: Macmillan, 1952.

Rowe, David Nelson. *Modern China: A Brief History*. Princeton: Van Nostrand, 1959, paperback.

Schwartz, Benjamin. *Chinese Communism and the Rise of Mao*. Cambridge: Harvard University Press, 1951.

Snow, Edgar. *Red Star over China*. New York: Random House, 1944.

Stuart, John Leighton. *Fifty Years in China: The Memoirs of John Leighton Stuart, Missionary and Ambassador*. New York: Random House, 1954.

Tsou, Tang. *America's Failure in China, 1949–50*. Chicago: University of Chicago Press, 1963.

United States Department of State. *United States Relations with China, with Special Reference to the Period 1944–1949* [The China White Paper]. Washington, D.C.: Government Printing Office, 1949.

Utley, Freda. *Last Chance in China*. New York: Bobbs-Merrill, 1947.

Wales, Nym. *Red Dust*. Stanford: Stanford University Press, 1952.

Wedemeyer, Albert C. *Wedemeyer Reports!* New York: Holt, Rinehart and Winston, 1958.

White, Theodore H., and Jacoby, Annalee. *Thunder out of China*. New York: Sloane, 1946.

X

Conflict in Korea

The Cairo Declaration had promised that following Japan's defeat, Korea would "in due course" become independent. In September, 1945, Japanese troops south of the thirty-eighth parallel surrendered to American forces, and Japanese troops north of the thirty-eighth parallel surrendered to Soviet forces. The bulk of Korean industry was located in the Soviet-occupied North, and the economy of southern Korea suffered from the division of the country and from lack of technical and managerial skills, which had formerly been supplied by the Japanese. The joint U.S.-U.S.S.R. Commission meeting in Seoul in 1946 and 1947 failed to bring about the unification of the country. The United States presented the Korean problem to the United Nations General Assembly, which established a Temporary Commission on Korea to unify the country and supervise elections for a constituent assembly. North Korean authorities, however, refused to recognize the Commission's authority or allow it to visit the North. In 1948 U.N.-supervised elections were held in southern Korea and Syngman Rhee was elected President of the newly formed Republic of Korea (ROK, "South Korea"). In the meantime, a Communist-dominated Democratic People's Republic of Korea (DPRK, "North Korea") was established north of the thirty-eighth parallel with the encouragement of Russian forces.

On June 25, 1950, the Russian-trained troops of the North Korean regime marched southward across the thirty-eighth parallel, driving before them the poorly armed South Korean forces. The United Nations Security Council immediately passed a U.S.-sponsored resolution calling on the North Korean forces to withdraw. On June 27, President Truman ordered American air and naval forces to resist the Communist aggression in Korea. He also instructed the navy to neutralize Formosa by preventing Nationalist attacks on the Communist-held mainland and Communist attacks on the Nationalist-held Formosa (Selection 58). On the same day, the U.N. Security Council called upon member nations to aid in repelling the

North Korean aggression (Selection 59). Three days later, Truman ordered United States land forces transferred from Japan to Korea. The legality of the U.N. resolutions and the American intervention was scathingly attacked by North Korea, Communist China, and the Soviet Union, which had been boycotting the meetings of the Security Council (Selection 60).

General Douglas MacArthur was made commander of the U.N. forces, which were composed predominantly of American and South Korean troops. (Neither North nor South Korea were U.N. members.) When the U.N. forces had been nearly driven off the Korean peninsula, on September 15 a surprise landing by United States Marines at Inchon, in the rear of the enemy, forced the Communists to retreat in confusion. On October 7, the U.N. General Assembly passed a resolution calling for the unification of Korea. The U.N. troops then moved northward across the thirty-eighth parallel, captured the North Korean capital (Pyongyang), and drove the enemy almost to the Manchurian (Chinese) border.

An entirely new war began in late October when "volunteers" from Communist China entered the struggle. On February 1, 1951, the U.N. General Assembly stated that the Communist Chinese were engaged in aggression (Selection 61). The Communists pushed the U.N. forces back southward across the parallel, but the U.N. Command managed to rally sufficiently to regain Seoul. MacArthur publicly demanded that he be permitted to bomb the "privileged sanctuary" (Manchuria) from which Communist aircraft and supplies were flowing, to establish a blockade against Communist China, and to unleash Chiang Kai-shek's forces against the Communists. The attitude of President Truman's military advisers and of America's NATO allies was that MacArthur's proposals might not lead to the quick victory which he promised but might so commit American strength on the Asiatic continent that Western Europe would be left undefended. General Omar Bradley, of the Joint Chiefs of Staff, said that the result of MacArthur's proposals would be "the wrong war, at the wrong place, at the wrong time, and with the wrong enemy." In April, 1951, President Truman unceremoniously removed General MacArthur from all of his commands in the Far East. In May the U.N. General Assembly adopted a resolution calling for an embargo on the shipment of arms and strategic materials to Communist China.

Protracted truce negotiations, begun in July, 1951, finally brought about an end to hostilities in Korea in July 1953 (Selection 62). The cease-fire line was at approximately the thirty-eighth parallel. The armistice agreement was strenuously opposed by President Rhee, who feared that it would perpetuate the division of the country and would give the Communists a new opportunity to attack South Korea. The armistice was signed by the U.N., Communist Chinese, and North Korean military authorities, but not by South Korean officials. It was notable that 75,000

North Korean and 14,000 Communist Chinese prisoners of war chose not to return to their Communist homelands. In October the United States and South Korea concluded a mutual defense treaty. The Geneva Conference of April to June, 1954, was unable to agree upon a formula for the reunification of Korea, and the division of that country between ideologically antagonistic regimes continues to this day.

In 1952 a constitutional amendment provided for direct popular election of the ROK president, instead of election by the National Assembly as hitherto. As a result, President Rhee was repeatedly reelected and remained in office until 1960. Gross procedural irregularities in the National Assembly and police interference and balloting frauds in the 1960 election provoked student-led popular demonstrations against the Rhee government throughout the country. A number of students were killed in clashes with police. As the crisis intensified, the ROK Army and the United States Embassy assumed an attitude of benevolent neutrality towards the demonstrators. Rhee was finally forced to resign and was given refuge in Hawaii. Following new elections, in which the Democratic Party won notable victories over the incumbent Liberals, a parliamentary-cabinet system of government was established, with Yun Po Sun as President and Chang Myun (John M. Chang) as Premier.

The new regime (Second Republic) proved incapable of coping with economic problems, political corruption, and constantly recurring student demonstrations. The rise of neutralist and pro-Communist agitation and the government's announced policy of reducing the military forces and seeking reunification through U.N.-sponsored elections in all of Korea aroused dissatisfaction in the army. Although the population of South Korea is relatively small (about 30,000,000), the ROK Army of 600,000 men is the fifth largest in the world. ROK Army and Marine troops led by Generals Park Chung Hee and Chang Do Young overthrew the government of Premier Chang in 1961 (Selection 63). The United Nations commander and the American chargé d'affaires in Seoul insisted that control be turned back to the civilian government. However, General Chang addressed a letter to President Kennedy assuring him of his adherence to the U.N. Charter and anticommunism and promising to return authority to a "conscientious" civilian government at a later date. General Park visited President Kennedy in Washington in the following November. Park Chung Hee, who became a civilian, was elected to the presidency by a narrow plurality in October 1963, and in December civilian government was reestablished.

It appears that stable democratic government in Korea will be possible only when ideological tensions subside and the artificial division of the country is ended. The truculence of Communist China, which greatly influences the North Korean regime, and the determination of the United States to resist the spread of communism in Asia, as shown in American

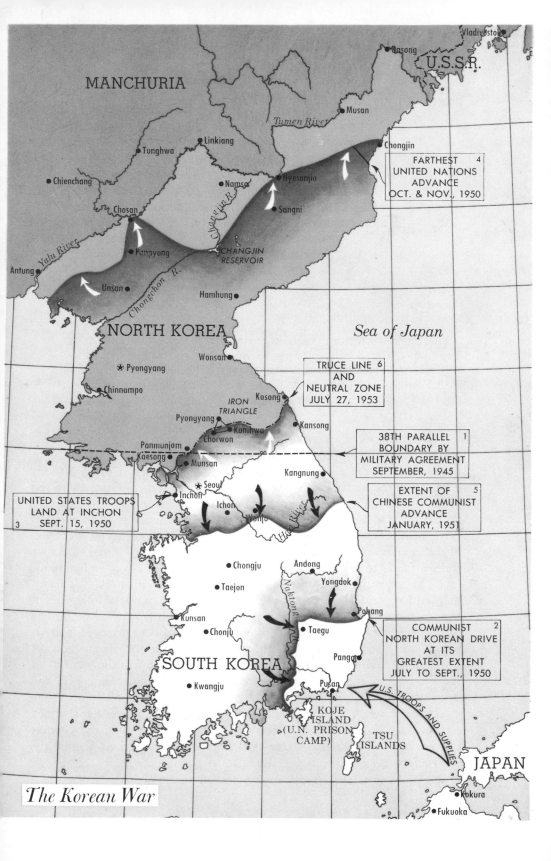

VLADIVOSTOK

MANCHURIA

U.S.S.R.

• Onsong

• Musan

Tumen River

• Tunghwa

• Linkiang

• Chongjin

• Chienchang

• Namsa

• Hyesanjin

FARTHEST
UNITED NATIONS
ADVANCE
OCT. & NOV., 1950   4

Changjin R.

• Sangni

• Chosan

• Panpyong

CHANGJIN
RESERVOIR

Yalu River

Antung •

• Unsan

Chongchon R.

• Hamhung

NORTH KOREA

Sea of Japan

• Wonsan

★ Pyongyang

TRUCE LINE   6
AND
NEUTRAL ZONE
JULY 27, 1953

• Chinnampo

*IRON
TRIANGLE*

• Kosong

Pyongyang •

• Kansong

• Kumhwa

38TH PARALLEL   1
BOUNDARY BY
MILITARY AGREEMENT
SEPTEMBER, 1945

• Chorwon

• Panmunjom

• Kaesong

• Munsan

• Kangnung

UNITED STATES TROOPS
LAND AT INCHON
3   SEPT. 15, 1950

★ Seoul

• Inchon

• Ichon

• Wonju

Han River

EXTENT OF   5
CHINESE COMMUNIST
ADVANCE
JANUARY, 1951

• Chongju

Andong •

• Taejon

• Yongdok

Naktong

• Kunsan

• Pohang

• Chonju

• Taegu

SOUTH KOREA

COMMUNIST   2
NORTH KOREAN DRIVE
AT ITS
GREATEST EXTENT
JULY TO SEPT., 1950

• Pango

• Kwangju

• Pusan

KOJE
ISLAND
(U.N. PRISON
CAMP)

TSU
ISLANDS

U.S. TROOPS AND SUPPLIES

JAPAN

The Korean War

• Kokura

• Fukuoka

support of the South Vietnamese as well as the South Korean government, suggest that the establishment of a stable regime in a unified Korea will not come about in the foreseeable future.

58

Statement by President Truman Dispatching American Forces to Korea

June 27, 1950

> The North Korean attack on South Korea resulted not only in the dispatch of American forces to Korea but also in the resumption of American military assistance to the Chinese Nationalists on Formosa and a stepping up of aid to the Philippine government and to the French forces in Indochina.

In Korea the Government forces, which were armed to prevent border raids and to preserve internal security, were attacked by invading forces from North Korea. The Security Council of the United Nations called upon the invading troops to cease hostilities and to withdraw to the 38th parallel. This they have not done but on the contrary have pressed the attack. The Security Council called upon all members of the United Nations to render every assistance to the United Nations in the execution of this resolution. In these circumstances I have ordered United States air and sea forces to give the Korean Government troops cover and support.

The attack upon Korea makes it plain beyond all doubt that Communism has passed beyond the use of subversion to conquer independent nations and will now use armed invasion and war. It has defied the orders of the Security Council of the United Nations issued to preserve international peace and security. In these circumstances the occupation of Formosa by Communist forces would be a direct threat to the security of the Pacific area and to United States forces performing their lawful and necessary functions in that area.

Accordingly I have ordered the Seventh Fleet to prevent any attack on Formosa. As a corollary of this action I am calling upon the Chinese Government on Formosa to cease all air and sea operations against the

From United States Department of State, *United States Policy in the Korean Crisis* (Washington, D.C.: Government Printing Office, 1950), p. 18.

mainland. The Seventh Fleet will see that this is done. The determination of the future status of Formosa must await the restoration of security in the Pacific, a peace settlement with Japan, or consideration by the United Nations.

I have also directed that United States Forces in the Philippines be strengthened and that military assistance to the Philippine Government be accelerated.

I have similarly directed acceleration in the furnishing of military assistance to the forces of France and the Associated States in Indochina and the dispatch of a military mission to provide close working relations with those forces.

I know that all members of the United Nations will consider carefully the consequences of this latest aggression in Korea in defiance of the Charter of the United Nations. A return to the rule of force in international affairs would have far-reaching effects. The United States will continue to uphold the rule of law.

I have instructed Ambassador Austin, as the Representative of the United States to the Security Council, to report these steps to the Council.

59

Resolution Adopted by the United Nations Security Council, June 27, 1950

The intervention by American forces in Korea was legalized by this resolution of the United Nations Security Council, passed in the absence of the Soviet representative (see Selection 60). The promptness of the United Nations to act in Korea contrasts with the ineffectiveness of the League of Nations in the Manchurian crisis of 1931.

The Security Council,

Having determined that the armed attack upon the Republic of Korea by forces from North Korea constitutes a breach of the peace,

Having called for an immediate cessation of hostilities, and

Having called upon the authorities of North Korea to withdraw forthwith their armed forces to the 38th parallel, and

From United States Department of State, *United States Policy in the Korean Crisis* (Washington, D.C.: Government Printing Office, 1950), p. 24.

Having noted from the report of the United Nations Commission for Korea that the authorities in North Korea have neither ceased hostilities nor withdrawn their armed forces to the 38th parallel and that urgent military measures are required to restore international peace and security, and

Having noted the appeal from the Republic of Korea to the United Nations for immediate and effective steps to secure peace and security,

Recommends that the Members of the United Nations furnish such assistance to the Republic of Korea as may be necessary to repel the armed attack and to restore international peace and security in the area.

60

Message from the Deputy Minister of Foreign Affairs of the Union of Soviet Socialist Republics to the Secretary General of the United Nations

June 29, 1950

The legality of the U.N. Security Council decision was attacked by the Soviet Union and other members of the Soviet bloc on the ground that the decision did not have the necessary concurrence of China (meaning Communist China) and the Soviet Union. The American view was that China (meaning Nationalist China) had concurred and that the abstention of the Soviet Union from voting did not count as a veto. The Soviet Union and, after December, 1950, Communist China gave massive aid to the North Koreans, never recognizing the legality of the United Nations military effort in Korea.

The Soviet Government has received from you the text of the Security Council resolution of 27 June 1950 calling the attention of Members of the United Nations to the necessity of intervening in Korean affairs in the interests of the South Korean authorities. The Soviet Gov-

From United States Department of State, *United States Policy in the Korean Crisis* (Washington, D.C.: Government Printing Office, 1950), p. 56.

ernment notes that this resolution was adopted by six votes, the seventh vote being that of the Kuomintang representative Dr. Tingfu F. Tsiang who has no legal right to represent China, whereas the United Nations Charter requires that a Security Council resolution must be adopted by seven votes including those of the five permanent members of the Council namely the United States, the United Kingdom, France, the Union of Soviet Socialist Republics and China. As is known, moreover, the above resolution was passed in the absence of two permanent members of the Security Council, the Union of Soviet Socialist Republics and China, whereas under the United Nations Charter a decision of the Security Council on an important matter can only be made with the concurring votes of all five permanent members of the Council, viz. the United States, the United Kingdom, France, the Union of Soviet Socialist Republics and China. In view of the foregoing it is quite clear that the said resolution of the Security Council on the Korean question has no legal force.

A. Gromyko

61

Resolution Adopted by the United Nations General Assembly, February 1, 1951

This resolution declaring the Peking regime guilty of aggression in Korea is one of the obstacles to Communist Chinese representation in the United Nations.

The General Assembly,

Noting that the Security Council, because of lack of unanimity of the permanent members, has failed to exercise its primary responsibility for the maintenance of international peace and security in regard to Chinese Communist intervention in Korea;

Noting that the Central People's Government of the People's Republic of China has not accepted United Nations proposals to bring about a cessation of hostilities in Korea with a view to peaceful settlement, and

Introduced before the First Committee by the United States on January 20, 1951; adopted by the First Committee on January 30. From United States Department of State, *United States Policy in the Korean Conflict, July 1950–February 1951* (Washington, D.C.: Government Printing Office, 1951), p. 37.

that its armed forces continue their invasion of Korea and their large-scale attacks upon United Nations forces there;

Finds that the Central People's Government of the People's Republic of China, by giving direct aid and assistance to those who were already committing aggression in Korea and by engaging in hostilities against United Nations forces there, has itself engaged in aggression in Korea;

Calls upon the Central People's Government of the People's Republic of China to cause its forces and nationals in Korea to cease hostilities against the United Nations forces and to withdraw from Korea;

Affirms the determination of the United Nations to continue its action in Korea to meet the aggression;

Calls upon all States and authorities to continue to lend every assistance to the United Nations action in Korea;

Calls upon all States and authorities to refrain from giving any assistance to the aggressors in Korea;

Requests a committee composed of the Members of the Collective Measures Committee as a matter of urgency to consider additional measures to be employed to meet this aggression and to report thereon to the General Assembly; it being understood that the Committee is authorized to defer its report if the Good Offices Committee, referred to in the following paragraph, reports satisfactory progress in its efforts.

Affirms that it continues to be the policy of the United Nations to bring about a cessation of hostilities in Korea and the achievement of United Nations objectives in Korea by peaceful means, and requests the President of the General Assembly to designate forthwith two persons who would meet with him at any suitable opportunity to use their good offices to this end.

62

The Korean Armistice Agreement

July 27, 1953

Although this truce ended the fighting in Korea, none of the political issues leading to the war have yet been settled. Because the truce did not provide for unification, South Korea did not sign it, but agreed to honor its terms in exchange for a security agreement with the United States.

PREAMBLE

The undersigned, the Commander-in-Chief, United Nations Command, on the one hand, and the Supreme Commander of the Korean People's Army and the Commander of the Chinese People's Volunteers, on the other hand, in the interest of stopping the Korean conflict, with its great toll of suffering and bloodshed on both sides, and with the objective of establishing an armistice which will insure a complete cessation of hostilities and of all acts of armed force in Korea until a final peaceful settlement is achieved, do individually, collectively, and mutually agree to accept and to be bound and governed by the conditions and terms of armistice set forth in the following Articles and Paragraphs, which said conditions and terms are intended to be purely military in character and to pertain solely to the belligerents in Korea.

ARTICLE I

MILITARY DEMARCATION LINE AND DEMILITARIZED ZONE

1. A Military Demarcation Line shall be fixed and both sides shall withdraw two (2) kilometers from this line so as to establish a Demilitarized Zone between the opposing forces. A Demilitarized Zone shall be established as a buffer zone to prevent the occurrence of incidents which might lead to a resumption of hostilities.

From United States Department of State, *American Foreign Policy, 1950–1955, Basic Documents* (Washington, D.C.: Government Printing Office, 1957), pp. 724–750. Only the initial portions of the agreement are printed here.

2. The Military Demarcation Line is located as indicated on the attached map (Map1).[1]

3. The Demilitarized Zone is defined by a northern and a southern boundary as indicated on the attached map (Map 1).

4. The Military Demarcation Line shall be plainly marked as directed by the Military Armistice Commission hereinafter established. The Commanders of the opposing sides shall have suitable markers erected along the boundary between the Demilitarized Zone and their respective areas. The Military Armistice Commission shall supervise the erection of all markers placed along the Military Demarcation Line and along the boundaries of the Demilitarized Zone.

5. The waters of the Han River Estuary shall be open to civil shipping of both sides wherever one bank is controlled by one side and the other bank is controlled by the other side. The Military Armistice Commission shall prescribe rules for the shipping in that part of the Han River Estuary indicated on the attached map (Map 2). Civil shipping of each side shall have unrestricted access to the land under the military control of that side.

6. Neither side shall execute any hostile act within, from, or against the Demilitarized Zone.

7. No person, military or civilian, shall be permitted to cross the Military Demarcation Line unless specifically authorized to do so by the Military Armistice Commission.

8. No person, military or civilian, in the Demilitarized Zone shall be permitted to enter the territory under the military control of either side unless specifically authorized to do so by the Commander into whose territory entry is sought.

9. No person, military or civilian, shall be permitted to enter the Demilitarized Zone except persons concerned with the conduct of civil administration and relief and persons specifically authorized to enter by the Military Armistice Commission.

10. Civil administration and relief in that part of the Demilitarized Zone which is south of the Military Demarcation Line shall be the responsibility of the Commander-in-Chief, United Nations Command; and civil administration and relief in that part of the Demilitarized Zone which is north of the Military Demarcation Line shall be the joint responsibility of the Supreme Commander of the Korean People's Army and the Commander of the Chinese People's Volunteers. The number of persons, military or civilian, from each side who are permitted to enter the Demilitarized Zone for the conduct of civil administration and relief shall be as determined by the respective Commanders, but in no case shall the total

[1] The originals of the maps, large-scale in size, are deposited with the signed original agreement in the archives of the Department of State where they are available for reference.

number authorized by either side exceed one thousand (1,000) persons at any one time. The number of civil police and the arms to be carried by them shall be as prescribed by the Military Armistice Commission. Other personnel shall not carry arms unless specifically authorized to do so by the Military Armistice Commission.

11. Nothing contained in this Article shall be construed to prevent the complete freedom of movement to, from, and within the Demilitarized Zone by the Military Armistice Commission, its assistants, its Joint Observer Teams with their assistants, the Neutral Nations Supervisory Commission hereinafter established, its assistants, its Neutral Nations Inspection Teams with their assistants, and of any other persons, materials, and equipment specifically authorized to enter the Demilitarized Zone by the Military Armistice Commission. Convenience of movement shall be permitted through the territory under the military control of either side over any route necessary to move between points within the Demilitarized Zone where such points are not connected by roads lying completely within the Demilitarized Zone.

ARTICLE II

CONCRETE ARRANGEMENTS FOR CEASE-FIRE AND ARMISTICE

A. General

12. The Commanders of the opposing sides shall order and enforce a complete cessation of all hostilities in Korea by all armed forces under their control, including all units and personnel of the ground, naval, and air forces, effective twelve (12) hours after this Armistice Agreement is signed. (See Paragraph 63 hereof for effective date and hour of the remaining provisions of this Armistice Agreement.)

13. In order to insure the stability of the Military Armistice so as to facilitate the attainment of a peaceful settlement through the holding by both sides of a political conference of a higher level, the Commanders of the opposing sides shall:

a. Within seventy-two (72) hours after this Armistice Agreement becomes effective, withdraw all of their military forces, supplies, and equipment from the Demilitarized Zone except as otherwise provided herein. All demolitions, minefields, wire entanglements, and other hazards to the safe movement of personnel of the Military Armistice Commission or its Joint Observer Teams, known to exist within the Demilitarized Zone after the withdrawal of military forces therefrom, together with lanes known to be free of all such hazards, shall be reported to the Military Armistice Commission by the Commander of the side whose forces emplaced such hazards. Subsequently, additional safe lanes shall be cleared; and eventually, within forty-five (45) days after the termination of the seventy-two (72) hour period, all such hazards shall be removed from the Demilitarized Zone as directed by and under the supervision of the Military Armistice Commission. At the termination of the seventy-two (72) hour period, except for unarmed troops authorized a forty-five (45) day period to complete salvage operations under Military Armistice Commission supervision, such units of a police nature as may be specifically requested by the Military Armistice Commission and agreed to by the Commanders of the opposing sides, and personnel authorized under Paragraphs 10 and 11 hereof, no personnel of either side shall be permitted to enter the Demilitarized Zone.

b. Within ten (10) days after this Armistice Agreement becomes effective, withdraw all of their military forces, supplies, and equipment from the rear and the coastal islands and waters of Korea of the other side. If such military forces are not withdrawn within the stated time limit, and there is no mutually agreed and valid reason for the delay, the other side shall have the right to take any action which it deems necessary for the maintenance of security and order. The term "coastal islands," as used above, refers to those islands which, though occupied by one side at the time when this Armistice Agreement becomes effective, were controlled by the other side on 24 June 1950; provided, however, that all the islands lying to the north and west of the provincial boundary line between HWANGHAE-DO and KYONGGI-DO shall be under the military control of the Supreme Commander of the Korean People's Army and the Commander of the Chinese People's Volunteers, except the island groups of PAENGYONG-DO (37°58′N, 124°40′E), TAECHONG-DO (37°50′N, 124°42′E), SOCHONG-DO (37°46′N, 124°46′E), YONPYONG-DO (37°38′N, 125°40′E), and U-DO (37°36′N, 125°58′E), which shall remain under the military control of the Commander-in-Chief, United Nations Command. All the islands on the west coast of Korea lying south of the above-mentioned boundary line shall remain under the military control of the Commander-in-Chief, United Nations Command. (See Map 3.) [2]

c. Cease the introduction into Korea of reinforcing military personnel; provided, however, that the rotation of units and personnel, the arrival in Korea of personnel on a temporary duty basis, and the return to Korea of personnel after short periods of leave or temporary duty outside of Korea shall be permitted within the scope prescribed below. "Rotation" is defined as the replacement of units or personnel by other units or personnel who are commencing a tour of duty in Korea. Rotation personnel shall be introduced into and evacuated from Korea only through the ports of entry enumerated in Paragraph 42 hereof. Rotation shall be conducted on a man-for-man basis; provided, however, that no more than thirty-five thousand (35,000) persons in the military service

[2] Not reprinted here.

shall be admitted into Korea by either side in any calendar month under the rotation policy. No military personnel of either side shall be introduced into Korea if the introduction of such personnel will cause the aggregate of the military personnel of that side admitted into Korea since the effective date of this Armistice Agreement to exceed the cumulative total of the military personnel of that side who have departed from Korea since that date. Reports concerning arrivals in and departures from Korea of military personnel shall be made daily to the Military Armistice Commission and the Neutral Nations Supervisory Commission; such reports shall include places of arrival and departure and the number of persons arriving at or departing from each such place. The Neutral Nations Supervisory Commission, through its Neutral Nations Inspection Teams, shall conduct supervision and inspection of the rotation of units and personnel authorized above, at the ports of entry enumerated in Paragraph 43 hereof.

d. Cease the introduction into Korea of reinforcing combat aircraft, armored vehicles, weapons, and ammunition; provided, however, that combat aircraft, armored vehicles, weapons, and ammunition which are destroyed, damaged, worn out, or used up during the period of the armistice may be replaced on the basis of piece-for-piece of the same effectiveness and the same type. Such combat aircraft, armored vehicles, weapons, and ammunition shall be introduced into Korea only through the ports of entry enumerated in Paragraph 43 hereof. In order to justify the requirement for combat aircraft, armored vehicles, weapons, and ammunition to be introduced into Korea for replacement purposes, reports concerning every incoming shipment of these items shall be made to the Military Armistice Commission and the Neutral Nations Supervisory Commission; such reports shall include statements regarding the disposition of the items being replaced. Items to be replaced which are removed from Korea shall be removed only through the ports of entry enumerated in Paragraph 43 hereof. The Neutral Nations Supervisory Commission, through its Neutral Nations Inspection Teams, shall conduct supervision and inspection of the replacement of combat aircraft, armored vehicles, weapons, and ammunition authorized above, at the ports of entry enumerated in Paragraph 43 hereof.

e. Insure that personnel of their respective commands who violate any of the provisions of this Armistice Agreement are adequately punished.

f. In those cases where places of burial are a matter of record and graves are actually found to exist, permit graves registration personnel of the other side to enter, within a definite time limit after this Armistice Agreement becomes effective, the territory of Korea under their military control, for the purpose of proceeding to such graves to recover and evacuate the bodies of the deceased military personnel of that side, including deceased prisoners of war. The specific procedures and the time limit for the performance of the above task shall be determined by the Military Armistice Commission. The Commanders of the opposing sides shall furnish to the other side all available information pertaining to the places of burial of the deceased military personnel of the other side.

g. Afford full protection and all possible assistance and cooperation to the Military Armistice Commission, its Joint Observer Teams, the Neutral Nations Supervisory Commission, and its Neutral Nations Inspection Teams, in the carrying out of their functions and responsibilities hereinafter assigned; and accord to the Neutral Nations Supervisory Commission, and to its Neutral Nations Inspection Teams, full convenience of movement between the headquarters of the Neutral Nations Supervisory Commission and the ports of entry enumerated in Paragraph 43 hereof over main lines of communication agreed upon by both sides (See Map 4), and between the headquarters of the Neutral Nations Supervisory Commission and the places where violations of this Armistice Agreement have been reported to have occurred. In order to prevent unnecessary delays, the use of alternate routes and means of transportation will be permitted whenever the main lines of communication are closed or impassable.

h. Provide such logistic support, including communications and transportation facilities, as may be required by the Military Armistice Commission and the Neutral Nations Supervisory Commission and their Teams.

i. Each construct, operate, and maintain a suitable airfield in their respective parts of the Demilitarized Zone in the vicinity of the headquarters of the Military Armistice Commission, for such uses as the Commission may determine.

j. Insure that all members and other personnel of the Neutral Nations Supervisory Commission and of the Neutral Nations Repatriation Commission hereinafter established shall enjoy the freedom and facilities necessary for the proper exercise of their functions, including privileges, treatment, and immunities equivalent to those ordinarily enjoyed by accredited diplomatic personnel under international usage.

14. This Armistice Agreement shall apply to all opposing ground forces under the military control of either side, which ground forces shall respect the Demilitarized Zone and the area of Korea under the military control of the opposing side.

15. This Armistice Agreement shall apply to all opposing naval forces, which naval forces shall respect the waters contiguous to the Demilitarized Zone and to the land area of Korea under the military control of the opposing side, and shall not engage in blockade of any kind of Korea.

16. This Armistice Agreement shall apply to all opposing air forces,

which air forces shall respect the air space over the Demilitarized Zone and over the area of Korea under the military control of the opposing side, and over the waters contiguous to both.

17. Responsibility for compliance with and enforcement of the terms and provisions of this Armistice Agreement is that of the signatories hereto and their successors in command. The Commanders of the opposing sides shall establish within their respective commands all measures and procedures necessary to insure complete compliance with all of the provisions hereof by all elements of their commands. They shall actively cooperate with one another and with the Military Armistice Commission and the Neutral Nations Supervisory Commission in requiring observance of both the letter and the spirit of all of the provisions of this Armistice Agreement.

18. The costs of the operations of the Military Armistice Commission and of the Neutral Nations Supervisory Commission and of their Teams shall be shared equally by the two opposing sides.

63

What Made the Revolution Succeed

Park Chung Hee

(Paraphrased by *Kyung Cho Chung*)

The collapse of the Rhee regime in 1960 and the overthrow of the Chang government in 1961 are here explained by the present President of Korea.

The question "What has made the military revolution successful?" is likely to cause misunderstanding. The revolution has just started with the seizure of power by the military force; its full-scale development is now about to begin. The *coup d'état* has, of course, proved to be successful. The question of whether the military revolution will be successful or not, however, belongs to the future. In this sense it might be more appropriate to ask "Will the military revolution prove to be successful?" The success of the military revolution can be said to be a result of the failure

Reprinted with permission of The Macmillan Company from *New Korea: New Land of the Morning Calm* by Kyung Cho Chung. Copyright © Kyung Cho Chung 1962.

of democracy in Korea. Therefore, the question "What has made the military revolution successful" really means "Why has democracy failed in the Republic of Korea?" Now let us review various aspects of Korean democracy in the past.

The history of Korean democracy was one of fifteen short years of successive failures. It was on August 15, 1945, that the Japanese imperialistic colonial rule over Korea was put to an end and democracy was "imported" to this country. Never before had the Korean people experienced Western democracy. Hence, Korea was a barren land for democracy. It was hardly possible that democracy transplanted here could reach fruition. In other words, Korea lacked the fundamental requirements for the sound growth of democracy. What are the fundamental requirements? We may look at them from four different angles: social and economic conditions, the national psychological attitude, the national moral conception, and finally, external tension.

For democracy to flourish, a nation should, first of all, maintain excellent social and economic conditions, and wipe out discontent among its people. In other words, democracy is bound to thrive where national life is stabilized and the educational standard is high. This is far from the case in Korea. Korea is a nation whose foundation has long been sustained by agriculture. What is the actual condition of the farming populace of this country?

According to the 1958 *Agricultural Year-Book*, published by the Agricultural Bank of Korea, the farming populace accounted for 62.8 per cent of the entire population of this country, totaling 21,909,742 persons. Those farming households who came under the category of from 0.245 acres up to less than 2.451 acres amounted to 1,610,521, or 72.6 per cent of all farming households, totaling 2,010,900. The income of farmers constituted only 37 per cent of that of the entire Korean populace. This shows vividly what a miserable life the Korean farmers are leading. Such poverty exists not only in rural areas but also in urban areas. If one reads a UNESCO report that the annual per capita income of this country runs below $80 in American money, he cannot but deplore the fact that Koreans are among the poorest peoples in the world.

It is only too natural that democracy should fail to prosper in Korea, where the per capita income and the living standard of the people are so low. Korea has received enormous amounts of aid from the United States and other friendly nations of the free world. Thanks to this assistance the Korean people have barely avoided starving to death. Korea has received approximately $3 billion in aid from the United States. But what contribution has the aid money made toward the attainment of a self-sufficient economy in the country? The structural ratio of the nation's gross national product in 1953–1959 runs at 40.5 per cent in primary industry, 15.8 per cent in secondary industry, and 43.6 per cent in tertiary industry.

This is a crippled structure. To think that tertiary industry should far outweigh primary industry in a nation that relies heavily on agriculture! Korea has neither adequate electricity nor ample water supplies. The man in the street satirizes this, saying, "The Korean reconstruction is a reconstruction of teashops, billiard halls, and bars."

Needless to say, reconstruction has been attained mainly with the aid from the United States. In other words, United States aid merely helped Korea to increase the tendency to consumption, rather than production, and fostered a consumption-first economy with an eye to attaining a demonstration effect. This ran diametrically counter to the direction the Korean economy should have taken for the attainment of self-sufficiency.

The nation's politicians gambled on this antinational course, and so did a good many businessmen, financiers, judicial officers, and government officials. Add to this, various types of corruption and irregularities in collusion with finance and politics. Judicial officers protected the "order" of corruption and irregularities with the process of law; educators advocated it among their students; and government officials bolstered it with their administrative privileges. In a nutshell, it was an order based on unsavory patronage and *sabasaba*, or disposition of matters by using underhanded means.

People called this "politics." All these things were done under the cloak of democracy. Such "politics," however, had nothing to do with the poverty-stricken multitudes of the nation. Neither did such "politics" have anything to do with democracy, even though it disguised itself under the cloak of democracy. Obviously, it was no more than an oligarchy bolstered by monetary influence.

From this stems the phenomenon of separation of the multitude from the ruling class, including politicians, who should have defended the people's rights. The discontent of the populace filled the nation. The statesmen were not aware of this. On the contrary, they were intoxicated with power, engulfed in self-complacency, and more engrossed in political swindling. The gap between the people and the statesmen grew wider and wider. Politics, when it loses the support of the people, is bound to fall back upon the terrorism of rifles and bayonets as a last resort. If things go on like this, signs appear signaling the downfall of the regime. A good example of this was the fourth-term and the fifth-term presidential and vice-presidential elections. The Liberal party, which desperately tried to maintain power by means of terrorism and blackmail, in the long run was expelled from power.

Then came into power the Democratic party, which played nothing more than the role of opposition group of the Liberal party. But though the Democratic party was an opponent of the Liberal party, it was in reality a collaborator with an oligarchy bolstered by monetary influence. No sooner had the Democratic party seized power than it showed the cloven hoof. Things had been better under the reign of the Liberal party than they were during the Democratic regime. The Liberal party could sustain itself in one way or another, thanks to a central figure, the bigoted old man Dr. Syngman Rhee, who was once looked up to by the Korean people as a great leader because of his career as an anti-Japanese fighter during Japanese rule. Unfortunately, there was no such leader as Dr. Rhee during the reign of the Democratic party.

The true nature of Democratic plutocracy appeared on the surface even more clearly in the early stage of its reign, and the people's hope became despair, which later developed into indifference. This indifference was vividly demonstrated in the elections for provincial councilors, including those of the City of Seoul, held less than four months after the government of John M. Chang was born; more than half the voters did not participate in the elections. This was a sort of silent resistance. The Chang regime's days were already numbered, and not only those of the Chang regime, but those of Korean democracy also.

The death sentence was declared from the Speaker's rostrum of the National Assembly Hall. The declaration was made, not by the House Speaker, but by a wounded April hero. In protest against the unfair ruling of the judicial authorities on the masterminds of the rigged mid-March presidential and vice-presidential elections in 1960, scores of wounded April heroes invaded the House of Representatives while it was in session, occupied the Speaker's rostrum, and declared the dissolution of the National Assembly.

It is said that in England even the queen cannot enter Parliament without permission. Yet in Korea, a riotous group swarmed into the Assembly Hall, sacred headquarters of the representatives of the will of the people, and occupied the Speaker's rostrum to declare the dissolution of the National Assembly! For this incident the Chang cabinet refused to shoulder responsibility. Such were the incapable and irresponsible politicians of this country in the past. It is not too much to say that with this incident the Second Republic, which was born of the April Revolution, was already doomed. Needless to say, amidst such social impoverishment, political irresponsibility, incapability, and corruption, the people could not display a high regard for individual responsibility in public life. In Korea, however, those who advocated individual rights and faithfully performed their duties and responsibilities were regarded as fools. But democracy can be achieved only when the entire nation is awakened to the fact that responsibilities always accompany rights.

What Koreans should bear in mind is the fact that their country is divided and constantly menaced by international Communism. No one knows when Korea might fall into a trap of direct or indirect aggression. At this very moment indirect Communist aggression is present in Korea, visibly or invisibly. In the past, the shortsighted politicians did nothing but strive to win political contests. They failed to strengthen the nation's anti-Communist front, and South Korea was forced into crisis. But South Koreans are not isolated in their fight against Communism. Friendly democratic nations are standing with them, and during the Korean War sixteen friendly nations heroically fought with them against the Communist aggressors. In the event of choice between Democracy and Communism, there can be no room for Koreans to consider both North-South negotiations and neutralism.

The history of Korean democracy is, frankly, a history of failures. The success of the May 16th military revolution was the result of the failure of Korean democracy. But is the success of the military revolution intended to erase democracy for good in this part of the world? No. The revolution was designed only to revive democracy in this country. Is it not proper to say that when Communism has been expelled from Korean soil, corruption and irregularities and hunger have been wiped out, and the national morality has been awakened to the significance of freedom, responsibilities, and duty, democracy can revive in this country?

The revolution is designed to perform a full-dress operation for the revival of the freedom and rights of the state and the people at a time when the nation is confronted with destruction and the people's rights have been trampled down. The military revolution is not intended to strangle democracy in this country, but to suspend it temporarily; it is a remedial measure intended to restore democracy to its healthy function.

South Korea will have to undergo a series of drastic reforms of its economic structure in the endeavor to increase per capita income, invigorate the national life, and build up national education and culture. South Korea will have to do away with the easygoing consumption-first national philosophy, and make desperate efforts to lay a firm foundation for the attainment of a self-sufficient economy.

The sources of past social evils—corruption, irregularities, and injustices—should be rooted out, and a clean national morality encouraged. A free society, firmly founded on order, justice, and responsibility is the destination we are headed for.

South Korea must also bear in mind that their country is cut in half by the 38th parallel and that the northern half of the country is being illegally occupied by the tools of world Communism. South Koreans must ready themselves, physically and mentally, for the possibility of fighting, together with friendly democratic nations, to overcome the Communists. There lies ahead only one road that leads to victory over Communism. It is neither negotiation nor evasion. To win, South Korea must make its strength superior to that of Communism.

SUGGESTED READING

Allen, Richard C. *Korea's Syngman Rhee: An Unauthorized Portrait.* Rutland, Vermont: Charles E. Tuttle Company, 1960.

Berger, Carl. *The Korea Knot: A Military-Political History*, rev. ed. Philadelphia: University of Pennsylvania Press, 1964.

Chung, Kyung Cho. *New Korea: New Land of the Morning Calm*. New York: Macmillan, 1962.

Higgins, Marguerite. *War in Korea: The Report of a Woman Correspondent*. Garden City, N.Y.: Doubleday, 1951.

MacArthur, Douglas. *Reminiscences*. New York: McGraw-Hill, 1964.

McCune, George M. *Korea Today*. Cambridge: Harvard University Press, 1950.

McCune, Shannon. *Korea's Heritage: A Regional and Social Geography*. Rutland, Vt.: Charles E. Tuttle Company, 1956.

Meade, E. Grant. *American Military Government in Korea*. New York: King's Crown, 1951.

Oliver, Robert T. *Syngman Rhee: The Man Behind the Myth*. New York: Dodd, Mead, 1954.

Oliver, Robert T. *Why War Came to Korea*. New York: Fordham University Press, 1950.

Osgood, Cornelius. *The Koreans and Their Culture*. New York: Ronald, 1951.

Rees, David. *Korea: The Limited War*. New York: St. Martin's, 1964.

Reeve, W. D. *The Republic of Korea: A Political and Economic Study*. London: Oxford University Press, 1963.

Rovere, Richard H., and Schlesinger, Arthur M., Jr. *The General and the President and the Future of American Foreign Policy*. New York: Farrar, Straus & Giroux, 1951.

Scalapino, Robert, ed. *North Korea Today*. New York: Frederick A. Praeger, 1963.

Spanier, John W. *The Truman-MacArthur Controversy and the Korean War*. Cambridge: Harvard University Press, 1959.

Vatcher, William H. Jr. *Panmunjom: The Story of the Korean Military Armistice Negotiations*. New York: Frederick A. Praeger, 1958.

Vetter, Hal. *Mutiny at Koji Island*. Rutland, Vt., and Tokyo, Japan: Charles E. Tuttle Company, 1965.

Whiting, Allen S. *China Crosses the Yalu: The Decision to Enter the Korean War*. New York: Macmillan, 1960.

XI

Communist
Rule in China

When the Communists took power in 1949, they were not sufficiently numerous to rule the country without the assistance and support, overt or tacit, of many non-Communists. The regime which they set up in Peking on October 1, 1949, therefore, was in form a "coalition of revolutionary classes," or united front, which included non-Communist parties and groups. The state form of the People's Republic of China was said to be a "people's democratic dictatorship"; that is to say, the "people" (working class, peasantry, petty bourgeoisie, and national bourgeoisie) would enjoy democratic freedoms and elect a government to enforce a dictatorship over the "reactionaries" (the bureaucratic bourgeoisie and the landlords) (Selection 64). As the Communists consolidated their control in China they were increasingly able to manipulate or destroy the groups which had originally collaborated with them in the United Front regime.

The agrarian reform act of 1950 was at first enforced leniently, but after a few months was directed against the "middle peasants" as well as the landlords and was characterized by much cruelty. Although the declared purpose of the agrarian reform was to give the land to the tiller, in 1955 individual farms were for the most part replaced by cooperatives.

In 1951, a Three Anti Movement against "corruption, waste, and bureaucracy" brought about the removal of politically unreliable elements from the government. Later, a Five Anti Movement against "tax-evasion, bribery, cheating in government contracts, theft of economic intelligence, and stealing national property" resulted in trials, fines, imprisonments, and suicides for many businessmen, and private enterprise ceased to remain as a serious obstacle to complete governmental control of trade and industry. Through physical coercion, propaganda, thought control (brainwashing), and the manipulation of mass organizations, the Communists were able to prevent any effective individual or organized resistance to their regime.

Communist China in 1961

TANNU TUVA

OUT

L. Balkhash

Aktogai

RAILWAY

TURKSIB

ALTAI

Altai
A. C.

BOROTALA
MONGOL A.C.

Karamai
oilfields

Frunze

Alma Ata

A K

Wusu

Issyk Kul

Andizhan

Kuldja

T I E N

S H A N

Urumchi (Tihwa)

MULEI
(Kazak)

Kashgar

KIZIL SU
A.C.
KIRGHIZ

Akosu R.

BAYIN GOL
MONGOL A.C.

YENKI
(Ch.Moslem)

CHANGKI CHINESE MOSLEM
A.C.

Turfan

Hami

PAMIR

PULI (TASH KURGHAN)
(Tadzhik)

Tarim R.

SINKIANG UIGUR A.R.

Taklamakan Desert

OCHINA (EDSIN) BANNE
MONGOL A.C.

Yumen

Kiuchüan

Chon

Wakhan R.

Guma

TARIM   BASIN

Khotan (Hotien)

Erhch'iang

Ansi

N. KANSU
(Mongol)

KASHMIR

K U N L U N

HAISI MONGOL -TIBETAN-KAZAK
A. C.

Kilien
Mts

Wu

Ladakh

Aksai
Chin.

HAIPEI TIBETAN A.C.

Koko
Nor

TIENC
(Tibet

Rudoch

M T S.

HAINAN TIBETAN A.C.

TSINGHAI

HWANGNAN
TIBETAN A.C.

Lo

Gartok

T

I

B

E

YUSHU TIBETAN A.C.

Yangtse R.

GOLOG
TIBETAN
A. C.

Yellow R.

Yushu

Ahpa

SZE

TI

H

Tsangpo (Brahmaputra) R.

Lhasa

Chamdo
(Changtu)

KANTSE
TIBETAN A.C.

Ch

M

A

Shigatse

CHAMDO AREA

FORMER SIKANG BOUNDARY

NEPAL

Gyangtse

L

A

Longju

S

Kangting

INDIA

BHUTAN

Khinzemane

MULI
(Tibetan
LIANGSHAN

Ganges R.

R.

WI
(Yi-

E. PAKISTAN

Brahmaputra

R.

KIANG HSIN P

MEKONG R.

BURMA ROAD

TEHHUNG THAI-
CHINGPO A.C.

Paoshan &
Pentsao

Kunming

NAMVAN
ASSIGNED TRACT

Lashio

YUNNAN

Kokiu

LANTSANG
(Lahu)

Pisec

HSI-SHUANG-

PAN-NA-THA
A.C.

BURMA

LA

Salween R.

Mekong R.

	Chinese Irredenta (now in U.S.S.R.)
	Former Chinese Irredenta (now in Burma)
	Unsettled boundaries
+++	Principal railways
+-+-+	Railways projected or under construction
==	New highways (in western provinces)
⚓	Principal ports
A.C.	Autonomous Chou (prefecture)
□	Autonomous Hsien (County, Nationality)
A.R.	Autonomous region
L.	League (in Inner Mongolia)

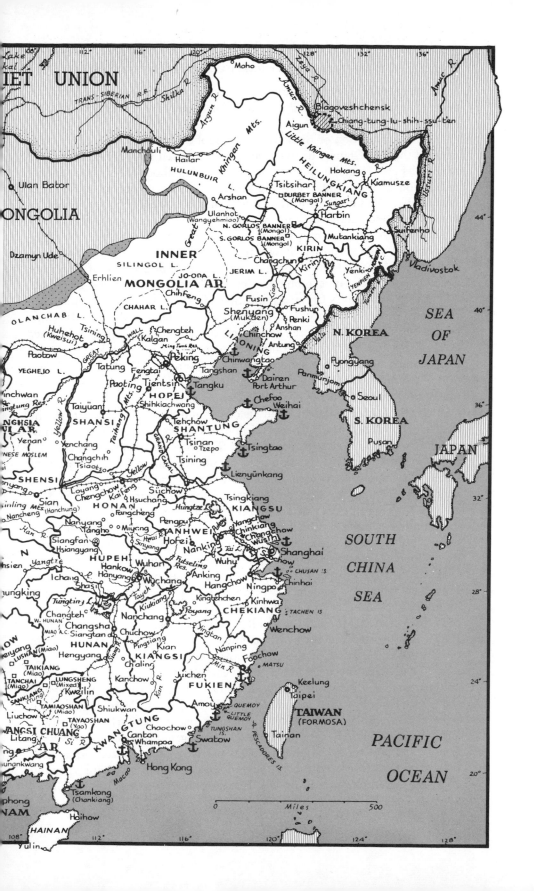

It has been alleged by the Chinese Nationalists that about fifteen million people were killed during the land reform and the drive against class enemies.

The Constitution of the People's Republic of China, adopted in 1954, asserted that the Chinese people's democratic united front would continue to play its part in mobilizing the people to bring about the socialist industrialization of the country and the socialist transformation of agriculture (Appendix B). The Constitution established a system of government in some ways resembling, in some ways differing from, that of the Soviet Union. The National People's Congress, a unicameral body, was the highest organ of state authority. It was to meet once a year, elect a chairman and vice-chairman of the Republic, and choose the premier of the State Council (cabinet) on recommendation of the chairman of the Republic. The National People's Congress and State Council were at the apex of a hierarchy of local, county, and provincial congresses and councils. Congresses on lower levels elected members to serve on congresses on higher levels. Delegates to the local congresses were elected by the local population from candidates nominated by the Communist Party, there being only one candidate for each seat. Although autonomous regions were designated for minority peoples, there was no claim that the system was federal or that major political subdivisions could legally secede from the system, as provided in the Constitution of the Soviet Union. The Communist Party was in complete control of the government on all levels, although a minority of posts were held by non-Communists. The structure of the Communist Party embodied the Leninist principle of "democratic centralism," which in effect meant strong control from the top.

In 1956, in an effort to counter disaffection among intellectuals, the government cautiously encouraged public discussion and criticism of Communist policies. In February, 1957, Mao Tse-tung, in his famous "Hundred Flowers" speech, held that free discussion, within certain limits, was necessary for the correct handling of "contradictions among the people." However, when the unexpectedly bitter denunciation of the regime and its leaders appeared to endanger Communist rule, a severe repression of the critics ensued. Hu Shih has vividly recounted the story (Selection 65). Pu Yi, the former Emperor of China and of Manchoukuo, was induced to declare his enthusiasm for the Communist regime (Selection 66).

The policies of the Peking regime veered further leftward, and a campaign against Rightists was launched. In 1958 the government inaugurated the Great Leap Forward in industry, with the goal of "catching up with Britain in fifteen years." Backyard blast furnaces were set up in towns and villages to increase steel production. The agricultural cooperatives, in which land and tools had already been partially collectivized on a semivoluntary basis, were now consolidated into communes, where virtually complete collectivization prevailed. The work in communes was organized along quasi-military lines, and preparations were begun to break up families: parents were to live in separate barracks, children in nurseries, and oldsters in "Happy Homes." The party-dominated communes replaced local government units, and the Chinese claimed that the communes represented a closer approximation to the Communist ideal of the withering away of the state and complete socialism than did the collective farms in the Soviet Union.

By 1959 the perilous disorganization of both industry and agriculture made it clear that forced industrialization and collectivism had gone too far. The tremendous drop in agricultural production and the widespread food shortages in the following two years were blamed by the regime on adverse weather conditions. The leadership partially retreated from extreme collectivization and renounced its overambitious plans for industrialization, to give priority to the improvement of agriculture. Peking leaders laid some of the blame for their economic woes on the niggardliness of Soviet assistance.

In 1966, the Great Proletarian Cultural Revolution swept China. A purge and reshuffling of top leadership was begun, and Marshal Lin Piao replaced Liu Shao-ch'i as second in command under Mao. In August, the Central Committee of the Communist Party called for an intensification of the revolution. Almost immediately, hundreds of thousands of teenagers organized as Red Guards appeared in Peking and other cities. They physically attacked local party officers, bureaucrats, and others suspected of revisionism or bourgeois tendencies. Occasionally they clashed with the workers in their effort to wipe out old ideas, old culture, old customs, and old habits. It appeared that the aged Mao was using the Red Guards to reinfuse the country with revolutionary idealism and to assure that his successors would be men committed to hold high the great red banner of Mao Tse-tung's thought.

In Taiwan the Nationalists carried out a program of rent reduction and land distribution which differed from the Communists' land reform: landlords were compensated for their land and the new landowners were not required to give up their land to cooperatives or communes (Selection 67).

64

On People's Democratic Dictatorship

July 1, 1949

Mao Tse-tung

Shortly before completing the conquest of mainland China, Mao described the Communist-led coalition government which he intended to establish. The people's democratic dictatorship would serve as the state form in the period of the "new democracy." See also *On New Democracy* (Chapter IX, Selection 51) and the Constitution of the People's Republic of China (Appendix B).

"You are dictatorial." My dear sirs, what you say is correct. That is just what we are. All the experiences of the Chinese people, accumulated in the course of successive decades, tell us to carry out a people's democratic dictatorship.

This means that the reactionaries must be deprived of the right to voice their opinions; only the people have that right.

Who are the "people"? At the present stage in China, they are the working class, the peasantry, the petty bourgeoisie and the national bourgeoisie.

Under the leadership of the working class and the Communist Party, these classes unite to create their own state and elect their own government so as to enforce their dictatorship over the henchmen of imperialism —the landlord class and bureaucratic capitalist class, as well as the reactionary clique of the Kuomintang, which represents these classes, and their accomplices. The people's government will suppress such persons. It will only permit them to behave themselves properly. It will not allow them to speak or act wildly. Should they do so, they will be instantly curbed and punished. The democratic system is to be carried out within the ranks of the people, giving them freedom of speech, assembly and association. The right to vote is given only to the people, not to the reactionaries.

These two things, democracy for the people and dictatorship for the reactionaries, when combined, constitute the people's democratic dictatorship.

From Mao Tse-tung, *On People's Democratic Dictatorship* (Peking: Foreign Languages Press, 1950), pp. 15–19.

Why must things be done in this way? Everyone is very clear on this point. If things were not done like this, the revolution would fail, the people would suffer and the state would perish.

"Don't you want to abolish state power?" Yes, we want to, but not at the present time. We cannot afford to abolish state power just now. Why not? Because imperialism still exists. Because, internally, reactionaries still exist and classes still exist.

Our present task is to strengthen the people's state apparatus—meaning principally the people's army, the people's police and the people's courts—thereby safeguarding national defence and protecting the people's interests. Given these conditions, China, under the leadership of the working class and the Communist Party, can develop steadily from an agricultural into an industrial country and from a New Democratic into a Socialist and, eventually, Communist society, eliminating classes and realizing universal harmony.

Such state apparatus as the army, the police and the courts are instruments with which one class oppresses another. As far as the hostile classes are concerned, these are instruments of oppression. They are violent and certainly not "benevolent" things.

"You are not benevolent." Exactly. We definitely have no benevolent policies toward the reactionaries or the counter-revolutionary activities of the reactionary classes. Our benevolent policy does not apply to such deeds or such persons, who are outside the ranks of the people; it applies only to the people.

The people's state is for the protection of the people. Once they have a people's state, the people then have the possibility of applying democratic methods on a nationwide and comprehensive scale to educate and reform themselves, so that they may get rid of the influences of domestic and foreign reactionaries. (These influences are still very strong at present and will remain for a long time to come; they cannot be eradicated quickly.) Thus the people can reform their bad habits and thoughts derived from the old society, so that they will not take the wrong road pointed out to them by the reactionaries, but will continue to advance and develop toward a Socialist and then Communist society.

The methods we use in this respect are democratic, that is, methods of persuasion and not of compulsion. If people break the law they will be punished, imprisoned or even sentenced to death. But these will be individual cases, differing in principle from the dictatorship imposed against the reactionaries as a class.

As for those belonging to reactionary classes or groups, after their political power has been overthrown, we will also give them land and work, permitting them to make a living and to reform themselves through labour into new persons—but only on condition that they do not rebel, sabotage or create disturbances. If they do not want to work, the people's state will force them to do so. Furthermore, the propaganda and educational work directed toward them will be carried out with the same care and thoroughness as the work already conducted among captured army officers. This may also be spoken of as a "benevolent policy," but it will be compulsorily imposed upon those originally from enemy classes. This can in no way be compared to our work along self-educational lines among the ranks of the revolutionary people.

This job of reforming the reactionary classes can be handled only by a state having a people's democratic dictatorship. When the work has been completed, China's major exploiting classes—the landlord class and the bureaucratic capitalist class, i.e., the monopoly capitalist class—will have been finally eliminated.

Then there will remain only the national bourgeoisie. In the present stage a great deal of suitable educational work can be done among them. When the time comes to realise Socialism, that is, to nationalise private enterprise, we will go a step further in our work of educating and reforming them. The people have a strong state apparatus in their hands, and they do not fear rebellion on the part of the national bourgeoisie.

65

A Month of Free Speech in Communist China

Hu Shih

Dr. Hu Shih tells how Peking's policy of "Letting a hundred flowers blossom and letting a hundred schools of thought contend" suddenly turned into a campaign to persecute and purge Rightists.

The student unrest, protest and riot formed one of the two great manifestations of the anti-Communist feelings of my people in the mainland. The other great manifestation was the one full month of outspoken and scathing criticism of the Communist party by Chinese intellectuals. That holiday of one month of freedom began with May 8 and abruptly ended on June 7, 1957. It was a month of free speech specially granted by

Excerpt from an address by Dr. Hu Shih at the Plenary Meeting of the Twelfth Regular Session of the General Assembly of the United Nations on September 26, 1957, as printed in *China Yearbook, 1958–59* (Taipei: China Publishing Company, 1958), pp. 747–750. Reprinted by permission of the China Publishing Company.

"instruction of the Central Committee of the Chinese Communist Party."

To have exactly one month of specially granted freedom of speech throughout eight long years of Communist rule—that in itself constitutes a sufficient commentary on the barbarity of the Communist regime.

Now, why was that one month of free speech granted at all? Was it granted because otherwise these non-Communist intellectuals and politicians would remain silent? No. For, under the Communist tyranny, the people have no freedom of silence—which is often more important than freedom of speech. In the old days, as long as a man remained silent, he would not be molested. But, under the Communist tyranny, there is no freedom to remain silent. You are called to the microphone to broadcast a speech prepared for you, or you are required to sign your name to an article written for you.

There is no freedom of silence. And, because they have no freedom of silence, the Chinese intellectuals have been compelled to speak insincerely, untruthfully, to pay compliment when compliment is undeserved, or to condemn friends or teachers whom they could not possibly have the heart to condemn. In short, the absence of the freedom of silence has forced many Chinese intellectuals to tell political lies, which is the only possible escape from this new tyranny and which, by the way, is also the only effective weapon to defeat the purposes of that tyranny.

For instance, when the Communist regime, some years ago, ordered a nation-wide purge of the poisonous effects of the thoughts of Hu Shih—that's me—every friend or student of mine had to speak his piece in refutation and condemnation of me, knowing very well that I would surely understand that he or she had no freedom of silence.

So, in the same manner, when the Communist dictators announced a year ago that, from now on, the Communist regime would carry out a policy of liberalism in dealing with science, literature and art, a policy of "Letting a hundred flowers blossom and letting a hundred schools of thought contend"—when that announcement was made, everybody smiled and applauded and said aloud: "How wonderful!"

So, in the same manner, when the dictators announced last year that the regime's new policy in dealing with the "democratic parties" was to be a policy of "Long-term Co-existence and Mutual Supervision"—when that announcement was made, again everybody smiled and applauded and said aloud: "How wonderful! How generous of you!"

But the stirring events in Hungary last October and the great unrest among the Chinese students brought about a great change in all this. The intellectuals and politicians were now prepared to speak out, prepared to say for the first time what they really wanted to say in plain and honest language. And the Communist leadership, too, was conscious of the wide and deep repercussions of the Hungarian revolution in the thought and feelings of the Chinese people. The Communists also wanted to find out the real feelings of the people, the intellectuals and the democratic politicians. The Communist leadership was so confident of its own power that it thought it could afford a little freedom for the intellectuals to speak up. In his February 27 speech, Mao Tse-tung made this savage brag:

"Since those Hungarian events, some of our intellectuals did lose their balance, but they did not stir up any storm in the country. Why? One reason, it must be said, was that we had succeeded in suppressing counter-revolution quite thoroughly."

Mao Tse-tung was so confident of his thoroughness in suppressing the counter-revolution that he was now ready to invite the intellectuals and politicians of the "democratic parties" to assist the Communist party in the coming campaign of "rectification" within the party. The non-Communist politicians and intellectuals were invited to speak out frankly about what they had observed as the defects and mistakes of the Communist regime. And, it is reported in the original version of Mao's speech of February 27 there were explicit assurances of complete freedom of speech.

So the great experiment of free speech began in early May. For a full month, everybody was free to voice his criticism of the party and the Communist regime; the few newspapers of the "democratic parties" were temporarily freed from Communist control and were able to print any news or opinion, however unfavourable to the Communist regime. Even the official press of the regime was instructed to print critical opinions without adverse comment.

But the tremendous volume of outspoken criticism against the regime and the great vehemence and bitterness of it all were far beyond the complacent expectations of the Communist leadership.

The Communist party was accused openly of believing and practising the notion that "the entire country belongs to the party as its war booty." The dictatorship of the Proletariat, for which Mao Tse-tung has coined the absurd name, "the People's democratic dictatorship," and which is no less than the absolute dictatorship of the Communist party over the people, was openly attacked as the root and the source of all the mistakes and evils of the Communist regime.

These critics stated openly that 90 per cent of past and present cases of "suppression of counter-revolution" were the result of wrong judgment and miscarried justice, and the democratic parties proposed that a higher commission of appeal and redress be established to re-examine all cases of suppression of counter-revolution. Many phases of the so-called socialist construction were severely criticized, and some critics said frankly that bureaucracy was a far more dangerous enemy than capitalism itself.

The Communist regime was attacked as a slavish imitation of the Soviet Union. The sincerity of Soviet friendship was questioned openly and the opinion was voiced that the Soviet Union should not be paid for the arms and ammunition which it had supplied to Red China in the Korean War.

And, of course, the criticism most frequently voiced was that, under the Communist rule, there were no freedom, no human rights, and no free elections.

All these were anti-Communist, anti-regime, and even "counter-revolutionary" voices which it was difficult for the Communist leadership to answer or to refute. And there was no doubt, during the whole month of outspoken criticism, that the Communist party was greatly discredited in the eyes of the people.

So the Communist leadership became very angry and regretted the whole affair as having given aid and comfort to the enemies of the socialist revolution. On June 7 the "freedom holiday" came to an abrupt end. The *People's Daily* now declared that there had been a political conspiracy on the part of the leaders of the democratic parties to extend their own spheres of influence and to overthrow the power of the Communist party. It further declared that the wise leadership of the Communist party had foreseen all this and had actually planned this period of open airing of grievances, complaints and criticisms as a method of sifting the fragrant flowers from the poisonous weeds. An editorial in the *People's Daily* of July 1 contained these interesting revelations:

"Carrying out the instructions of the Central Committee of the Chinese Communist Party, the *People's Daily* and all other papers of the party published little or no opinion from the positive side during the period between May 8 and June 7. The purpose was to let all the ghosts and evil spirits "bloom and contend" to their utmost, to let the poisonous weeds grow as tall as they could. This is to say that the Communist party, realizing that a class struggle between the bourgeoisie and the proletariat is inevitable, let the bourgeoisie and the bourgeois intellectuals initiate this battle.

"Some people said this was a secret trap. We say this is an open strategy. For we have told our enemies beforehand that we would hoe the poisonous weeds only after letting them grow out of the earth."

Thus, the movement of "Letting a hundred flowers blossom and letting a hundred schools of thought contend" suddenly turned into a campaign to persecute and purge the "Rightists"—a campaign which is still going on on the Chinese mainland, with a dozen leading intellectuals selected to be the targets of public interrogation, persecution, humiliation and degradation.

66

Ex-Emperor of China Happy Under Red Rule

Aisin Giorro Pu Yi

> Here Henry Pu Yi, who had been the last Emperor of China (as Hsüan-t'ung, 1909–1912), the restored Emperor of China for two weeks (July, 1917), the Chief Executive of Manchoukuo (1932–1934), and Emperor of Manchoukuo (1934–1945), contrasts his present happiness under the Communist regime with his miserable life as a monarch during feudalistic times. (See also Chapter I, Selection 8.)

The most memorable day of my life was December 4, 1959. Before then I had been the Emperor Hsuan Tung, the last ruler of the feudal monarchy that had existed in China for 3,000 years. Later I had become Emperor of the Japanese puppet state of Manchukuo and a war criminal.

On that day in 1959, after 10 years of re-education, I was granted a special pardon and released by the People's Government. Since then I have become an ordinary citizen of the People's Republic, one who lives by his own labor. Through the years I have gradually come to see how thoroughly soaked in crime and evil the first half of my life had been.

I was made Emperor of the Ching dynasty at the age of two. Three years later, in 1911, the revolution led by Sun Yat-sen overthrew the monarchy. Though the Ching court gave up its political power, the Republicans agreed to let me retain my title, palace and retinue, and appropriated an annual sum of 4 million taels, or 125,000 kilograms of silver for my expenses.

1,000 EUNUCHS

So I continued the ritual of sitting on the throne inside the thick vermilion-colored walls of the Forbidden City. I was attended by 1,000 eunuchs, more than 100 physicians, some 200 chefs and cooks, and protected by several hundred guards.

From Washington *Sunday Star*, March 8, 1964. Reprinted by permission of the North American Newspaper Alliance.

I owned a fabulous collection of jewels and other wealth. Any time I wanted to do so, I could order a diamond costing 30,000 yuan, or spend 2,000 yuan to buy a German police dog. At every meal, I sat down to a spread of some 60 dishes, and seldom did I wear the same clothes twice.

I was told by the nobles, the ministers and my tutors—and fully believed—that I was the sacred "Son of Heaven"; that "all land under Heaven is the property of the sovereign, all the people in the realm are subjects of the sovereign."

This mentality of "I am above all," instilled in me since childhood, gave birth to the most reactionary political ambition. I could not reconcile myself to the downfall of the Ching dynasty. I was determined to restore the rule of the Aisin Giorros (the Manchu family name of the Ching dynasty).

In 1924, when I had come of age and began attending to Court affairs myself, the nationalist troops led by the patriotic General Feng Yu-hsiang occupied Peking for a time. I was driven out of the Forbidden City—a move that intensified my fear and hatred of the revolutionaries, and intensified my liking for foreigners—actually, only for European, American and Japanese imperialists.

GREETED WITH "BANZAIS!"

At the Japanese Legation in Peking, my first place of refuge, and later in the Japanese Concession of Tientsin, I was still addressed as "Emperor of the Great Ching" by the consul-generals, the garrison commanders and capitalists of the United States, Britain, Japan, France and Italy. I was invited to review their troops on their national days, and received New Year and birthday greetings from them.

Indeed, things seemed to be turning out as I had wished. In 1931 the Japanese created "Manchukuo" in China's northeast (the home of the Manchu people and the cradle of the Ching dynasty) and put me on the throne as its puppet head.

To restore the "honor and glory" of the Aisin Giorro house throughout China, I considered it no shame to betray my country, to give my loyalty to the enemy, to commit innumerable bloody crimes against the people of the northeast.

My private life was completely degenerate. I was suspicious of everyone, I flew into a rage over the merest trifles. Dissipation and a perpetual nervous state, had weakened me so much, that—though still in my 30s—I had to be kept going with the aid of drugs.

With the collapse of Japanese imperialism in China, death became a real danger to me. I was arrested, together with my retinue and other officials of the puppet state, by the Soviet army, which helped to free the northeast.

We were taken to the Soviet Union and held under detention for five years. In 1950, we were sent back to China. As the train carrying us entered Chinese territory, I almost went crazy with fear, thinking of the unbearable humiliations and bloody revenge awaiting me.

But the horrors I feared never happened, when the train stopped at Shenyang, we were escorted to the Public Security Department, where an official of the People's Government urged us to study and re-educate ourselves. From Shenyang, we were taken to Fushun. There, at the center where the Japanese puppet "Manchukuo" and Kuomintang war criminals were held separately, we labored four hours, and studied four hours more, every day.

We had wholesome food and warm clothing, enjoyed the facilities of a clinic and bathhouse, and could engage in various recreations.

No one—from warden to guards—ever insulted or abused us: beating and scolding were simply nonexistent. A Burmese visitor exclaimed in astonishment: "Why, this is not a prison at all—it's more like a big school!"

STUDIES MARXISM

In such an environment, I began a life I'd never experienced before. For the first time ever, I was addressed by my name, lived in a group, and tried my hand at physical labor. I began to study something entirely different from the doctrines of Confucius and Mencius.

We had courses on China's feudal history over the past 100 years, which I compared with my knowledge of the late Ching dynasty and my own experiences and activities. Whether I liked it or not, I could not deny the fact that China had sunk from a sovereign state to a semi-colony and colony, during the last century.

Painfully, I recalled the appalling misery my actions had caused. At this point, the administrators of the center thought we were ready to be shown our country, about which we really knew nothing.

We visited factories, mines, farms, welfare institutions, cultural organizations and many other places in the northeast. The contrast between past and present deepened my understanding of my crimes. It showed me that the only way to a bright and useful life was to reform myself, so that I might become one of the people.

Since the first day of my life, I had—literally—opened my mouth to be fed, and stretched out my arms to be dressed. Even in the first days at Fushun, I still considered it beneath my "dignity" to fill my own rice bowl, fetch my own water and wash my own clothes. I was waited on by my nephews, who were also war criminals.

HIS FIRST EARNINGS

But in time I began to feel embarrassed at being the only one sitting around and doing nothing, while everybody else was busy with some work. I started attending to my own everyday needs. Then I took my turn of duty at cleaning the room and washing the bowls and dishes.

In 1953, we had our first try at productive labor—making paper boxes for a pencil factory. But I soon found out that, in the time it took me to make one box, the others finished several, and that mine were of poor quality. After several days, I achieved my best total of eight stand-ard-quality boxes in two hours. That day, the warden bought us candy with our earnings. Somehow, the candy—the first thing I earned with my own labor—tasted better than all the sweets I'd ever eaten!

The discouragement I felt at my own stupidity and clumsiness had gradually passed away by the second half of 1955, when we began growing vegetables. I actually distinguished myself in hoeing the field and fetching water and I also insisted on carrying coal by shoulder-pole, although the warden tried to dissuade me, thinking that this work might be too heavy. To my own—and others'—surprise, I did almost as well as some of the young people there.

One day the warden saw me and asked, with a smile: "How is your appetite these days?"

"Three big bowls of rice at each meal."

The guards and fellow-inmates who heard the conversation all burst into hearty laughter. I laughed too, feeling very happy.

Labor not only improved my health; more important, it gradually brought changes in my thinking and outlook. My own experiences in physical labor proved to me that parasites who live off others are stupid; that only those who work are clever and intelligent.

HIS NEW LIFE

In the past four years, I have embarked on a new life as a citizen of the People's Republic of China. First, as a gardener in the Peking Botani-cal Gardens, and now on the Committee for the Collection and Com-pilation of Historical Materials under the National Committee of the People's Political Consultative Conference, I have been doing some use-ful work for the people.

Until I went to prison, my relationship with others—including my own relatives—had been the impersonal and cold one that exists between "Sovereign" and "subjects," between "master" and "servant," with both sides practicing deceit.

Never had I known true friendship and love. Now, I have many comrades and friends. Last May Day, I married Li Shu-hsien, a nurse; and for the first time in my life, I have a happy home of my own.

Other members of the Aisin Giorro clan also live a different life. Today, among its descendants, are: a delegate to the National People's Congress; a member of the People's Consultative Conference; distinguished veterans of the Chinese People's Volunteers in Korea; doctors working in hospitals of the People's Liberation Army; teachers, a leading motorcyclist; and a famous fencing instructor.

Some of them are Communists, some are members of the Young Communist League and Young Pioneers.

Now, can I help but feel the joy of this bright new existence? Though I am already 58 years old, I feel my real life has just begun.

67

Differences Between Land Reform in Taiwan and the Communist "Land Reform"

Chen Cheng

Here the late General Chen Cheng, Vice-President of Nationalist China from 1954 to 1965, contrasts the land reform in Taiwan under his administration with that in Communist China.

. . . From the foregoing, it is clear that the land reform in Taiwan and that of the Chinese Communists are entirely different. By way of comparison, the following summary notes the differences with respect to their purposes, the methods used, and results achieved.

PURPOSE OF REFORM

1. In Taiwan:

a. In order to realize the ideal "of the people" as embodied in the Three Principles of the People, the ownership of farm lands has been gradually turned over to the farmers themselves.

b. In order to realize the ideal of "by the people" as embodied in

From Chen Cheng, *Land Reform in Taiwan* (Taipei: China Publishing Company, 1961), pp. 125–129. Reprinted by permission of the China Publishing Company.

the Three Principles of the People, such tasks as the distribution, utilization, and management of farm land are turned over, as far as feasible, to the farmers in accordance with the spirit of self-government.

c. In order to realize the ideal of "for the people" as embodied in the Three Principles of the People, all the income derived from farm production, except part of it to be used for payment of taxes according to law, goes to the farmers.

2. On the Chinese mainland:

a. In the name of land nationalization, all land has become the property of the Communist Party.

b. In the name of production through "cooperation" and "collectivization," the Peiping regime takes over all fruits of production.

c. In the name of liberating the oppressed farmers, all farmers on the mainland have been turned into productive tools of the Peiping regime.

d. In the name of "making all people into soldiers," mainland farmers have become tools of war for the Peiping regime.

METHODS OF REFORM

1. In Taiwan:

a. Concerning land reform:

  1. Implementation of the 37.5% farm rent limitation program.
  2. Implementation of sale of public lands.
  3. Implementation of the Land-to-the-Tiller Program.

    a. Purchase of excess farm land from landlords and payment of compensation to them.

    b. Retention by the landlords of a part of their tenanted land in accordance with law.

    c. Resale by the government of compulsorily purchased land to its incumbent cultivator.

    d. Payment of the purchase price by the farmer-purchaser either in kind or with land bonds by installments spread over a period of ten years.

    e. Prior right of purchase of landlords' land by incumbent cultivator and right of asking the Land Bank for loan in making such purchase.

b. Concerning development and utilization of land:

  1. Development of new tidal lands.
  2. Development of marginal lands.
  3. Promotion of water conservation projects.
  4. Land replotting and consolidation.
  5. Promotion of mechanized farming.
  6. Scientific farming.
  7. Promotion of the farmers' capacity for self-government.

2. On the Chinese mainland:

a. Methods used in the earlier stage:

1. Farmers were forced to engage in struggle and the liquidation of landlords, to create a reign of terror, to divide the lands of landlords, to destroy the families of landlords, and even to demand their heads.

2. There was unceasing checking and rechecking of the people and their lands in an effort to intensify the class struggle so that poor peasants were raised to the status of middle peasants, middle peasants to the status of rich peasants, and rich peasants to the status of landlords. The end result was that all genuine farmers became objects of liquidation and struggle and ran the risk of having their families broken up and even losing their own lives.

b. Methods used in the middle stage:

1. Agricultural collectivization was practiced to force farmers to join collective farms and deprive them of their landownership.

2. In the name of the "leadership of the Party and Government," full control was exercised over both the cooperatives and the farmers.

3. In the name of subordinating "individual interest" to "collective interests" and "collective interests" to the "interests of the state," agricultural cooperatives were turned into tools for the exploitation and enslavement of farmers by the Communists.

c. Methods used at present:

1. To carry out the "people's commune" system in order to deprive the people of all their possessions and turn them into "worker ants of an ant colony."

2. To practice "collective living," "to make all activities partake of the nature of a combat," and "to organize the people like an army" so that the Peiping regime may drive and enslave the people under its domination to do what it wants them to do and turn them into tools of war.

RESULTS ACHIEVED

1. In Taiwan:

a. Production has increased and the rural areas are thriving. Nurtured by agriculture, industry has flourished. Stimulated by industry's need for farm products, agriculture has been making steady progress.

b. With the amelioration of their living conditions, farmers have gained a better understanding of the importance to themselves of politics and culture, thereby laying the foundations for a democratic life and self-government and raising the general cultural level of the people.

c. Industrial and agricultural development has led to social stability and progress, thereby laying a solid foundation for a counterattack against the Communist-controlled mainland and for national recovery.

2. On the Chinese mainland:

a. Under the rule of Communist tyranny, the people have had nothing for themselves except their physical existence and have lost interest in life.

b. The so-called "land reform" carried out by the Chinese Communists is really a changing of the farmer's status. Farmers have been transformed into serfs. How can serfs be expected to take any interest in production? That is why agricultural production of the mainland has been on the decline. Besides, natural disasters flow one after another in rapid succession and famine has become a universal phenomenon and more and more serious.

c. The Communist Party has become a new class with special privileges, and exploits the people for the furtherance of its own interests. To carry out its plans to exploit the people, it has to resort to such ruthless measures as repression, persecution, and mass massacre. Groaning under the weight of this tyrannical rule, the people on the mainland have come to a point at which they are ready to die together with their oppressors.

To summarize briefly, the goal of land reform in Taiwan is to promote the welfare of the people through changes in the land system and increase of land productivity. On the other hand, the so-called "land reform" of the Chinese Communists has as its chief goal the seizure of political power and the consolidation of their rule. "Land reform" has been used as a cloak to cover up their deception, persecution, massacre, and other acts of violence committed by baiting the people with land and entrapping them thereby. No contrast can be sharper than that between the land reform in Taiwan and the so-called "land reform" of the Chinese Communists.

SUGGESTED READING

Barnett, A. Doak. *Communist China: The Early Years.* New York: Frederick A. Praeger, 1964, paperback.

Bowie, Robert R., and Fairbank, John K., eds. *Communist China, 1955–1959: Policy Documents with Analysis.* Cambridge: Harvard University Press, 1962.

Buss, Claude A. *The People's Republic of China.* Princeton: Van Nostrand, 1962, paperback.

Chandra-Sekhar, Sripati. *Red China: An Asian View.* New York: Frederick A. Praeger, 1961, paperback.

Chao, Kuo-chun. *Agrarian Policies of Mainland China: A Documentary Study, 1949–1956.* Cambridge: Cambridge University Press, 1957.

Chen, Theodore H. E. *Thought Reform of the Chinese Intellectuals.* Hong Kong: Hong Kong University Press, 1960.

Cohen, Arthur A. *The Communism of Mao Tse-tung.* Chicago: University of Chicago Press, 1964, paperback.

Cole, Allen B. *Forty Years of Chinese Communism: Selected Readings with Commentary.* Washington: Service Center for Teachers of History, American Historical Association, 1962, paperback.

Evans, Robert E., ed. *Reports from Red China.* New York: Bantam, 1962, paperback.

Feuerwerker, Albert, ed. *Modern China.* Englewood Cliffs, N.J.: Prentice-Hall, 1964, paperback.

Gluckstein, Ygael. *Mao's China: Economic and Political Survey.* Boston: Beacon Press, 1957.

Greene, Felix. *China: The Country Americans Are Not Allowed to Know.* New York: Ballantine Books, 1960, paperback.

Hu, Chang-tu, et al. *China: Its People, Its Society, Its Culture.* New Haven: Human Relations Area Files Press, 1960.

Hughes, T. J., and Luard, D. E. T. *Economic Development of Communist China.* London: Oxford University Press, 1961.

Hunter, Edward. *Brain-Washing in Red China: The Calculated Destruction of Men's Minds.* New York: Vanguard, 1951.

Jacobs, Dan N., and Baerwald, Hans H. *Chinese Communism: Selected Documents.* New York: Harper & Row, 1963, paperback.

Jan, George P., ed. *Government of Communist China.* San Francisco: Chandler Publishing Company, 1966, paperback.

Kahin, George McT., ed. *Major Governments of Asia,* 2nd ed. Ithaca: Cornell University Press, 1963.

Lewis, John Wilson, ed. *Major Doctrines of Communist China.* New York: Norton, 1964, paperback.

Li Choh-ming. *Economic Development of Communist China: An Appraisal of the First Five Years of Industrialization.* Berkeley: University of California Press, 1959.

Lifton, Robert J. *Thought Reform and the Psychology of Totalism: A Study of "Brainwashing" in China.* New York: Norton, 1963, paperback.

MacFarquhar, Roderick. *The Hundred Flowers Campaign and the Chinese Intellectuals.* New York: Frederick A. Praeger, 1960.

Mu Fu-sheng. *The Wilting of the Hundred Flowers: The Chinese Intelligentsia under Mao.* New York: Frederick A. Praeger, 1963, paperback.

Quigley, Harold S. *China's Politics in Perspective.* Minneapolis: University of Minnesota Press, 1960.

Schram, Stuart R. *The Political Thought of Mao Tse-tung.* New York: Frederick A. Praeger, 1963, paperback.

Schurmann, Franz. *Ideology and Organization in Communist China.* Berkeley: University of California Press, 1966.

Snow, Edgar. *Other Side of the River: Red China Today.* New York: Random House, 1962.

Tang, Peter S. H. *Communist China Today.* Washington, D.C.: Research Institute on the Sino-Soviet Bloc, 1961.

Tung, William L. *The Political Institutions of Modern China.* The Hague: Martinius Nijhoff, 1964.

Walker, Richard L. *China under Communism: The First Five Years.* New Haven: Yale University Press, 1955.

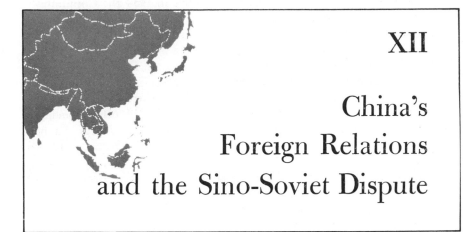

XII

China's
Foreign Relations
and the Sino-Soviet Dispute

Following the establishment of the Communist regime in Peking and its recognition by the Soviet Union, Great Britain, and many other countries, the question of seating Communist China in the United Nations has been perennially raised. China is one of the five permanent members of the Security Council and is therefore entitled to a seat. The problem is one of credentials: whether the seat is to be occupied by the representative of the Nationalist government or of the Communist government. The Soviet Union boycotted the Security Council from January to August, 1950, in order to pressure other members into seating the Chinese Communists. After the Peking regime intervened in the Korean War, Communist China was condemned as an aggressor by the United Nations General Assembly (Chapter X, Selection 61), and so long as this condemnation continues to stand, the question of Peking's eligibility to enter the United Nations remains in doubt. Compromise proposals envisage the seating of both the Nationalists and the Communists by, for example, giving the Nationalists a vote in the General Assembly and giving the Communists the seat in the Security Council. However, "two Chinas" solutions, intended to pacify the Formosa Strait as well as solve the U.N. seating question, are emphatically rejected by both the Nationalists and the Communists as destructive of the unity of China.

In February, 1950, Communist China and the Soviet Union made a treaty of alliance, which later served as the diplomatic base for the North Korean attack on South Korea and the subsequent intervention of Soviet-armed Chinese "volunteers" in the conflict (Selection 68). Although Moscow gave significant aid to Peking in its land warfare in Korea, it did not provide China with the air and naval strength needed to "liberate" Taiwan from the Chinese Nationalists. Thus in 1954 the Communists bombarded the offshore islands (Quemoy and Matsu) without dislodging the Nationalists defenders, who benefited from American logistical support. In 1955 the United States Congress passed a resolution authorizing the President to employ American forces to defend Taiwan, the Pescadores, and "related positions and territories," such as, presumably, the offshore islands. In the same year a mutual defense treaty between the United States and Nationalist China was ratified. On the other hand, the United States Navy, rather than help the Nationalists defend the Tachen Islands, assisted them in evacuating the islands, which were considered indefensible.

The Nationalist leader, Chiang Kai-shek, repeatedly proclaims his intention to recapture the mainland. Once the Nationalist forces land on the continent, he says, the Chinese people, who hate Communist oppression, will rise up against their masters. Foreign troops, therefore, would not be required for the liberation of the mainland, but American logistical support would be necessary. The recent acquisition of an atomic weapon by the Chinese Communists, the Nationalists assert, has made it more urgent than ever for the nations of the world to eliminate the Peking regime. The United States, however, has shown no enthusiasm for involvement in a war in China proper, and its policies are not based upon the assumption that the Peking regime will soon be overthrown. The unwillingness of the Soviet Union to assist the Chinese Communists to liberate Taiwan and the unwillingness of the United States to help the Nationalists to recapture the mainland have resulted in a *de facto* truce, broken from time to time by Communist artillery bombardments of the offshore islands and Nationalist commando raids and U-2 overflights of the mainland.

The Chinese Communists were not pleased by Premier Khrushchev's denunciation of Stalin and advocacy of peaceful transition to socialism and peaceful coexistence at the Twentieth Congress of the Communist Party of the Soviet Union in 1956 (Selection 69). Rivalry for influence in Korea, Mongolia, and Southeast Asia and for leadership in the world Communist movement, fundamental differences over the Sino-Indian border question and the nuclear test-ban treaty, and the niggardliness of Soviet economic and military aid contributed to bitter feelings in Peking towards Moscow. By mid-1963 it appeared that there were no limits to the charges which the Chinese were willing to make directly against the leaders of the Kremlin, their "revisionist" and "capitulationist" policies, and their willingness to "gang up" with the American "imperialists" against the Chinese people (Selection 70). Peking claimed that the fall of Khrushchev in 1964 represented a defeat for his policies, but within a few weeks, the Chinese denounced the Kremlin for continuing Khrushchev's policies and demanded that his successors resign. The Chinese have been giving support to revolutionary elements in Asia and Africa, often in opposition to the somewhat more moderate orientation of Soviet policy, which has tended to support neutralist regimes. Notwithstanding the intense bitterness of the Sino-Soviet dispute, the two countries have continued to maintain diplomatic relations and from time to time have reminded the world of their unshakable alliance.

India's anti-imperialism and pacifism inclined her to assume a friendly attitude towards Communist China in the early 1950's. The vast buffer zone of Tibet and the Himalayas seemed to guarantee against political and military tensions along the Sino-Indian frontier. Prime Minister Jawaharlal Nehru advocated the seating of the Peking regime in the U.N., took a neutral position in the Korean conflict, and acquiesced in the Chinese conquest of Tibet. The Sino-Indian treaty concerning Tibet in 1954 provided for the relinquishment of Indian rights in Tibet and for the *Panchshila*, or Five Principles of Coexistence: (1) mutual respect for territorial integrity and sovereignty, (2) nonaggression, (3) noninterference in internal affairs, (4) equality and mutual benefit, and (5) peaceful coexistence.

However, the Indians were deeply shocked by the harshness of the Chinese suppression of the anti-Communist Tibetans in 1959, leading to the flight of the Dalai Lama to India. Then in October, 1963, during the height of the United States-Soviet confrontation in the Cuban missile crisis, Chinese troops began a massive offensive in the disputed border regions between China and India. The hitherto neutral Indian leaders were now grateful to receive American and British, as well as Soviet, military equipment. Soviet efforts toward mediating the Sino-Indian War were regarded as unfriendly by China, which insisted that it was defending itself from India and the imperialists. The Chinese march into India came to a halt in November when the Chinese unilaterally declared the terms for a cease-fire. The Indians were unhappy with the Chinese terms, but the alternative was to continue losing the war to the rapidly advancing Chinese, and India tacitly accepted the cease-fire provisions.

In 1963 the Peking regime made a border treaty with Pakistan, India's archenemy, intensifying New Delhi's distrust of Peking. In September, 1965, when war broke out between India and Pakistan over Kashmir, Communist China announced its support of Pakistan's territorial claims and sent troops to the Indian frontier, claiming that Indian troops had entered Chinese territory. The U.N. Security Council called for a cease-fire, which was accepted by India and Pakistan, and the Soviet Union helped to arrange an India-Pakistan truce, which was signed at Tashkent,

Northwest China

in Soviet central Asia. The Soviet diplomatic efforts in the India-Pakistan settlement enjoyed the sympathy of the United States and was condemned by Peking as part of a plot by the imperialists and revisionists to encircle China.

In 1964 France's recognition of the Chinese People's Republic and the explosion of the first Chinese-made atomic weapon enhanced Communist China's prestige throughout the world, especially in the underdeveloped countries. The Peking-oriented Communist Party of Indonesia, the largest Marxist-Leninist party outside the Soviet Union and China, became a dominant influence in the domestic and foreign policies of President Sukarno's "guided democracy." Peking encouraged Indonesia's "crush Malaysia" war and her dramatic resignation from the United Nations. Comrade Lin Piao, in September, 1965, published an article, "Long Live the Victory of the People's War," which spoke of surrounding North America and Europe with revolutions patterned after China's in Asia, Africa, and Latin America (Selection 71). However, in October, 1965, an attempted Communist coup d'état in Indonesia provoked a counter coup by the Indonesian army. Urged on by the military, the enraged populace killed tens of thousands of Communists and alleged Communists. A military-dominated regime was established, Sukarno was reduced to a figurehead, and the pro-Chinese Foreign Minister was forced out of office. Peking's influence in the underdeveloped world suffered another setback when Kwame Nkrumah, the pro-Chinese President of Ghana, was deposed during his visit to Peking in February, 1966.

The escalation of the war in Vietnam in 1966 intensified rather than lessened the Sino-Soviet dispute, as China accused the Soviet Union of betraying North Vietnam and the Viet Cong to the American imperialists. The purge of revisionists and the excesses of the Red Guards in China in 1966 exposed a bitter power struggle within the Chinese Communist Party and damaged Peking's image.

68

Treaty of Friendship, Alliance and Mutual Assistance Between the People's Republic of China and the Union of Soviet Socialist Republics

February 14, 1950

This Sino-Soviet treaty was directed against "aggression on the part of Japan or any other state that may collaborate in any way with Japan in acts of aggression." Since Japan at that time was disarmed, it appears that the parties to this treaty had in mind the United States, which maintained substantial land, sea, and air bases in Japan. War broke out in Korea five months later.

The Central People's Government of the People's Republic of China and the Presidium of the Supreme Soviet of the Union of Soviet Socialist Republics, fully determined to prevent jointly, by strengthening friendship and co-operation between the People's Republic of China and the Union of Soviet Socialist Republics, the revival of Japanese imperialism and the resumption of aggression on the part of Japan or any other state that may collaborate in any way with Japan in acts of aggression; imbued with the desire to consolidate lasting peace and universal security in the

From Chinese People's Institute of Foreign Affairs, *Oppose the Revival of Japanese Militarism (A Selection of Important Documents and Commentaries)* (Peking: Foreign Languages Press, 1960), pp. 1–4.

Far East and throughout the world in conformity with the aims and principles of the United Nations; profoundly convinced that the consolidation of good neighbourly relations and friendship between the People's Republic of China and the Union of Soviet Socialist Republics meets the vital interests of the peoples of China and the Soviet Union, have towards this end decided to conclude the present Treaty and have appointed as their plenipotentiary representatives: Chou En-lai, Premier of the Government Administration Council and Minister of Foreign Affairs of China, acting for the Central People's Government of the People's Republic of China; and Andrei Yanuaryevich Vyshinsky, Minister of Foreign Affairs of the U.S.S.R., acting for the Presidium of the Supreme Soviet of the Union of Soviet Socialist Republics. Both plenipotentiary representatives, having communicated their full powers and found them in good and due form, have agreed upon the following:

ARTICLE 1

Both Contracting Parties undertake jointly to adopt all necessary measures at their disposal for the purpose of preventing the resumption of aggression and violation of peace on the part of Japan or any other state that may collaborate with Japan directly or indirectly in acts of aggression. In the event of one of the Contracting Parties being attacked by Japan or any state allied with her and thus being involved in a state of war, the other Contracting Party shall immediately render military and other assistance by all means at its disposal.

The Contracting Parties also declare their readiness to participate in a spirit of sincere co-operation in all international actions aimed at ensuring peace and security throughout the world and to contribute their full share to the earliest implementation of these tasks.

ARTICLE 2

Both Contracting Parties undertake in a spirit of mutual agreement to bring about the earliest conclusion of a peace treaty with Japan jointly with other powers which were Allies in the Second World War.

ARTICLE 3

Each Contracting Party undertakes not to conclude any alliance directed against the other Contracting Party and not to take part in any coalition or in any actions or measures directed against the other Contracting Party.

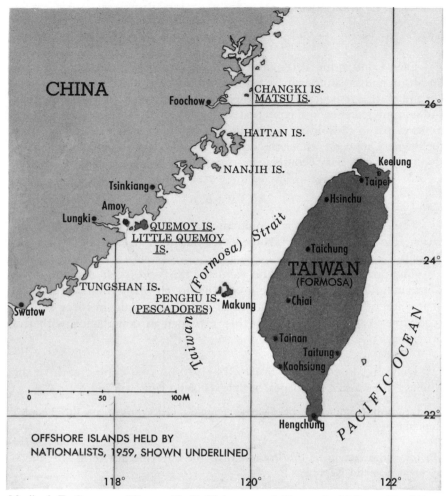

Meribeth E. Cameron, Thomas H. D. Mahoney and George E. McReynolds—*China, Japan and the Powers*, Second Edition   Copyright © 1960   The Ronald Press Company, New York.

Taiwan and the Nationalist Offshore Islands

ARTICLE 4

Both Contracting Parties, in the interests of consolidating peace and universal security, will consult with each other in regard to all important international problems affecting the common interests of China and the Soviet Union.

ARTICLE 5

Each Contracting Party undertakes, in a spirit of friendship and co-operation and in conformity with the principles of equality, mutual benefit and mutual respect for the national sovereignty and territorial integrity and non-interference in the internal affairs of the other Contracting Party, to develop and consolidate economic and cultural ties between China and the Soviet Union, to render the other all possible economic assistance and to carry out necessary economic co-operation.

ARTICLE 6

The present Treaty shall come into force immediately after its ratification; the exchange of instruments of ratification shall take place in Peking.

The present Treaty shall be valid for thirty years. If neither of the Contracting Parties gives notice a year before the expiration of this term of its intention to denounce the Treaty, it shall remain in force for another five years and shall be further extended in compliance with this provision.

Done in Moscow on February 14, 1950, in two copies, each in the Chinese and Russian languages, both texts being equally valid.

On the authorization of the Central People's Government of the People's Republic of China

Chou En-Lai

On the authorization of the Presidium of the Supreme Soviet of the Union of Soviet Socialist Republics

A. Y. Vyshinsky

69

Outline of Views on the Question of Peaceful Transition

November 10, 1957

Unhappy with the Soviet line of peaceful transition to socialism, the Chinese leaders gave the following statement to the Central Committee of the Communist Party of the Soviet Union at the 1957 Meeting of Representatives of Communist and Workers Parties in Moscow. This document makes it clear that the beginning of the Sino-Soviet dispute dates back at least to 1957.

I. On the question of the transition from capitalism to socialism, it would be more flexible to refer to the two possibilities, peaceful transition and non-peaceful transition, than to just one, and this would place us in a position where we can have the initiative politically at any time.

1. Referring to the possibility of peaceful transition indicates that for us the use of violence is primarily a matter of self-defence. It enables the Communist Parties in the capitalist countries to sidestep attacks on them on this issue, and it is politically advantageous—advantageous for winning the masses and also for depriving the bourgeoisie of its pretexts for such attacks and isolating it.

2. If practical possibilities for peaceful transition were to arise in individual countries in the future when the international or domestic situation changes drastically, we could then make timely use of the opportunity to win the support of the masses and solve the problem of state power by peaceful means.

3. Nevertheless, we should not tie our own hands because of this desire. The bourgeoisie will not step down from the stage of history voluntarily. This is a universal law of class struggle. In no country should the proletariat and the Communist Party slacken their preparations for the revolution in any way. They must be prepared at all times to repulse

From Editorial Departments of *Renmin Ribao* (People's Daily) and *Hongqi* (Red Flag), *The Origin and Development of the Differences between the Leadership of the CPSU and Ourselves—Comment on the Open Letter of the Central Committee of the CPSU* (Peking: Foreign Languages Press, 1963), pp. 58–62.

counter-revolutionary attacks and, at the critical juncture of the revolution when the working class is seizing state power, to overthrow the bourgeoisie by armed force if it uses armed force to suppress the people's revolution (generally speaking, it is inevitable that the bourgeoisie will do so).

II. In the present situation of the international communist movement, it is advantageous from the point of view of tactics to refer to the desire for peaceful transition. But it would be inappropriate to over-emphasize the possibility of peaceful transition. The reasons are:

1. Possibility and reality, the desire and whether or not it can be fulfilled, are two different matters. We should refer to the desire for peaceful transition, but we should not place our hopes mainly on it and therefore should not over-emphasize this aspect.

2. If too much stress is laid on the possibility of peaceful transition, and especially on the possibility of seizing state power by winning a majority in parliament it is liable to weaken the revolutionary will of the proletariat, the working people and the Communist Party and disarm them ideologically.

3. To the best of our knowledge, there is still not a single country where this possibility is of any practical significance. Even if it is slightly more apparent in a particular country, over-emphasizing this possibility is inappropriate because it does not conform with the realities in the overwhelming majority of countries. Should such a possibility actually occur in some country, the Communist Party there must on the one hand strive to realize it, and on the other hand always be prepared to repulse the armed attacks of the bourgeoisie.

4. The result of emphasizing this possibility will neither weaken the reactionary nature of the bourgeoisie nor lull them.

5. Nor will such emphasis make the social democratic parties any more revolutionary.

6. Nor will such emphasis make Communist Parties grow any stronger. On the contrary, if some Communist Parties should as a result obscure their revolutionary features and thus become confused with the social democratic parties in the eyes of the people, they would only be weakened.

7. It is very hard to gather forces and prepare for the revolution, and after all parliamentary struggle is easy in comparison. We must fully utilize the parliamentary form of struggle, but its role is limited. What is most important is to proceed with the hard work of gathering the revolutionary forces.

III. To obtain a majority in parliament is not the same as smashing the old state machinery (chiefly the armed forces) and establishing new state machinery (chiefly the armed forces). Unless the military-bureaucratic state machinery of the bourgeoisie is smashed, a parliamentary

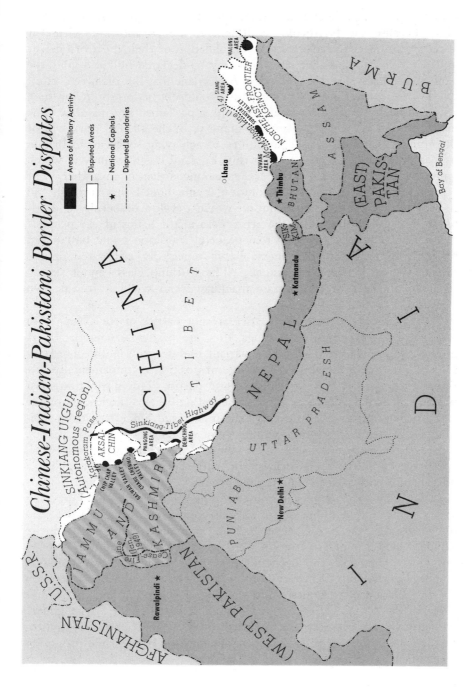

Chinese-Indian-Pakistani Border Disputes

- Areas of Military Activity
- Disputed Areas
★ National Capitals
- ∙∙∙ Disputed Boundaries

U.S.S.R.

AFGHANISTAN

SINKIANG UIGUR
(Autonomous region)

Karakorum Pass

AKSAI CHIN

Sinkiang-Tibet Highway

CHINA

TIBET

○ Lhasa

PANGONG AREA

CHANG CHENMO VALLEY

DEMCHOK AREA

GALWAN VALLEY

CHIP CHAP VALLEY

JAMMU AND KASHMIR

Line of Control (India 1949)

Cease-fire Line (1949)

Rawalpindi ★

(WEST) PAKISTAN

PUNJAB

New Delhi ★

UTTAR PRADESH

NEPAL

★ Katmandu

SIK-KIM

BHUTAN

★ Thimbu

NEFA

NORTH-EAST FRONTIER AGENCY

McMahon Line (1914)

SIANG AREA

WALONG AREA

TOWANG AREA

KAMENG VALLEY

SUBANSIRI VALLEY

ASSAM

(EAST) PAKIS-TAN

INDIA

BURMA

Bay of Bengal

majority for the proletariat and their reliable allies will either be impossible (because the bourgeoisie will amend the constitution whenever necessary in order to facilitate the consolidation of their dictatorship) or undependable (for instance, elections may be declared null and void, the Communist Party may be outlawed, parliament may be dissolved, etc.).

IV. Peaceful transition to socialism should not be interpreted in such a way as solely to mean transition through a parliamentary majority. The main question is that of the state machinery. In the 1870's, Marx was of the opinion that there was a possibility of achieving socialism in Britain by peaceful means, because "at that time England was a country in which militarism and bureaucracy were less pronounced than in any other." For a period after the February Revolution, Lenin hoped that through "all power to the Soviets" the revolution would develop peacefully and triumph, because at that time "the arms were in the hands of the people." Neither Marx nor Lenin meant that peaceful transition could be realized by using the old state machinery. Lenin repeatedly elaborated on the famous saying of Marx and Engels, "The working class cannot simply lay hold of the ready-made state machinery and wield it for its own purposes."

V. The social democratic parties are not parties of socialism. With the exception of certain Left wings, they are parties serving the bourgeoisie and capitalism. They are a variant of bourgeois political parties. On the question of socialist revolution, our position is fundamentally different from that of the social democratic parties. This distinction must not be obscured. To obscure this distinction only helps the leaders of the social democratic parties to deceive the masses and hinders us from winning the masses away from the influence of the social democratic parties. However, it is unquestionably very important to strengthen our work with respect to the social democratic parties and strive to establish a united front with their left and middle groups.

VI. Such is our understanding of this question. We do hold differing views on this question, but out of various considerations we did not state our views after the 20th Congress of the Communist Party of the Soviet Union. Since a joint Declaration is to be issued, we must now explain our views. However, this need not prevent us from attaining common language in the draft Declaration. In order to show a connection between the formulation of this question in the draft Declaration and the formulation of the 20th Congress of the Communist Party of the Soviet Union, we agree to take the draft put forward today by the Central Committee of the Communist Party of the Soviet Union as a basis, while proposing amendments in certain places.

70

An Adverse Current That Is Opposed to Marxism-Leninism and Is Splitting the International Communist Movement

By 1963 the Chinese Communists were accusing their Soviet comrades of frequent lying and much worse, such as "attempting to deprive China of the right to possess nuclear weapons to resist the U.S. nuclear threat" and carrying out "large-scale subversive activities" in China. Here are the "iron-clad facts," numbered from 1 through 10.

In the Open Letter the leaders of the CPSU try hard to make people believe that after the 22nd Congress they "undertook new attempts" to improve relations between the Chinese and Soviet Parties and to strengthen unity among the fraternal Parties and countries.

This is another lie.

What are the facts?

They show that since the 22nd Congress the leadership of the CPSU has become more unbridled in violating the principles guiding relations among fraternal Parties and countries and in pursuing policies of great-power chauvinism, sectarianism and splittism in order to promote its own line of systematic revisionism, which is in complete violation of Marxism-Leninism. This has brought about a continuous deterioration in Sino-Soviet relations and grave damage to the unity of the fraternal Parties and countries.

The following are the main facts about how the leaders of the CPSU have sabotaged Sino-Soviet unity and the unity of fraternal Parties and countries since the 22nd Congress:

1. The leaders of the CPSU have tried hard to impose their erroneous line upon the international communist movement and to replace the Declaration and the Statement with their own revisionist programme.

From Editorial Departments of *Renmin Ribao* (People's Daily) and *Hongqi* (Red Flag), *The Origin and Development of the Differences between the Leadership of the CPSU and Ourselves—Comment on the Open Letter of the Central Committee of the CPSU* (Peking: Foreign Languages Press, 1963), pp. 44–51.

They describe their erroneous line as the "whole set of Leninist policies of the international communist movement of recent years," and they call their revisionist programme the "real Communist Manifesto of our time" and the "common programme" of the "Communist and Workers' Parties and of the people of countries of the socialist community."

Any fraternal Party which rejects the erroneous line and programme of the CPSU and perseveres in the fundamental theories of Marxism-Leninism and the revolutionary principles of the Declaration and the Statement is looked upon as an enemy by the leaders of the CPSU, who oppose, attack and injure it and try to subvert its leadership by every possible means.

2. Disregarding everything, the leadership of the CPSU broke off diplomatic relations with socialist Albania, an unprecedented step in the history of relations between fraternal Parties and countries.

3. The leadership of the CPSU has continued to exert pressure on China and to make outrageous attacks on the Chinese Communist Party. In its letter of February 22, 1962 to the Central Committee of the CPC, the Central Committee of the CPSU accused the CPC of taking a "special stand of their own" and pursuing a line at variance with the common course of the fraternal Parties, and even made a crime out of our support for the Marxist-Leninist Albanian Party of Labour. As pre-conditions for improving Sino-Soviet relations, the leaders of the CPSU attempted to compel the CPC to abandon its Marxist-Leninist and proletarian internationalist stand, abandon its consistent line, which is in full conformity with the revolutionary principles of the Declaration and the Statement, accept their erroneous line, and also accept as a *fait accompli* their violation of the principles guiding relations among fraternal Parties and countries. In its Open Letter, the Central Committee of the CPSU boasted of its letters to the Central Committee of the CPC during this period, of Khrushchov's remarks about his desire for unity in October 1962 to our Ambassador to the Soviet Union and so on, but in fact these were all acts for realizing their base attempt.

4. The Central Committee of the CPSU rejected the proposal made by the fraternal Parties of Indonesia, Vietnam, New Zealand, etc., that a meeting of representatives of the fraternal Parties should be convened, as well as the five positive proposals made by the Central Committee of the CPC in its letter of April 7, 1962 to the Central Committee of the CPSU for the preparation for the meeting of fraternal Parties. In its reply of May 30, 1962 to the Central Committee of the CPC, the Central Committee of the CPSU went so far as to make the demand that the Albanian comrades abandon their own stand as a pre-condition for improving Soviet-Albanian relations and also for convening a meeting of the fraternal Parties.

5. In April and May 1962 the leaders of the CPSU used their organs

and personnel in Sinkiang, China, to carry out large-scale subversive activities in the Ili region and enticed and coerced several tens of thousands of Chinese citizens into going to the Soviet Union. The Chinese Government lodged repeated protests and made repeated representations, but the Soviet Government refused to repatriate these Chinese citizens on the pretext of "the sense of Soviet legality" and "humanitarianism." To this day this incident remains unsettled. This is indeed an astounding event, unheard of in the relations between socialist countries.

6. In August 1962 the Soviet Government formally notified China that the Soviet Union would conclude an agreement with the United States on the prevention of nuclear proliferation. This was a joint Soviet-U.S. plot to monopolize nuclear weapons and an attempt to deprive China of the right to possess nuclear weapons to resist the U.S. nuclear threat. The Chinese Government lodged repeated protests against this.

7. The leadership of the CPSU has become increasingly anxious to strike political bargains with U.S. imperialism and has been bent on forming a reactionary alliance with Kennedy, even at the expense of the interests of the socialist camp and the international communist movement. An outstanding example was the fact that, during the Caribbean crisis, the leadership of the CPSU committed the error of capitulationism by submitting to the nuclear blackmail of the U.S. imperialists and accepting the U.S. government's demand for "international inspection" in violation of Cuban sovereignty.

8. The leadership of the CPSU has become increasingly anxious to collude with the Indian reactionaries and has been bent on forming a reactionary alliance with Nehru against socialist China. The leadership of the CPSU and its press openly sided with Indian reaction, condemned China for its just stand on the Sino-Indian border conflict and defended the Nehru government. Two-thirds of Soviet economic aid to India have been given since the Indian reactionaries provoked the Sino-Indian border conflict. Even after large-scale armed conflict on the Sino-Indian border began in the autumn of 1962, the leadership of the CPSU has continued to extend military aid to the Indian reactionaries.

9. The leadership of the CPSU has become increasingly anxious to collude with the Tito clique of Yugoslavia and has been bent on forming a reactionary alliance with the renegade Tito to oppose all Marxist-Leninist parties. After the 22nd Congress, it took a series of steps to reverse the verdict on the Tito clique and thus openly tore up the 1960 Statement.

10. Since November 1962 the leadership of the CPSU has launched still fiercer attacks, on an international scale, against the Chinese Communist Party and other Marxist-Leninist Parties and whipped up a new adverse current in order to split the socialist camp and the international communist movement. Khrushchov made one statement after another

and the Soviet press carried hundreds of articles attacking the Chinese Communist Party on a whole set of issues. Directed by the leaders of the CPSU, the Congresses of the fraternal Parties of Bulgaria, Hungary, Czechoslovakia, Italy and the Democratic Republic of Germany became stages for anti-China performances, and more than forty fraternal Parties published resolutions, statements or articles attacking the Chinese Communist Party and other Marxist-Leninist Parties.

The facts cited above cannot possibly be denied by the leaders of the CPSU. These iron-clad facts prove that the "new attempts" they made after the 22nd Congress of the CPSU were aimed, not at improving Sino-Soviet relations and strengthening unity between the fraternal Parties and countries, but on the contrary, at further ganging up with the U.S. imperialists, the Indian reactionaries and the renegade Tito clique in order to create a wider split in the socialist camp and the international communist movement.

In these grave circumstances, the Chinese Communist Party had no alternative but to make open replies to the attacks of some fraternal Parties. Between December 15, 1962 and March 8, 1963 we published seven such replies. In these articles we continued to leave some leeway and did not criticize the leadership of the CPSU by name.

Despite the serious deterioration in Sino-Soviet relations resulting from the errors of the leadership of the CPSU, the Chinese Communist Party agreed to send its delegation to Moscow for the talks between the Chinese and Soviet Parties, and, in order that there might be a systematic exchange of views in the talks, put forward its proposal concerning the general line of the international communist movement in its letter of reply to the Central Committee of the CPSU dated June 14.

As subsequent facts have shown, the leaders of the CPSU were not only insincere about eliminating differences and strengthening unity, but used the talks as a smokescreen for covering up their activities to further worsen Sino-Soviet relations.

On the eve of the talks, the leaders of the CPSU publicly attacked the Chinese Communist Party by name, through statements and resolutions. At the same time, they unjustifiably expelled a number of Chinese Embassy personnel and research students from the Soviet Union.

On July 14, that is, on the eve of the U.S.-British-Soviet talks, while the Sino-Soviet talks were still in progress, the leadership of the CPSU hastily published the Open Letter of the Central Committee of the CPSU to Party Organizations and All Communists in the Soviet Union and launched unbridled attacks on the Chinese Communist Party. This was another precious presentation gift made by the leaders of the CPSU to the U.S. imperialists in order to curry favour with them.

Immediately afterwards in Moscow, the leadership of the CPSU signed the treaty on the partial halting of nuclear tests with the United

States and Britain in open betrayal of the interests of the Soviet people, the people in the socialist camp including the Chinese people, and the peace-loving people of the world; there was a flurry of contacts between the Soviet Union and India; Khrushchov went to Yugoslavia for a "vacation"; the Soviet press launched a frenzied anti-China campaign; and so on and so forth. This whole train of events strikingly demonstrates that, disregarding everything, the leadership of the CPSU is allying with the imperialists, the reactionaries of all countries and the renegade Tito clique in order to oppose fraternal socialist countries and fraternal Marxist-Leninist Parties. All this completely exposes the revisionist and splitting line which the leadership of the CPSU is following.

At present, the "anti-China chorus" of the imperialists, the reactionaries of all countries and the revisionists is making a lot of noise. And the campaign led by Khrushchov to oppose Marxism-Leninism and split the socialist camp and the international communist ranks is being carried on with growing intensity.

71

Long Live the Victory of the People's War!

Lin Piao

Vice-Chairman of the Central Committee of the
Communist Party of China, Vice-Premier
and Minister of National Defense

Comrade Lin Piao published this long article in September, 1965. It attracted world-wide attention because it formally proclaims China's global strategy to defeat "United States imperialism." Just as the Communists had won the civil war in China by conquering the countryside and encircling the cities, so the people's armies of the oppressed peoples of Asia, Africa, and Latin America ("rural areas of the world") would encircle and defeat North America and Western Europe ("the cities of the world"). In the same article, Lin charges the Soviet leaders with betraying the revolutionary peoples. Lin cites Vietnam as "the most convincing

The first half of this article, which primarily concerns the war against Japan, and the last section, which attacks the Khrushchev revisionists as traitors to the world revolution, are omitted here. The footnotes are also omitted. From *Peking Review*, Vol. VIII, No. 36 (September 3, 1965), 22–27.

example of a victim of aggression defeating U.S. imperialism by a people's war." The struggle in Vietnam has evidently come to be regarded by both Peking and Washington as part of a Chinese-led global revolution against any form of American influence in the developing areas.

THE INTERNATIONAL SIGNIFICANCE OF COMRADE MAO TSE-TUNG'S THEORY OF PEOPLE'S WAR

The Chinese revolution is a continuation of the Great October Revolution. The road of the October Revolution is the common road for all people's revolutions. The Chinese revolution and the October Revolution have in common the following basic characteristics: (1) Both were led by the working class with a Marxist-Leninist party as its nucleus. (2) Both were based on the worker-peasant alliance. (3) In both cases state power was seized through violent revolution and the dictatorship of the proletariat was established. (4) In both cases the socialist system was built after victory in the revolution. (5) Both were component parts of the proletarian world revolution.

Naturally, the Chinese revolution had its own peculiar characteristics. The October Revolution took place in imperialist Russia, but the Chinese revolution broke out in a semi-colonial and semi-feudal country. The former was a proletarian socialist revolution, while the latter developed into a socialist revolution after the complete victory of the new-democratic revolution. The October Revolution began with armed uprisings in the cities and then spread to the countryside, while the Chinese revolution won nation-wide victory through the encirclement of the cities from the rural areas and the final capture of the cities.

Comrade Mao Tse-tung's great merit lies in the fact that he has succeeded in integrating the universal truth of Marxism-Leninism with the concrete practice of the Chinese revolution and has enriched and developed Marxism-Leninism by his masterly generalization and summation of the experience gained during the Chinese people's protracted revolutionary struggle.

Comrade Mao Tse-tung's theory of people's war has been proved by the long practice of the Chinese revolution to be in accord with the objective laws of such wars and to be invincible. It has not only been valid for China, it is a great contribution to the revolutionary struggles of the oppressed nations and peoples throughout the world.

The people's war led by the Chinese Communist Party, comprising the War of Resistance and the Revolutionary Civil Wars, lasted for twenty-two years. It constitutes the most drawn-out and most complex people's war led by the proletariat in modern history, and it has been the richest in experience.

In the last analysis, the Marxist-Leninist theory of proletarian revolution is the theory of the seizure of state power by revolutionary violence, the theory of countering war against the people by people's war. As Marx so aptly put it, "Force is the midwife of every old society pregnant with a new one."

It was on the basis of the lessons derived from the people's wars in China that Comrade Mao Tse-tung, using the simplest and the most vivid language, advanced the famous thesis that "political power grows out of the barrel of a gun."

He clearly pointed out:

The seizure of power by armed force, the settlement of the issue by war, is the central task and the highest form of revolution. This Marxist-Leninist principle of revolution holds good universally, for China and for all other countries.

War is the product of imperialism and the system of exploitation of man by man. Lenin said that "war is always and everywhere begun by the exploiters themselves, by the ruling and oppressing classes." So long as imperialism and the system of exploitation of man by man exist, the imperialists and reactionaries will invariably rely on armed force to maintain their reactionary rule and impose war on the oppressed nations and peoples. This is an objective law independent of man's will.

In the world today, all the imperialists headed by the United States and their lackeys, without exception, are strengthening their state machinery, and especially their armed forces. U.S. imperialism, in particular, is carrying out armed aggression and suppression everywhere.

What should the oppressed nations and the oppressed people do in the face of wars of aggression and armed suppression by the imperialists and their lackeys? Should they submit and remain slaves in perpetuity? Or should they rise in resistance and fight for their liberation?

Comrade Mao Tse-tung answered this question in vivid terms. He said that after long investigation and study the Chinese people discovered that all the imperialists and their lackeys "have swords in their hands and are out to kill. The people have come to understand this and so act after the same fashion." This is called doing unto them what they do unto us.

In the last analysis, whether one dares to wage a tit-for-tat struggle against armed aggression and suppression by the imperialists and their lackeys, whether one dares to fight a people's war against them, is tantamount to whether one dares to embark on revolution. This is the most effective touchstone for distinguishing genuine from fake revolutionaries and Marxist-Leninists.

In view of the fact that some people were afflicted with the fear of the imperialists and reactionaries, Comrade Mao Tse-tung put forward his famous thesis that "the imperialists and all reactionaries are paper tigers." He said,

All reactionaries are paper tigers. In appearance, the reactionaries are terrifying, but in reality they are not so powerful. From a long-term point of view, it is not the reactionaries but the people who are really powerful.

The history of people's war in China and other countries provides conclusive evidence that the growth of the people's revolutionary forces from weak and small beginnings into strong and large forces is a universal law of development of people's war. A people's war inevitably meets with many difficulties, with ups and downs and setbacks in the course of its development, but no force can alter its general trend towards inevitable triumph.

Comrade Mao Tse-tung points out that we must despise the enemy strategically and take full account of him tactically.

To despise the enemy strategically is an elementary requirement for a revolutionary. Without the courage to despise the enemy and without daring to win, it will be simply impossible to make revolution and wage a people's war, let alone to achieve victory.

It is also very important for revolutionaries to take full account of the enemy tactically. It is likewise impossible to win victory in a people's war without taking full account of the enemy tactically, and without examining the concrete conditions, without being prudent and giving great attention to the study of the art of struggle, and without adopting appropriate forms of struggle in the concrete practice of the revolution in each country and with regard to each concrete problem of struggle.

Dialectical and historical materialism teaches us that what is important primarily is not that which at the given moment seems to be durable and yet is already beginning to die away, but that which is arising and developing, even though at the given moment it may not appear to be durable, for only that which is arising and developing is invincible.

Why can the apparently weak new-born forces always triumph over the decadent forces which appear so powerful? The reason is that truth is on their side and that the masses are on their side, while the reactionary classes are always divorced from the masses and set themselves against the masses.

This has been borne out by the victory of the Chinese revolution, by the history of all revolutions, the whole history of class struggle and the entire history of mankind.

The imperialists are extremely afraid of Comrade Mao Tse-tung's thesis that "imperialism and all reactionaries are paper tigers," and the revisionists are extremely hostile to it. They all oppose and attack this thesis and the philistines follow suit by ridiculing it. But all this cannot in the least diminish its importance. The light of truth cannot be dimmed by anybody.

Comrade Mao Tse-tung's theory of people's war solves not only the problem of daring to fight a people's war, but also that of how to wage it.

Comrade Mao Tse-tung is a great statesman and military scientist, proficient at directing war in accordance with its laws. By the line and policies, the strategy and tactics he formulated for the people's war, he led the Chinese people in steering the ship of the people's war past all hidden reefs to the shores of victory in most complicated and difficult conditions.

It must be emphasized that Comrade Mao Tse-tung's theory of the establishment of rural revolutionary base areas and the encirclement of the cities from the countryside is of outstanding and universal practical importance for the present revolutionary struggles of all the oppressed nations and peoples, and particularly for the revolutionary struggles of the oppressed nations and peoples in Asia, Africa and Latin America against imperialism and its lackeys.

Many countries and peoples in Asia, Africa and Latin America are now being subjected to aggression and enslavement on a serious scale by the imperialists headed by the United States and their lackeys. The basic political and economic condition in many of these countries have many similarities to those that prevailed in old China. As in China, the peasant question is extremely important in these regions. The peasants constitute the main force of the national-democratic revolution against the imperialists and their lackeys. In committing aggression against these countries, the imperialists usually begin by seizing the big cities and the main lines of communication, but they are unable to bring the vast countryside completely under their control. The countryside, and the countryside alone, can provide the broad areas in which the revolutionaries can manoeuvre freely. The countryside, and the countryside alone, can provide the revolutionary bases from which the revolutionaries can go forward to final victory. Precisely for this reason, Comrade Mao Tse-tung's theory of establishing revolutionary base areas in the rural districts and encircling the cities from the countryside is attracting more and more attention among the people in these regions.

Taking the entire globe, if North America and Western Europe can be called "the cities of the world," then Asia, Africa and Latin America constitute "the rural areas of the world." Since World War II, the proletarian revolutionary movement has for various reasons been temporarily held back in the North American and West European capitalist countries, while the people's revolutionary movement in Asia, Africa and Latin America has been growing vigorously. In a sense, the contemporary world revolution also presents a picture of the encirclement of cities by the rural areas. In the final analysis, the whole cause of world revolution hinges on the revolutionary struggles of the Asian, African and Latin American peoples who make up the overwhelming majority of the world's population. The socialist countries should regard it as their internationalist duty to support the people's revolutionary struggles in Asia, Africa and Latin America.

The October Revolution opened up a new era in the revolution of the oppressed nations. The victory of the October Revolution built a bridge between the socialist revolution of the proletariat of the West and the national-democratic revolution of the colonial and semi-colonial countries of the East. The Chinese revolution has successfully solved the problem of how to link up the national-democratic with the socialist revolution in the colonial and semi-colonial countries.

Comrade Mao Tse-tung has pointed out that, in the epoch since the October Revolution, anti-imperialist revolution in any colonial or semi-colonial country is no longer part of the old bourgeois, or capitalist world revolution, but is part of the new world revolution, the proletarian-socialist world revolution.

Comrade Mao Tse-tung has formulated a complete theory of the new-democratic revolution. He indicated that this revolution, which is different from all others, can only be, nay must be, a revolution against imperialism, feudalism and bureaucrat-capitalism waged by the broad masses of the people under the leadership of the proletariat.

This means that the revolution can only be, nay must be, led by the proletariat and the genuinely revolutionary party armed with Marxism-Leninism, and by no other class or party.

This means that the revolution embraces in its ranks not only the workers, peasants and the urban petty bourgeoisie, but also the national bourgeoisie and other patriotic and anti-imperialist democrats.

This means, finally, that the revolution is directed against imperialism, feudalism and bureaucrat-capitalism.

The new-democratic revolution leads to socialism, and not to capitalism.

Comrade Mao Tse-tung's theory of the new-democratic revolution is the Marxist-Leninist theory of revolution by stages as well as the Marxist-Leninist theory of uninterrupted revolution.

Comrade Mao Tse-tung made a correct distinction between the two revolutionary stages, i.e., the national-democratic and the socialist revolutions; at the same time he correctly and closely linked the two. The national-democratic revolution is the necessary preparation for the socialist revolution, and the socialist revolution is the inevitable sequel to the national-democratic revolution. There is no Great Wall between the two revolutionary stages. But the socialist revolution is only possible after the completion of the national-democratic revolution. The more thorough the national-democratic revolution, the better the conditions for the socialist revolution.

The experience of the Chinese revolution shows that the tasks of the national-democratic revolution can be fulfilled only through long and tortuous struggles. In this stage of revolution, imperialism and its lackeys are the principal enemy. In the struggle against imperialism and its lackeys, it is necessary to rally all anti-imperialist patriotic forces, including the national bourgeoisie and all patriotic personages. All those patriotic personages from among the bourgeoisie and other exploiting classes who join the anti-imperialist struggle play a progressive historical role; they are not tolerated by imperialism but welcomed by the proletariat.

It is very harmful to confuse the two stages, that is, the national-democratic and the socialist revolutions. Comrade Mao Tse-tung criticized the wrong idea of "accomplishing both at one stroke," and pointed out that this utopian idea could only weaken the struggle against imperialism and its lackeys, the most urgent task at that time. The Kuomintang reactionaries and the Trotskyites they hired during the War of Resistance deliberately confused these two stages of the Chinese revolution, proclaiming the "theory of a single revolution" and preaching so-called "socialism" without any Communist Party. With this preposterous theory they attempted to swallow up the Communist Party, wipe out any revolution and prevent the advance of the national-democratic revolution, and they used it as a pretext for their non-resistance and capitulation to imperialism. This reactionary theory was buried long ago by the history of the Chinese revolution.

The Khrushchov revisionists are now actively preaching that socialism can be built without the proletariat and without a genuinely revolutionary party armed with the advanced proletarian ideology, and they have cast the fundamental tenets of Marxism-Leninism to the four winds. The revisionists' purpose is solely to divert the oppressed nations from their struggle against imperialism and sabotage their national-democratic revolution, all in the service of imperialism.

The Chinese revolution provides a successful lesson for making a thoroughgoing national-democratic revolution under the leadership of the proletariat; it likewise provides a successful lesson for the timely transition from the national-democratic revolution to the socialist revolution under the leadership of the proletariat.

Mao Tse-tung's thought has been the guide to the victory of the Chinese revolution. It has integrated the universal truth of Marxism-Leninism with the concrete practice of the Chinese revolution and creatively developed Marxism-Leninism, thus adding new weapons to the arsenal of Marxism-Leninism.

Ours is the epoch in which world capitalism and imperialism are heading for their doom and socialism and communism are marching to victory. Comrade Mao Tse-tung's theory of people's war is not only a product of the Chinese revolution, but has also the characteristics of our epoch. The new experience gained in the people's revolutionary struggles in various countries since World War II has provided continuous evidence that Mao Tse-tung's thought is a common asset of the revolutionary people of the whole world. This is the great international significance of the thought of Mao Tse-tung.

DEFEAT U.S. IMPERIALISM AND ITS LACKEYS BY PEOPLE'S WAR

Since World War II, U.S. imperialism has stepped into the shoes of German, Japanese and Italian fascism and has been trying to build a great American empire by dominating and enslaving the whole world. It is actively fostering Japanese and West German militarism as its chief accomplices in unleashing a world war. Like a vicious wolf, it is bullying and enslaving various peoples, plundering their wealth, encroaching upon their countries' sovereignty and interfering in their internal affairs. It is the most rabid aggressor in human history and the most ferocious common enemy of the people of the world. Every people or country in the world that wants revolution, independence and peace cannot but direct the spearhead of its struggle against U.S. imperialism.

Just as the Japanese imperialists' policy of subjugating China made it possible for the Chinese people to form the broadest possible united front against them, so the U.S. imperialists' policy of seeking world domination makes it possible for the people throughout the world to unite all the forces that can be united and form the broadest possible united front for a converging attack on U.S. imperialism.

At present, the main battlefield of the fierce struggle between the people of the world on the one side and U.S. imperialism and its lackeys on the other is the vast area of Asia, Africa and Latin America. In the world as a whole, this is the area where the people suffer worst from imperialist oppression and where imperialist rule is most vulnerable. Since World War II, revolutionary storms have been rising in this area, and today they have become the most important force directly pounding U.S. imperialism. The contradiction between the revolutionary peoples of Asia, Africa and Latin America and the imperialists headed by the United States is the principal contradiction in the contemporary world. The development of this contradiction is promoting the struggle of the people of the whole world against U.S. imperialism and its lackeys.

Since World War II, people's war has increasingly demonstrated its power in Asia, Africa and Latin America. The peoples of China, Korea, Viet Nam, Laos, Cuba, Indonesia, Algeria and other countries have waged people's wars against the imperialists and their lackeys and won great victories. The classes leading these people's wars may vary, and so may the breadth and depth of mass mobilization and the extent of victory, but the victories in these people's wars have very much weakened and pinned down the forces of imperialism, upset the U.S. imperialist plan to launch a world war, and become mighty factors defending world peace.

Today, the conditions are more favourable than ever before for the waging of people's wars by the revolutionary peoples of Asia, Africa and Latin America against U.S. imperialism and its lackeys.

Since World War II and the succeeding years of revolutionary upsurge, there has been a great rise in the level of political consciousness and the degree of organization of the people in all countries, and the resources available to them for mutual support and aid have greatly increased. The whole capitalist-imperialist system has become drastically weaker and is in the process of increasing convulsion and disintegration. After World War I, the imperialists lacked the power to destroy the new-born socialist Soviet state, but they were still able to suppress the people's revolutionary movements in some countries in the parts of the world under their own rule and so maintain a short period of comparative stability. Since World War II, however, not only have they been unable to stop a number of countries from taking the socialist road, but they are no longer capable of holding back the surging tide of the people's revolutionary movements in the areas under their own rule.

U.S. imperialism is stronger, but also more vulnerable, than any imperialism of the past. It sets itself against the people of the whole world, including the people of the United States. Its human, military, material and financial resources are far from sufficient for the realization of its ambition of dominating the whole world. U.S. imperialism has further weakened itself by occupying so many places in the world, overreaching itself, stretching its fingers out wide and dispersing its strength, with its rear so far away and its supply lines so long. As Comrade Mao Tse-tung has said, "Whenever it commits aggression, it puts a new noose around its neck. It is besieged ring upon ring by the people of the whole world."

When committing aggression in a foreign country, U.S. imperialism can only employ part of its forces, which are sent to fight an unjust war far from their native land and therefore have a low morale, and so U.S. imperialism is beset with great difficulties. The people subjected to its aggression are having a trial of strength with U.S. imperialism neither in Washington nor New York, neither in Honolulu nor Florida, but are fighting for independence and freedom on their own soil. Once they are mobilized on a broad scale, they will have inexhaustible strength. Thus superiority will belong not to the United States but to the people subjected to its aggression. The latter, though apparently weak and small, are really more powerful than U.S. imperialism.

The struggles waged by the different peoples against U.S. imperialism reinforce each other and merge into a torrential world-wide tide of opposition to U.S. imperialism. The more successful the development of people's war in a given region, the larger the number of U.S. imperialist forces that can be pinned down and depleted there. When the U.S. aggressors are hard pressed in one place, they have no alternative but to loosen their grip on others. Therefore, the conditions become more favourable for the people elsewhere to wage struggles against U.S. imperialism and its lackeys.

Everything is divisible. And so is this colossus of U.S. imperialism. It can be split up and defeated. The peoples of Asia, Africa, Latin America and other regions can destroy it piece by piece, some striking at its head and others at its feet. That is why the greatest fear of U.S. imperialism is that people's wars will be launched in different parts of the world, and particularly in Asia, Africa and Latin America, and why it regards people's war as a mortal danger.

U.S. imperialism relies solely on its nuclear weapons to intimidate people. But these weapons cannot save U.S. imperialism from its doom. Nuclear weapons cannot be used lightly. U.S. imperialism has been condemned by the people of the whole world for its towering crime of dropping two atom bombs on Japan. If it uses nuclear weapons again, it will become isolated in the extreme. Moreover, the U.S. monopoly of nuclear weapons has long been broken; U.S. imperialism has these weapons, but others have them too. If it threatens other countries with nuclear weapons, U.S. imperialism will expose its own country to the same threat. For this reason, it will meet with strong opposition not only from the people elsewhere but also inevitably from the people in its own country. Even if U.S. imperialism brazenly uses nuclear weapons, it cannot conquer the people, who are indomitable.

However highly developed modern weapons and technical equipment may be and however complicated the methods of modern warfare, in the final analysis the outcome of a war will be decided by the sustained fighting of the ground forces, by the fighting at close quarters on battlefields, by the political consciousness of the men, by their courage and spirit of sacrifice. Here the weak points of U.S. imperialism will be completely laid bare, while the superiority of the revolutionary people will be brought into full play. The reactionary troops of U.S. imperialism cannot possibly be endowed with the courage and the spirit of sacrifice possessed by the revolutionary people. The spiritual atom bomb which the revolutionary people possess is a far more powerful and useful weapon than the physical atom bomb.

Viet Nam is the most convincing current example of a victim of aggression defeating U.S. imperialism by a people's war. The United States has made south Viet Nam a testing ground for the suppression of people's war. It has carried on this experiment for many years, and everybody can now see that the U.S. aggressors are unable to find a way of coping with people's war. On the other hand, the Vietnamese people have brought the power of people's war into full play in their struggle against the U.S. aggressors. The U.S. aggressors are in danger of being swamped in the people's war in Viet Nam. They are deeply worried that their defeat in Viet Nam will lead to a chain reaction. They are expanding the war in an attempt to save themselves from defeat. But the more they expand the war, the greater will be the chain reaction. The more they escalate the war, the heavier will be their fall and the more disastrous their defeat. The people in other parts of the world will see still more clearly that U.S. imperialism can be defeated, and that what the Vietnamese people can do, they can do too.

History has proved and will go on proving that people's war is the most effective weapon against U.S. imperialism and its lackeys. All revolutionary people will learn to wage people's war against U.S. imperialism and its lackeys. They will take up arms, learn to fight battles and become skilled in waging people's war, though they have not done so before. U.S. imperialism like a mad bull dashing from place to place, will finally be burned to ashes in the blazing fires of the people's wars it has provoked by its own actions.

SUGGESTED READING

Barnett, A. Doak. *Communist China and Asia: Challenge to American Policy.* New York: Vintage Books, 1961, paperback.

Barnett, A. Doak, ed. *Communist Strategies in Asia: A Comparative Analysis of Governments and Parties.* New York: Frederick A. Praeger, 1963, paperback.

Beloff, Max. *Soviet Policy in the Far East, 1944–1951.* London: Oxford University Press, 1953.

Boorman, Howard L., et al. *Moscow-Peking Axis: Strengths and Strains.* New York: Harper & Row, 1957.

Boyd, R. G. *Communist China's Foreign Policy.* New York: Frederick A. Praeger, 1962, paperback.

Bromke, Adam, ed. *The Communist States at the Crossroads: Between Moscow and Peking.* New York: Frederick A. Praeger, 1965.

Chakravarti, P. C. *India's China Policy.* Bloomington: University of Indiana Press, 1962.

Crankshaw, Edward. *The New Cold War: Moscow v. Peking.* Baltimore: Penguin, 1963, paperback.

Dallin, David J. *Soviet Russia and the Far East.* New Haven: Yale University Press, 1948.

Dallin, David J. *The Rise of Russia in Asia.* New Haven: Yale University Press, 1949.

Fairbank, John K. *The United States and China,* rev. ed. Cambridge: Harvard University Press, 1958, paperback.

Fitzgerald, C. P. *The Chinese View of Their Place in the World*. New York: Oxford University Press, 1963, paperback.

Floyd, David. *Mao Against Khrushchev: A Short History of the Sino-Soviet Conflict*. New York: Frederick A. Praeger, 1963, paperback.

Halperin, Morton H., and Perkins, Dwight H. *Communist China and Arms Control*. New York: Frederick A. Praeger, 1966.

Halpern, A. M., ed. *Policies toward China: Views from Six Continents*. New York: McGraw-Hill, 1966, paperback.

Hinton, Harold C. *Communist China in World Politics*. Boston: Houghton Mifflin, 1966.

Hsieh, Alice Langley. *Communist China's Strategy in the Nuclear Era*. Englewood Cliffs, N.J.: Prentice-Hall, 1962, paperback.

Hudson, G. F., Lowenthal, Richard, and MacFarquhar, Roderick, eds. *The Sino-Soviet Dispute*. New York: Frederick A. Praeger, 1961, paperback.

Jackson, W. A. *Russo-Chinese Borderlands*. Princeton: Van Nostrand, 1962, paperback.

Jacobs, Dan N., and Baerwald, Hans H., eds. *Chinese Communism: Selected Documents*. New York: Harper & Row, 1963, paperback.

Klochko, Mikhail A. *Soviet Scientist in Red China*. New York: Frederick A. Praeger, 1964.

Lamb, Alastair. *The China-India Border: Origins of the Disputed Boundary*. London: Oxford University Press, 1964, paperback.

Lattimore, Owen. *Nomads and Commissars: Mongolia Revisited*. New York: Oxford University Press, 1962.

Lindsay, Michael. *China and the Cold War*. Melbourne: University of Melbourne Press, 1955.

London, Kurt, ed. *Unity and Contradiction: Major Aspects of Sino-Soviet Relations*. New York: Frederick A. Praeger, 1962.

McLane, Charles B. *Soviet Policy and the Chinese Communists, 1931–1946*. New York: Columbia University Press, 1964.

Mehnert, Klaus. *Peking and Moscow*. New York: New American Library, 1964, paperback.

Murphy, George G. S. *Soviet Mongolia: A Study of the Oldest Political Satellite*. Berkeley: University of California Press, 1966.

Newman, Robert P. *Recognition of Communist China? A Study in Argument*. New York: Macmillan, 1961, paperback.

Passin, Herbert. *China's Cultural Diplomacy*. New York: Frederick A. Praeger, 1962.

Pavlovsky, Michel N. *Chinese-Russian Relations*. New York: Philosophical Library, 1949.

Pentony, DeVere E., ed. *Red World in Tumult*. San Francisco: Chandler Publishing Company, 1962, paperback.

Reischauer, Edwin O. *Wanted: An Asian Policy*. New York: Knopf, 1955.

Schwartz, Harry. *Tsars, Mandarins, and Commissars: A History of Chinese-Russian Relations*. Philadelphia: Lippincott, 1964.

Tang, Peter S. H. *Russian and Soviet Policy in Manchuria and Outer Mongolia, 1911–1931*. Durham: Duke University Press, 1959.

Wheeler, G. E. *The Modern History of Soviet Central Asia.* New York: Frederick A. Praeger, 1964.

Whiting, Allen S., and General Sheng Shih-ts'ai. *Sinkiang: Pawn or Pivot?* East Lansing: Michigan State University Press, 1958.

Wint, Guy. *Communist China's Crusade: Mao's Road to Power and the New Campaign for World Revolution.* New York: Frederick A. Praeger, 1964.

Wu, Aitchen K. *China and the Soviet Union: A Study of Sino-Soviet Relations.* New York: John Day, 1950.

Zagoria, Donald S. *The Sino-Soviet Conflict, 1956–1961.* Princeton: Princeton University Press, 1962. (Paperback: Atheneum)

XIII

The War in Vietnam

In 1940, Japan, with the acquiescence of the Vichy government of France, sent troops into northern French Indochina. Japanese forces occupied southern Indochina in July 1941, threatening British, Dutch, and American possessions in Southeast Asia. In response, the United States froze Japanese assets. Indochina figured prominently in the ensuing negotiations, which ended with the Japanese attack on Pearl Harbor. (See Chapter VI, Selections 33, 34, and 35.)

In March, 1945, as the Axis cause was becoming hopeless, the Japanese disarmed the French garrisons and set up native governments headed by Emperor Bao Dai of Annam and the Kings of Cambodia and Laos. Thus the Japanese severely damaged European prestige and encouraged the nationalist movement in Indochina. The Japanese-sponsored regimes, however, were not recognized by the Vietminh (Vietnamese Independent League), led by Ho Chi Minh. With their superior organizational skills, Ho Chi Minh and his fellow Communists had assumed the leadership of the nationalist movement.

In August Ho's forces managed to seize much of the country and induced Bao Dai to abdicate. On September 2, 1945, the date of the Japanese surrender, the independence of the Democratic Republic of Vietnam, with its capital in Hanoi, was proclaimed by Ho and his followers (Selection 72).

For the purpose of accepting the surrender of Japanese troops, in mid-September Chinese Nationalist forces occupied Indochina north of the sixteenth parallel and British forces occupied the area south of the sixteenth parallel. With British acquiescence, the Free French took control of Saigon from the Vietminh. By January, when the British left, the French had reoccupied the principal cities, roads, and plantations, but much of the countryside remained in the hands of the Vietminh. In the North, on the other hand, the Chinese permitted the Vietminh to continue their administration, and when the Chinese left, the Vietminh were in full control. As in Germany, the military dispositions at the end of World War II were to prove decisive for future political developments.

The French began negotiations with the Democratic Republic of Vietnam, and in March, 1946, an agreement was reached providing, in principle, for an independent Vietnam within the French Union. The agreement broke down before the year was over, and fighting erupted between the French, who were determined to restore their empire, and the Vietminh. In 1949 the French established the State of Vietnam, headed by former Emperor Bao Dai as Chief of State. However, Bao Dai, a playboy who spent most of his time on the French Riviera, was unable to garner support among the Vietnamese. War continued between the French-supported government and the Vietminh, who after 1950 were receiving aid from Communist China. The United States, interested in cultivating its NATO ally, France, and in containing communism in Asia, began supplying money and equipment to the French-sponsored State of Vietnam.[1] In 1950 the State of Vietnam, Cambodia, and Laos became independent but "associated" states in the French Union. This belated concession to nationalist sentiment failed to halt the military conflict between the French and the guerrilla forces of the Vietminh.

The expenditure of great sums of lives and money—much of the money came from the United States—proved inadequate to save Indochina for France, as was demonstrated by the catastrophic French defeat at Dien Bien Phu in 1954. The French negotiated a military truce with the Vietminh at the Geneva Conference, leaving the area north of the seventeenth parallel in the hands of the Communist-dominated Democratic Republic of Vietnam and the area south in the hands of the weak, French-oriented State of Vietnam. It was agreed at the conference that an election would be held throughout Vietnam in 1956 for the purpose of unifying the country (Selection 73). The partitioning of Vietnam between north and south is often said to have stemmed from the Geneva settlement, but the basic causes, of course, were the rise of nationalism and communism and the decline of European imperialism in Southeast Asia.

The military and diplomatic situation following the Geneva Conference appeared to favor the subsequent unification of Vietnam under the auspices of the Communist-ruled Democratic Republic of Vietnam, but American intervention was foreshadowed by the critical attitude of the United States towards the Geneva accords (Selection 74). In order to halt the further spread of communism in Asia, the United States immediately organized the Southeast Asia Treaty Organization (SEATO), adhered to by the United States, Great Britain, France, Australia, New Zealand, the Philippine Republic, Thailand, and Pakistan (Selection 75).

In October, 1955, Premier Ngo Dinh Diem of the State of Vietnam (South Vietnam) arranged a referendum bringing about the deposition

[1] See Chapter X, Selection 58.

of Bao Dai and the establishment of the Republic of Vietnam, with Diem as President. French influence in Saigon was largely replaced by American influence. President Diem was able to bring under control the armed religious sects and gangster elements in South Vietnam. In July, 1956, the elections in preparation for national unification which had been provided in the Geneva accords were cancelled. Diem, with American backing, pleaded that his government had not been a party to the Geneva settlement and was therefore not bound by it. Such an election would likely have favored Ho Chi Minh's regime in Hanoi, in view of the existence of the Communist dictatorship in the North and Ho Chi Minh's prestige as a nationalist leader throughout all of Vietnam. Enjoying generous economic and military aid from the United States, South Vietnam (the Republic of Vietnam) for a few years made surprising progress towards political stability. However, in 1958 the Viet Cong (Communist-led Vietnamese guerrillas) stepped up their attacks on South Vietnamese officials and soldiers (Selection 76).

President Diem came increasingly under the influence of his brother, Ngo Dinh Nhu, the head of the secret police and the National Revolutionary Movement, and his sister-in-law, the domineering and unpopular Madame Nhu. The government became an oppressive family dictatorship, based upon intrigue, corruption, and force rather than popular support. The fact that another of Diem's brothers, Ngo Dinh Thuc, was the Roman Catholic Archbishop of Hue lent plausibility to the belief of the Buddhists that the Ngo family was using its political power to destroy Buddhism, the faith of the majority of the population. In 1963 President Kennedy publicly criticized the policies of the Diem regime, suggesting that political, social, and economic reforms were needed to establish a popular base for the South Vietnamese government. Peaceful Buddhist demonstrations were harshly suppressed, and a number of monks burned themselves to death in protest against the dictatorship. Finally, in November, 1963, a military coup, reportedly encouraged by American army officers, overthrew the Diem regime, killing Diem and his brother Nhu and establishing a military junta. Following Diem's overthrow, there were repeated Buddhist, Catholic, and student demonstrations. Military coups d'état occurred every few months until the establishment of the junta headed by General Nguyen Cao Ky in June, 1965. In the meantime, the Viet Cong intensified their attacks on the South Vietnamese army. American soldiers, including Special Forces (Green Berets) trained in guerrilla tactics, had been serving as "advisers" to the South Vietnamese troops.

In August, 1964, North Vietnamese PT boats attacked American naval vessels patrolling the Gulf of Tonkin in the vicinity of hostilities between North and South Vietnamese forces. United States airplanes not only drove off attacking units, but, on orders from President Johnson, bombed North Vietnamese bases and naval craft. On August 10, the

United States Congress passed almost unanimously a joint resolution requested by President Johnson approving the President's determination
"to take all necessary measures to repel any armed attack against the
forces of the United States and *to prevent further aggression* [italics
added]" (Selection 77).

During the 1964 presidential election campaign, the Republican
candidate, Barry Goldwater, advocated that the United States Air Force
bomb targets in North Vietnam. President Johnson, however, said that
the situation in Vietnam did not require such an enlargement of the
conflict, which might commit American boys to fighting a war. Nevertheless, after Johnson had been reelected (partly because he was regarded as less trigger-happy than his opponent), his Vietnam policy
hardened. Following a Viet Cong attack on American troops in South
Vietnam on February 7, 1965, the United States commenced continuous
air attacks on military installations in North Vietnam used for the training and infiltration of Viet Cong into the South (Selection 78). Soviet
Prime Minister Aleksei Kosygin was visiting Hanoi when the raids began,
and he promised increased aid to the Democratic Republic of Vietnam.
The bombing raids were explained as an effort to make clear to the Communists the American determination to protect South Vietnam from aggression. Secretary of State Dean Rusk said that the raids would be
halted as soon as the Hanoi regime stopped infiltrating men and supplies
into the South. Shocked by the warlike moves of the President, a small
but articulate minority in the United States protested against the escalation of the war. At teach-ins in colleges and universities, students and
professors debated many aspects of the administration's Vietnam policy
(Selection 79).

By the spring of 1965 the military and political situation of South
Vietnam had deteriorated to the point that perhaps only one-fourth of
the territory and less than half of the population were under the control
of the Saigon government. In a speech at Johns Hopkins University in
April, 1965, President Johnson said that the United States was prepared
to take part in "unconditional discussions" to end the war and indicated
that if Hanoi made peace, North as well as South Vietnam could share
in a massive American-sponsored aid program in Southeast Asia (Selection 80). However, a cease-fire at this time would have halted the Viet
Cong advance, and the Hanoi government, confident of victory, proposed terms for a peace which would amount to the Communist conquest
of South Vietnam (Selection 81).

By June, 1965, the role of American forces in South Vietnam ceased
to be merely advisory, and they became directly involved in the fighting.
The massive American intervention in 1965 probably prevented the fall
of South Vietnam to the Communists that year, but the war continued
on a larger scale than before. It became evident that the United States
was determined to prevent a Viet Cong victory in Vietnam even if it

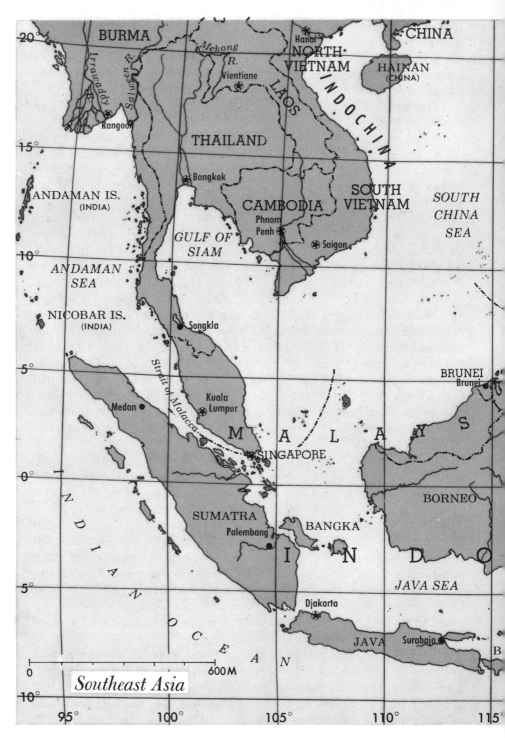

Southeast Asia

FORMOSA
(NAT. CHINA)

LUZON

● Baguio

PHILIPPINE
REPUBLIC

Manila ✳

NDORO

SAMAR

PANAY

LEYTE

NEGROS

ALAWAN

MINDANAO

ULU SEA

Davao ●

CELEBES SEA

Menado ●

HALMAHERA

M O L U C C A S

SOELA

CELEBES

E S I A

CERAM

ssar ●

BANDA SEA

BAWA

FLORES

(PORT.)

TIMOR

P A C I F I C

O C E A N

YAP ●

CAROLINE ISLANDS

PALAU

U.N. TRUSTEESHIP
(U.S.A. ADMIN.)

WEST IRIAN

ARAFURA SEA

Makassar

120°   125°   130°   135°   140°

327

meant a very substantial escalation of the conflict. Increasingly, also, regular elements of the North Vietnamese army became engaged in the fighting in South Vietnam. Fears grew in the United States and Europe that the conflict might escalate into an all-out war as it had in Korea, with the possible intervention of Chinese forces.

Critics of the administration's policy in Vietnam became more vocal. The "hawks" called for the mining of the port of Haiphong and an intensification of the air attacks against North Vietnam, including the bombing of Hanoi, or even Peking, in order to hasten the defeat of the Communists. There was great disappointment with the lack of support in Vietnam shown by America's NATO allies, some of whom were trading with Communist China and North Vietnam. Since there had been no declaration of war and no explicit U.N. sanction for the American intervention in Vietnam, the legal basis for American policy came under attack. The Republican Party issued a white paper accusing the Democratic administration of unclear policies which had encouraged Communist belligerency and of lack of candor with the American people concerning the seriousness of the military situation in Vietnam (Selection 82).

In January, 1966, the annual Christmas truce in Vietnam was extended and the bombing of the North was suspended by the United States in order to provide a climate for peace talks and make the American desire for peace more credible (Selection 83). However, as expected in Washington, this gesture by the United States produced no results. North Vietnam continued infiltrating men and supplies into the South, and the United States resumed bombing the North. The Communists seemed little interested in a compromise peace so long as it appeared that they stood a good chance of winning the war. It appeared that the United States had become committed to a long drawn-out land war in Asia with neither peace nor victory in the foreseeable future (Selection 84).

In February, 1966, the United States Senate Foreign Relations Committee, chaired by Senator J. William Fulbright, conducted televised hearings on the Vietnam War. The Chairman of the Committee assumed, on the whole, a critical attitude towards State Department policies, while Senator Wayne Morse attacked the expediency, the morality, and the legality of the American involvement in Vietnam. It was evident that there were fundamental disagreements in Washington concerning the nature of the world Communist threat, the present and future role of Communist China in Southeast Asia, the relationships among the Viet Cong, Hanoi, Peking, and Moscow, basic questions of military and diplomatic strategy, and finally the kind of settlement necessary to achieve a satisfactory peace in Southeast Asia. Praised as highly educational to the American public, the Senate hearings, while critical of administration policy, failed to come up with a clear and plausible alternative.

By February, 1967, there were more than 400,000 American fighting men in Vietnam, and tens of thousands more were on their way. Many Americans took the attitude that the United States should either fight to win or get out; but the achievement of either of these apparently simple objectives would be difficult and dangerous. The United States had become embroiled in war in Asia for the third time in a single generation.

72

Declaration of Independence of the Democratic Republic of Vietnam

September 2, 1945

On the day that Japan formally surrendered to the Allies, the Democratic Republic of Vietnam, headed by Ho Chi Minh, declared its independence from France. Note the appeal to democratic and nationalist aspirations.

"All men are created equal. They are endowed by their Creator with certain inalienable rights, among these are Life, Liberty and the pursuit of Happiness."

This immortal statement was made in the Declaration of Independence of the United States of America in 1776. In a broader sense, this means:

"All the peoples on the earth are equal from birth, all the peoples have a right to live, be happy and free."

The Declaration of the French Revolution made in 1791 on the Rights of Man and the Citizen also states: "All men are born free and with equal rights, and must always remain free and have equal rights."

Those are undeniable truths.

Nevertheless, for more than eighty years, the French imperialists abusing the standard of Liberty, Equality and Fraternity, have violated our Fatherland and oppressed our fellow-citizens. They have acted contrary to the ideals of humanity and justice.

In the field of politics, they have deprived our people of every democratic liberty.

They have enforced inhuman laws; they have set up three distinct political regimes in the North, the Centre and the South of Vietnam in order to wreck our national unity and prevent our people from being united.

They have built more prisons than schools. They have mercilessly slain our patriots; they have drowned our uprisings in rivers of blood. They have fettered public opinion; they have promoted illiteracy. To weaken our race they have forced us to use opium and alcohol.

In the province of economics, they have fleeced us to the backbone, impoverished our people and devastated our land.

They have robbed us of our ricefields, our mines, our forests, our raw materials. They have monopolized the issuance of banknotes and the export trade.

They have invented numerous injustifiable taxes, and reduced our people, especially our peasantry to a state of extreme poverty.

They have hampered our national bourgeoisie from prospering; they have mercilessly exploited our workers.

In the Autumn of 1940, when the Japanese fascists violated Indochina's territory to establish new bases in their fight against the Allies, the French imperialists fell on bended knees and handed over our country to them.

Thus from that date, our people were subjected to a double yoke from French and Japanese. Their sufferings and miseries increased. The result was that from the end of last year to the beginning of this year, from Quang-Tri Province to the North of Vietnam, more than two millions of our fellow-citizens died from starvation. On the 9th of March, the French troops were disarmed by the Japanese. The French colonialists either fled or surrendered: showing that not only were they incapable of "protecting" us, but that, in the span of five years, they twice sold our country to the Japanese.

On several occasions before the 9th of March, the Viet-Minh League had urged the French to ally with them against the Japanese. Instead of answering this proposal, the French colonialists, on the contrary, intensified their terrorist activities against the Viet-Minh members to such an extent that before fleeing they massacred a great number of our political internees detained at Yen-Bay and Cao-Bang.

Notwithstanding all this, our fellow-citizens have always manifested towards the French a tolerant and humane attitude. Even after the Japanese putsch of March 1945, the Viet-Minh League helped many Frenchmen to cross the frontier, rescued some of them from Japanese jails and protected French lives and property.

From the autumn of 1940, our country had in fact ceased to be a French colony and had become a Japanese possession.

After the Japanese had surrendered to the Allies, our whole people rose to regain its national sovereignty and to found the Democratic Republic of Vietnam.

The truth is that we have wrested our independence from the Japanese and not from the French.

The French have fled, the Japanese have capitulated, emperor Bao-

Dai has abdicated. Our people have broken the chains which for nearly a century have fettered us and won independence for the Fatherland. Our people at the same time have overthrown the monarchic regime that has reigned supreme for tens of centuries. In its place has been established the present Democratic Republic.

For these reasons, we, members of the Provisional Government, representing the whole Vietnamese people, declare that from now on we break off all relations of a colonial character with France; we repeal all the international obligations that France had so far subscribed to on behalf of Vietnam and we abolish all the special rights the French have unlawfully acquired in our Fatherland.

The whole Vietnamese people animated by a common purpose, are determined to fight to the bitter end against any attempt by the French colonialists to reconquer our country.

We are convinced that the Allied nations which at Teheran and San Francisco have acknowledged the principles of self-determination and equality of nations, will not refuse to acknowledge the independence of Vietnam.

A people that has courageously opposed French domination for more than eighty years, a people that has fought side by side with the Allies against the fascists during these last years, such a people must be free and independent.

For these reasons we, members of the Provisional Government of the Democratic Republic of Vietnam solemnly declare to the world that Vietnam has the right to be a free and independent country—and in fact it is so already. The entire Vietnamese people are determined to mobilise all their physical and mental strength, to sacrifice their lives and property in order to safeguard their independence and liberty.

Hanoi, the Second of September 1945

Ho-Chi-Minh, President
Tran-Huy-Lieu
Vo-Nguyen-Giap
Chu-Van-Tan
Pham-Van-Dong
Duong-Duc-Hien
Nguyen-Van-To
Nguyen-Manh-Ha
Cu-Huy-Can
Pham-Ngoc-Thach
Nguyen-Van-Xuan
Vu-Trong-Khanh
Dao-Trong-Kim
Vu-Dinh-Hoe
Le-Van-Hien

73

Final Declaration of the Geneva Conference on the Problem of Restoring Peace in Indo-China

July 21, 1954

The Geneva accords consist of armistice documents signed by military commanders and make no mention of a political boundary between a North Vietnam and a South Vietnam. Instead they fix a provisional military demarcation line, on either side of which the forces of the People's Army of Vietnam and the forces of the French Union would withdraw. The following declaration summarizes the agreements. The United States refused to join in this declaration. (See Selection 74.) In 1965 both the United States and North Vietnam cited the Geneva accords as a basis for settlement of the conflict which raged at that time in Vietnam. However, from the beginning there were various interpretations concerning the substance of these agreements and who was bound by them.

FINAL DECLARATION, dated the 21st July, 1954, of the Geneva Conference on the problem of restoring peace in Indo-China, in which the representatives of Cambodia, the Democratic Republic of Viet-Nam, France, Laos, the People's Republic of China, the State of Viet-Nam, the Union of Soviet Socialist Republics, the United Kingdom, and the United States of America took part.

1. The Conference takes note of the agreements ending hostilities in Cambodia, Laos and Viet-Nam and organizing international control and the supervision of the execution of the provisions of these agreements.

2. The Conference expresses satisfaction at the ending of hostilities in Cambodia, Laos and Viet-Nam; the Conference expresses its conviction that the execution of the provisions set out in the present declaration and

The lengthy and detailed military truce agreements are not reproduced here. From United States Department of State, *American Foreign Policy, 1950–1955: Basic Documents* (Washington, D.C.: Government Printing Office, 1957), I, 785–787.

in the agreements on the cessation of hostilities will permit Cambodia, Laos and Viet-Nam henceforth to play their part, in full independence and sovereignty, in the peaceful community of nations.

3. The Conference takes note of the declarations made by the Governments of Cambodia and of Laos of their intention to adopt measures permitting all citizens to take their place in the national community, in particular by participating in the next general elections, which, in conformity with the constitution of each of these countries, shall take place in the course of the year 1955, by secret ballot and in conditions of respect for fundamental freedoms.

4. The Conference takes note of the clauses in the agreement on the cessation of hostilities in Viet-Nam prohibiting the introduction into Viet-Nam of foreign troops and military personnel as well as of all kinds of arms and munitions. The Conference also takes note of the declarations made by the Governments of Cambodia and Laos of their resolution not to request foreign aid, whether in war material, in personnel or in instructors except for the purpose of the effective defence of their territory and, in the case of Laos, to the extent defined by the agreements on the cessation of hostilities in Laos.

5. The Conference takes note of the clauses in the agreement on the cessation of hostilities in Viet-Nam to the effect that no military base under the control of a foreign State may be established in the regrouping zones of the two parties, the latter having the obligation to see that the zones allotted to them shall not constitute part of any military alliance and shall not be utilized for the resumption of hostilities or in the service of an aggressive policy. The Conference also takes note of the declarations of the Governments of Cambodia and Laos to the effect that they will not join in any agreement with other States if this agreement includes the obligation to participate in a military alliance not in conformity with the principles of the Charter of the United Nations or, in the case of Laos, with the principles of the agreement on the cessation of hostilities in Laos or, so long as their security is not threatened, the obligation to establish bases on Cambodian or Laotian territory for the military forces of foreign Powers.

6. The Conference recognizes that the essential purpose of the agreement relating to Viet-Nam is to settle military questions with a view to ending hostilities and that the military demarcation line is provisional and should not in any way be interpreted as constituting a political or territorial boundary. The Conference expresses its conviction that the execution of the provisions set out in the present declaration and in the agreement on the cessation of hostilities creates the necessary basis for the achievement in the near future of a political settlement in Viet-Nam.

7. The Conference declares that, so far as Viet-Nam is concerned, the settlement of political problems, effected on the basis of respect for the

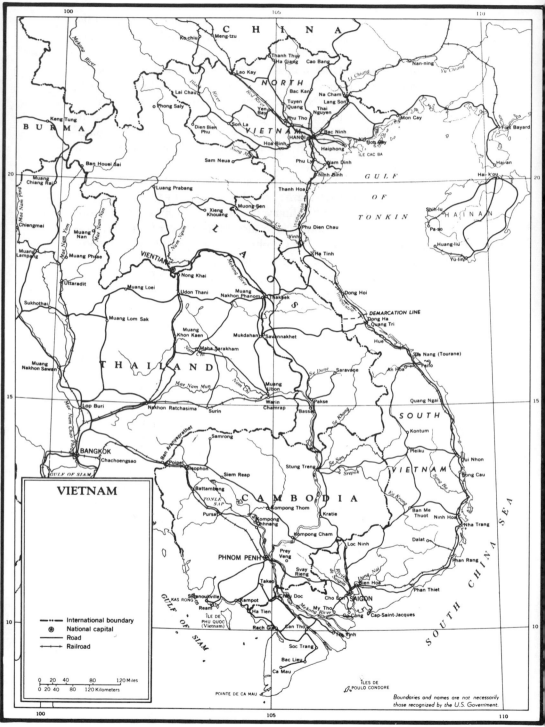

VIETNAM

Legend:
- ·–·–· International boundary
- ⊛ National capital
- —— Road
- +++++ Railroad

Scale:
0 20 40   80   120 Miles
0 20 40   80   120 Kilometers

Boundaries and names are not necessarily those recognized by the U.S. Government.

334

principles of independence, unity and territorial integrity, shall permit the Viet-Namese people to enjoy the fundamental freedoms, guaranteed by democratic institutions established as a result of free general elections by secret ballot. In order to ensure that sufficient progress in the restoration of peace has been made, and that all the necessary conditions obtain for free expression of the national will, general elections shall be held in July 1956, under the supervision of an international commission composed of representatives of the Member States of the International Supervisory Commission,[1] referred to in the agreement on the cessation of hostilities. Consultations will be held on this subject between the competent representative authorities of the two zones from 20 July 1955 onwards.

8. The provisions of the agreements on the cessation of hostilities intended to ensure the protection of individuals and of property must be most strictly applied and must, in particular, allow everyone in Viet-Nam to decide freely in which zone he wishes to live.

9. The competent representative authorities of the Northern and Southern zones of Viet-Nam, as well as the authorities of Laos and Cambodia, must not permit any individual or collective reprisals against persons who have collaborated in any way with one of the parties during the war, or against members of such persons' families.

10. The Conference takes note of the declaration of the Government of the French Republic to the effect that it is ready to withdraw its troops from the territory of Cambodia, Laos and Viet-Nam, at the request of the governments concerned and within periods which shall be fixed by agreement between the parties except in the cases where, by agreement between the two parties, a certain number of French troops shall remain at specified points and for a specified time.

11. The Conference takes note of the declaration of the French Government to the effect that for the settlement of all the problems connected with the re-establishment and consolidation of peace in Cambodia, Laos and Viet-Nam, the French Government will proceed from the principle of respect for the independence and sovereignty, unity and territorial integrity of Cambodia, Laos and Viet-Nam.

12. In their relations with Cambodia, Laos and Viet-Nam, each member of the Geneva Conference undertakes to respect the sovereignty, the independence, the unity and the territorial integrity of the above-mentioned states, and to refrain from any interference in their internal affairs.

13. The members of the Conference agree to consult one another on any question which may be referred to them by the International Supervisory Commission, in order to study such measures as may prove necessary to ensure that the agreements on the cessation of hostilities in Cambodia, Laos and Viet-Nam are respected.

[1] The member states are Canada, India, and Poland.

74

Statement by the United States Under Secretary of State at the Concluding Plenary Session of the Geneva Conference

July 21, 1954

> The United States refused to join in the Final Declaration of the Geneva Conference (Selection 73). Under Secretary of State Walter Bedell Smith issued the following statement, which recognizes the French-sponsored State of Vietnam and mentions the American position that peoples are entitled to determine their own future. Thus from the beginning, the United States position on the Geneva accords differed from that of the other powers, including France.

As I stated on July 18, my Government is not prepared to join in a declaration by the Conference such as is submitted. However, the United States makes this unilateral declaration of its position in these matters:

DECLARATION

The Government of the United States being resolved to devote its efforts to the strengthening of peace in accordance with the principles and purposes of the United Nations takes note of the agreements concluded at Geneva on July 20 and 21, 1954 between (a) the Franco-Laotian Command and the Command of the Peoples Army of Viet-Nam; (b) the Royal Khmer Army Command and the Command of the Peoples Army of Viet-Nam; (c) Franco-Vietnamese Command and the Command of the Peoples Army of Viet-Nam and of paragraphs 1 to 12 inclusive of the declaration presented to the Geneva Conference on July 21, 1954 declares with regard to the aforesaid agreements and paragraphs that (i)

From United States Department of State, *American Foreign Policy, 1950–1955: Basic Documents* (Washington, D.C.: Government Printing Office, 1957), I, 787–788.

it will refrain from the threat or the use of force to disturb them in accordance with Article 2 (4) of the Charter of the United Nations dealing with the obligation of members to refrain in their international relations from the threat or use of force; and (ii) it would view any renewal of the aggression in violation of the aforesaid agreements with grave concern and as seriously threatening international peace and security.

In connection with the statement in the declaration concerning free elections in Viet-Nam my Government wishes to make clear its position which it has expressed in a declaration made in Washington on June 29, 1954, as follows:

In the case of nations now divided against their will, we shall continue to seek to achieve unity through free elections supervised by the United Nations to insure that they are conducted fairly.

With respect to the statement made by the representative of the State of South Viet-Nam,[1] the United States reiterates its traditional position that peoples are entitled to determine their own future and that it will not join in an arrangement which would hinder this. Nothing in its declaration just made is intended to or does indicate any departure from this traditional position.

We share the hope that the agreements will permit Cambodia, Laos and Viet-Nam to play their part, in full independence and sovereignty, in the peaceful community of nations, and will enable the peoples of that area to determine their own future.

---

[1] Statement made July 21, 1954, at the closing session of the Geneva Conference. For an English-language text, see Peter V. Curl, *Documents on American Foreign Relations, 1954* (New York: Harper & Row, 1955), pp. 315–316.

75

Southeast Asia Collective Defense Treaty (Manila Pact)

September 8, 1954

Immediately after the Geneva Conference, the United States, in order to halt the spread of communism in Asia, took the initiative in the formulation of the Manila Pact and the establishment of the Southeast Asia Treaty Organization (SEATO). The non-adherence of such major Asian states as India, Indonesia, and Japan, and the participation of the European colonial powers, Great Britain and France, raised doubts as to the effectiveness of the alliance.

The Parties to this Treaty,

Recognizing the sovereign equality of all the Parties,

Reiterating their faith in the purposes and principles set forth in the Charter of the United Nations and their desire to live in peace with all peoples and all governments,

Reaffirming that, in accordance with the Charter of the United Nations, they uphold the principle of equal rights and self-determination of peoples, and declaring that they will earnestly strive by every peaceful means to promote self-government and to secure the independence of all countries whose peoples desire it and are able to undertake its responsibilities,

Desiring to strengthen the fabric of peace and freedom and to uphold the principles of democracy, individual liberty and the rule of law, and to promote the economic well-being and development of all peoples in the treaty area,

Intending to declare publicly and formally their sense of unity, so that any potential aggressor will appreciate that the Parties stand together in the area, and

Desiring further to coordinate their efforts for collective defense for the preservation of peace and security,

Therefore agree as follows:

From United States Department of State, *American Foreign Policy, 1950–1955: Basic Documents* (Washington, D.C.: Government Printing Office, 1957), I, 912–915.

ARTICLE I

The Parties undertake, as set forth in the Charter of the United Nations, to settle any international disputes in which they may be involved by peaceful means in such a manner that international peace and security and justice are not endangered, and to refrain in their international relations from the threat or use of force in any manner inconsistent with the purposes of the United Nations.

ARTICLE II

In order more effectively to achieve the objectives of this Treaty, the Parties, separately and jointly, by means of continuous and effective self-help and mutual aid will maintain and develop their individual and collective capacity to resist armed attack and to prevent and counter subversive activities directed from without against their territorial integrity and political stability.

ARTICLE III

The Parties undertake to strengthen their free institutions and to cooperate with one another in the further development of economic measures, including technical assistance, designed both to promote economic progress and social well-being and to further the individual and collective efforts of governments toward these ends.

ARTICLE IV

1. Each Party recognizes that aggression by means of armed attack in the treaty area against any of the Parties or against any State or territory which the Parties by unanimous agreement may hereafter designate, would endanger its own peace and safety, and agrees that it will in that event act to meet the common danger in accordance with its constitutional processes. Measures taken under this paragraph shall be immediately reported to the Security Council of the United Nations.

2. If, in the opinion of any of the Parties, the inviolability or the integrity of the territory or the sovereignty or political independence of any Party in the treaty area or of any other State or territory to which the provisions of paragraph 1 of this Article from time to time apply is threatened in any way other than by armed attack or is affected or threatened by any fact or situation which might endanger the peace of the area, the Parties shall consult immediately in order to agree on the measures which should be taken for the common defense.

3. It is understood that no action on the territory of any State

designated by unanimous agreement under paragraph 1 of this Article or on any territory so designated shall be taken except at the invitation or with the consent of the government concerned.

ARTICLE V

The Parties hereby establish a Council, on which each of them shall be represented, to consider matters concerning the implementation of this Treaty. The Council shall provide for consultation with regard to military and any other planning as the situation obtaining in the treaty area may from time to time require. The Council shall be so organized as to be able to meet at any time.

ARTICLE VI

This Treaty does not affect and shall not be interpreted as affecting in any way the rights and obligations of any of the Parties under the Charter of the United Nations or the responsibility of the United Nations for the maintenance of international peace and security. Each Party declares that none of the international engagements now in force between it and any other of the Parties or any third party is in conflict with the provisions of this Treaty, and undertakes not to enter into any international engagement in conflict with this Treaty.

ARTICLE VII

Any other State in a position to further the objectives of this Treaty and to contribute to the security of the area may, by unanimous agreement of the Parties, be invited to accede to this Treaty. Any State so invited may become a Party to the Treaty by depositing its instrument of accession with the Government of the Republic of the Philippines. The Government of the Republic of the Philippines shall inform each of the Parties of the deposit of each such instrument of accession.

ARTICLE VIII

As used in this Treaty, the "treaty area" is the general area of Southeast Asia, including also the entire territories of the Asian Parties, and the general area of the Southwest Pacific not including the Pacific area north of 21 degrees 30 minutes north latitude. The Parties may, by unanimous agreement, amend this Article to include within the treaty area the territory of any State acceding to this Treaty in accordance with Article VII or otherwise to change the treaty area.

ARTICLE IX

1. This Treaty shall be deposited in the archives of the Government of the Republic of the Philippines. Duly certified copies thereof shall be transmitted by that government to the other signatories.

2. The Treaty shall be ratified and its provisions carried out by the Parties in accordance with their respective constitutional processes. The instruments of ratification shall be deposited as soon as possible with the Government of the Republic of the Philippines, which shall notify all of the other signatories of such deposit.[1]

3. The Treaty shall enter into force between the States which have ratified it as soon as the instruments of ratification of a majority of the signatories shall have been deposited, and shall come into effect with respect to each other State on the date of the deposit of its instrument of ratification.

ARTICLE X

This Treaty shall remain in force indefinitely, but any Party may cease to be a Party one year after its notice of denunciation has been given to the Government of the Republic of the Philippines, which shall inform the Governments of the other Parties of the deposit of each notice of denunciation.

ARTICLE XI

The English text of this Treaty is binding on the Parties, but when the Parties have agreed to the French text thereof and have so notified the Government of the Republic of the Philippines, the French text shall be equally authentic and binding on the Parties.

UNDERSTANDING OF THE UNITED STATES OF AMERICA

The United States of America in executing the present Treaty does so with the understanding that its recognition of the effect of aggression and armed attack and its agreement with reference thereto in Article IV, paragraph 1, apply only to communist aggression but affirms that in the event of other aggression or armed attack it will consult under the provisions of Article IV, paragraph 2.

---

[1] Thailand deposited its instrument of ratification Dec. 2, 1954; the remaining signatories (the United States, Australia, France, New Zealand, Pakistan, the Philippines, and the United Kingdom) deposited their instruments Feb. 19, 1955.

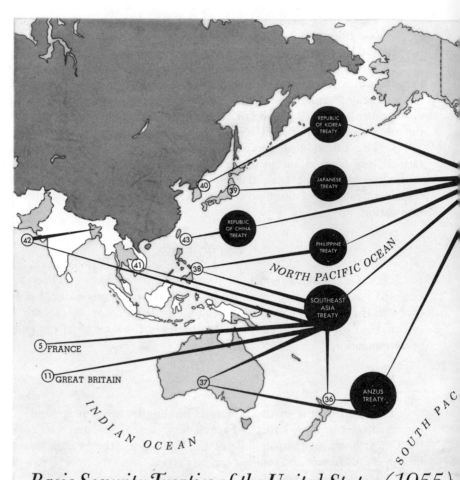

Basic Security Treaties of the United States (1955)

NORTH ATLANTIC TREATY (15 NATIONS)

A treaty signed April 4, 1949, by which "the parties agree that an armed attack against one or more of them in Europe or North America shall be considered an attack against them all; and...each of them...will assist the . . . attacked by taking forthwith, individually and in concert with the other Parties, such action as it deems necessary including the use of armed force..."

1 UNITED STATES	9 LUXEMBOURG
2 CANADA	10 PORTUGAL
3 ICELAND	11 FRANCE
4 NORWAY	12 ITALY
5 UNITED	13 GREECE
KINGDOM	14 TURKEY
6 NETHERLANDS	15 FEDERAL
7 DENMARK	REPUBLIC
8 BELGIUM	OF GERMANY

RIO TREATY (21 NATIONS)

A treaty signed September 2, 1947, which provides that an armed attack against any American State "shall be considered as an attack against all the American States and...each one . . . undertakes to assist in meeting the attack . . ."

1 UNITED STATES	25 PANAMA
16 MEXICO	26 COLOMBIA
17 CUBA	27 VENEZUELA
18 HAITI	28 ECUADOR
19 DOMINICAN	29 PERU
REPUBLIC	30 BRAZIL
20 HONDURAS	31 BOLIVIA
21 GUATEMALA	32 PARAGUAY
22 EL SALVADOR	33 CHILE
23 NICARAGUA	34 ARGENTINA
24 COSTA RICA	35 URUGUAY

ANZUS (Australia—New Zealand—United States) TREATY (3 NATIONS)

A treaty signed September 1, 1951, whereby each of the parties "recognizes that an armed attack in the Pacific Area on any of the Parties would be dangerous to its own peace and safety and declares that it would act to meet the common danger in accordance with its constitutional processes."

   1 UNITED STATES
36 NEW ZEALAND
37 AUSTRALIA

PHILIPPINE TREATY (BILATERAL)

A treaty signed August 30, which the parties recognize armed attack in the Pacifi either of the Parties woul gerous to its own peace ar and each party agrees that "to meet the common d accordance with its cons processes."

   1 UNITED STATE
38 PHILIPPINES

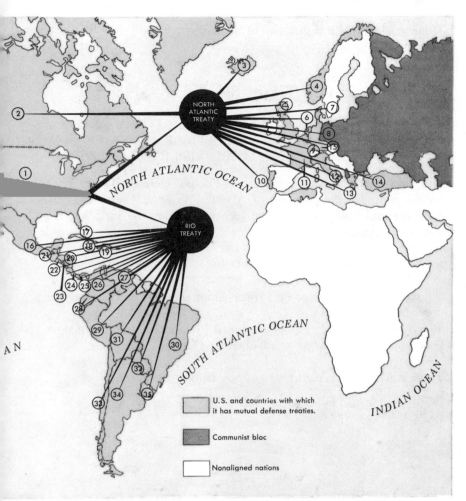

U.S. and countries with which
it has mutual defense treaties.

Communist bloc

Nonaligned nations

...ESE TREATY (...ERAL)

...signed September 8, 1951,
...Japan on a provisional basis
..., and the United States
...to "maintain certain of its
...rces in and about Japan . . .
...o deter armed attack upon

    1 UNITED STATES
    39 JAPAN

REPUBLIC OF KOREA (South Korea) TREATY (BILATERAL)

A treaty signed October 1, 1953,
whereby each party "recognizes that
an armed attack in the Pacific area
on either of the Parties . . . would be
dangerous to its own peace and
safety" and that each Party "would
act to meet the common danger in
accordance with its constitutional
processes."

    1 UNITED STATES
    40 REPUBLIC OF KOREA

SOUTHEAST ASIA TREATY (8 NATIONS)

A treaty signed September 8, 1954,
whereby each Party "recognizes that
aggression by means of armed attack
in the treaty area against any of the
Parties . . . would endanger its own
peace and safety" and each will "in
that event act to meet the common
danger in accordance with its constitutional processes."

    1 UNITED STATES
    5 UNITED KINGDOM
    11 FRANCE
    36 NEW ZEALAND
    37 AUSTRALIA
    38 PHILIPPINES
    41 THAILAND
    42 PAKISTAN

REPUBLIC OF CHINA (Formosa) TREATY (BILATERAL)

A treaty signed December 2, 1954,
whereby each of the parties "recognizes that an armed attack in the
West Pacific Area directed against
the territories of either of the Parties would be dangerous to its own
peace and safety," and that each
"would act to meet the common danger in accordance with its constitutional processes." The territory of
the Republic of China is defined as
"Taiwan (Formosa) and the Pescadores."

    1 UNITED STATES
    43 REPUBLIC OF CHINA
       (FORMOSA)

In witness whereof, the undersigned Plenipotentiaries have signed this Treaty.

Done at Manila, this eighth day of September, 1954.

.   .   .   .

Protocol to the Treaty, September 8, 1954 [2]

DESIGNATION OF STATES AND TERRITORY AS TO WHICH PROVISIONS OF ARTICLE IV AND ARTICLE III ARE TO BE APPLICABLE

The Parties to the Southeast Asia Collective Defense Treaty unanimously designate for the purposes of Article IV of the Treaty the States of Cambodia and Laos and the free territory under the jurisdiction of the State of Vietnam.

The Parties further agree that the above mentioned states and territory shall be eligible in respect of the economic measures contemplated by Article III.

This Protocol shall enter into force simultaneously with the coming into force of the Treaty.

IN WITNESS WHEREOF, the undersigned Plenipotentiaries have signed this Protocol to the Southeast Asia Collective Defense Treaty.

Done at Manila, this eighth day of September, 1954.

[2] Ratification advised by the Senate Feb. 1, 1955; ratified by the President Feb. 4, 1955; entered into force Feb. 19, 1955.

76

The Pattern of Viet Cong Activity in the South

In 1961 the United States Department of State issued the following account of Viet Cong activity. The document concludes with the warning that "A government or a people who now think that 'Viet-Nam is so far away from us' may well discover that they are the South Vietnamese of tomorrow. Then they may wish they had done more now. But then it will be late, very late, perhaps too late!"

A. THE MILITARY PATTERN

The pattern varies from village to village, from district to district, depending on the extent of Viet Cong control. But the variations are minor. In general, the organizational framework of the Viet Cong military units is quite standardized throughout South Vietnam.

There are three kinds of Viet Cong soldier. One is based on the village. He receives no pay. Generally he works at his job—usually as a farmer or fisherman or laborer—during the day. At night or in emergencies he is available for assignment by his superiors. The Viet Cong like to have at least 5 and preferably 10 guerrillas of this type in each village. In villages largely controlled by the Viet Cong, a full squad (10 to 16 men) is usual. A village squad is likely to have a few land mines at its disposal and two or three rifles or submachineguns. Knives, machetes, spears, or other weapons are more common than modern firearms.

Halftime, irregular forces are organized by the Viet Cong at the district level. There are generally several companies of 50 or more men in each district. These troops receive half pay and so must work at least part time to eke out a living. They are both better equipped and better trained than the village guards.

It would be a mistake to assume that the Vietnamese villagers are searching out Viet Cong agents in order to enlist as local guards or irregular soldiers. Undoubtedly there are some volunteers. But the record shows that many young Vietnamese are dragooned into service with the

From *A Threat to the Peace: North Viet-Nam's Effort to Conquer South Viet-Nam* (Washington, D.C.: Government Printing Office, 1961), pp. 7–13.

VC. Some are kidnapped; others are threatened; still others join to prevent their families from being harmed.

Last summer, an American radio correspondent (CBS) interviewed a young Vietnamese who had been captured in an action against the Viet Cong in Kien Phong Province. The "volunteer," Pham Van Dau, was only 17 years old. The reporter asked him why he had joined the Communists. He replied: "Because they took my father away for 10 days and tried to force him to join their organization. But my father refused. Then they took me and forced me to cooperate. They threatened to kill my father if I refused. That is why I joined them."

Similar statements have been made by hundreds of young men who either deserted the VC ranks or surrendered to the Republic of Viet-Nam forces.

The hard core of the Viet Cong (VC) military organization is the full-time regular unit usually based on a province or region. These are well-trained and highly disciplined guerrilla fighters. Soldiering is their job and they do it effectively. They follow a rigid training schedule that is roughly two-thirds military and one-third political in content. This compares with the 50–50 proportion for district units and the 70 per cent political and 30 per cent military content of the village guerrilla's training.

Some of the regular VC forces have been introduced from the North in units. Moreover, the leaders of regular VC units are almost exclusively men trained in North Viet-Nam although many are natives of the South.

Money to pay the regular VC units comes from a variety of sources. "Taxes" are extorted from the local population. Landowners and plantation operators often must pay a tribute to the VC as the price for not having their lands devastated. Similarly, transportation companies have been forced to pay the VC or face the threat of having their buses or boats sabotaged. Officials and wealthy people have been kidnapped for ransom by the VC. The VC have often stopped buses, taken the money and valuables of all on board, given them a lecture on the "glories of communism," and turned them loose.

For the most part the VC have concentrated their attention on individuals and isolated or poorly defended outposts. They have killed hundreds of village chiefs and other local officials. In the past year, however, and particularly in the last few months, the VC have moved into larger unit operations. Several attacks have been carried out in battalion strength or more against fairly large units of the South Vietnamese Army.

Among the favored targets of the VC have been police stations, self-defense corps units, civil guard outposts, and small units of the South Viet-Nam Army. By hitting such targets suddenly and in superior force, the VC are able to assure themselves a supply of arms and ammunition. This reduces their dependence on the long supply line from the North.

The weapons of the VC are largely French- or U.S.-made, or handmade on primitive forges in the jungles.

The Communists have avoided any large-scale introduction of Soviet-bloc arms into South Viet-Nam, for this would be too clear evidence of their direct involvement. However, as the armed forces of the so-called Democratic Republic of Viet-Nam have been reequipped with new weapons from the Sino-Soviet bloc, their old weapons have helped supply the Viet Cong in the South.

The size of the Viet Cong regular units has grown steadily in recent years. Once estimated at approximately 3,000 men, the strength of the full-time Viet Cong elite fighting force is now believed to be at least 8,000 or 9,000 organized in some 30 battalions. An additional 8,000 or more troops operate under the leadership of regular Viet Cong officers at the provincial or district level. These figures do not include many thousands of village guards, political cadres, special agents, bearers, and the like. The pace of infiltration of officers and men has jumped markedly since Pathet Lao victories in Laos have assured a relatively safe corridor through that country into western South Viet-Nam.

There are good reasons to think that Laos now provides not only a route into South Viet-Nam but also a safe haven from which Viet Cong units operate. Laos-based units of the Viet Cong are believed to have played an important role in large-scale attacks by the VC in the highlands north of Kontum and near Ban Me Thuot this summer and fall and perhaps in assaults in the northern Provinces of Quang Nam and Quang Ngai.

In addition to providing a channel for troops and agents, the infiltration routes from North Viet-Nam into the South are used to transfer supplies and equipment. Much of the food needed by the VC is acquired locally through "taxation" or outright seizure. Armed attacks provide many of the weapons and much of the ammunition. But shipments from the North supplement these sources. There is also regular traffic across the mountain trails and by seagoing junks which supplies the VC with material for clothing and uniforms, medical supplies, communications equipment, tools, generators, and all the many things required by a fighting force in the field.

B. THE POLITICAL PATTERN

The content and methods of Viet Cong political activity leave no doubt as to its Communist orientation. In a transparent effort to give their movement a cloak of respectability and of popular support, the so-called "Front for Liberation of the South" was formed late last year. Within the front are separate "liberation" organizations—for youth, for the peasants, for workers, for intellectuals, for women, indeed for every significant segment of society in South Viet-Nam.

However, seized documents, propaganda pamphlets, and indoctrination leaflets picked up throughout South Viet-Nam make clear that the Lao Dong (Workers) Party, that is, the Communist Party, is the vanguard of the "liberation" movement. As those familiar with the Communist movement know, this means that the "liberation" movement is directed by the Communist Party. The Lao Dong Party of the South is part of and controlled by Ho Chi Minh's Lao Dong Party in the North.

The Viet Cong organization in the South follows the familiar Communist pattern. The basic unit is the cell of a few persons in a village or neighborhood. Village units are subordinate to the district headquarters and these in turn are controlled by the provincial party headquarters. Above the latter are the regional or zonal headquarters which take their directions from Hanoi.

The pattern of political indoctrination is what one would expect—concentration on studies of "socialism," meaning communism; praise for and identification with the program and progress of the Ho regime in the North; promises of support for the "liberation" movement by the "socialist camp"; criticism of the "imperialists," "warmongers," and "colonialists" and their "puppets."

Through their propaganda the Viet Cong seek to appeal to every group in the South with promises of special attention—"autonomy" for minority tribal groups, land and freedom from usury for the peasants, education for the youth, "freedom" for the intellectuals, and so forth.

In addition to the party organization itself, close ties are maintained with the military units through a system of political officers assigned to all units down to the platoon. Party members often serve as part-time guerrillas. They provide additional eyes and ears for the military units, supplying reports on GVN military establishments and troop movements. They may be assigned to collect money or to gather food for the Viet Cong.

C. THE USE OF TERROR

While professing sympathy for the needs and hopes of the people, the Viet Cong has resorted to the most brutal forms of force and coercion in carrying out its program. It has sought by every available means to frustrate the efforts of the authorities in South Viet-Nam to provide the people with social services. It has made no secret of its determination to destroy if possible the legally elected Government in South Viet-Nam and to place that country and its people under the control of Hanoi. It promises improvements but does what it can to prevent those very improvements if they are carried out by the non-Communist authorities.

Assassination, often after the most brutal torture, is a favored Viet Cong tactic. Government officials, schoolteachers, even wives and children have been the victims. Literally hundreds of village chiefs have been murdered in order to assert Viet Cong power and to instill fear in the populace. The list of atrocities is long. A catalog of these activities has been assembled in annual installments by the Saigon authorities.[1] They make gruesome reading, even for a generation that is jaded with accounts of man's inhumanity.

A particularly brutal example was reported from Vinh Binh Province the first week in November. The chief of the Cau Ke district, Le Van Nghia, was killed when his car hit a Viet Cong mine. Killed with the district chief were his wife and two other persons. The official's two children, aged one and three, miraculously survived the blast, but they were killed on the spot by the Viet Cong who had prepared the ambush.

Kidnapping is another criminal technique commonly used by the Viet Cong. Often the victims are never heard from again. Sometimes they are returned after sufficient ransom has been paid. At times this method is used to get recruits when efforts at persuasion fail.

Recently, in a gesture of utter contempt for the International Control Commission (I.C.C.) which is charged with overseeing enforcement of the Geneva Accords in Viet-Nam, the Viet Cong kidnapped Col. Hoang Thuy Nam, chief of the South Viet-Nam liaison mission with the I.C.C. He was seized by a group of armed men at his farm less than 10 miles from Saigon. Appeals for his release went unheeded. The I.C.C. refused to raise its voice in protest. Ten days later his body was found floating in the Saigon River. It bore the marks of awful torture inflicted before his death. It was a ghastly crime that shocked Viet-Nam and civilized people everywhere.

Any official, worker, or establishment that represents a service to the people by the Government in Saigon is fair game for the Viet Cong. Schools have been among their favorite targets. Through harassment, the murder of teachers, and sabotage of buildings the Viet Cong succeeded in closing more than 200 primary schools in South Viet-Nam in 1960, interrupting the education of more than 25,000 students. The number is reported to have risen to almost 400 in recent months.

Hospitals and medical clinics have often been attacked as part of the anti-Government campaign and also because such attacks provide the Viet Cong with needed medical supplies. The Communists have encouraged people in rural areas to oppose the work of the Government's anti-malaria teams, and some of the workers have been killed. Village and

[1] See "Violations of the Geneva Agreements by the Viet-Minh Communists," published by the Government of the Republic of Viet-Nam and dated July 1959, July 1960, and May 1961.

town offices, police stations, and agricultural research stations are high on the list of preferred targets for the Viet Cong.

In short, anything that spells order or security for the people of the South is anathema to the Viet Cong (VC) unless it be VC "order" or VC "security," anything that represents service or public welfare becomes a target, and a man who serves his Government and his people is likely to have his name inscribed on the Viet Cong's "wanted" list.

In 1960 the Government of the Republic of Viet-Nam claimed that about 1,400 local Government officials and civilians were assassinated by the Viet Cong. Approximately 700 persons were kidnapped during the year. In the first 6 months of 1961 more than 500 murders of officials and civilians were reported and about 1,000 persons were kidnapped. The number of acts of terrorism carried out by the Viet Cong in recent months exceeds last year's levels according to authorities in Saigon.

77

The Tonkin Gulf Resolution

August 10, 1964

Following the Tonkin incident, in August, 1964, the United States House of Representatives passed unanimously and the Senate passed by a vote of 88 to 2 (only Senators Wayne Morse, Democrat from Oregon, and Ernest Gruening, Democrat from Alaska dissenting) the following resolution. In the course of the debate, Morse challenged the legality and expediency of American military and naval activity in Indochina and termed the resolution unconstitutional and a "predated declaration of war."

Whereas naval units of the Communist regime in Vietnam, in violation of the principles of the Charter of the United Nations and of international law, have deliberately and repeatedly attacked United States

H. J. Res. 1145, from United States of America, *Congressional Record* (Washington, D.C.: Government Printing Office, 1964), Vol. 110, Part 14, p. 18471.

These maps, published by the Communist Chinese in June, 1965, purport to show the expansion of Viet Cong control in South Vietnam between 1961 and 1965. "Liberated areas" refers to Viet Cong controlled areas, and "enemy-occupied areas" refers to areas controlled by the South Vietnamese government. The present editor cannot vouch for the accuracy of the details in these maps, but there is no question that the political and military situation had grossly deteriorated for the Saigon regime by the spring of 1965.

EXPANDING LIBERATED AREAS IN S. VIET NAM

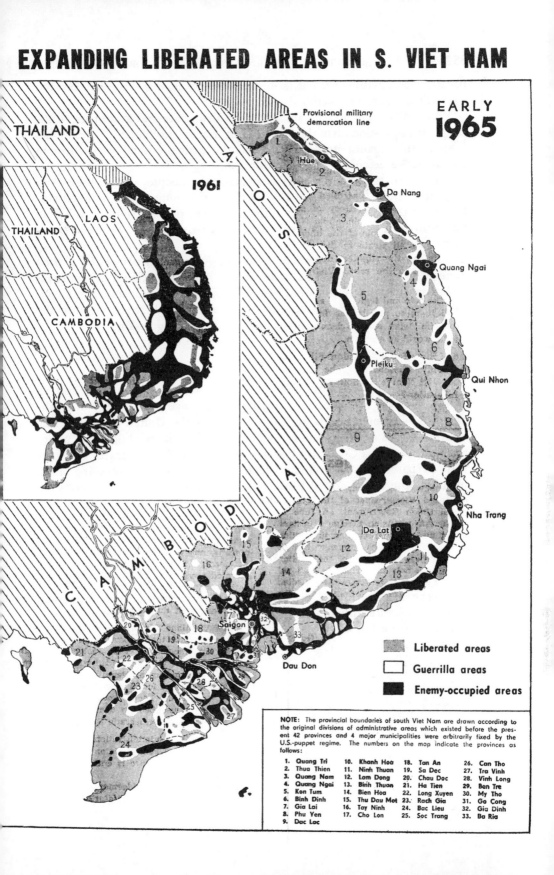

EARLY **1965**

1961

Provisional military demarcation line

THAILAND

L A O S

LAOS

THAILAND

CAMBODIA

C A M B O D I A

Hue

Da Nang

Quang Ngai

Pleiku

Qui Nhon

Nha Trang

Da Lat

Saigon

Dau Don

Liberated areas

Guerrilla areas

Enemy-occupied areas

NOTE: The provincial boundaries of south Viet Nam are drawn according to the original divisions of administrative areas which existed before the present 42 provinces and 4 major municipalities were arbitrarily fixed by the U.S.-puppet regime. The numbers on the map indicate the provinces as follows:

1. Quang Tri	10. Khanh Hoa	18. Tan An	26. Can Tho
2. Thua Thien	11. Ninh Thuan	19. Sa Dec	27. Tra Vinh
3. Quang Nam	12. Lam Dong	20. Chau Doc	28. Vinh Long
4. Quang Ngai	13. Binh Thuan	21. Ha Tien	29. Ben Tre
5. Kon Tum	14. Bien Hoa	22. Long Xuyen	30. My Tho
6. Binh Dinh	15. Thu Dau Mot	23. Rach Gia	31. Go Cong
7. Gia Lai	16. Tay Ninh	24. Bac Lieu	32. Gia Dinh
8. Phu Yen	17. Cho Lon	25. Soc Trang	33. Ba Ria
9. Dac Lac			

naval vessels lawfully present in international waters, and thereby created a serious threat to international peace; and

Whereas these attacks are part of a deliberate and systematic campaign of aggression that the Communist regime in North Vietnam has been waging against its neighbors and the nations joined with them in the collective defense of their freedom; and

Whereas the United States is assisting the peoples of southeast Asia to protect their freedom and has no territorial, military or political ambitions in that area, but desires only that these peoples should be left in peace to work out their own destinies in their own way: Now, therefore, be it

Resolved by the Senate and House of Representatives of the United States of America in Congress assembled, That the Congress approves and supports the determination of the President, as Commander in Chief, to take all necessary measures to repel any armed attack against the forces of the United States and to prevent further aggression.

SECTION 2.

The United States regards as vital to its national interest and to world peace the maintenance of international peace and security in southeast Asia. Consonant with the Constitution of the United States and the Charter of the United Nations and in accord with its obligations under the Southeast Asia Collective Defense Treaty, the United States is, therefore, prepared, as the President determines, to take all necessary steps, including the use of armed force, to assist any member or protocol state of the Southeast Asia Collective Defense Treaty requesting assistance in defense of its freedom.

SECTION 3.

This resolution shall expire when the President shall determine that the peace and security of the area is reasonably assured by international conditions created by action of the United Nations or otherwise, except that it may be terminated earlier by concurrent resolution of the Congress.

78

A White House Statement

February 7, 1965

In February, 1965, unable to stop the Viet Cong in South Vietnam, the United States and South Vietnam unleashed their superior air power against North Vietnam. It was becoming increasingly difficult to keep the war localized.

On Feb. 7, U.S. and South Vietnamese air elements were directed to launch joint retaliatory attacks against barracks and staging areas in the southern area of North Viet Nam which intelligence has shown to be actively used by Hanoi for training and infiltration of Viet Cong personnel into South Viet Nam.

Results of the attack and further operational details will be announced as soon as they are reported from the field.

Today's action by the U.S. and South Vietnamese governments was in response to provocations ordered and directed by the Hanoi regime.

Commencing at 2 a.m. on Feb. 7, Saigon time (1 p.m. Saturday EST) two South Vietnamese air fields, two U.S. barracks areas, several villages and one town in South Viet Nam were subjected to deliberate, surprise attacks. Substantial casualties resulted.

Our intelligence has indicated, and this action confirmed, that Hanoi had ordered a more aggressive course of action against both South Vietnamese and American installations.

Moreover, these attacks were only made possible by the continuing infiltration of personnel and equipment from North Viet Nam. This infiltration markedly increased during 1964 and continues to increase.

To meet these attacks the governments of South Viet Nam and the U.S. government agreed to appropriate reprisal action against North Vietnamese targets. The President's approval of this action was given after the action was discussed with and recommended by the National Security Council last night.

Issued by George Reedy, White House Press Secretary, at 8:30 A.M., Eastern Standard Time, February 7, 1965.

Today's joint response was carefully limited to military areas which are supplying men and arms for attacks in South Viet Nam.

As in the case of the North Vietnamese attacks in the Gulf of Tonkin last August, the response is appropriate and fitting.

As the U.S. government has frequently stated, we seek no wider war. Whether or not this course can be maintained lies with the North Vietnamese aggressors.

The key to the situation remains the cessation of infiltration from North Viet Nam and the clear indication by the Hanoi regime that it is prepared to cease aggression against its neighbors.

79

Speech at the National Teach-In on the Vietnam War

May 15, 1965

Professor George McTurnan Kahin

The rash of teach-ins reached a climax when an all-day session, broadcast to campuses across the United States, was held at the Sheraton Park Hotel in Washington, D.C., on May 15, 1965. One of the leading academic critics of the American policy, George McTurnan Kahin, an authority on Southeast Asia at Cornell University, delivered the following speech, which emphasizes the importance of nationalism in Southeast Asia.

Since the end of the war American officials have made such grave errors in policy towards Southeast Asia that we have every right to be sceptical about their ability to respond intelligently to the present situation in Vietnam. Their most consistent failure has been an inability both to appreciate the importance of Asian nationalism and to work with rather than against that powerful force. This is a major reason why Burma, Cambodia, and Indonesia have become so distrustful of the U.S. and why they have either broken or come close to breaking relations

Text as released to the press, May 15, 1965, mimeographed.

with us. Moreover the obsession of American policy-makers with what they still see as monolithic communism has blinded them to the fact that communism in Asia has adapted itself to nationalism. They have confused the broad, but nationally differentiated, force and potential of communism with the threat of specifically Chinese power.

Despite the immense informational-gathering facilities of the government, serious policy mistakes have been made because decisions have been taken on the basis of inappropriate criteria, wrong analyses, and disregard of the relevant facts. At the same time, essential information has been withheld from the American public, and crucial policy decisions on Southeast Asia have been made before the public has even been aware that a problem exists. Once taken, these decisions have set in motion events which severely circumscribe any moderating influence which an informed public might bring to bear. Moreover, in recent months the tendency has increased to dismiss even thoughtful criticism of government policy as irresponsible meddling.

In Vietnam, American policy has been wrong from the outset. In the decade following World War II, because of our illusory hope that we could induce France to become the keystone of an American-designed European military organization, we temporized with our commitment to national self-determination and backed France in her effort to reestablish control over Vietnam. By supporting her attempt to establish a Vietnamese regime which lacked nationalist support, we helped to ensure that Vietnamese patriots would have no real alternative but to rally to the banner of Ho Chi Minh. France's humiliating defeat at Dien Bien Phu in 1954 was a military defeat, but it was made inevitable by the political failure that preceded it.

Then came the Geneva Agreements. Clearly specifying that Vietnam was one country, they stipulated that the 17th parallel was a temporary demarcation line, "not in any way to be interpreted as constituting a political or territorial boundary." In its own unilateral declaration at Geneva the U.S. spoke only of Vietnam, not of a South or a North Vietnam, and with respect to the Conference's provision for national elections the U.S. also stated that it would "continue to seek to achieve unity through free elections supervised by the United Nations."

Nevertheless the U.S. soon after set out to build up a separate state in the South. And again we made the mistake of thinking we could establish a viable government on an inadequate nationalist base.

The U.S. supported Ngo Dinh Diem, giving him massive amounts of economic assistance. But American aid was no substitute for the nationalist support Diem's regime never really acquired, despite what our officials told Congress and the American public. Diem himself had said in 1953 that Ho Chi Minh "gained in popularity as a leader of the resistance, not as a Communist" and that "the vast majority of his followers" were "nationalist and in no way pro-communist." What the U.S. failed to recognize was that in these conditions Ho Chi Minh, who for at least nine years had been the acknowledged head of the Vietnamese nationalist movement, could not be replaced as the leader of the Vietnamese people by a man supported from the outside—a man little known and who had spent the critical years of the independence struggle abroad.

America's failure to build up an effective government under Diem is now well known. But this was not immediately apparent. For after Geneva his regime enjoyed several years of grace, during which Ho Chi Minhs' followers left it pretty much alone. Essentially this was due to the fact that the Geneva Agreements had promised nation-wide elections for 1956. It was primarily because of this provision, and because the Agreements also stipulated that France would be responsible for carrying out the accords in the South and would remain there until the elections were held, that the Vietminh withdrew its armies from the South and for a considerable period suspended revolutionary activity there. But, with American encouragement, Diem refused to permit the elections in 1956; and France washed her hands of the responsibilities she had assumed at Geneva. Regardless of what sophistry has been employed to demonstrate otherwise, by encouraging Diem to defy this central provision of the Geneva Agreements, the U.S. reneged on the position it had taken there in its own unilateral declaration. Civil war in Vietnam became inevitable. For, when a military struggle for power ends on the agreed condition that the competition will be transferred to the political level, can the side which violates the agreed conditions legitimately expect that the military struggle will not be resumed?

Despite the initial period of insulation from Vietminh militancy and despite unstinting American economic and political backing, Diem failed to develop a real base of popular support. Programs urged by the U.S. for social and economic reform and for winning the allegiance of the non-Vietnamese hill-dwelling peoples were never effectively carried out. The Saigon government remained all too isolated from the peasantry. As a result, it was unable to compete with the Vietcong guerrillas when, from 1958 on, they adopted increasingly militant policies. And in the nineteen months since the assassination of Diem the situation has continued to deteriorate, and the shifting combinations of army officers and bureaucrats controlling the government have remained just as isolated from the villages of Vietnam.

Faced with this decline in political cohesion and the evident inability of the South Vietnamese military to stave off the Vietcong, the present administration has enlarged the war in Vietnam by bombing the North and increasing American military activity in the South. It has endeavored to compensate for the continuing erosion of Saigon's political and military base by introducing more American troops and more American air power. And it has justified this in terms of our pledge to support South Vietnam, a commitment which the administration regards as a test case.

Here we should recall the caveat of Secretary Acheson in 1950. America, he said, could not by itself create politically stable states in Asia. "The United States," he stated, "cannot furnish the determination, it cannot furnish will-power, and cannot furnish the loyalty of a people to its government." Where such factors were absent, he said, American efforts would be totally wasted. President Kennedy also recognized these limitations when, in September 1963, he said of the South Vietnamese: "In the final analysis, it's their war. They're the ones who have to win it or lose it. We can help them, give them equipment, we can send our men there as advisers, but they have to win it."

In the context of these cautions, does an unconditional American military pledge to a weak and factious regime which lacks popular backing make common sense? Is our pledge of support completely unqualified? Does it not demand a minimum degree of performance and coopera- tion from Saigon—political as well as military? Is our pledge automatically to any military or civilian group that happens to control Saigon?

What happens if our current policy of brinksmanship induces Hanoi to send its 300,000-man army into South Vietnam? For this it may very well do if the damage inflicted by the U.S. becomes so great that the North has little to lose by undertaking a retaliatory attack and little to save through compromise and negotiation. The well-known military analyst Hanson Baldwin has estimated that to cope effectively with such a force the U.S. might have to use as many as a million men. The U.S. does not have these forces immediately available, and even to send in a small proportion would take our entire strategic reserve.

A full-scale confrontation between American troops and the North Vietnamese army, even if no Chinese forces were also involved, would probably exact a toll in American lives at least as great as that suffered in Korea. How responsible a policy would this be? Would it be com- patible with our global interests and our long-standing commitments to other countries throughout the world? What of our commitments in Europe? And what of our increasing commitments in this hemisphere? Surely, too, we must consider the implications for our long-term policies toward Russia and China. The sane trend towards a rapprochement with Russia started by President Eisenhower and continued by President Ken- nedy has already been seriously affected by our policy in Vietnam and will be further undermined if we continue on our present course. Among Communist parties throughout Asia, as well as among the non-aligned states, China's scornful derision of Russia's policy of peaceful coexistence has been gaining ever-wider approval. The possibility of cooperation be- tween the U.S. and Russia to contain China's power and influence in

Southeast Asia is becoming ever more remote. Our major aim in Asia is to contain China and thus to provide the opportunity for the states of South and Southeast Asia to develop free of Peking's dominating influence. And it is this consideration which should govern American policy towards Vietnam.

No matter how much military power we send into Vietnam, the present American policy of trying to sustain a separate state in the South may very well fail. For the local political factors necessary to insure success are simply not there. If we are to salvage anything in Vietnam, we will achieve more through a cease-fire and a negotiated political settlement than through the futile infusion of more and more American military power. The U.S. must recognize that the historic Vietnamese fear of and antagonism towards China continues despite the common adherence to Communist ideology. Inasmuch as the character of Vietnamese communism is inseparable from Vietnamese nationalism, Vietnamese power will not necessarily be exerted in concert with Chinese power.

Those who are still impressed by the simplistic Domino Theory must realize that the non-Communist governments of Southeast Asia will not automatically collapse if the Communists should come to control all of Vietnam. So long as Southeast Asian governments are in harmony with their countries' nationalism, and so long as they are wise enough to meet the most pressing economic and social demands of their peoples, they are not likely to succumb to communism. Nationalism and the demand for social and economic progress are the dominant forces in Southeast Asia today. If we can work with these forces we will make a major contribution to maintaining the territorial integrity of the states of Southeast Asia and provide them with a better opportunity to develop along non-communist lines.

The first step in this direction must be to negotiate a settlement in Vietnam. What has been our position thus far? The Administration tells us that it is prepared to negotiate *unconditionally*, but in effect *on condition* that the Vietcong cease all operations immediately, and *on condition* that the state of South Vietnam continue its separate existence, in permanent violation of the Geneva Agreements. Furthermore, we have made clear that the Vietcong and its political arm the National Liberation Front, cannot be party to negotiations. Not only is this one more condition, but it flies squarely in the face of political reality. For it is widely acknowledged that at least half of the South is under the control of the Vietcong. Is it not Utopian to assume that Hanoi is in a position to insist upon the Vietcong's yielding up the position it has won there? In 1954 the Vietminh could induce its numerous supporters in the South to accept Vietnam's partition and to abandon their gains south of the 17th parallel because partition was regarded as a temporary measure, to last only until elections. But we cannot assume that once again the insurgents

in the South will give up what they have won through a long and difficult campaign. Over the last five years the doctrine of uncompromising
struggle and a real expectation of victory have been assiduously nurtured
among the Vietcong. While there undoubtedly is a considerable congru-
ence of interest between Hanoi and the Vietcong, under these circumstances we cannot assume that Hanoi can abruptly call off the Southerners'
resistance. And whatever influence Hanoi has over the Vietcong, we cannot expect it to exert this so long as we continue our bombing of the
North.

The morale of the North Vietnamese is no more likely to be broken
by bombs than was that of the British or the Russians in World War II.
Indeed their will is likely to be stiffened. President Johnson said after
our embassy in Saigon had been bombed that, "Outrages like this will
only reinforce the determination of the American people and Government." What is true for Americans is true for the Vietnamese.

Halting our bombardment of the North would be our first genuine
indication of an interest in negotiations. Our cavalier dismissal of the
U.N. Secretary General's efforts hardly constituted an earnest of serious
American interest in negotiations. We should give him an unequivocal
mandate to pursue negotiations, and we should make clear that we want
not just discussions but serious negotiations. Concurrently we should give
much more encouragement than we have to those non-aligned Asian and
African states which wish to help promote a peaceful settlement in
Vietnam.

Finally, for those many Americans who still regard full public discussion of vitally important national issues as essential to our brand of
democracy, there is a particularly disquieting domestic aspect of this situation. Realizing as they do that an informed public discussion requires
access to all the relevant facts, they can only be deeply disturbed when
a spokesman for the newspaper editors of this country feels compelled to
state, as he did last month, that the American "press in Vietnam face
stronger restrictions than it ever has in wartime" and that we are getting
"contradictions, double talk and half truths" from the government concerning the situation in Vietnam. And surely Americans have grounds
for concern when *The New York Times* can editorialize, as it did not
long afterwards, that "high ranking representatives of government in
Washington and in Saigon" have so "obscured, confused or distorted
news from Vietnam" or have made such "fatuously erroneous evaluations
about the course of the war" that the credibility of the United States
Government has been sacrificed.

When the American public faces the prospect of war, it has the right
to full and honest answers. I ask Mr. Bundy to respond to a few of the
most urgent questions:

1. Can the recent suspension of bombings be interpreted as an earnest of the United States' sincerity in seeking negotiations?
2. Would the U.S. be prepared to cooperate with other powers, including China, with the object of attaining a political settlement in Vietnam in conjunction with a guarantee of the territorial boundaries of the states of continental Southeast Asia?
3. To what level does the administration calculate it would be necessary to expand the draft in order to achieve a military victory over both the Vietcong and the as yet uncommitted North Vietnamese forces?
4. We have been in favor of elections to unify Germany and Korea. Why have we opposed them in Vietnam?
5. What position are we prepared to take if the Government in Saigon decides to negotiate unilaterally with Hanoi, and what is our response if it asks us to go home?

80

Pattern for Peace in Southeast Asia

April 7, 1965

President Lyndon Johnson

In this address delivered at Johns Hopkins University, the President outlines the aims of American policy and lays the blame for the fighting in South Vietnam on North Vietnam and Communist China, which were encouraging and aiding the Viet Cong. At the same time that he emphasizes the American determination to halt Communist aggression, Johnson also indicates America's willingness to enter peace negotiations "with the governments concerned," apparently ruling out direct negotiations with the Viet Cong.

Last week 17 nations sent their views to some two dozen countries having an interest in Southeast Asia. We are joining those 17 countries and stating our American policy tonight, which we believe will contribute toward peace in this area of the world.

I have come here to review once again with my own people the views of the American Government.

Tonight Americans and Asians are dying for a world where each people may choose its own path to change.

Text as delivered, released by the United States Department of State, April, 1965.

This is the principle for which our ancestors fought in the valleys of Pennsylvania. It is a principle for which our sons fight tonight in the jungles of Viet-Nam.

Viet-Nam is far away from this quiet campus. We have no territory there, nor do we seek any. The war is dirty and brutal and difficult. And some 400 young men, born into an America that is bursting with opportunity and promise, have ended their lives on Viet-Nam's steaming soil.

Why must we take this painful road?

Why must this nation hazard its ease, its interest, and its power for the sake of a people so far away?

We fight because we must fight if we are to live in a world where every country can shape its own destiny, and only in such a world will our own freedom be finally secure.

This kind of world will never be built by bombs or bullets. Yet the infirmities of man are such that force must often precede reason and the waste of war, the works of peace.

We wish that this were not so. But we must deal with the world as it is, if it is ever to be as we wish.

The world as it is in Asia is not a serene or peaceful place.

The first reality is that North Viet-Nam has attacked the independent nation of South Viet-Nam. Its object is total conquest.

Of course, some of the people of South Viet-Nam are participating in attack on their own government. But trained men and supplies, orders and arms, flow in a constant stream from North to South.

This support is the heartbeat of the war.

And it is a war of unparalleled brutality. Simple farmers are the targets of assassination and kidnaping. Women and children are strangled in the night because their men are loyal to their government. And helpless villages are ravaged by sneak attacks. Large-scale raids are conducted on towns, and terror strikes in the heart of cities.

The confused nature of this conflict cannot mask the fact that it is the new face of an old enemy.

Over this war—and all Asia—is another reality: the deepening shadow of Communist China. The rulers in Hanoi are urged on by Peiping. This is a regime which has destroyed freedom in Tibet, which has attacked India, and has been condemned by the United Nations for aggression in Korea. It is a nation which is helping the forces of violence in almost every continent. The contest in Viet-Nam is part of a wider pattern of aggressive purposes.

WHY ARE WE IN SOUTH VIET-NAM?

Why are these realities our concern? Why are we in South Viet-Nam?

We are there because we have a promise to keep. Since 1954 every

American President has offered support to the people of South Viet-Nam. We have helped to build, and we have helped to defend. Thus, over many years, we have made a national pledge to help South Viet-Nam defend its independence.

And I intend to keep that promise.

To dishonor that pledge, to abandon this small and brave nation to its enemies, and to the terror that must follow, would be an unforgivable wrong.

We are also there to strengthen world order. Around the globe, from Berlin to Thailand, are people whose well-being rests in part on the belief that they can count on us if they are attacked. To leave Viet-Nam to its fate would shake the confidence of all these people in the value of an American commitment and in the value of America's word. The result would be increased unrest and instability, and even wider war.

We are also there because there are great stakes in the balance. Let no one think for a moment that retreat from Viet-Nam would bring an end to conflict. The battle would be renewed in one country and then another. The central lesson of our time is that the appetite of aggression is never satisfied. To withdraw from one battlefield means only to prepare for the next. We must say in Southeast Asia—as we did in Europe—in the words of the Bible: "Hitherto shalt thou come, but no further."

There are those who say that all our efforts there will be futile—that China's power is such that it is bound to dominate all Southeast Asia. But there is no end to that argument until all of the nations of Asia are swallowed up.

There are those who wonder why we have a responsibility there. Well, we have it there for the same reason that we have a responsibility for the defense of Europe. World War II was fought in both Europe and Asia, and when it ended we found ourselves with continued responsibility for the defense of freedom.

Our objective is the independence of South Viet-Nam and its freedom from attack. We want nothing for ourselves—only that the people of South Viet-Nam be allowed to guide their own country in their own way.

We will do everything necessary to reach that objective, and we will do only what is absolutely necessary.

In recent months attacks on South Viet-Nam were stepped up. Thus it became necessary for us to increase our response and to make attacks by air. This is not a change of purpose. It is a change in what we believe that purpose requires.

We do this in order to slow down aggression.

We do this to increase the confidence of the brave people of South Viet-Nam who have bravely borne this brutal battle for so many years with so many casualties.

And we do this to convince the leaders of North Viet-Nam—and all who seek to share their conquest—of a simple fact:

We will not be defeated.

We will not grow tired.

We will not withdraw, either openly or under the cloak of a meaningless agreement.

We know that air attacks alone will not accomplish all of these purposes. But it is our best and prayerful judgment that they are a necessary part of the surest road to peace.

THE PATH OF PEACEFUL SETTLEMENT

We hope that peace will come swiftly. But that is in the hands of others besides ourselves. And we must be prepared for a long continued conflict. It will require patience as well as bravery—the will to endure as well as the will to resist.

I wish it were possible to convince others with words of what we now find it necessary to say with guns and planes: armed hostility is futile —our resources are equal to any challenge—because we fight for values and we fight for principle, rather than territory or colonies, our patience and our determination are unending.

Once this is clear, then it should also be clear that the only path for reasonable men is the path of peaceful settlement.

Such peace demands an independent South Viet-Nam—securely guaranteed and able to shape its own relationships to all others—free from outside interference—tied to no alliance—a military base for no other country.

These are the essentials of any final settlement.

We will never be second in the search for such a peaceful settlement in Viet-Nam.

There may be many ways to this kind of peace: in discussion or negotiation with the governments concerned; in large groups or in small ones; in the reaffirmation of old agreements or their strengthening with new ones.

We have stated this position over and over again 50 times and more to friend and foe alike. And we remain ready with this purpose for unconditional discussions.

And until that bright and necessary day of peace we will try to keep conflict from spreading. We have no desire to see thousands die in battle —Asians or Americans. We have no desire to devastate that which the people of North Viet-Nam have built with toil and sacrifice. We will use our power with restraint and with all the wisdom that we can command.

But we will use it.

A COOPERATIVE EFFORT FOR DEVELOPMENT

This war, like most wars, is filled with terrible irony. For what do the people of North Viet-Nam want? They want what their neighbors also desire—food for their hunger, health for their bodies, a chance to learn, progress for their country, and an end to the bondage of material misery. And they would find all these things far more readily in peaceful association with others than in the endless course of battle.

These countries of Southeast Asia are homes for millions of impoverished people. Each day these people rise at dawn and struggle through until the night to wrest existence from the soil. They are often wracked by diseases, plagued by hunger, and death comes at the early age of 40.

Stability and peace do not come easily in such a land. Neither independence nor human dignity will ever be won though by arms alone. It also requires the works of peace. The American people have helped generously in times past in these works, and now there must be a much more massive effort to improve the life of man in that conflict-torn corner of our world.

The first step is for the countries of Southeast Asia to associate themselves in a greatly expanded cooperative effort for development. We would hope that North Viet-Nam would take its place in the common effort just as soon as peaceful cooperation is possible.

The United Nations is already actively engaged in development in this area, and as far back as 1961 I conferred with our authorities in Viet-Nam in connection with their work there. And I would hope tonight that the Secretary-General of the United Nations could use the prestige of his great office and his deep knowledge of Asia to initiate, as soon as possible, with the countries of that area, a plan for cooperation in increased development.

For our part I will ask the Congress to join in a billion-dollar American investment in this effort as soon as it is underway.

And I would hope that all other industrialized countries, including the Soviet Union, will join in this effort to replace despair with hope and terror with progress.

The task is nothing less than to enrich the hopes and existence of more than a hundred million people. And there is much to be done.

The vast Mekong River can provide food and water and power on a scale to dwarf even our own TVA. The wonders of modern medicine can be spread through villages where thousands die every year from lack of care. Schools can be established to train people in the skills needed to manage the process of development. And these objectives, and more, are within the reach of a cooperative and determined effort.

I also intend to expand and speed up a program to make available our farm surpluses to assist in feeding and clothing the needy in Asia.

We should not allow people to go hungry and wear rags while our own warehouses overflow with an abundance of wheat and corn and rice and cotton.

So I will very shortly name a special team of outstanding, patriotic, and distinguished Americans to inaugurate our participation in these programs. This team will be headed by Mr. Eugene Black, the very able former President of the World Bank.

THE DREAM OF OUR GENERATION

This will be a disorderly planet for a long time. In Asia, and elsewhere, the forces of the modern world are shaking old ways and uprooting ancient civilizations. There will be turbulence and struggle and even violence. Great social change—as we see in our own country—does not always come without conflict.

We must also expect that nations will on occasion be in dispute with us. It may be because we are rich, or powerful, or because we have made some mistakes, or because they honestly fear our intentions. However, no nation need ever fear that we desire their land, or to impose our will, or to dictate their institutions.

But we will always oppose the effort of one nation to conquer another nation.

We will do this because our own security is at stake.

But there is more to it than that. For our generation has a dream. It is a very old dream. But we have the power, and now we have the opportunity to make that dream come true.

For centuries nations have struggled among each other. But we dream of a world where disputes are settled by law and reason. And we will try to make it so.

For most of history men have hated and killed one another in battle. But we dream of an end to war. And we will try to make it so.

For all existence most men have lived in poverty, threatened by hunger. But we dream of a world where all are fed and charged with hope. And we will help to make it so.

The ordinary men and women of North Viet-Nam and South Viet-Nam, of China and India, of Russia and America, are brave people. They are filled with the same proportions of hate and fear, of love and hope. Most of them want the same things for themselves and their families. Most of them do not want their sons to ever die in battle, or to see their homes, or the homes of others, destroyed.

Well, this can be their world yet. Man now has the knowledge—always before denied—to make this planet serve the real needs of the people who live on it.

I know this will not be easy. I know how difficult it is for reason to guide passion, and love to master hate. The complexities of this world do not bow easily to pure and consistent answers.

But the simple truths are there just the same. We must all try to follow them as best we can.

POWER, WITNESS TO HUMAN FOLLY

We often say how impressive power is. But I do not find it impressive at all. The guns and the bombs, the rockets and the warships, are all symbols of human failure. They are necessary symbols. They protect what we cherish. But they are witness to human folly.

A dam built across a great river is impressive.

In the countryside where I was born, and where I live, I have seen the night illuminated, and the kitchen warmed, and the home heated, where once the cheerless night and the ceaseless cold held sway. And all this happened because electricity came to our area along the humming wires of the REA. Electrification of the countryside—yes, that, too, is impressive.

A rich harvest in a hungry land is impressive.

The sight of healthy children in a classroom is impressive.

These—not mighty arms—are the achievements which the American nation believes to be impressive.

And if we are steadfast, the time may come when all other nations will also find it so.

Every night before I turn out the lights to sleep I ask myself this question: Have I done everything that I can do to unite this country? Have I done everything I can to help unite the world, to try to bring peace and hope to all the peoples of the world? Have I done enough?

Ask yourselves that question in your homes—and in this hall tonight. Have we, each of us, all done all we can do? Have we done enough?

We may well be living in the time foretold many years ago when it was said: "I call heaven and earth to record this day against you, that I have set before you life and death, blessing and cursing: therefore choose life, that both thou and thy seed may live."

This generation of the world must choose: destroy or build, kill or aid, hate or understand.

We can do all these things on a scale that has never been dreamed of before.

Well, we will choose life. And so doing, we will prevail over the enemies within man, and over the natural enemies of all mankind.

81

The Four-Point Stand of the Government of the Democratic Republic of Vietnam

April 8, 1965

In April, 1965, when most of the territory of South Vietnam seemed to be under the control of the Viet Cong, the North Vietnamese government announced its proposals for a peaceful settlement of the conflict. The Hanoi regime was apparently confident of a Communist victory and was in no mood for a compromise peace.

It is the unswerving policy of the Government of the Democratic Republic of Vietnam to strictly respect the 1954 Geneva agreements on Vietnam, and to correctly implement their basic provisions as embodied in the following points:

1. Reaffirmation of the basic national rights of the Vietnamese people: peace, independence, sovereignty, unity and territorial integrity. In accordance with the Geneva agreements, the U.S. Government must withdraw all U.S. troops, military personnel and weapons of all kinds from south Vietnam, dismantle all U.S. military bases there, cancel its "military alliance" with south Vietnam. The U.S. Government must end its policy of intervention and aggression in south Vietnam. In accordance with the Geneva agreements, the U.S. Government must stop its acts of war against north Vietnam, cease all encroachments on the territory and sovereignty of the Democratic Republic of Vietnam.

2. Pending the peaceful reunification of Vietnam, while Vietnam is still temporarily divided into two zones, the military provisions of the 1954 Geneva agreements on Vietnam must be strictly respected: the two zones must refrain from joining any military alliance with foreign countries, and there must be no foreign military bases, troops and military personnel on their respective territory.

3. The internal affairs of south Vietnam must be settled by the

From the Report of Premier Pham Van Dong at the session of the National Assembly of the Democratic Republic of Vietnam on April 8, 1965, as printed in *Peking Review*, Vol. IX, No. 6 (February 4, 1966), p. 8.

people of south Vietnam themselves, in accordance with the programme of the South Vietnam National Front for Liberation without any foreign interference.

4. The peaceful reunification of Vietnam is to be settled by the Vietnamese people in both zones, without any foreign interference.

This stand unquestionably enjoys the approval and support of all peace- and justice-loving governments and peoples in the world.

The Government of the Democratic Republic of Vietnam is of the view that the above-expounded stand is the basis for the soundest political settlement of the Vietnam problem. If this basis is recognized, favourable conditions will be created for the peaceful settlement of the Vietnam problem and it will be possible to consider the reconvening of an international conference along the pattern of the 1954 Geneva Conference on Vietnam.

The Government of the Democratic Republic of Vietnam declares that any approach contrary to the above-mentioned stand is inappropriate; any approach tending to secure a U.N. intervention in the Vietnam situation is also inappropriate because such approaches are basically at variance with the 1954 Geneva agreements on Vietnam.

82

Republican Reaction to the Johnson Administration's Handling of the Vietnam War

> The Republicans supported a strong stand in Vietnam, but they could not resist the temptation to lay some of the blame for the unhappy events in Indochina on the Democrats, as is shown in this excerpt from their white paper on Vietnam.

The administration of Lyndon Johnson has greatly increased the involvement of American military forces, raising the number of troops from 16,000 to 125,000 with further increases anticipated. In February of 1965, it began bombing targets in North Vietnam. In spite of protestations to the contrary, it is changing the nature of American participation

From House of Representatives, Republican Conference, Committee on Planning and Research, *Vietnam: Some Neglected Aspects of the Historical Record* (August 25, 1965), pp. 18–22.

in the war by committing substantial numbers of American troop units to ground combat with the Vietcong.

At the same time, the Johnson administration has taken extraordinary steps to bring about negotiations to end the fighting. It has announced its willingness to enter unconditional negotiations. It suspended bombing of North Vietnam for 6 days. It has blessed the efforts of other nations and of public and private intermediaries to bring about a conference to discuss peace. It has offered "a billion dollar American investment" for the regional development of southeast Asia including the development of the Mekong River—a plan similar to one proposed by the Eisenhower administration 10 years ago.

DEESCALATION OF THE OBJECTIVE OF THE UNITED STATES

As the military effort of the United States in Vietnam has burgeoned, the pronouncements of President Johnson defining the objective of the United States have been progressively watered down.

On December 31, 1963, the President, in a letter to Gen. Duong Van Minh, said the objective was "achieving victory." On July 28, 1965, the President said "our goal . . . [is] . . . to convince the Communists that we cannot be defeated by force of arms."

In more specific terms, the President on April 20, 1964, expressed willingness to accept "any settlement which assures the independence of South Vietnam and its freedom to seek help for its protection." His speech of April 7, 1965, at Johns Hopkins University seemed to discard the freedom of South Vietnam to seek help for its protection, for on that occasion the President defined the objective in contradictory terms as "an independent South Vietnam—securely guaranteed and able to shape its own relationships to all others—free from outside interference—tied to no alliance—a military base for no other country." Clearly South Vietnam would not have freedom to shape its relationship to other countries if it were barred from ties with alliances or from providing a military base to another country. Experience suggests that without an ally South Vietnam would not be securely guaranteed.

Finally, on July 28, 1965, the President seemed to discard the independence of South Vietnam as an objective. Declaring that the "purposes" of the 1954 Geneva agreements "are still our own," he asserted that "the people of South Vietnam shall have the right to shape their own destiny in free elections—in the South or throughout all Vietnam under international supervision. . . ." This raises the disquieting possibility of accepting now in Vietnam the type of election which the United States rejected a decade ago—an election which, in the words of John F. Kennedy, would be "stacked and subverted in advance."

MISCALCULATION

The President now tells the Nation, "This is really war."

To what degree miscalculation on the part of the enemy has brought about this state of affairs, no one can be sure. It is clear, however, that many of the words and deeds of the past 4 years could only have encouraged underestimation of the constancy and firmness of the Nation in the pursuit of its foreign policy goals.

The whole handling of the problem of Laos could have no result other than the conclusion that the United States would not match its words with deeds.

The administration said that it would not permit aggression against Laos to succeed, but it did.

The administration said that it would not begin negotiating about Laos until a cease-fire had been put into effect, but it did.

The administration indicated that it would not accept a peace settlement in Laos which granted a veto to any member of the Commission established to supervise the peace, but it did.

Miscalculation was the natural result of the withdrawal of American backing for the Diem government. For the United States had pledged its support to Diem "all the way," in Lyndon Johnson's phrase in 1961. Abrupt reversal of policy leading to the overthrow of the leader whom the Government of the United States had been ardently supporting and whose downfall was a major Vietcong objective could appear only as evidence of weakening of the resolve of this Nation. Whether the error was the commitment to support Diem "all the way" or connivance in Diem's downfall, the net effect was to cast doubt on the value and durability of a pledge of support by the United States.

Miscalculation was encouraged by President Johnson's campaign oratory of 1964. In order to make his opponent appear reckless and trigger happy, the President in several statements set limits to American participation in the Vietnamese conflict which were to be exceeded after the election. For example, on August 12, 1964, he said:

"Some others are eager to enlarge the conflict. They call upon us to supply American boys to do the job that Asian boys should do."

Again, on August 29, the President declared:

"I have had advice to load our planes with bombs and to drop them on certain areas that I think would enlarge the war, and result in our committing a good many American boys to fighting a war that I think ought to be fought by the boys of Asia to help protect their own land. And for that reason, I haven't chosen to enlarge the war."

In Hanoi and Peiping all this could be interpreted only as an assurance that they need not fear fuller use of the power of the United States in Vietnam beyond the type of assistance provided to the South Vietnamese in the summer of 1964.

"Perhaps," Secretary Rusk was quoted in *The New York Times* as saying, "the Communist world misunderstood our Presidential campaign." [1] Perhaps, indeed, it did. But whose fault was that?

Miscalculation is encouraged by threats that are not followed up by appropriate action.

Such was the case when President Johnson on February 21, 1964, said, "Those engaged in external direction and supply [in Vietnam] would do well to remember that this type of aggression is a deeply dangerous game." This remark was advertised as a major foreign policy declaration by White House aides who called the words "dangerous game" highly significant. The impression was given to the press that the President was suggesting a strike at North Vietnam. But nothing happened. The Communists did not slow down, and the administration did nothing to demonstrate the danger in their game.

In June of 1964, at Honolulu, Secretary Rusk asked newsmen to report that the U.S. commitment to Vietnam was unlimited, comparable with West Berlin. President Johnson declared, "If a nation is to keep its freedom, it must be prepared to risk war. When necessary, we will take that risk." These threats were followed up by the campaign oratory which set limits to the American commitment by appearing to rule out action against North Vietnam and any extension of the American role in combat.

LACK OF CANDOR ON THE PART OF THE ADMINISTRATION

Miscalculation is encouraged—and the American people are confused —when the administration glosses over a messy situation with optimistic pronouncements and predictions.

Consider such statements as the following:

Lyndon B. Johnson: "We do not have [a problem in] Laos." (Feb. 11, 1964.)

Robert S. McNamara:

"Actions taken there have proved effective and will prove more effective as time goes on." (Jan. 17, 1962.)

"Progress in the last 8 to 10 weeks has been great. . . . The Government has asked only for logistical support. . . . Nothing but progress and hopeful indications of further progress in the future." (May 12, 1962.)

"Our military assistance to Vietnam is paying off. I continue to be

[1] Henry F. Graff, "How Johnson Makes Foreign Policy," *The New York Times Magazine*, July 4, 1965, p. 16.

encouraged. There are many signs indicating progress." (July 25, 1962.)

"There is a new feeling of confidence that victory is possible in South Vietnam." (Jan. 31, 1963.)

"The major part of the U.S. military task can be completed by the end of 1965, although there may be continuing requirement for a limited number of U.S. training personnel." (Oct. 2, 1963.)

"We have every reason to believe that [U.S. military] plans will be successful in 1964." (Dec. 12, 1963.)

"With these further measures, we felt that a start could be made in reducing the number of U.S. military personnel in Vietnam as their training missions were completed. Accordingly, we announced that about 1,000 men were to be withdrawn by the end of 1963, and expressed the hope that the major part of the U.S. military task could be completed by the end of 1965, although we recognized that there might be a continuing requirement for a limited number of U.S. advisory personnel." (Jan. 30, 1964.)

"We are confident these plans point the way to victory." (March 1964.) [2]

It would be tedious to detail the facts that showed how remote each of these pronouncements was from grim reality. One example will suffice. Secretary Rusk declared in the course of a visit to Vietnam on April 20, 1964, that things were showing "steady improvement." The headline in *The New York Times* 2 days later read, "Reds inflict heaviest toll on South Vietnam Army." It had been the bloodiest week of the war, the Times reported, with 1,000 Vietnamese Government and 23 American casualties.

Now once again, the public is being told by the White House that there is reason for "cautious optimism."

Neither the Congress nor the public is being accurately and fully informed about the Nation's involvement in Vietnam. American military personnel were called advisers long after they became combatants. Today their "primary mission," the Nation is told, "is to secure and safeguard important installations like the airbase at Da Nang. . . ." [3]

The President announced on July 28 that the stationing of 125,000 American troops in Vietnam did "not imply any change in policy whatever."

Yet, Secretary McNamara testified on August 4, 1965, "The principal role of U.S. ground combat forces will be to supplement this reserve [of the South Vietnamese Army] in support of the frontline forces of the South Vietnamese Army."

[2] McNamara's statements were reported in *The New York Times* on the dates indicated.
[3] White House statement, Background, p. 230.

The able Saigon correspondent of the Los Angeles Times, Jack Foisie, has written:

"Although the decision to commit large-scale American combat units in Vietnam is apparent, and is obvious to the enemy through the buildup of logistical bases on the central coast, authorities in Washington try to pretend that we really are not committed to land warfare in Asia, to casualties as large or larger than suffered during the Korean war." [4]

As the military effort of the United States was stepped up, adequate funds for its support were not requested of the Congress. Now an attempt to hide the cost is made by asking for added funds in two installments—one now, the other in January of 1966.

The figures that are fed to the press and the public by the administration contradict each other and surpass belief. In June of 1965, Secretary Rusk gave a figure for South Vietnamese casualties since 1960 that was 50 per cent higher than the figure General Wheeler gave 1 month earlier.[5] It is hard to believe that casualties in 1 month in 1965 increased so dramatically. It is hard, too, to accept estimates of Vietcong combat deaths which indicate that 20 to 25 per cent of the estimated Vietcong military strength was wiped out in each of 2 successive recent years.

The astute correspondent of the Washington Post, Howard Margolis, after surveying casualty figures released by the administration, concludes:

"The impression all this leaves is that the publicly released statistics are more a selection of numbers intended to paint a picture that supports whatever the official view is at the moment than a realistic indication of how things are going." [6]

The greatest shortage which the Vietnamese war has so far produced is a shortage of candor and accuracy.

The Nation, by the President's admission, is now engaged in a war. All Americans must support whatever action is needed to put a stop to Communist aggression and to make safe the freedom and independence of South Vietnam.

Criticism of administration actions, when well-founded, is not inconsistent with support of this objective nor of the methods needed to attain it. Indeed, such criticism can help in the attainment of the Nation's objective without unnecessary loss or delay.

[4] *Los Angeles Times*, July 25, 1965.

[5] Rusk speech, American Foreign Service Association, Washington, D.C., June 23, 1965—"From 1961 to the present . . . South Vietnamese armed forces have lost some 25,000 dead and 51,000 wounded." Wheeler speech, San Francisco, May 7, 1965, "More than 50,000 South Vietnamese soldiers have been killed or wounded in battle since 1960."

[6] *Washington Post*, Aug. 16, 1965.

83

Fourteen Points for Peace in Southeast Asia

January 7, 1966

United States State Department

During the Christmas truce and a suspension of bombing raids on North Vietnam, the State Department issued the following peace proposals.

The following statements are on the public record about elements which the U.S. believes can go into peace in Southeast Asia:

1. The Geneva Agreements of 1954 and 1962 are an adequate basis for peace in Southeast Asia;

2. We would welcome a conference on Southeast Asia or on any part thereof;

3. We would welcome "negotiations without preconditions" as the 17 nations put it;

4. We would welcome unconditional discussions as President Johnson put it;

5. A cessation of hostilities could be the first order of business at a conference or could be the subject of preliminary discussions;

6. Hanoi's four points could be discussed along with other points which others might propose;

7. We want no U.S. bases in Southeast Asia;

8. We do not desire to retain U.S. troops in South Viet Nam after peace is assured;

9. We support free elections in South Viet Nam to give the South Vietnamese a government of their own choice;

10. The question of the reunification of Viet Nam should be determined by the Vietnamese through their own free decision;

11. The countries of Southeast Asia can be non-aligned or neutral if that is their option;

12. We would much prefer to use our resources for the economic reconstruction of Southeast Asia than in war. If there is peace, North

Press release, as printed in United States Department of State, *Viet-Nam: The 38th Day* (Washington, D.C.: Government Printing Office, 1966), p. 5.

Viet Nam could participate in a regional effort to which we would be prepared to contribute at least one billion dollars;

13. The President has said, "The Viet Cong would not have difficulty being represented and having their views represented if for a moment Hanoi decided she wanted to cease aggression. I don't think that would be an insurmountable problem."

14. We have said publicly and privately that we could stop the bombing of North Viet Nam as a step toward peace although there has not been the slightest hint or suggestion from the other side as to what they would do if the bombing stopped.

84

Senators' Report on Vietnam

January 7, 1966

In January, 1966, neither peace nor victory was in prospect for the foreseeable future, according to this gloomy report to the Senate Foreign Relations Committee by five Senators recently returned from Southeast Asia. Only the conclusion of the report is given here.

A rapid solution to the conflict in Viet Nam is not in immediate prospect. This would appear to be the case whether military victory is pursued or negotiations do, in fact, materialize.

Insofar as the military situation is concerned, the large-scale introduction of U.S. forces and their entry into combat has blunted but not turned back the drive of the Viet Cong. The latter have responded to the increased American role with a further strengthening of their forces by local recruitment in the South and reinforcements from the North and a general stepping up of military activity.

As a result the lines remain drawn in South Viet Nam in substantially the same pattern as they were at the outset of the increased U.S. commitment. What has changed basically is the scope and intensity of the struggle and the part which is being played by the forces of the United States and those of North Viet Nam.

The Senators were Mike Mansfield (Democrat, Montana), Edmund S. Muskie (Democrat, Maine), Daniel K. Inouye (Democrat, Hawaii), J. Caleb Boggs (Republican, Delaware), and George Aiken (Republican, Vermont).

Despite the great increase in American military commitment, it is doubtful in view of the acceleration of Viet Cong efforts that the constricted position now held in Viet Nam by the Saigon government can continue to be held for the indefinite future, let alone extended, without a further augmentation of American forces on the ground.

Indeed, if present trends continue, there is no assurance as to what ultimate increase in American military commitment will be required before the conflict is terminated. For the fact is that under present terms of reference and as the war has evolved, the question is not one of applying increased U.S. pressure to a defined military situation but rather of pressing against a military situation which is, in effect, openended. How open is dependent on the extent to which North Viet Nam and its supporters are willing and able to meet increased force by increased force.

All of mainland Southeast Asia, at least, cannot be ruled out as a potential battlefield. As noted, the war has already expanded significantly into Laos and is beginning to lap over the Cambodian border while pressure increased in the northeast of Thailand.

Even if the war remains substantially within its present limits, there is little foundation for the expectation that the government of Viet Nam in Saigon will be able, in the near future, to carry a much greater burden than it is now carrying.

This is in no sense a reflection on the caliber of the current leaders of Viet Nam. But the fact is that they are, as other Vietnamese governments have been over the past decade, at the beginning of a beginning in dealing with the problems of popular mobilization in support of the government.

They are starting, moreover, from a point considerably behind that which prevailed at the time of President (Ngo Dinh) Diem's assassination. Under present concepts and plans, then, what lies ahead is, literally, a vast and continuing undertaking in social engineering in the wake of such military progress as may be registered. And for many years to come this task will be very heavily dependent on U.S. foreign aid.

The basic concept of present American policy with respect to Viet Nam casts the United States in the role of support of the Vietnamese government and people. This concept becomes more difficult to maintain as the military participation of the United States undergoes rapid increase. Yet a change in the basic concept could have a most unfortunate impact upon the Vietnamese people and the world at large.

What is involved here is the necessity for the greatest restraint in word and action, lest the concept be eroded and the war drained of a purpose with meaning in the concept of Viet Nam.

This danger is great, not only because of the military realities of the situation but also because, with a few exceptions, assistance has not been and is not likely to be forthcoming for the war effort in South Viet Nam from nations other than the United States. On the contrary, as it now appears, the longer the war continues in its present pattern and the more expands in scope, the greater will become the strain placed upon the relations of the United States with allies both in the Far East and in Europe.

Many nations are deeply desirous of an end to this conflict as quickly as possible. Few are specific as to the manner in which this end can be brought about or the shape it is likely to take.

In any event, even though other nations, in certain circumstances, may be willing to play a third-party role in bringing about negotiations, any prospects for effective negotiations at this time—and they are slim—are likely to be largely dependent on the initiatives and efforts of the combatants.

Negotiations at this time, moreover, if they do come about, and if they are accompanied by a cease-fire and standfast, would serve to stabilize a situation in which the majority of the population remains under nominal government control but in which dominance of the countryside rests largely in the hands of the Viet Cong. What might eventually materialize through negotiations from this situation cannot be foreseen at this time with any degree of certainty.

That is not, to say the least, a very satisfactory prospect. What needs also to be borne in mind, however, is that the visible alternative at this time and under present terms of reference is the indefinite expansion and intensification of the war which will require the continuous introduction of additional U.S. forces.

The end of that course cannot be foreseen, either, and there are no grounds for optimism that the end is likely to be reached within the confines of South Viet Nam or within the very near future.

In short, such choices as may be open are not simply choices. They are difficult and painful choices and they are beset with many imponderables. The situation, as it now appears, offers only the very slim prospects of a just settlement by negotiations or the alternative prospect of a continuance of the conflict in the direction of a general war on the Asian mainland.

SUGGESTED READING

Bone, Robert C. *Contemporary Southeast Asia*. New York: Random House, 1962, paperback.

Burchett, Wilfred G. *Vietnam: Inside Story of the Guerilla War*, 2nd ed. New York: International Publishers, 1965, paperback.

Burchett, Wilfred G. *Vietnam North: A First-Hand Report*. New York: International Publishers, 1966, paperback.

Butwell, Richard. *Southeast Asia Today—And Tomorrow: A Political Analysis*, rev. ed. New York: Frederick A. Praeger, 1964, paperback.

Cole, Allen B., ed. *Conflict in Indo-China and International Repercussions: A Documentary History 1945–1955*. Ithaca: Cornell University Press, 1956.

Du Berrier, Hilaire. *Background to Betrayal: The Tragedy of Vietnam*. Boston: Western Islands, 1965, paperback.

Elsbree, Willard H. *Japan's Role in Southeast Asian Nationalist Movements*. Cambridge: Harvard University Press, 1953.

Emerson, Rupert. *From Empire to Nation: The Rise to Self-Assertion of Asian and African Peoples*. Cambridge: Harvard University Press, 1960.

Fall, Bernard. *Hell in a Very Small Place: The Siege of Dien Bien Phu*. Philadelphia: Lippincott, 1967.

Fall, Bernard. *The Two Viet-Nams: A Political and Military Analysis*, rev. ed. New York: Frederick A. Praeger, 1964.

Fall, Bernard. *Viet-Nam Witness, 1953–1966*. New York: Frederick A. Praeger, 1966.

Fifield, Russell H. *Southeast Asia in United States Policy*. New York: Frederick A. Praeger, 1963, paperback.

Fishel, Wesley R. *Vietnam: Is Victory Possible?* New York: The Foreign Policy Association, 1964, paperback.

Fulbright, J. William. *The Arrogance of Power*. New York: Random House, 1967.

Gettleman, Marvin E. *Vietnam: History, Documents, and Opinions on a Major World Crisis*. Greenwich, Conn.: Fawcett Publications, 1965, paperback.

Goodwin, Richard N. *Triumph or Tragedy: Reflections on Vietnam*. New York: Random House, 1966, paperback.

Halberstam, David. *The Making of a Quagmire*. New York: Random House, 1964.

Hall, G. D. H. *A History of Southeast Asia*, 2nd ed. New York: St. Martin's, 1963.

Hammer, Ellen J. *The Struggle for Indochina, 1940–1955: Viet Nam and the French Experience*. Stanford: Stanford University Press, 1966, paperback.

Hammer, Ellen J. *Vietnam: Yesterday and Today*. New York: Holt, Rinehart and Winston, 1966, paperback.

Harrison, Brian. *A Short History of South-East Asia*. New York: St. Martin's, 1954.

Honey, P. J. *Communism in North Vietnam*. Cambridge: M.I.T. Press, 1963.

Kahin, George McT., ed. *Governments and Politics of Southeast Asia*, 2nd ed. Ithaca: Cornell University Press, 1964.

Lacouture, Jean. *Vietnam: Between Two Truces*. New York: Vintage Books, 1966, paperback.

Peace in Vietnam: A New Approach in Southeast Asia, A Report Prepared for the American Friends Service Committee. New York: Hill and Wang, 1966, paperback.

Pike, Douglas. *Viet Cong: The Organization and Techniques of the National Liberation Front of South Vietnam*. Cambridge: M.I.T. Press, 1966.

Purcell, Victor. *The Chinese in Southeast Asia*. London: Oxford University Press, 1951.

Pye, Lucian W. *Guerrilla Communism in Malaya: Its Social and Political Meaning*. Princeton: Princeton University Press, 1954.

Raskin, Marcus G., and Fall, Bernard F., eds. *The Viet-Nam Reader: Articles and Documents on American Foreign Policy and the Viet-Nam Crisis*. New York: Vintage Books, paperback.

Roy, Jules. *The Battle of Dienbienphu*. New York: Pyramid Books, 1966, paperback.

Schlesinger, Arthur M., Jr. *The Bitter Heritage: Vietnam and American Democracy, 1941–1966*. Boston: Houghton Mifflin, 1967.

Scigliano, Robert. *South Vietnam: Nation under Stress*. Boston: Houghton Mifflin, 1963, paperback.

Trager, Frank N., ed. *Marxism in Southeast Asia*. Stanford: Stanford University Press, 1959.

Vandenbosch, Amry, and Butwell, Richard. *The Changing Face of Southeast Asia*. Lexington: University of Kentucky Press, 1966.

Vietnam: Why, 2d ed. New York: The Reporter, 1966.

von der Mehden, Fred R. *Religion and Nationalism in Southeast Asia: Burma, Indonesia, and the Philippines*. Madison: University of Wisconsin Press, 1963.

Warner, Denis. *The Last Confucian: Vietnam, Southeast Asia, and the West*. Baltimore: Penguin, 1964, paperback.

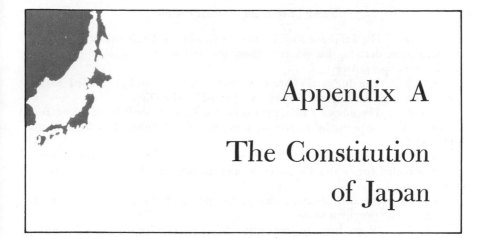

Appendix A

The Constitution

of Japan

We, the Japanese people, acting through our duly elected representatives in the National Diet, determined that we shall secure for ourselves and our posterity the fruits of peaceful cooperation with all nations and the blessings of liberty throughout this land, and resolved that never again shall we be visited with the horrors of war through the action of government, do proclaim that sovereign power resides with the people and do firmly establish this Constitution. Government is a sacred trust of the people, the authority for which is derived from the people, the powers of which are exercised by the representatives of the people, and the benefits of which are enjoyed by the people. This is a universal principle of mankind upon which this Constitution is founded. We reject and revoke all constitutions, laws, ordinances, and rescripts in conflict herewith.

We, the Japanese people, desire peace for all time and are deeply conscious of the high ideals controlling human relationship, and we have determined to preserve our security and existence, trusting in the justice and faith of the peace-loving peoples of the world. We desire to occupy an honored place in an international society striving for the preservation of peace, and the banishment of tyranny and slavery, oppression and intolerance for all time from the earth. We recognize that all peoples of the world have the right to live in peace, free from fear and want.

We believe that no nation is responsible to itself alone, but that laws of political morality are universal; and that obedience to such laws is incumbent upon all nations who would sustain their own sovereignty and justify their sovereign relationship with other nations.

We, the Japanese people, pledge our national honor to accomplish these high ideals and purposes with all our resources.

Effective May 3, 1947. Text as given in Supreme Commander for the Allied Powers, Government Section, *Political Reorientation of Japan: September 1945 to September 1948* (Washington, D.C.: Government Printing Office, n.d.), II, 671–677.

CHAPTER I. THE EMPEROR

Article 1. The Emperor shall be the symbol of the State and of the unity of the people, deriving his position from the will of the people with whom resides sovereign power.

Article 2. The Imperial Throne shall be dynastic and succeeded to in accordance with the Imperial House Law passed by the Diet.

Article 3. The advice and approval of the Cabinet shall be required for all acts of the Emperor in matters of state, and the Cabinet shall be responsible therefor.

Article 4. The Emperor shall perform only such acts in matters of state as are provided for in this Constitution and he shall not have powers related to government.

The Emperor may delegate the performance of his acts in matters of state as may be provided by law.

Article 5. When, in accordance with the Imperial House Law, a Regency is established, the Regent shall perform his acts in matters of state in the Emperor's name. In this case, paragraph one of the preceding article will be applicable.

Article 6. The Emperor shall appoint the Prime Minister as designated by the Diet.

The Emperor shall appoint the Chief Judge of the Supreme Court as designated by the Cabinet.

Article 7. The Emperor, with the advice and approval of the Cabinet, shall perform the following acts in matters of state on behalf of the people:

Promulgation of amendments of the constitution, laws, cabinet orders and treaties.

Convocation of the Diet.

Dissolution of the House of Representatives.

Proclamation of general election of members of the Diet.

Attestation of the appointment and dismissal of Ministers of State and other officials as provided for by law, and of full powers and credentials of Ambassadors and Ministers.

Attestation of general and special amnesty, commutation of punishment, reprieve, and restoration of rights.

Awarding of honors.

Attestation of instruments of ratification and other diplomatic documents as provided for by law.

Receiving foreign ambassadors and ministers.

Performance of ceremonial functions.

Article 8. No property can be given to, or received by, the Imperial House, nor can any gifts be made therefrom, without the authorization of the Diet.

CHAPTER II. RENUNCIATION OF WAR

Article 9. Aspiring sincerely to an international peace based on justice and order, the Japanese people forever renounce war as a sovereign right of the nation and the threat or use of force as means of settling international disputes.

In order to accomplish the aim of the preceding paragraph, land, sea, and air forces, as well as other war potential, will never be maintained. The right of belligerency of the state will not be recognized.

CHAPTER III. RIGHTS AND DUTIES OF THE PEOPLE

Article 10. The conditions necessary for being a Japanese national shall be determined by law.

Article 11. The people shall not be prevented from enjoying any of the fundamental human rights. These fundamental human rights guaranteed to the people by this Constitution shall be conferred upon the people of this and future generations as eternal and inviolate rights.

Article 12. The freedoms and rights guaranteed to the people by this Constitution shall be maintained by the constant endeavor of the people, who shall refrain from any abuse of these freedoms and rights and shall always be responsible for utilizing them for the public welfare.

Article 13. All of the people shall be respected as individuals. Their right to life, liberty, and the pursuit of happiness shall, to the extent that it does not interfere with the public welfare, be the supreme consideration in legislation and in other governmental affairs.

Article 14. All of the people are equal under the law and there shall be no discrimination in political, economic or social relations because of race, creed, sex, social status or family origin.

Peers and peerage shall not be recognized.

No privilege shall accompany any award of honor, decoration or any distinction, nor shall any such award be valid beyond the lifetime of the individual who now holds or hereafter may receive it.

Article 15. The people have the inalienable right to choose their public officials and to dismiss them.

All public officials are servants of the whole community and not of any group thereof.

Universal adult suffrage is guaranteed with regard to the election of public officials.

In all elections, secrecy of the ballot shall not be violated. A voter shall not be answerable, publicly or privately, for the choice he has made.

Article 16. Every person shall have the right of peaceful petition for the redress of damage, for the removal of public officials, for the enactment, repeal or amendment of laws, ordinances or regulations and for other matters; nor shall any person be in any way discriminated against for sponsoring such a petition.

Article 17. Every person may sue for redress as provided by law from the State or a public entity, in case he has suffered damage through illegal act of any public official.

Article 18. No person shall be held in bondage of any kind. Involuntary servitude, except as punishment for crime, is prohibited.

Article 19. Freedom of thought and conscience shall not be violated.

Article 20. Freedom of religion is guaranteed to all. No religious organization shall receive any privileges from the State, nor exercise any political authority.

No person shall be compelled to take part in any religious act, celebration, rite or practice.

The State and its organs shall refrain from religious education or any other religious activity.

Article 21. Freedom of assembly and association as well as speech, press and all other forms of expression are guaranteed.

No censorship shall be maintained, nor shall the secrecy of any means of communication be violated.

Article 22. Every person shall have freedom to choose and change his residence and to choose his occupation to the extent that it does not interfere with the public welfare.

Freedom of all persons to move to a foreign country and to divest themselves of their nationality shall be inviolate.

Article 23. Academic freedom is guaranteed.

Article 24. Marriage shall be based only on the mutual consent of both sexes and it shall be maintained through mutual cooperation with the equal rights of husband and wife as a basis.

With regard to choice of spouse, property rights, inheritance, choice of domicile, divorce and other matters pertaining to marriage and the family, laws shall be enacted from the standpoint of individual dignity and the essential equality of the sexes.

Article 25. All people shall have the right to maintain the minimum standards of wholesome and cultured living.

In all spheres of life, the State shall use its endeavors for the promotion and extension of social welfare and security, and of public health.

Article 26. All people shall have the right to receive an equal education correspondent to their ability, as provided by law.

All people shall be obligated to have all boys and girls under their protection receive ordinary education as provided for by law. Such compulsory education shall be free.

Article 27. All people shall have the right and the obligation to work.

Standards for wages, hours, rest and other working conditions shall be fixed by law.

Children shall not be exploited.

Article 28. The right of workers to organize and bargain and act collectively is guaranteed.

Article 29. The right to own or to hold property is inviolable.

Property rights shall be defined by law, in conformity with the public welfare.

Private property may be taken for public use upon just compensation therefor.

Article 30. The people shall be liable to taxation as provided by law.

Article 31. No person shall be deprived of life or liberty, nor shall any other criminal penalty be imposed, except according to procedure established by law.

Article 32. No person shall be denied the right of access to the courts.

Article 33. No person shall be apprehended except upon warrant issued by a competent judicial officer which specifies the offense with which the person is charged, unless he is apprehended, the offense being committed.

Article 34. No person shall be arrested or detained without being at once informed of the charges against him or without the immediate privilege of counsel; nor shall he be detained without adequate cause; and upon demand of any person such cause must be immediately shown in open court in his presence and the presence of his counsel.

Article 35. The right of all persons to be secure in their homes, papers and effects against entries, searches and seizures shall not be impaired except upon warrant issued for adequate cause and particularly describing the place to be searched and things to be seized, or except as provided by Article 33.

Each search or seizure shall be made upon separate warrant issued by a competent judicial officer.

Article 36. The infliction of torture by any public officer and cruel punishments are absolutely forbidden.

Article 37. In all criminal cases the accused shall enjoy the right to a speedy and public trial by an impartial tribunal.

He shall be permitted full opportunity to examine all witnesses, and he shall have the right of compulsory process for obtaining witnesses on his behalf at public expense.

At all times the accused shall have the assistance of competent counsel who shall, if the accused is unable to secure the same by his own efforts, be assigned to his use by the State.

Article 38. No person shall be compelled to testify against himself.

Confession made under compulsion, torture or threat, or after prolonged arrest or detention shall not be admitted in evidence.

No person shall be convicted or punished in cases where the only proof against him is his own confession.

Article 39. No person shall be held criminally liable for an act which was lawful at the time it was committed, or of which he has been acquitted, nor shall he be placed in double jeopardy.

Article 40. Any person, in case he is acquitted after he has been arrested or detained, may sue the State for redress as provided by law.

CHAPTER IV. THE DIET

Article 41. The Diet shall be the highest organ of state power, and shall be the sole law-making organ of the State.

Article 42. The Diet shall consist of two Houses, namely the House of Representatives and the House of Councillors.

Article 43. Both Houses shall consist of elected members, representative of all the people.

The number of the members of each House shall be fixed by law.

Article 44. The qualifications of members of both Houses and their electors shall be fixed by law. However, there shall be no discrimination because of race, creed, sex, social status, family origin, education, property or income.

Article 45. The term of office of members of the House of Representatives shall be four years. However, the term shall be terminated before the full term is up in case the House of Representatives is dissolved.

Article 46. The term of office of members of the House of Councillors shall be six years, and election for half the members shall take place every three years.

Article 47. Electoral districts, method of voting and other matters pertaining to the method of election of members of both Houses shall be fixed by law.

Article 48. No person shall be permitted to be a member of both Houses simultaneously.

Article 49. Members of both Houses shall receive appropriate annual payment from the national treasury in accordance with law.

Article 50. Except in cases provided by law, members of both Houses shall be exempt from apprehension while the Diet is in session, and any members apprehended before the opening of the session shall be freed during the term of the session upon demand of the House.

Article 51. Members of both Houses shall not be held liable outside the House for speeches, debates or votes cast inside the House.

Article 52. An ordinary session of the Diet shall be convoked once per year.

Article 53. The Cabinet may determine to convoke extraordinary sessions of the Diet. When a quarter or more of the total members of either House makes the demand, the Cabinet must determine on such convocation.

Article 54. When the House of Representatives is dissolved, there must be a general election of members of the House of Representatives within forty (40) days from the date of dissolution, and the Diet must be convoked within thirty (30) days from the date of the election.

When the House of Representatives is dissolved, the House of Councillors is closed at the same time. However, the Cabinet may in time of national emergency convoke the House of Councillors in emergency session.

Measures taken at such session as mentioned in the proviso of the preceding paragraph shall be provisional and shall become null and void unless agreed to by the House of Representatives within a period of ten (10) days after the opening of the next session of the Diet.

Article 55. Each House shall judge disputes related to qualifications of its members. However, in order to deny a seat to any member, it is necessary to pass a resolution by a majority of two-thirds or more of the members present.

Article 56. Business cannot be transacted in either House unless one-third or more of total membership is present.

All matters shall be decided, in each House, by a majority of those present, except as elsewhere provided in the Constitution, and in case of a tie, the presiding officer shall decide the issue.

Article 57. Deliberation in each House shall be public. However, a secret meeting may be held where a majority of two-thirds or more of those members present passes a resolution therefor.

Each House shall keep a record of proceedings. This record shall be published and given general circulation, excepting such parts of proceedings of secret session as may be deemed to require secrecy.

Upon demand of one-fifth or more of the members present, votes of the members on any matter shall be recorded in the minutes.

Article 58. Each House shall select its own president and other officials.

Each House shall establish its rules pertaining to meetings, proceedings and internal discipline, and may punish members for disorderly conduct. However, in order to expel a member, a majority of two-thirds or more of those members present must pass a resolution thereon.

Article 59. A bill becomes a law on passage by both Houses, except as otherwise provided by the Constitution.

A bill which is passed by the House of Representatives, and upon which the House of Councillors makes a decision different from that of the House of Representatives, becomes a law when passed a second time by the House of Representatives by a majority of two-thirds or more of the members present.

The provision of the preceding paragraph does not preclude the House of Representatives from calling for the meeting of a joint committee of both Houses, provided for by law.

Failure by the House of Councillors to take final action within sixty (60) days after receipt of a bill passed by the House of Representatives, time in recess excepted, may be determined by the House of Representatives to constitute a rejection of the said bill by the House of Councillors.

Article 60. The budget must first be submitted to the House of Representatives.

Upon consideration of the budget, when the House of Councillors makes a decision different from that of the House of Representatives, and when no agreement can be reached even through a joint committee of both Houses, provided for by law, or in the case of failure by the House of Councillors to take final action within thirty (30) days, the period of recess excluded, after the receipt of the budget passed by the House of Representatives, the decision of the House of Representatives shall be the decision of the Diet.

Article 61. The second paragraph of the preceding article applies also to the Diet approval required for the conclusion of treaties.

Article 62. Each House may conduct investigations in relation to government, and may demand the presence and testimony of witnesses, and the production of records.

Article 63. The Prime Minister and other Ministers of State may, at any time, appear in either House for the purpose of speaking on bills, regardless of whether they are members of the House or not. They must appear when their presence is required in order to give answers or explanations.

Article 64. The Diet shall set up an impeachment court from among the members of both Houses for the purpose of trying those judges against whom removal proceedings have been instituted.

Matters relating to impeachment shall be provided by law.

CHAPTER V. THE CABINET

Article 65. Executive power shall be vested in the Cabinet.

Article 66. The Cabinet shall consist of the Prime Minister, who shall be its head, and other Ministers of State, as provided for by law.

The Prime Minister and other Ministers of State must be civilians.

The Cabinet, in the exercise of executive power, shall be collectively responsible to the Diet.

Article 67. The Prime Minister shall be designated from among the members of the Diet by a resolution of the Diet. This designation shall precede all other business.

If the House of Representatives and the House of Councillors disagree and if no agreement can be reached even through a joint committee of both Houses, provided for by law, or the House of Councillors fails to make designation within ten (10) days, exclusive of the period of recess, after the House of Representatives has made designation, the decision of the House of Representatives shall be the decision of the Diet.

Article 68. The Prime Minister shall appoint the Ministers of State. However, a majority of their number must be chosen from among the members of the Diet.

The Prime Minister may remove the Ministers of State as he chooses.

Article 69. If the House of Representatives passes a non-confidence resolution, or rejects a confidence resolution, the Cabinet shall resign en masse, unless the House of Representatives is dissolved within ten (10) days.

Article 70. When there is a vacancy in the post of Prime Minister, or upon the first convocation of the Diet after a general election of members of the House of Representatives, the Cabinet shall resign en masse.

Article 71. In the cases mentioned in the two preceding articles, the Cabinet shall continue its functions until the time when a new Prime Minister is appointed.

Article 72. The Prime Minister, representing the Cabinet, submits bills, reports on general national affairs and foreign relations to the Diet and exercises control and supervision over various administrative branches.

Article 73. The Cabinet, in addition to other general administrative functions, shall perform the following functions:

Administer the law faithfully; conduct affairs of state.

Manage foreign affairs.

Conclude treaties. However, it shall obtain prior or, depending on circumstances, subsequent approval of the Diet.

Administer the civil service, in accordance with standards established by law.

Prepare the budget, and present it to the Diet.

Enact cabinet orders in order to execute the provisions of this Constitution and of the law. However, it cannot include penal provisions in such cabinet orders unless authorized by such law.

Decide on general amnesty, special amnesty, commutation of punishment, reprieve, and restoration of rights.

Article 74. All laws and cabinet orders shall be signed by the competent Minister of State and countersigned by the Prime Minister.

Article 75. The Ministers of State, during their tenure of office, shall not be subject to legal action without the consent of the Prime Minister. However, the right to take that action is not impaired hereby.

CHAPTER VI. JUDICIARY

Article 76. The whole judicial power is vested in a Supreme Court and in such inferior courts as are established by law.

No extraordinary tribunal shall be established, nor shall any organ or agency of the Executive be given final judicial power.

All judges shall be independent in the exercise of their conscience and shall be bound only by this Constitution and the laws.

Article 77. The Supreme Court is vested with the rule-making power under which it determines the rules of procedure and of practice, and of matters relating to attorneys, the internal discipline of the courts and the administration of judicial affairs.

Public procurators shall be subject to the rule-making power of the Supreme Court.

The Supreme Court may delegate the power to make rules for inferior courts to such courts.

Article 78. Judges shall not be removed except by public impeachment unless judicially declared mentally or physically incompetent to perform official duties. No disciplinary action against judges shall be administered by any executive organ or agency.

Article 79. The Supreme Court shall consist of a Chief Judge and such number of judges as may be determined by law; all such judges excepting the Chief Judge shall be appointed by the Cabinet.

The appointment of the judges of the Supreme Court shall be reviewed by the people at the first general election of members of the House of Representatives following their appointment, and shall be reviewed again at the first general election of members of the House of Representatives after a lapse of ten (10) years, and in the same manner thereafter.

In cases mentioned in the foregoing paragraph, when the majority of the voters favors the dismissal of a judge, he shall be dismissed.

Matters pertaining to review shall be prescribed by law.

The judges of the Supreme Court shall be retired upon the attainment of the age as fixed by law.

All such judges shall receive, at regular stated intervals, adequate compensation which shall not be decreased during their terms of office.

Article 80. The judges of the inferior courts shall be appointed by the Cabinet from a list of persons nominated by the Supreme Court. All such judges shall hold office for a term of ten (10) years with privilege of reappointment, provided that they shall be retired upon the attainment of the age as fixed by law.

The judges of the inferior courts shall receive, at regular stated intervals, adequate compensation which shall not be decreased during their terms of office.

Article 81. The Supreme Court is the court of last resort with power to determine the constitutionality of any law, order, regulation or official act.

Article 82. Trials shall be conducted and judgment declared publicly.

Where a court unanimously determines publicity to be dangerous to public order or morals, a trial may be conducted privately, but trials of political offenses, offenses involving the press or cases wherein the rights of people as guaranteed in Chapter III of this Constitution are in question shall always be conducted publicly.

CHAPTER VII. FINANCE

Article 83. The power to administer national finances shall be exercised as the Diet shall determine.

Article 84. No new taxes shall be imposed or existing ones modified except by law or under such conditions as law may prescribe.

Article 85. No money shall be expended, nor shall the State obligate itself, except as authorized by the Diet.

Article 86. The Cabinet shall prepare and submit to the Diet for its consideration and decision a budget for each fiscal year.

Article 87. In order to provide for unforeseen deficiencies in the budget, a reserve fund may be authorized by the Diet to be expended upon the responsibility of the Cabinet.

The Cabinet must get subsequent approval of the Diet for all payments from the reserve fund.

Article 88. All property of the Imperial Household shall belong to the State. All expenses of the Imperial Household shall be appropriated by the Diet in the budget.

Article 89. No public money or other property shall be expended or appropriated for the use, benefit or maintenance of any religious institution or association, or for any charitable, educational or benevolent enterprises not under the control of public authority.

Article 90. Final accounts of the expenditures and revenues of the State shall be audited annually by a Board of Audit and submitted by the Cabinet to the Diet, together with the statement of audit, during the fiscal year immediately following the period covered.

The organization and competency of the Board of Audit shall be determined by law.

Article 91. At regular intervals and at least annually the Cabinet shall report to the Diet and the people on the state of national finances.

CHAPTER VIII. LOCAL SELF-GOVERNMENT

Article 92. Regulations concerning organization and operations of local public entities shall be fixed by law in accordance with the principle of local autonomy.

Article 93. The local public entities shall establish assemblies as their deliberative organs, in accordance with law.

The chief executive officers of all local public entities, the members of their assemblies, and such other local officials as may be determined by law shall be elected by direct popular vote within their several communities.

Article 94. Local public entities shall have the right to manage their property, affairs and administration and to enact their own regulations within law.

Article 95. A special law, applicable only to one local public entity, cannot be enacted by the Diet without the consent of the majority of the local public entity concerned, obtained in accordance with law.

CHAPTER IX. AMENDMENTS

Article 96. Amendments to this Constitution shall be initiated by the Diet, through a concurring vote of two-thirds or more of all the members of each House and shall thereupon be submitted to the people for ratification, which shall require the affirmative vote of a majority of all votes cast thereon, at a special referendum or at such election as the Diet shall specify.

Amendments when so ratified shall immediately be promulgated by the Emperor in the name of the people, as an integral part of this Constitution.

CHAPTER X. SUPREME LAW

Article 97. The fundamental human rights by this Constitution guaranteed to the people of Japan are fruits of the age-old struggle of man to be free; they have survived the many exacting tests for durability and are conferred upon this and future generations in trust, to be held for all time inviolate.

Article 98. This Constitution shall be the supreme law of the nation and no law, ordinance, imperial rescript or other act of government, or part thereof, contrary to the provisions hereof, shall have legal force or validity.

The treaties concluded by Japan and established laws of nations shall be faithfully observed.

Article 99. The Emperor or the Regent as well as Ministers of State, members of the Diet, judges, and all other public officials have the obligation to respect and uphold this Constitution.

CHAPTER XI. SUPPLEMENTARY PROVISIONS

Article 100. This Constitution shall be enforced as from the day when the period of six months will have elapsed counting from the day of its promulgation.

The enactment of laws necessary for the enforcement of this Constitution, the election of members of the House of Councillors and the procedure for the convocation of the Diet and other preparatory procedures necessary for the enforcement of this Constitution may be executed before the day prescribed in the preceding paragraph.

Article 101. If the House of Councillors is not constituted before the effective date of this Constitution, the House of Representatives shall function as the Diet until such time as the House of Councillors shall be constituted.

Article 102. The term of office for half the members of the House of Councillors serving in the first term under this Constitution shall be three years. Members falling under this category shall be determined in accordance with law.

Article 103. The Ministers of State, members of the House of Representatives and judges in office on the effective date of this Constitution, and all other public officials who occupy positions corresponding to such positions as are recognized by this Constitution shall not forfeit their positions automatically on account of the enforcement of this Constitution unless otherwise specified by law. When, however, successors are elected or appointed under the provisions of this Constitution, they shall forfeit their positions as a matter of course.

Appendix B

The Constitution of the People's Republic of China

PREAMBLE

In the year 1949, after more than a century of heroic struggle, the Chinese people, led by the Communist Party of China, finally achieved their great victory in the people's revolution against imperialism, feudalism and bureaucrat-capitalism; and so brought to an end a long history of oppression and enslavement and founded the People's Republic of China, a people's democratic dictatorship. The system of people's democracy—new democracy—of the People's Republic of China guarantees that China can in a peaceful way banish exploitation and poverty and build a prosperous and happy socialist society.

From the founding of the People's Republic of China to the attainment of a socialist society is a period of transition. During the transition the fundamental task of the state is, step by step, to bring about the socialist industrialization of the country and, step by step, to accomplish the socialist transformation of agriculture, handicrafts and capitalist industry and commerce. In the last few years our people have successfully carried out a series of large-scale struggles: the reform of the agrarian system, resistance to American aggression and aid to Korea, the suppression of counter-revolutionaries and the rehabilitation of the national economy. As a result, the necessary conditions have been created for planned economic construction and gradual transition to socialism.

The First National People's Congress of the People's Republic of China,

Adopted on September 20, 1954, by the First National People's Congress of the People's Republic of China. Text as given in Liu Shao-chi, *Report on the Draft Constitution of the People's Republic of China: Constitution of the People's Republic of China* (Peking: Foreign Languages Press, 1954), pp. 69–101.

at its first session held in Peking, the capital, solemnly adopted the Constitution of the People's Republic of China on September 20, 1954. This Constitution is based on the Common Programme of the Chinese People's Political Consultative Conference of 1949, and is an advance on it. It consolidates the gains of the Chinese people's revolution and the political and economic victories won since the founding of the People's Republic of China; and, moreover, it reflects the basic needs of the state in the period of transition, as well as the general desire of the people as a whole to build a socialist society.

In the course of the great struggle to establish the People's Republic of China, the people of our country forged a broad people's democratic united front, composed of all democratic classes, democratic parties and groups, and popular organizations, and led by the Communist Party of China. This people's democratic united front will continue to play its part in mobilizing and rallying the whole people in common struggle to fulfil the fundamental task of the state during the transition and to oppose enemies within and without.

All nationalities of our country are united in one great family of free and equal nations. This unity of China's nationalities will continue to gain in strength, founded as it is on ever-growing friendship and mutual aid among themselves, and on the struggle against imperialism, against public enemies of the people within the nationalities, and against both dominant-nation chauvinism and local nationalism. In the course of economic and cultural development, the state will concern itself with the needs of the different nationalities, and, in the matter of socialist transformation, pay full attention to the special characteristic in the development of each.

China has already built an indestructible friendship with the great Union of Soviet Socialist Republics and the People's Democracies; and the friendship between our people and peace-loving people in all other countries is growing day by day. Such friendship will be constantly strengthened and broadened. China's policy of establishing and extending diplomatic relations with all countries on the principle of equality, mutual benefit and mutual respect for each other's sovereignty and territorial integrity, which has already yielded success, will continue to be carried out. In international affairs our firm and consistent policy is to strive for the noble cause of world peace and the progress of humanity.

CHAPTER 1. GENERAL PRINCIPLES

Article 1. The People's Republic of China is a people's democratic state led by the working class and based on the alliance of workers and peasants.

Article 2. All power in the People's Republic of China belongs to the people. The organs through which the people exercise power are the National People's Congress and the local people's congresses.

The National People's Congress, the local people's congresses and other organs of state practise democratic centralism.

Article 3. The People's Republic of China is a single multi-national state.

All the nationalities are equal. Discrimination against, or oppression of, any nationality, and acts which undermine the unity of the nationalities are prohibited.

All the nationalities have freedom to use and foster the growth of their spoken and written languages, and to preserve or reform their own customs or ways.

Regional autonomy applies in areas where people of national minorities live in compact communities. National autonomous areas are inalienable parts of the People's Republic of China.

Article 4. The People's Republic of China, by relying on the organs of state and the social forces, and by means of socialist industrialization and socialist transformation, ensures the gradual abolition of systems of exploitation and the building of a socialist society.

Article 5. At present, the following basic forms of ownership of means of production exist in the People's Republic of China: state ownership, that is, ownership by the whole people; co-operative ownership, that is, collective ownership by the working masses; ownership by individual working people; and capitalist ownership.

Article 6. The state sector of the economy is a socialist sector, owned by the whole people. It is the leading force in the national economy and the material basis on which the state carries out socialist transformation. The state ensures priority for the development of the state sector of the economy.

All mineral resources and waters, as well as forests, undeveloped land and other resources which the state owns by law, are the property of the whole people.

Article 7. The co-operative sector of the economy is either socialist, when collectively owned by the working masses, or semi-socialist, when in part collectively owned by the working masses. Partial collective ownership by the working masses is a transitional form by means of which individual peasants, individual handicraftsmen and other individual working people organize themselves in their advance towards collective ownership by the working masses.

The state protects the property of the co-operatives, encourages, guides and helps the development of the co-operative sector of the economy. It regards the promotion of producers' co-operatives as the chief means for the transformation of individual farming and individual handicrafts.

Article 8. The state protects the right of peasants to own land and other means of production according to law.

The state guides and helps individual peasants to increase production and encourages them to organize producers', supply and marketing, and credit co-operatives voluntarily.

The policy of the state towards rich-peasant economy is to restrict and gradually eliminate it.

Article 9. The state protects the right of handicraftsmen and other non-agricultural individual working people to own means of production according to law.

The state guides and helps individual handicraftsmen and other non-agricultural individual working people to improve their enterprise and encourages them to organize producers', and supply and marketing co-operatives voluntarily.

Article 10. The state protects the right of capitalists to own means of production and other capital according to law.

The policy of the state towards capitalist industry and commerce is to use, restrict and transform them. The state makes use of the positive sides of capitalist industry and commerce which are beneficial to national welfare and the people's livelihood, restricts their negative sides which are not beneficial to national welfare and the people's livelihood, encourages and guides their transformation into various forms of state-capitalist economy, gradually replacing capitalist ownership with ownership by the whole people; and this it does by means of control exercised by administrative organs of state, the leadership given by the state sector of the economy, and supervision by the workers.

The state forbids capitalists to engage in unlawful activities which injure the public interest, disrupt the social-economic order, or undermine the economic plan of the state.

Article 11. The state protects the right of citizens to own lawfully-earned incomes, savings, houses and other means of life.

Article 12. The state protects the right of citizens to inherit private property according to law.

Article 13. The state may, in the public interest, buy, requisition or nationalize land and other means of production both in cities and countryside according to provisions of law.

Article 14. The state forbids any person to use his private property to the detriment of the public interest.

Article 15. By economic planning, the state directs the growth and transformation of the national economy to bring about the constant increase of productive forces, in this way enriching the material and cultural life of the people and consolidating the independence and security of the country.

Article 16. Work is a matter of honour for every citizen of the People's Republic of China who is able to work. The state encourages citizens to take an active and creative part in their work.

Article 17. All organs of state must rely on the masses of the people, constantly maintain close contact with them, heed their opinions and accept their supervision.

Article 18. All servants of the state must be loyal to the people's democratic system, observe the Constitution and the law and strive to serve the people.

Article 19. The People's Republic of China safeguards the people's democratic system, suppresses all treasonable and counter-revolutionary activities and punishes all traitors and counter-revolutionaries.

The state deprives feudal landlords and bureaucrat-capitalists of political rights for a specific period of time according to law; at the same time it provides them with a way to earn a living, in order to enable them to reform through work and become citizens who earn their livelihood by their own labour.

Article 20. The armed forces of the People's Republic of China belong to the people; their duty is to safeguard the gains of the people's revolution and the achievements of national construction, and to defend the sovereignty, territorial integrity and security of the country.

CHAPTER 2. THE STATE STRUCTURE

SECTION I. THE NATIONAL PEOPLE'S CONGRESS

Article 21. The National People's Congress is the highest organ of state authority in the People's Republic of China.

Article 22. The National People's Congress is the only legislative authority in the country.

Article 23. The National People's Congress is composed of deputies elected by provinces, autonomous regions, municipalities directly under the central authority, the armed forces and Chinese resident abroad.

The number of deputies to the National People's Congress, including those representing national minorities, and the manner of their election, are prescribed by electoral law.

Article 24. The National People's Congress is elected for a term of four years.

Two months before the term of office of the National People's Congress expires, its Standing Committee must complete the election of deputies to the succeeding National People's Congress. Should exceptional circumstances arise preventing such an election, the term of office of the sitting National People's Congress may be prolonged until the first session of the succeeding National People's Congress.

Article 25. The National People's Congress meets once a year, convened by its Standing Committee. It may also be convened whenever its Standing Committee deems this necessary or one-fifth of the deputies so propose.

Article 26. When the National People's Congress meets it elects a presidium to conduct its sittings.

Article 27. The National People's Congress exercises the following functions and powers:

1. to amend the Constitution;
2. to enact laws;
3. to supervise the enforcement of the Constitution;
4. to elect the Chairman and the Vice-Chairman of the People's Republic of China;
5. to decide on the choice of the Premier of the State Council upon recommendation by the Chairman of the People's Republic of China, and of the component members of the State Council upon recommendation by the Premier;
6. to decide on the choice of the Vice-Chairmen and other members of the Council of National Defence upon recommendation by the Chairman of the People's Republic of China;
7. to elect the President of the Supreme People's Court;
8. to elect the Chief Procurator of the Supreme People's Procuratorate;
9. to decide on the national economic plans;
10. to examine and approve the state budget and the financial report;
11. to ratify the status and boundaries of provinces, autonomous regions, and municipalities directly under the central authority;
12. to decide on general amnesties;
13. to decide on questions of war and peace; and

14. to exercise such other functions and powers as the National People's Congress considers necessary.

Article 28. The National People's Congress has power to remove from office:

1. the Chairman and the Vice-Chairman of the People's Republic of China;

2. the Premier and Vice-Premiers, Ministers, Heads of Commissions and the Secretary-General of the State Council;

3. the Vice-Chairmen and other members of the Council of National Defence;

4. the President of the Supreme People's Court; and

5. the Chief Procurator of the Supreme People's Procuratorate.

Article 29. Amendments to the Constitution require a two-thirds majority vote of all the deputies to the National People's Congress.

Laws and other bills require a simple majority vote of all the deputies to the National People's Congress.

Article 30. The Standing Committee of the National People's Congress is a permanently acting body of the National People's Congress.

The Standing Committee is composed of the following members, elected by the National People's Congress:

> the Chairman;
> the Vice-Chairmen;
> the Secretary-General; and
> other members.

Article 31. The Standing Committee of the National People's Congress exercises the following functions and powers:

1. to conduct the election of deputies to the National People's Congress;

2. to convene the National People's Congress;

3. to interpret the laws;

4. to adopt decrees;

5. to supervise the work of the State Council, the Supreme People's Court and the Supreme People's Procuratorate;

6. to annul decisions and orders of the State Council which contravene the Constitution, laws or decrees;

7. to revise or annul inappropriate decisions issued by the government authorities of provinces, autonomous regions, and municipalities directly under the central authority;

8. to decide on the appointment or removal of any Vice-Premier, Minister, Head of Commission or the Secretary-General of the State Council when the National People's Congress is not in session;

9. to appoint or remove the Vice-Presidents, judges, and other members of the Judicial Committee of the Supreme People's Court;

10. to appoint or remove the Deputy Chief Procurators, procurators, and other members of the Procuratorial Committee of the Supreme People's Procuratorate;

11. to decide on the appointment or recall of plenipotentiary representatives to foreign states;

12. to decide on the ratification or abrogation of treaties concluded with foreign states;

13. to institute military, diplomatic and other special titles and ranks;

14. to institute and decide on the award of state orders, medals and titles of honour;

15. to decide on the granting of pardons;

16. to decide, when the National People's Congress is not in session, on the proclamation of a state of war in the event of armed attack on the country or in fulfilment of international treaty obligations concerning common defence against aggression;

17. to decide on general or partial mobilization;

18. to decide on the enforcement of martial law throughout the country or in certain areas; and

19. to exercise such other functions and powers as are vested in it by the National People's Congress.

Article 32. The Standing Committee of the National People's Congress exercises its functions and powers until a new Standing Committee is elected by the succeeding National People's Congress.

Article 33. The Standing Committee of the National People's Congress is responsible to the National People's Congress and reports to it.

The National People's Congress has power to recall members of its Standing Committee.

Article 34. The National People's Congress establishes a Nationalities Committee, a Bills Committee, a Budget Committee, a Credentials Committee and other necessary committees.

The Nationalities Committee and the Bills Committee are under the direction of the Standing Committee of the National People's Congress when the National People's Congress is not in session.

Article 35. The National People's Congress, or its Standing Committee if the National People's Congress is not in session, may, if necessary, appoint commissions of inquiry for the investigation of specific questions.

All organs of state, people's organizations and citizens concerned are obliged to supply necessary information to these commissions when they conduct investigations.

Article 36. Deputies to the National People's Congress have the right to address questions to the State Council, or to the Ministries and Commissions of the State Council, which are under obligation to answer.

Article 37. No deputy to the National People's Congress may be arrested or placed on trial without the consent of the National People's Congress or, when the National People's Congress is not in session, of its Standing Committee.

Article 38. Deputies to the National People's Congress are subject to the supervision of the units which elect them. These electoral units have power to replace at any time the deputies they elect, according to the procedure prescribed by law.

SECTION II. THE CHAIRMAN OF THE PEOPLE'S REPUBLIC OF CHINA

Article 39. The Chairman of the People's Republic of China is elected by the National People's Congress. Any citizen of the People's Republic of China who has the right to vote and stand for election and has reached the age of thirty-five is eligible for election as Chairman of the People's Republic of China.

The term of office of the Chairman of the People's Republic of China is four years.

Article 40. The Chairman of the People's Republic of China, in pursuance of decisions of the National People's Congress or the Standing Committee of the National People's Congress, promulgates laws and decrees; appoints or removes the Premier, Vice-Premiers, Ministers, Heads of Commissions and the Secretary-General of the State Council; appoints or removes the Vice-Chairmen and other members of the Council of National Defence; confers state orders, medals and titles of honour; proclaims general amnesties and grants pardons; proclaims martial law; proclaims a state of war; and orders mobilization.

Article 41. The Chairman of the People's Republic of China represents the People's Republic of China in its relations with foreign states, receives foreign diplomatic representatives and, in pursuance of decisions of the Standing Committee of the National People's Congress, appoints or recalls plenipotentiary representatives to foreign states and ratifies treaties concluded with foreign states.

Article 42. The Chairman of the People's Republic of China commands the armed forces of the country, and is Chairman of the Council of National Defence.

Article 43. The Chairman of the People's Republic of China, whenever necessary, convenes a Supreme State Conference and acts as its chairman.

The Vice-Chairman of the People's Republic of China, the Chairman of the Standing Committee of the National People's Congress, the Premier of the State Council and other persons concerned take part in the Supreme State Conference.

The Chairman of the People's Republic of China submits the views of the Supreme State Conference on important affairs of state to the National People's Congress, its Standing Committee, the State Council, or other bodies concerned for their consideration and decision.

Article 44. The Vice-Chairman of the People's Republic of China assists the Chairman in his work. The Vice-Chairman may exercise such part of the functions and powers of the Chairman as the Chairman may entrust to him.

The provisions of Article 39 of the Constitution governing the election and term of office of the Chairman of the People's Republic of China apply also to the election and term of office of the Vice-Chairman of the People's Republic of China.

Article 45. The Chairman and the Vice-Chairman of the People's Republic of China exercise their functions and powers until the new Chairman and Vice-Chairman elected by the succeeding National People's Congress take office.

Article 46. Should the Chairman of the People's Republic of China be incapacitated for a prolonged period by reason of health, the functions of Chairman shall be exercised by the Vice-Chairman.

Should the office of Chairman of the People's Republic of China fall vacant, the Vice-Chairman succeeds to the office of Chairman.

SECTION III. THE STATE COUNCIL

Article 47. The State Council of the People's Republic of China, that is, the Central People's Government, is the executive organ of the highest state authority; it is the highest administrative organ of state.

Article 48. The State Council is composed of the following members:

the Premier;

the Vice-Premiers;

the Ministers;

the Heads of Commissions; and

the Secretary-General.

The organization of the State Council is determined by law.

Article 49. The State Council exercises the following functions and powers:

1. to formulate administrative measures, issue decisions and orders and verify their execution, in accordance with the Constitution, laws and decrees;

2. to submit bills to the National People's Congress or its Standing Committee;

3. to co-ordinate and lead the work of Ministries and Commissions;

4. to co-ordinate and lead the work of local administrative organs of state throughout the country;

5. to revise or annul inappropriate orders and directives issued by Ministers or by Heads of Commissions;

6. to revise or annul inappropriate decisions and orders issued by local administrative organs of state;

7. to put into effect the national economic plans and provisions of the state budget;

8. to control foreign and domestic trade;

9. to direct cultural, educational and public health work;

10. to administer affairs concerning the nationalities;

11. to administer affairs concerning Chinese resident abroad;

12. to protect the interests of the state, to maintain public order and to safeguard the rights of citizens;

13. to direct the conduct of external affairs;

14. to guide the building up of the defence forces;

15. to ratify the status and boundaries of autonomous *chou*, counties, autonomous counties, and municipalities;

16. to appoint or remove administrative personnel according to provisions of law; and

17. to exercise such other functions and powers as are vested in it by the National People's Congress or its Standing Committee.

Article 50. The Premier directs the work of the State Council and presides over its meetings.

The Vice-Premiers assist the Premier in his work.

Article 51. The Ministers and Heads of Commissions direct the work of their respective departments. They may issue orders and directives within the jurisdiction of their respective departments and in accordance with laws and decrees, and decisions and orders of the State Council.

Article 52. The State Council is responsible to the National People's Congress and reports to it, or, when the National People's Congress is not in session, to its Standing Committee.

SECTION IV. THE LOCAL PEOPLE'S CONGRESSES AND LOCAL PEOPLE'S COUNCILS

Article 53. The administrative division of the People's Republic of China is as follows:

1. The country is divided into provinces, autonomous regions, and municipalities directly under the central authority;

2. Provinces and autonomous regions are divided into autonomous *chou*, counties, autonomous counties, and municipalities; and

3. Counties and autonomous counties are divided into *hsiang*, nationality *hsiang*, and towns.

Municipalities directly under the central authority and other large municipalities are divided into districts. Autonomous *chou* are divided into counties, autonomous counties, and municipalities.

Autonomous regions, autonomous *chou* and autonomous counties are all national autonomous areas.

Article 54. People's congresses and people's councils are established in provinces, municipalities directly under the central authority, counties, municipalities, municipal districts, *hsiang*, nationality *hsiang*, and towns.

Organs of self-government are established in autonomous regions, autonomous *chou* and autonomous counties. The organization and work of organs of self-government are specified in Section V of Chapter Two of the Constitution.

Article 55. Local people's congresses at all levels are the organs of government authority in their respective localities.

Article 56. Deputies to the people's congresses of provinces, municipalities directly under the central authority, counties, and municipalities divided into districts are elected by the people's congresses of the next lower level; deputies to the people's congresses of municipalities not divided into districts, municipal districts, *hsiang*, nationality *hsiang* and towns are directly elected by the voters.

The number of deputies to local people's congresses and the manner of their election are prescribed by electoral law.

Article 57. The term of office of the provincial people's congresses is four years. The term of office of the people's congresses of municipalities directly under the central authority, counties, municipalities, municipal districts, *hsiang*, nationality *hsiang*, and towns is two years.

Article 58. The local people's congresses at every level ensure the observance and execution of laws and decrees in their respective administrative areas; draw up plans for local economic and cultural development and for public works; examine and approve local budgets and financial reports; protect public property; maintain public order; safeguard the rights of citizens and the equal rights of national minorities.

Article 59. The local people's congresses elect, and have power to recall, members of the people's councils at corresponding levels.

The people's congresses at county level and above elect, and have power to recall, the presidents of people's courts at corresponding levels.

Article 60. The local people's congresses adopt and issue decisions within the limits of the authority prescribed by law.

The people's congresses of nationality *hsiang* may, within the limits of the authority prescribed by law, take specific measures appropriate to the characteristic of the nationalities concerned.

The local people's congresses have power to revise or annul inappropriate decisions and orders issued by people's councils at corresponding levels.

The people's congresses at county level and above have power to revise or annul inappropriate decisions issued by people's congresses at the next lower level as well as inappropriate decisions and orders issued by people's councils at the next lower level.

Article 61. Deputies to the people's congresses of provinces, municipalities directly under the central authority, counties, and municipalities divided into districts are subject to supervision by the units which elect them; deputies to the people's congresses of municipalities not divided into districts, municipal districts, *hsiang*, nationality *hsiang*, and towns are subject to supervision by their electorates. The electoral units and electorates which elect the deputies to the local people's congresses have power at any time to recall their deputies according to the procedure prescribed by law.

Article 62. Local people's councils, that is, local people's governments, are the executive organs of local people's congresses at corresponding levels, and are the administrative organs of state in their respective localities.

Article 63. A local people's council is composed, according to its level, of the provincial governor and deputy provincial governors; or the mayor and deputy mayors; or the county head and deputy county heads; or the district head and deputy district heads; or the *hsiang* head and the deputy *hsiang* heads; or the town head and deputy town heads, as the case may be; together with council members.

The term of office of a local people's council is the same as that of the people's congress at corresponding level.

The organization of local people's councils is determined by law.

Article 64. The local people's councils administer their respective areas within the limits of the authority prescribed by law.

The local people's councils carry out the decisions issued by people's congresses at corresponding levels and decisions and orders issued by administrative organs of state at higher levels.

The local people's councils issue decisions and orders within the limits of the authority prescribed by law.

Article 65. The people's councils at county level and above direct the work of all their subordinate departments and of people's councils at lower levels, as well as appoint or remove personnel of organs of state according to provisions of law.

The people's councils at county level and above have power to suspend the carrying out of inappropriate decisions by people's congresses at the next lower level; and to revise or annul inappropriate orders and directives issued by their subordinate departments, and inappropriate decisions and orders issued by people's councils at lower levels.

Article 66. The local people's councils are responsible to the people's congresses at corresponding levels and to the administrative organs of state at the next higher level, and report to them.

The local people's councils throughout the country are administrative organs of state, and are subordinate to and under the co-ordinating direction of the State Council.

SECTION V. THE ORGANS OF SELF-GOVERNMENT OF
NATIONAL AUTONOMOUS AREAS

Article 67. The organs of self-government of all autonomous regions, autonomous *chou* and autonomous counties are formed in accordance with the basic principles governing the organization of local organs of state as specified in Section IV of Chapter Two of the Constitution. The form of each organ of self-government may be determined in accordance with the wishes of the majority of the people of the nationality or nationalities enjoying regional autonomy in a given area.

Article 68. In all autonomous regions, autonomous *chou* and autonomous counties where a number of nationalities live together, each nationality is entitled to appropriate representation on the organs of self-government.

Article 69. The organs of self-government of all autonomous regions, autonomous *chou* and autonomous counties exercise the functions and powers of local organs of state as specified in Section IV of Chapter Two of the Constitution.

Article 70. The organs of self-government of all autonomous regions, autonomous *chou* and autonomous counties exercise autonomy within the limits of the authority prescribed by the Constitution and the law.

The organs of self-government of all autonomous regions, autonomous *chou* and autonomous counties administer their own local finances within the limits of the authority prescribed by law.

The organs of self-government of all autonomous regions, autonomous *chou* and autonomous counties organize their local public security forces in accordance with the military system of the state.

The organs of self-government of all autonomous regions, autonomous *chou* and autonomous counties may draw up statutes governing the exercise of autonomy or separate regulations suited to the political, economic and cultural characteristics of the nationality or nationalities in a given area, which statutes and regulations are subject to endorsement by the Standing Committee of the National People's Congress.

Article 71. In performing their duties, organs of self-government of all autonomous regions, autonomous *chou* and autonomous counties employ the spoken and written language or languages commonly used in the locality.

Article 72. The higher organs of state should fully safeguard the right of organs of self-government of all autonomous regions, autonomous *chou* and autonomous counties to exercise autonomy, and should assist the various national minorities in their political, economic and cultural development.

SECTION VI. THE PEOPLE'S COURTS AND THE PEOPLE'S PROCURATORATE

Article 73. In the People's Republic of China judicial authority is exercised by the Supreme People's Court, local people's courts and special people's courts.

Article 74. The term of office of the President of the Supreme People's Court and presidents of local people's courts is four years.

The organization of people's courts is determined by law.

Article 75. The system of people's assessors applies, in accordance with law, to judicial proceedings in the people's courts.

Article 76. Cases in the people's courts are heard in public unless otherwise provided for by law. The accused has the right to defence.

Article 77. Citizens of all nationalities have the right to use their own spoken and written languages in court proceedings. The people's courts are to provide interpretation for any party unacquainted with the spoken or written language commonly used in the locality.

In an area where people of national minorities live in compact communities or where a number of nationalities live together, hearings in people's courts are conducted in the language commonly used in the locality, and judgments, notices and all other documents of the people's courts are made public in such language.

Article 78. In administering justice the people's courts are independent, subject only to the law.

Article 79. The Supreme People's Court is the highest judicial organ.

The Supreme People's Court supervises the judicial work of local people's courts and special people's courts; people's courts at higher levels supervise the judicial work of people's courts at lower levels.

Article 80. The Supreme People's Court is responsible to the National People's Congress and reports to it; or, when the National People's Congress is not in session, to its Standing Committee. Local people's courts are responsible to the local people's congresses at corresponding levels and report to them.

Article 81. The Supreme People's Procuratorate of the People's Republic of China exercises procuratorial authority over all departments of the State Council, all local organs of state, persons working in organs of state, and citizens, to ensure observance of the law. Local organs of the people's procuratorate and special people's procuratorates exercise procuratorial authority within the limits prescribed by law.

Local organs of the people's procuratorate and the special people's procuratorates work under the leadership of the people's procuratorates at higher levels, and all work under the co-ordinating direction of the Supreme People's Procuratorate.

Article 82. The term of office of the Chief Procurator of the Supreme People's Procuratorate is four years.

The organization of people's procuratorates is determined by law.

Article 83. In the exercise of their authority local organs of the people's procuratorate are independent and are not subject to interference by local organs of state.

Article 84. The Supreme People's Procuratorate is responsible to the National People's Congress and reports to it; or, when the National People's Congress is not in session, to its Standing Committee.

CHAPTER 3. FUNDAMENTAL RIGHTS AND DUTIES OF CITIZENS

Article 85. Citizens of the People's Republic of China are equal before the law.

Article 86. Citizens of the People's Republic of China who have reached the age of eighteen have the right to vote and stand for election whatever their nationality, race, sex, occupation, social origin, religious belief, education, property status, or length of residence, except insane persons and persons deprived by law of the right to vote and stand for election.

Women have equal rights with men to vote and stand for election.

Article 87. Citizens of the People's Republic of China enjoy freedom of speech, freedom of the press, freedom of assembly, freedom of association, freedom of procession and freedom of demonstration. The state guarantees to citizens enjoyment of these freedoms by providing the necessary material facilities.

Article 88. Citizens of the People's Republic of China enjoy freedom of religious belief.

Article 89. Freedom of the person of citizens of the People's Republic of China is inviolable. No citizen may be arrested except by decision of a people's court or with the sanction of a people's procuratorate.

Article 90. The homes of citizens of the People's Republic of China are inviolable, and privacy of correspondence is protected by law.

Citizens of the People's Republic of China enjoy freedom of residence and freedom to change their residence.

Article 91. Citizens of the People's Republic of China have the right to work. To guarantee enjoyment of this right, the state, by planned development of the national economy, gradually creates more employment, and better working conditions and wages.

Article 92. Working people in the People's Republic of China have the right to rest and leisure. To guarantee enjoyment of this right, the state prescribes working hours and holidays for workers and office employees; at the same time it gradually expands material facilities to enable working people to rest and build up their health.

Article 93. Working people in the People's Republic of China have the right to material assistance in old age, and in case of illness or disability. To guarantee enjoyment of this right, the state provides social insurance, social assistance and public health services and gradually expands these facilities.

Article 94. Citizens of the People's Republic of China have the right to education. To guarantee enjoyment of this right, the state establishes and gradually extends the various types of schools and other cultural and educational institutions.

The state pays special attention to the physical and mental development of young people.

Article 95. The People's Republic of China safeguards the freedom of citizens to engage in scientific research, literary and artistic creation and other cultural pursuits. The state encourages and assists creative work in science, education, literature, art and other cultural pursuits.

Article 96. Women in the People's Republic of China enjoy equal rights with men in all spheres of political, economic, cultural, social and domestic life.

The state protects marriage, the family, and the mother and child.

Article 97. Citizens of the People's Republic of China have the right to bring complaints against any person working in organs of state for transgression of law or neglect of duty by making a written or verbal statement to any organ of state at any level. People suffering loss by reason of infringement by persons working in organs of state of their rights as citizens have the right to compensation.

Article 98. The People's Republic of China protects the proper rights and interests of Chinese residents abroad.

Article 99. The People's Republic of China grants the right of asylum to any foreign national persecuted for supporting a just cause, for taking part in the peace movement or for engaging in scientific activity.

Article 100. Citizens of the People's Republic of China must abide by the Constitution and the law, uphold discipline at work, keep public order and respect social ethics.

Article 101. The public property of the People's Republic of China is sacred and inviolable. It is the duty of every citizen to respect and protect public property.

Article 102. It is the duty of citizens of the People's Republic of China to pay taxes according to law.

Article 103. It is the sacred duty of every citizen of the People's Republic of China to defend the homeland.

It is an honourable duty of citizens of the People's Republic of China to perform military service according to law.

CHAPTER 4. NATIONAL FLAG, NATIONAL EMBLEM, CAPITAL

Article 104. The national flag of the People's Republic of China is a red flag with five stars.

Article 105. The national emblem of the People's Republic of China is: in the centre, Tien An Men under the light of five stars, framed with ears of grain, and with a cogwheel at the base.

Article 106. The capital of the People's Republic of China is Peking.

Major Textbooks on Modern East Asia

Beckmann, George M. *The Modernization of China and Japan*. New York: Harper & Row, 1962.

Bingham, Woodbridge; Conroy, Hilary; Iklé, Frank. *A History of Asia*, vol. 2: *Old Empires, Western Penetration, and the Rise of New Nations since 1600*. Boston: Allyn and Bacon, 1965.

Buss, Claude A. *Asia in the Modern World: A History of China, Japan, and Southeast Asia*. New York: Macmillan, 1964.

Cameron, Meribeth E.; Mahoney, Thomas H. D.; and McReynolds, George E. *China, Japan and the Powers: A History of the Modern Far East*, 2nd ed. New York: Ronald, 1960.

Clyde, Paul H., and Beers, Burton H. *The Far East: A History of the Western Impact and the Eastern Response (1830–1965)*, 4th ed. Englewood Cliffs, N.J.: Prentice-Hall, 1966.

Crofts, Alfred, and Buchanan, Percy. *A History of the Far East*. New York: McKay, 1958.

Fairbank, John K.; Reischauer, Edwin O.; and Craig, Albert M. *East Asia: The Modern Transformation*. Boston: Houghton Mifflin, 1965.

Greene, Fred. *The Far East*. New York: Holt, Rinehart and Winston, 1961.

Kim, Young Hum. *East Asia's Turbulent Century: With Diplomatic Documents*. New York: Appleton-Century-Crofts, 1966.

Latourette, Kenneth Scott. *A Short History of the Far East*, 4th ed. New York: Macmillan, 1964.

MacNair, Harley Farnsworth, and Lach, Donald F. *Modern Far Eastern International Relations*, 2nd ed. New York: Van Nostrand, 1955.

Michael, Franz, and Taylor, George E. *The Far East in the Modern World*, rev. ed. New York: Holt, Rinehart and Winston, 1964.

Peffer, Nathaniel. *The Far East: A Modern History*. Ann Arbor: The University of Michigan Press, 1958.

Vinacke, Harold M. *A History of the Far East in Modern Times*, 6th ed. New York: Appleton-Century-Crofts, 1959.

CORRELATION CHART

Chapters in *Sources in Modern East Asian History and Politics* and Relevant Pages in Frequently Used Textbooks

Textbooks*	I Reform and Revolu- tion in China	II The Emer- gence of the Japanese Empire	III World War I and the Far East	IV The United Front in China	V Japanese Milita- rism	VI World War II in the Far East
Beckmann	118–243	244–351	352–393	396–433 453–462 654–664	339–453 559–622	466–501 580–622
Bingham, Conroy, and Iklé	201–226 277–294 335–359	295–334 390–382	514–531	527–536	537–559	560–587
Buss	98–103 109–141 237–246 256–270	27– 47 103–105 142–182 279–299	265–270 300–315	246–255 270–278	315–323 375–397 309–323	398–455 461–484
Cameron, Mahoney, and McReyn- olds	163–180 206–237 283–325 381–398	91–162 181–205 238–282	326–380	413–440	441–461 499–544	462–498 545–555
Clyde and Beers	51– 96 146–223 240–248	97–145 224–239 249–258	259–290	303–315 335–344	291–302 316–335	345–358 390–407
Crofts and Buchanan	110–249 311–333	87–109 153–184 250–286	334–353	320–333	374–397	398–421
Fairbank, Reischauer, and Craig	80–178 313–407 613–658	179–312 488–568	658–676	676–706	568–612 706–710	710–717 804–811
Greene	61–131 517–518	183–216	113–114 217–220 518–519	114–131	234–259	131–137 238–259 519–527

* See page 409 for titles of textbooks.

410

VII *The Defeat and Occupation of Japan*	VIII *Democracy in Japan*	IX *The Communist Victory in China*	X *Conflict in Korea*	XI *Communist Rule in China*	XII *China's Foreign Relations and the Sino-Soviet Dispute*	XIII *The War in Vietnam*
622–634	634–645	433–437 462–469 501–515	529–532	515–528 664–673	528–537	
588–602	631–633	602–606	614–631	606–613 634–641	636–639	485–513 663–667
456–460 509–527	623–644	389–392 412–419 528–541	600–619	541–549 646–688	662–670	575–599 715–741
577–597 605–613	613–615 648–653	556–576 598–605	620–642	658–690	642–648 653–657	
408–420	449–461	421–432	462–469	433–448 469–474	442–445	475–494
423–462 476–480	522–534	354–373 480–490	491–499	538–545		463–475 500–521
811–821	821–843	710–717 848–860	844–848	860–879	879–884	773–782
260–288 527–528	288–291	138–150 528–530	506–508 530–539	150–176	504–511 540–542	415–485 539–545

Textbooks*	I Reform and Revolution in China	II The Emergence of the Japanese Empire	III World War I and the Far East	IV The United Front in China	V Japanese Militarism	VI World War II in the Far East
Kim	5– 12 17– 24 39– 45	12– 16 24– 38 45– 49 53– 59	60– 74		74– 91	91–116
Latourette	78–187 368–386 423–459	190–261 387–421 504–515	459–468 515–526	468–502 591–596	526–590 596–600	600–649
MacNair and Lach	3– 15 30– 60 64– 88 113–126 242–253	17– 24 61– 64 99–113 270–294	126–216	218–228 253–269	217–218 228–241 297–358 362–404 415–432 436–441	358–362 404–414 432–436 441–514
Michael and Taylor	119–141 148–166 178–225 316–325	141–148 166–171 236–278	171–177 225–235 339–356	371–410	516–563 543–580 714–728 754–759	422–432 563–584 754–750
Peffer	103–119 155–188 200–213 229–241	81–102 120–154 189–199 214–228	242–266	252–334	335–370	371–409
Vinacke	3– 74 146–164 186–282 392–397	76–121 121–145 166–185 300–362	282–299 362–390 397–436	437–462	494–564	564–651

* See page 409 for titles of textbooks.

VII *The Defeat and Occupa- tion of Japan*	VIII *Democ- racy in Japan*	IX *The Communist Victory in China*	X *Conflict in Korea*	XI *Com- munist Rule in China*	XII *China's Foreign Relations and the Sino-Soviet Dispute*	XIII *The War in Vietnam*
116–119 138–148	161–163 172–174 182–184	120–137	149–158 163–168 174–176 185–188	168–171	176–181 188–198	
731–741	741–749	689–700	722–731	701–722		669–689
589–611	611–621	517–551	621–647	551–588		662–671
584–601 750–754	601–614 784–787	329–339 356–364 410–422 432–454 754–759 761–770	364–367 759–761 770–784	455–493	367–371 447–454 493–515	299–303 507–510 660–681 787–805
410–418 447–454		419–430 440–446 462–467	455–461	468–471		431–439 472–479
729–752	752–758	652–682	702–728	683–696	696–701	759–771

Index

(Italicized numbers indicate that the texts of the documents appear on these pages.)